A history of three of the judges of King Charles I. Major-General Whalley, Major-General Goffe, and Colonel Dixwell: who, at the Restoration, 1660, fled to America

Ezra Stiles

Eighteenth Century
Collections Online
Print Editions

Gale ECCO Print Editions

Relive history with *Eighteenth Century Collections Online*, now available in print for the independent historian and collector. This series includes the most significant English-language and foreign-language works printed in Great Britain during the eighteenth century, and is organized in seven different subject areas including literature and language; medicine, science, and technology; and religion and philosophy. The collection also includes thousands of important works from the Americas.

The eighteenth century has been called "The Age of Enlightenment." It was a period of rapid advance in print culture and publishing, in world exploration, and in the rapid growth of science and technology – all of which had a profound impact on the political and cultural landscape. At the end of the century the American Revolution, French Revolution and Industrial Revolution, perhaps three of the most significant events in modern history, set in motion developments that eventually dominated world political, economic, and social life.

In a groundbreaking effort, Gale initiated a revolution of its own: digitization of epic proportions to preserve these invaluable works in the largest online archive of its kind. Contributions from major world libraries constitute over 175,000 original printed works. Scanned images of the actual pages, rather than transcriptions, recreate the works *as they first appeared.*

Now for the first time, these high-quality digital scans of original works are available via print-on-demand, making them readily accessible to libraries, students, independent scholars, and readers of all ages.

For our initial release we have created seven robust collections to form one the world's most comprehensive catalogs of 18th century works.

Initial Gale ECCO Print Editions collections include:

History and Geography
Rich in titles on English life and social history, this collection spans the world as it was known to eighteenth-century historians and explorers. Titles include a wealth of travel accounts and diaries, histories of nations from throughout the world, and maps and charts of a world that was still being discovered. Students of the War of American Independence will find fascinating accounts from the British side of conflict.

Social Science

Delve into what it was like to live during the eighteenth century by reading the first-hand accounts of everyday people, including city dwellers and farmers, businessmen and bankers, artisans and merchants, artists and their patrons, politicians and their constituents. Original texts make the American, French, and Industrial revolutions vividly contemporary.

Medicine, Science and Technology

Medical theory and practice of the 1700s developed rapidly, as is evidenced by the extensive collection, which includes descriptions of diseases, their conditions, and treatments. Books on science and technology, agriculture, military technology, natural philosophy, even cookbooks, are all contained here.

Literature and Language

Western literary study flows out of eighteenth-century works by Alexander Pope, Daniel Defoe, Henry Fielding, Frances Burney, Denis Diderot, Johann Gottfried Herder, Johann Wolfgang von Goethe, and others. Experience the birth of the modern novel, or compare the development of language using dictionaries and grammar discourses.

Religion and Philosophy

The Age of Enlightenment profoundly enriched religious and philosophical understanding and continues to influence present-day thinking. Works collected here include masterpieces by David Hume, Immanuel Kant, and Jean-Jacques Rousseau, as well as religious sermons and moral debates on the issues of the day, such as the slave trade. The Age of Reason saw conflict between Protestantism and Catholicism transformed into one between faith and logic -- a debate that continues in the twenty-first century.

Law and Reference

This collection reveals the history of English common law and Empire law in a vastly changing world of British expansion. Dominating the legal field is the *Commentaries of the Law of England* by Sir William Blackstone, which first appeared in 1765. Reference works such as almanacs and catalogues continue to educate us by revealing the day-to-day workings of society.

Fine Arts

The eighteenth-century fascination with Greek and Roman antiquity followed the systematic excavation of the ruins at Pompeii and Herculaneum in southern Italy; and after 1750 a neoclassical style dominated all artistic fields. The titles here trace developments in mostly English-language works on painting, sculpture, architecture, music, theater, and other disciplines. Instructional works on musical instruments, catalogs of art objects, comic operas, and more are also included.

The BiblioLife Network

This project was made possible in part by the BiblioLife Network (BLN), a project aimed at addressing some of the huge challenges facing book preservationists around the world. The BLN includes libraries, library networks, archives, subject matter experts, online communities and library service providers. We believe every book ever published should be available as a high-quality print reproduction; printed on-demand anywhere in the world. This insures the ongoing accessibility of the content and helps generate sustainable revenue for the libraries and organizations that work to preserve these important materials.

The following book is in the "public domain" and represents an authentic reproduction of the text as printed by the original publisher. While we have attempted to accurately maintain the integrity of the original work, there are sometimes problems with the original work or the micro-film from which the books were digitized. This can result in minor errors in reproduction. Possible imperfections include missing and blurred pages, poor pictures, markings and other reproduction issues beyond our control. Because this work is culturally important, we have made it available as part of our commitment to protecting, preserving, and promoting the world's literature.

GUIDE TO FOLD-OUTS MAPS and OVERSIZED IMAGES

The book you are reading was digitized from microfilm captured over the past thirty to forty years. Years after the creation of the original microfilm, the book was converted to digital files and made available in an online database.

In an online database, page images do not need to conform to the size restrictions found in a printed book. When converting these images back into a printed bound book, the page sizes are standardized in ways that maintain the detail of the original. For large images, such as fold-out maps, the original page image is split into two or more pages

Guidelines used to determine how to split the page image follows:

• Some images are split vertically; large images require vertical and horizontal splits.
• For horizontal splits, the content is split left to right.
• For vertical splits, the content is split from top to bottom.
• For both vertical and horizontal splits, the image is processed from top left to bottom right.

EZRA STILES S.T.D. LL.D.

President of Yale College.

A

HISTORY

OF THREE OF THE

JUDGES

OF

KING CHARLES I.

MAJOR-GENERAL WHALLEY, MAJOR-GENE-
RAL GOFFE, and COLONEL DIXWELL:

WHO, AT THE RESTORATION, 1660, FLED TO AMERICA;
AND WERE SECRETED AND CONCEALED, IN
MASSACHUSETTS AND CONNECTICUT,
FOR NEAR THIRTY YEARS.

WITH AN ACCOUNT OF

Mr. THEOPHILUS WHALE, of Narraganſett,
Suppoſed to have been alſo one of the Judges.

By *PRESIDENT STILES.*

*They were lo'ed about—being deſtitute, afflicted, tormented—they wander-
ed in deſerts, and in mountains, and in dens and caves of the earth.*

—Of whom the world was not worthy.———

*Be not forgetful to entertain ſtrangers . for thereby ſome have entertained
Angls unawares.* Heb xi and xiii.

HARTFORD · PRINTED BY ELISHA BABCOCK.

1794.

TO

AIL THE PATRONS OF

REAL, PERFECT, AND UNPOLLUTED LIBERTY,

CIVIL AND RELIGIOUS,

THROUGHOUT THE WORLD;

THIS HISTORY

OF THREE OF ITS MOST ILLUSTRIOUS AND HEROIC,

BUT UNFORTUNATE DEFENDERS,

IS HUMBLY SUBMITTED,

AND DEDICATED,

BY A HITHERTO UNCORRUPTED FRIEND

TO UNIVERSAL LIBERTY.

EZRA STILES.

YALE COLLEGE,
Nov. 20, 1793. }

C O N T E N T S.

HISTORY

OF THREE OF THE JUDGES

OF KING CHARLES I.

WHO, ESCAPING ROYAL VENGEANCE, FOUND AN
ASYLUM IN NEW-ENGLAND, AND PARTICULARLY
IN CONNECTICUT.

CHAP. I.

Of the Three Judges separately, and before their Exile.

OF about one hundred and thirty Judges, appointed in the original commiſſion, by the commons'
Houſe of Parliament, for the tryal of King Charles I.
only ſeventy-four ſat, and of theſe, ſixty-ſeven were
preſent at the laſt ſeſſion, and were unanimous in paſſing the definitive ſentence upon the King ; and fifty-
nine ſigned the warrant for his execution, 1649. Of
theſe fifty-nine, about one-third, or twenty-four, were
dead at the Reſtoration, 1660. Twenty-ſeven perſons,
Judges and others, were then taken, tried and condemned, ſome of which were pardoned, and nine of
the Judges, and five others, as accomplices, were executed. Only ſixteen Judges fled, and finally eſcaped :
three of whom, Major-General EDWARD WHAL-
LEY, Major-General WILLIAM GOFFE, and Colonel
JOHN DIXWELL, fled and ſecreted themſelves in New-
England, and died here. One of the Judges piſtoled
himſelf in Holland, another fled to Lauſanna, and was

affaffinated there · what became of the reft is to me un-known, and perhaps is yet in undetected oblivion. I am to write the hiftory of thofe three only, who fled to America and died here. Thefe came to New-Eng-land, and found a friendly afylum and concealment in Maffachufetts and Connecticut : and Col Dixwell lies buried in New-Haven. I fhall collect and digeft the memoirs of thefe three Judges ; whofe hiftory being partly combined, and partly difconnected, may fome-times involve repetitions.

The æra is now arrived, when tribunals for the trial of delinquent Majefty, of Kings and Sovereign Rulers, will be provided for, in the future policies and confti-tutions of Sovereignties, Empires and Republics : when this heroic and high example of doing juftice to crimi-nal Royalty, of the adjudication of a King, will be re-curred to and contemplated with juftice and impartiality. And however it has been overwhelmed with infamy for a century and a half, will hereafter be approved, admired and imitated , and the memoirs of thefe fuffering exiles will be immortalized with honor.

A full account of them cannot yet be collected, as part of their hiftory lies ftill concealed on the other fide of the Atlantic. But although time and future refearch-es may amplify the information concerning them, it is however prefumed fo much may be now collected, as may enable pofterity and the world to form a juft and true idea and eftimate of the principles, defigns and characters of thefe illuftrious Worthies.

General Whalley.

" The Whalleys are of great antiquity," fays the Reverend Mark Noble, in his memoirs of the family of Cromwell. The General defcended from the family of Whalley, which figured in England in the reign of Henry the fixth. Richard Whalley, Efq. of Kirkton, in the county of Nottingham, was a man of great opulence , a member of parliament for Scarborough, 1 Edward VI. He died 1583, aged 84. His eldest son and heir, Thomas Whalley, Esq. by his wife Elizabeth, had several children; and among others, first, Richard, who married the Protector Oliver Cromwell's Aunt. Second, Walter Whalley, D. D. educated at Pembroke-Hall. Third, Thomas, educated in Trinity College, both of Cambridge. Richard Whalley, Esq. uncle to the Protector, succeeded his grandfather, of his name. He was a member of Parliament, 43. Eliz. He had three wives: His second was Frances, daughter of Sir Henry Cromwell, Hinckinbrooke, Knight, grandfather of the Protector, Oliver. He had issue only by the second, the Protector's aunt, who were, Thomas, Edward, one of King Charles' I. Judges, and Henry, the Judge Advocate. It is Edward, the second son of Richard by Frances, aunt to Oliver Cromwell, of whom I am now writing.

EDWARD WHALLEY, Esq. the Judge, being a second son, " was brought up to merchandize. No sooner did the contest between King Charles and his Parliament blaze out, than he (though in the middle age of life) took up arms in defence of the liberties of the subject: and this in opposition to the sentiments of his nearest relations. Probably his religious opinions determined him as much or more than any other consideration. And though the usage of arms must be new to him, yet he early distinguished himself in the parliament service, in many sieges and battles; but in none more than in the battle of Nasby, in 1645, in which he charged and entirely defeated two divisions of Langdale's horse, though supported by Prince Rupert, who commanded the reserve: for which Parliament, January 21, 1645—6, voted him to be a Colonel of Horse; and May 9, the following year, they gave him the thanks of the house, and £100. to purchase two horses, for his brilliant action at Banbury, which he took by storm, and afterwards marched to Worcester, which city surrendered to him July 23, following."

6/ " Feb. 3, 1647, the Commons granted him for his arrears, at the rate of fifteen years purchase, the manor of Flawborough, part of the estate of the Marquis of Newcastle, the annual rent of which was £400."* This was redeeming part of his father's estate purchased by the Marquis for a small part of its value.

" Cromwell confided so much in him, that he committed the person of the King to his care. The loyalists have charged him with severity to his royal prisoner, but the monarch himself, in a letter he left behind him, when he made his escape, fully exculpates him from that charge "

He was one of the commissioners appointed and authorised by Parliament, as the High Court of Justice, and sat in that august and awful Tribunal, to which Majesty was rendered amenable, and which had the intrepidity and fortitude to pass judgment on the life of a King; one of whose judges he thus was, and the warrant for whose execution he signed.

At the battle of Dunbar, September 3, 1650, he, with Monk, commanded the foot, and greatly contributed to the complete defeat of the Scotch army.— " Cromwell left him in Scotland with the rank of Commissary-General, and gave him the command of four regiments of horse, with which he performed many actions, that gained him great honor."

He continued a steady friend to his cousin Oliver, after he had raised himself to the sovereignty , and was entrusted by him with the government of the counties of Lincoln, Nottingham, Derby, Warwick, and Leicester, by the name of *Major-General.* He was one of the Representatives of Nottinghamshire, in the Parliament held in 1654 and 1656. The Protector made him Commissary-General for Scotland, and called him up to his other House.

* *Noble,* V. I. 179.

" He was looked upon with jealoufy by Parliament after the refignation of Richard the Protector, efpecial-ly as he leaned fo much to the interefts of the army. For this reafon they took from him his Commiffion.—This ftill endeared him the more to the army, who when Monk's conduct began to be problematical, de-puted him one of their commiffioners to agree to terms of peace and amity with that in Scotland. But Monk, who knew his hatred to the royal family, and how much reafon he had to dread their return, abfolutely refufed to treat with him."

" The Reftoration of monarchy foon after becom-ing vifible, he faw the danger of the fituation. For befides the lofs of the eftate he poffeffed of the Duke of Newcaftle, and the manors of Weft-Walton and Tor-rington, in the county of Norfolk, part of Queen Hen-rietta Maria's jointure, which he had purchafed, and whatever elfe eftate he had, he knew even his life would be offered up to the fhrine of the King, whom he had condemned to death: he therefore prudently retired —September 22, 1660, a proclamation was publifhed, fetting forth, that he had left the kingdom, but as there was great reafon to fuppofe he was returned, £100. was offered to any who fhould difcover him in any of the Britifh dominions, and caufe him to be brought in alive, or dead, if he made any refiftance. Colonel Goffe was included in this proclamation. †

Here the European hiftorians are loft. They repre-fent that thefe two exiles efcaped to the continent, and were at Lucerne, in Switzerland, in 1664, where fome fay that they died, others, that leaving that place, they privately wandered about for fome years, and died in a foreign clime, but when or where unknown. But truely their remaining hiftory, after they left England, 1660, is to be traced only in America.

† Noble. P. 184.

Mr. Noble gives this character of General Whalley: " His valor and military knowledge were confessedly great, his religious sentiments wild and enthusiastic. From a merchant's counter to rise to so many and so high offices in the state, and to conduct himself with propriety in them, sufficiently evinces that he had good abilities: nor is his honesty questioned by any, which, as one of the King's Judges, and a Major-General, would lay him open to a very narrow scrutiny. '

General Edward Whalley married the sister of Sir George Middleton, Knight, who was as great an enemy to King Charles I. as he was a friend to King Charles II. ' By her he had several children, and one born so late as 1656. What became of them is unknown, except John, his eldest son and heir, who was a cornet of horse, and who was returned member of Parliament for the town of Nottingham, 1658—9, and also for the borough of Shoreham. He married the daughter of Sir Herbert Springer, Knight, by whom he had Herbert Whalley, Esq. his eldest son and heir ; who, though King Charles II. granted the manor, the Parliament had given to the Major-General, once belonging to the Earl, then Marquis, then Duke of Newcastle, with all the rest of his own lands, forfeited to the Crown by any of the purchasers, yet this Herbert Whalley, Esq was, 1672, in possession of some of the pristern Inheritance of the Whalley's which had been purchased by his Grace's ancestors from them, but by mortgage which the Duke, when Earl, made to Sir Arnold Waring some years before, through assignments or heirship, became vested in this Herbert. '

Of Whalley's children, Noble knew none but John. But he had a daughter who was married to General Gffe, whom Goffe left in England, and with whom he kept up a correspondence, by the name of Mother Golding, while in exile in New-England.

The laſt of his letters to her was dated at Hadley, 1679. Goffe had ſeveral children by her, whom he left in England.

Henry Whalley, brother of the Major-General, is ſaid to have been an Alderman of London. From the regard his couſin Henry Cromwell, Lord-Deputy, had for him, he was promoted to the office of Judge-Advocate of the armies of England and Scotland before 1655. He continued in Scotland during the remainder of the protectorate of Oliver, and in 1656, repreſented the Sheriffdom of Selkirk and Peebles in the Britiſh Parliament : and was one of thoſe who ſigned the order for proclaiming his couſin Richard, Lord Protector.

In verification of Noble's account of the family and connections of Whalley, I add an extract from the *Faſti Oxonienſes*, P. 90. " Oliver Cromwell had ſeveral uncles, whoſe deſcendants taking not part with him, only one or two, they were not preferred by him. He had alſo five aunts, the eldeſt of which, named Joane, was married to Francis Barrington, whoſe ſon Robert was countenanced by Oliver. The ſecond named Elizabeth, was wife of John Hamden, of Hamden in Bucks, father of John Hamden, one of the five members of Parliament, excepted againſt by Charles I. and a Colonel for the Parliament in the beginning of the rebellion. Which John loſt his life in their ſervice in June 1643. By this match Oliver Cromwell came to be related to the Ingoldeſbies, and Goodwins, of Bucks. The third, named Frances, was the ſecond wife of Richard Whalley, of Kirton, in Nottinghamſhire, father to Edward Whalley, a Colonel in the Parliament army, one of the King's Judges, Commiſſary-General in Scotland, one of Oliver's Lords, and a Major-General. He fled from juſtice upon the approach of the return of King Charles II. and lived and died in a ſtrange land. '

The heroic acts and atchievements of Gen. Whalley

are to be found in all the histories of those times, in the records of Parliament, and the other original memoirs of Whitlock, Wellwood, Rushworth, and the periodical publications of that day, now before me. From all which it appears, that he was a man of true and real greatness of mind, and of abilities equal to any enterprize, and to the highest councils of the state, civil, political, and military : that he was a very active character in the national events, for twenty years in the great period from 1640 to 1660. He was a man of religion. It has been the manner of all the court historians, ever since the licentious æra of Charles II. to confound all the characters of religion with the irrational and extravagant fanaticism of that day, and of every age. But candour ought to confess, at least to believe, and even to know, that in the cause of liberty, in the Parliamentary cause, while there were many mad enthusiasts both in religion and politics, the great and noble transactions of that day, show there was also great wisdom, great abilities, great generalship, great learning, great knowledge of law and justice, great integrity, and rational sincere religion, to be found conversant among the most vigorous and active characters of that æra. Among these WHALLEY ought to be ranked , and to be considered as a man of firmness in a good cause, and like Daniel at the Court of Persia, of a religion of which he was not ashamed , of an open, but unostentatious zeal, of real rational and manly virtue, a determined servant and worshipper of the most high God , of exemplary holiness of life , of fervent indeed, but sincere and undissembled piety. The commissioners of Nottinghamshire give this testimony : " They think themselves happy in having a person of so high merit sent down to them as Major-General Whalley, who is their native countryman, a gentleman of an honorable family, and of singular justice, ability, and piety †

GENERAL GOFFE.

William Goffe, Efq. was a fon of the reverend Stephen Goffe, a Puritan Divine, Rector of Stanmer, in Suffex. He lived with Mr. Vaughan, a dry falter in London, a great partizan of the Parliament, and a zealous Prefbyterian. Difliking trade, and the war opening, he repaired to the parliament army ; where his merit raifed him to be a Quarter-Mafter, and then a Colonel of foot, and afterwards a General. He was a member of Parliament ; and one of thofe who took up accufation againft the eleven members, and who fentenced the King, and figned the warrant for his execution. He rendered the Protector great fervice, in affifting Colonel White in purging the parliament. For this and his other fervices he received Lambert's poft of Major-General of foot. He was returned for Great Yarmouth in the Parliament of 1654, and for the county of Southampton in 1656. Laft of all he was called up into the Protector's Houfe of Lords. He was grateful to the Cromwell intereft, and figned the order for proclaiming the Protector Richard. This attachment made him to be regarded by the Parliament, as well as army, with jealoufy, after they began to be difpofed to a return of monarchy. And Monk, who knew he was an enemy to the King's return, refufed to admit him to treat with him, though fent by the Englifh army. At the Reftoration he left the kingdom with Whalley, whofe daughter he married, and came with him to Bofton in New-England, 1660.

There happened a remarkable diverfity of religious fentiments in the family of Goffe. The father, the reverend Stephen Goffe was a ferious, pious and learned Puritan Divine ; and paid great attention to the education of his children. He gave an univerfity education to two of his fons, John and Stephen : and although his fon William was not liberally or academically educated, yet fuch were his abilities, and fo well were they cultivated and improved by reading, obfervation and converse with scientific subjects, and the great variety of literary life, that the University of Oxford conferred upon him the honorary degree of Master of Arts. In religion and piety he was very similar to his father-in-law, Whalley. Indeed, both Goffe and Whalley were exactly of the same religious sentiments with that eminent Puritan Divine, Dr. Owens, Vice-Chancellor of the University of Oxford, who was a Congregationalist. The Pœdobaptist part of the dissenting interest in England, was unhappily divided into Presbyterians and Congregationalists, both unanimously agreeing in doctrines, and differing only on forms of church government, and yet generally very amicably differing, as knowing they were harmoniously agreed in all the great, essential, and most important things in religion. If any thing, the Independents, or Congregationalists, were then the most catholic and fraternal of the two. Oliver Cromwell, and these two Judges, were Congregationalists. While General Goffe's father was a Puritan, his brother John was a clergyman of the established church : his brother Stephen became agent for Charles II. in France, Flanders, and Holland, turned Roman Catholic, and became a priest among the Oratorians in Paris, and afterwards a chaplain to Queen Henrietta Maria : while William himself was the pious Congregational Puritan, exactly agreeing in religious sentiments with the first settlers of Boston and New-Haven.

I subjoin some extracts from the *Fasti Oxonienses.* Page 79.

" May 19.   Colonel William Goffe, was then also presented by Zanchy, and created M. A. He was the son of Stephen Goffe, Rector of Stanmore in Sussex, and younger brother to John Goffe, mentioned among the writers, *An.* 1661, and to Stephen Goffe, mentioned in the Fasti, *An.* 1626. While this William was a youth, and averse to all kind of learning, he was bound an apprentice to one Vaughan, a salter in London, brother to Colonel Joseph Vaughan, a Parliamentarian, and a zealous Prefbyterian; whofe time being near, or newly out, he betook himfelf to be a foldier for the righteous caufe, inftead of fetting up his trade, went out a Quarter-Mafter of Foot, and continued in the wars till he forgot what he had fought for. At length, through feveral military grades, he became a Colonel, a frequent prayer maker, preacher, and preffer for righteoufnefs and freedom, which in outward fhew, was expreffed very zealoufly, and therefore in high efteem in the Parliament army. In 1648, he was one of the Judges of King Charles I. fate in judgment when he was brought before the High Court of Juftice, ftood up as confenting when fentence paffed upon him for his decollation, and afterwards fet his hand and feal to the warrant for his execution. Afterwards, having, like his General (Cromwell) an evil tincture of that fpirit that loved and fought after the favor and praife of man, more than that of God, as by woful experience in both of them it did afterwards appear, he could not further believe, or perfevere upon that account, by degrees fell off from the anti-monarchical principles of the cheif part of the army, and was the man, with Colonel William White, who brought Mufqueteers, and turned out the Anabaptiftical members that were left behind of the *Little*, or *Barebone's* Parliament, out of the houfe, *An.* 1654 Complying thus kindly with the defign and intereft of the faid General, he was by him, when made Protector, conftituted Major-General of Hampfhire, Suffex and Berks, a place of great profit, and afterwards was of one, if not of two Parliaments; did advance his intereft greatly, and was in fo great efteem and favor in Oliver's Court, that he was judged the only fit man to have Major-General John Lambert's place and command, as Major-General of the army of foot, and by fome to have the Protectorfhip fettled on him, in future time. He being thus made fo confiderable a perfon, was taken out of the Houfe to be a Lord, and to have a negative voice in the other Houfe, and the rather for this reafon, that he never in all his life (as he ufed to fay) fought against any fuch thing as a fingle perfon, or a negative voice, but only to pull down Charles and fet up Oliver, &c. in which he obtained his end. In 1660, a little before the reftoration of King Charles II. he betook himfelf to his heels to fave his neck, without any regard had to his Majefty's proclamation, wandered about, fearing every one that he met fhould flay him; and was living at Laufanna in 1664, with Edmond Ludlow, Edward Whalley, and other regicides, when John Lifle, another of that number, was there by certain generous royalifts difpatched. He afterwards lived feveral years in vagabondfhip, but when he died, or where his carcafs was lodged, is as yet unknown to me."

The following is extracted from *Athenæ Oxonienfes*. Page 261.

" John Goughe, commonly called Goffe, fon of the Rector of Stanmer, in Suffex, was born in that county, began to be converfant with the Mufes in Merton College, *An*. 1624, made Demi of that of S. Mar. Magd. 1627, aged feventeen years, or more, Perpetual Fellow 29 July, 1630, being then Bachelor of Arts. Afterwards proceeding in that faculty, he entered into orders, and became a preacher in thefe parts. In 1642, September 26, he was inducted into the Vicarage of Hackington, alias S. Stephen, near to the city of Canterbury, in the place of James Hirft, deceafed. From whence being ejected foon after for refufing the covenant, was, with other loyal clegymen, caft into the county prifon in S. Dunftan's parifh, in the fuburbs of the faid city. In 1652, he, by the endeavors of his brother William, whom I fhall anon mention, was inducted into the Rectory of Norton, near Sittingbourne, in Kent, on the thirteenth day of March, and in the year 1660, he being reftored to the Vicarage of S. Stephen, was actually created Doctor of Divinity in the beginning of December in the same year, and inducted again according to the ceremonies of the church of England, into the Rectory of Norton, on the fourth of March following, which were all the Spiritualities he enjoyed.

" He hath written a book entitled, *Exclefiæ Anglicanæ Threenodia in qua perturbatiffimus regni & ecclefiæ ftatus, fub Anabaptiftica tyrannide lugetur,* London, 1661. *Oct.* Also a large Latin Epiftle written to Doctor Edward Simfon, fet before a book written by him, entitled, *Chronicon Catholicum* &c. London, 1652. *Fol.* He concluded his laft day in the parifh of Norton before mentioned, and was buried in the chancel of the church of S. Alphage in Canterbury, on the 26th day of November, in fixteen hundred fixty and one. This perfon, who was a zealous fon of the Church of England, had an elder brother named Stephen Goffe, originally of Mert. Coll. afterwards of S. Alb. Hall, and a bigot of the Church of Rome ; and another brother named William, whether elder or younger I know not, who was originally a trader in London, afterwards a Prefbyterian, Independent, one of the Judges of King Charles I. and one of Oliver's Lords ; who, to fave his neck from the gallows, did, upon a forefight of the King's return, 1660, leave the nation, and died obfcurely in a ftrange land. The father of the faid Goffe, was Stephen Goffe, fome time Bachelor of Arts of Magd. College, a good logician and difputant, but a very fevere Puritan, eminent for his training up, while a tutor, feveral that proved afterwards very noted fcholars ; among whom muft not be forgotten, Robert Harris, D. D. fome time Prefident of Trinity College, in Oxon."

Further accounts of General Goffe, and his fhare and activity in the national adminiftration, efpecially during the Protectorate, are to be found in the memoirs and hiftories of thofe times. Thus we have given a fum-

mary account of General Whalley and General Goffe,
the parts they acted and the characters they sustained on
the European theatre of life, and antecedent to their
coming over to New-England.   And certainly they
were among the personages of the first eminence for
great and noble actions in their day.   They were both
of Oliver's House of Lords ; and when we consider his
singular penetration and sagacious judgment in discern-
ing characters, and the abundance of great and meritorious characters strongly attached to his cause, from
among which he had to select his counsellors, being in
no necessity of selecting inferior abilities, the presump-
tion is strong and just, that in themselves they were
very distinguished and meritorious characters.

They had moved in a great sphere ; they had acted in
a great cause, which might have been carried through,
had national instability permitted it.   But Monk, ever
of dubious principles, and who had never been at heart
a friend to the cause, turning up at the head of the army
in the course of events by a certain casualty and fatality ;
and resolving on a bold stroke for the abolition of this
and the restoration of the former government ; and at
the same time the nation, unhappily wearied out of the
convulsions and struggles of civil war, in the very critical moment of the parturition of empire, when indeed
had they been sensible of it the die was cast, the difficulty was over, and the policy already formed ; the
nation, I say, becoming prepared for a revolution, it
was obvious that great havock would be made among
the most distinguished and active characters, and that
these two judges must fall among the rest.   It is very
dangerous and unwise to trust supremacy into the hands
of those who are not cordial in a great cause, be that
cause just or unjust, and especially in a just and glorious cause.   If opportunity presents, instead of its conservation and defence, it will certainly be betrayed and
given up.   It was so by Monk.   The great cause of
liberty was lost, overwhelmed and gone.   The Judges

therefore feeing their fate inevitable, found it neceſſary to eſcape from England, exile themſelves from their native country, and evaniſh into oblivion. Accordingly, feeing the complexion of Parliament, and that the Reſtoration was in effect determined and fettled, juſt before it actually took place, they ſecretly withdrew themſelves, and abdicated into New-England in 1660 Here they lived fecreted together until they finiſhed life : and therefore their remaining hiftory muſt be confidered together.

CHAP. II.

Their Exile, and living together in their various Lodgments in New-England, to their death.

I Shall now proceed to the Hiftory of the two Judges, in their exile and pilgrimages after their arrival together in New-England : and trace them in their concealments at New-Haven, Milford, Guilford and Hadley, to the laſt notices of them. This ſhall be arranged in two ſections. 1. Their hiftory for the firſt eleven months after their arrival, while they appeared publicly here, and eſpecially the dangerous period of the two laſt months of their public appearance, when they entirely abdicated, and were ever after totally loſt from all knowledge of the public. 2. Their various pilgrimages in total oblivion and concealment from the public.

Sect 1. *The firſt eleven months of their public appearance, after their arrival at Boſton.*

The moſt authentic account is taken from Goffe's journal or diary, for ſeven years from their departure from London, 1660, to 1667. It confiſted of ſeveral pocket volumes in Goffe's own hand writing ; received

from the Ruffel family, and preferved in Dr. Cotton
Mather's library in Bofton. The Doctor's only fon,
Dr. Samuel Mather, married Governor Hutchinfon's fifter ; by which means the Governor obtained
Goffe's manufcript, and himfelf fhewed me, in 1766,
one of thefe little manufcript books in Goffe 's own hand.
It confifted of 55 leaves, or 110 pages, in fmall 12 *mo.*
It began the firft month of the year 1662, and was a
diary of one whole year and a little more. It was
written in characters, though not altogether in fhort
hand, being a mixture of inverted alphabet and characters, eafily decyphered : and contained news from Europe, and private occurrences with them at New-Haven
and Milford. From this I then made fome extracts.
Mr. Hutchinfon, from this and the other volumes, as
well as from their manufcript letters, fundry original
copies of which he fhewed me, formed the fummary
abftract, which he publifhed as a marginal note in the
firft volume of his Hiftory of Maffachufetts, p 215.
firft printed 1764. This may be depended upon as genuine information, and is as follows :

Governor Hutchinfon's Account of Whalley and Goffe.

" In the fhip. † which arrived at Bofton from London, the 27th of July, 1660, there came paffengers,
Colonel Whalley and Colonel Goffe, two of the late
King's Judges Colonel Goffe brought teftimonials
from Mr. John Row and Mr. Seth Wood, two minifters of a church in Weftminfter. Colonel Whalley
had been a member of Mr. Thomas Goodwin's church.
Goffe kept a journal or diary, from the day he left Weftminfter, May 4, until the year 1667, which together
with feveral other papers belonging to him, I have in
my poffeffion. Almoft the whole is in characters, or
fhort hand, not difficult to decypher. The ftory of
thefe perfons has never yet been publifhed to the world.
It has never been known in New-England. Their papers, after their death, were collected, and have re-

† *Capt. Purce.*

Goffe's diary?

mained near an hundred years in a library in Boston. It must give some entertainment to the curious. They left London before the King was proclaimed. It does not appear that they were among the most obnoxious of the Judges : but as it was expected vengeance would be taken of some of them, and a great many had fied, they did not think it safe to remain. They did not attempt to conceal their persons or characters when they arrived at Boston, but immediately went to the Governor, Mr. Endicot, who received them very courteously. They were visited by the principal persons of the town ; and among others, they take notice of Colonel Crown's coming to see them. He was a noted Royalist. Although they did not disguise themselves, yet they chose to reside at Cambridge, a village about four miles distant from the town, where they went the first day they arrived. They went publicly to meetings on the Lord's day, and to occasional lectures, fasts, and thanksgivings, and were admitted to the sacrament, and attended private meetings for devotion, visited many of the principal towns, and were frequently at Boston ; and once when insulted there, the person who insulted them was bound to his good behaviour. They appeared grave, serious and devout, and the rank they had sustained commanded respect. Whalley had been one of Cromwell's Lieutenant-Generals, and Goffe a Major-General. It is not strange that they should meet with this favorable reception, nor was this reception any contempt of the authority in England. They were known to have been two of the King's Judges ; but Charles the second was not proclaimed, when the ship that brought them left London. They had the news of it in the Channel. The reports afterwards, by way of Barbadoes, were that all the Judges would be pardoned but seven. The act of indemnity was not brought over till the last of November. When it appeared that they were not excepted, some of the principal persons in the Government were alarmed, pity and

compaffion prevailed with others.   They had affuran-
ces from fome that belonged to the General Court, that
they would ftand by them, but were advifed by others
to think of removing.   The 22d. of February, 1661,
the Governor fummoned a Court of affiftants, to confult about fecuring them, but the Court did not agree
to it.   Finding it unfafe to remain any longer, they
left Cambridge the 26th following, and arrived at New-
Haven the 7th of March, 1661.   One Captain Bree-
dan, who had feen them at Bofton, gave information
thereof upon his arrival in England   A few days after
their removal, a hue and cry, as they term it in their
diary, was brought by the way of Barbadoes ;   and
thereupon a warrant to fecure them iffued, the 8th of
March, from the Governor and Affiftant', which was
fent to Springfield and other towns in the weftern part
of the colony, but they were beyond the reach of it."

The Governor adds in a long marginal note, " They
were well treated at New-Haven by the minifters, [dagger]
and fome of the magiftrates, and for fome days feemed
to apprehend themfelves out of danger.   But the news
of the King's proclamation being brought to New-Haven, they were obliged to abfcond.   The 27th of
March they removed to New-Milford, and appeared
there in the day time, and made themfelves known ;
but at night returned privately to New-Haven, and
lay concealed in Mr Davenport the minifter's houfe,
until the 30th of April.   About this time news came
to Bofton, that ten of the Judges were executed, and
the Governor received a royal mandate, dated March
5, 1660. to caufe Whalley and Goffe to be fecured.
This greatly alarmed the country, and there is no
doubt that the court were now in earneft in their endea
vors to apprehend them : and to avoid all fufpicion,
they gave commiffion and inftruction to two young
merchants from England, Thomas Kellond and Thomas Kirk, zealous royalifts, to go through the colonies

[dagger] *Rev. John Davenport and Rev. Nicholas Street.*

as far as Manhados, in fearch of them. They had friends who informed them what was doing, and they removed from Mr. Davenport's to the houfe of one Jones, ‡ where they lay hid until the 11th of May, and then removed to a mill, and from thence, on the 13th into the woods, where they met Jones and two of his companions, Sperry and Burril, who firft condu&ed them to a place called Hatchet-Harbour, where they lay two nights, until a cave or hole in the fide of a hill was prepared to conceal them. This hill they called Providence-Hill: and there they continued from the 15th of May to the 11th of June, fometimes in the cave, and in very tempeftuous weather, in a houfe near to it. During this time the meffengers went through New-Haven to the Dutch fettlement, from whence they returned to Bofton by water. They made diligent fearch, and had full proof that the regicides had been feen at Mr. Davenport's, and offered great rewards to Englifh and Indians who fhould give information, that they might be taken , but by the fidelity of their three friends they remained undifcovered. Mr. Davenport was threatened with being called to an account, for concealing and comforting traitors, and might well be alarmed. They had engaged to furrender, rather than the country or any particular perfons fhould fuffer upon their account : and upon intimation of Mr. Davenport's danger, they generoufly refolved to go to New-Haven, and deliver themfelves up to the authority there. The miferies they had fuffered, and were ftill expofed to, and the little chance they had of finally efcaping, in a country where every ftranger is immediately known to be fuch, would not have been fufficient to have induced them. They let the Deputy-Governor, Mr. Leete know where they were , but he took no meafures to fecure them , and the next day fome perfons came to them to advife them not to furrender. Having publicly fhewn themfelves at New-Haven, they had cleared

‡ *William Jones, Efq. afterwards Depuy-Goveror of Connecticut.*

C

Mr. Davenport from the fufpicion of ftill concealing them, and the 24th of June went into the woods again to their cave. They continued there, fometimes venturing to a houfe near the cave, until the 19th of Auguft —when the fearch for them being pretty well over they ventured to the houfe of one Tomkins, near Milford meeting-houfe, where they remained two years, without fo much as going into the orchard. After that, they took a little more liberty, and made themfelves known to feveral perfons in whom they could confide, and each of them frequently prayed, and alfo exercifed, as they termed it, or preached at private meetings in their chamber. In 1664, the commiffioners from King Charles arrived at Bofton—Upon the news of it, they retired to their cave, where they tarried eight or ten days. Soon after, fome Indians in their hunting, difcovered the cave with the bed, and the report being fpread abroad, it was not fafe to remain near it. On the 13th of October, 1664, they removed to Hadley, near an hundred miles diftant, travelling only by night; where Mr. Ruffel, the minifter of the place, had previoufly agreed to receive them. Here they remained concealed fifteen or fixteen years, very few perfons in the colony being privy to it. The laft account of Goffe, is from a letter, dated *Ebenezer*, the name they gave their feveral places of abode, April 2, 1679. Whalley had been dead fome time before. The tradition at Hadleys, that two perfons unknown, were buried in the minifter's cellar. The minifter was no fufferer by his boarders. They received more or lefs remittances every year, for many years together, from their wives in England Thofe few perfons who knew where they were, made them frequent prefents. Richard Saltonftall, Efq. who was in the fecret, when he left the country and went to England in 1672, made them a prefent of fifty pounds at his departure, and they take notice of donations from feveral other friends. They were in conftant terror, though they had reafon to

hope, after some years, that the enquiry for them was
over.   They read with pleasure the news of their being
killed, with other judges, in Switzerland.   Their diary for six or seven years, contains every little occurrent
in the town, church, and particular families in the
neighborhood.   They had indeed, for five years of
their lives, been among the principal actors in the great
affairs of the nation : Goffe especially, who turned the
members of the little Parliament out of the house, and
who was attached to Oliver and to Richard to the last ;
but they were both of low birth and education.   They
had very constant and exact intelligence of every thing,
which passed in England, and were unwilling to give
up all hopes of deliverance.   Their greatest expectations were from the fulfilment of the prophecies.   They
had no doubt, that the execution of the Judges was the
slaying of the witnesses.   They were much disappointed,
when the year 1666 had passed without any remarkable
event, but flattered themselves that the Christian æra
might be erroneous.   Their lives were miserable and
constant burdens.   They complain of being banished
from all human society.   A letter from Goffe's wife,
who was Whalley's daughter, I think worth preserving.   After the second year, Goffe writes by the name
of *Walter Goldsmith*, and she of *Frances Goldsmith* ;
and the correspondence is carried on, as between a mother and son.   There is too much religion in their letters for the taste of the present day : but the distresses
of two persons, under these peculiar circumstances,
who appear to have lived very happily together, are
very strongly described.

Whilst they were at Hadley, February 10, 1664—5,
Dixwell, another of the Judges, came to them ; but
from whence, or in what part of America he first landed, is not known.   The first mention of him in their
journal, is by the name of Colonel Dixwell ; but ever
after they call him Mr. Davids.   He continued some
years at Hadley, and then removed to New-Haven.—

He was generally supposed to have been one of those who were obnoxious in England, but he never discovered who he was, until he was on his death-bed. I have one of his letters signed James Davids, dated March 23, 1683. He married at New-Haven, and left several children. After his death his son, who before had been called Davids, took the name of Dixwell, came to Boston, and lived in good repute; was a ruling elder of one of the churches there, and died in 1725, of the small-pox by inoculation. Some of his grand-children are now living. Colonel Dixwell was buried in New-Haven. His grave-stone still remains with this inscription,—" J. D. Esq. deceased March 18th, in the 82d year of his age, 1688."

It cannot be denied, that many of the principal persons in the colony greatly esteemed these persons for their professions of piety, and their grave deportment, who did not approve of their political conduct. Mr. Mitchel, the minister of Cambridge, who shewed them great friendship upon their first arrival, says in a manuscript which he wrote in his own vindication, " Since I have had opportunity, by reading and discourse, to look a little into that action for which these men suffer, I could never see that it was justifiable." After they were declared traitors, they certainly would have been sent to England, if they could have been taken. It was generally thought that they had left the country; and even the consequence of their escape was dreaded, lest when they were taken, those who had harbored them should suffer for it. Mr. Endicot, the Governor, writes to the Earl of Manchester, that he supposes they went towards the Dutch at Manhados, and took shipping for Holland: and Mr. Bradstreet, then Governor, in December 1684, writes to Edward Randolph, " that after their being at New-Haven, he could never hear what became of them." Randolph, who was sent to search into the secrets of the government, could obtain no more knowledge of them, than that they had been

Ridot Harbour Lodge Fort.
Left this Aug. 19. 1661.

Thomas...

Mr. Rich.ᵈ Sperry

Lodge

Mr. Ralph Lines

West River or Aboute

Mill Judges here May 11. 1661

Bea

MAP of NEW-HAVEN
and the Environs

Scale of Miles
1   2   3

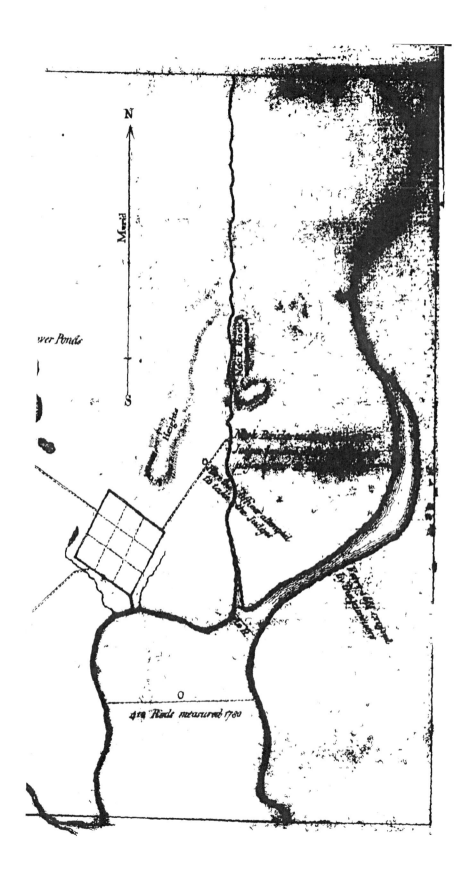

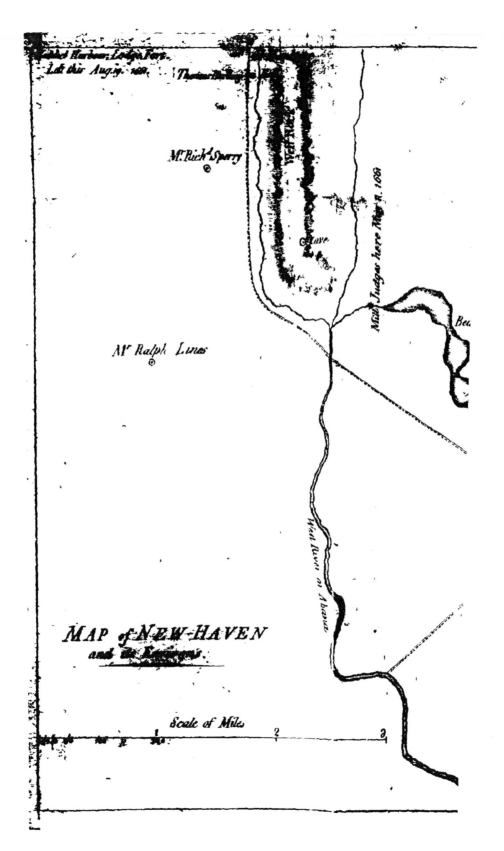

...that Harbour, Lodge, Fort.
Left this Aug.19. 1661. Thomas...

Mr Rich.d Sperry

West Rock

Cave

Mr.d Judges here May 11. 1661

Bea...

Mr Ralph Lines

West River or Abavu

MAP of NEW-HAVEN
and the Environs.

Scale of Miles

2   3

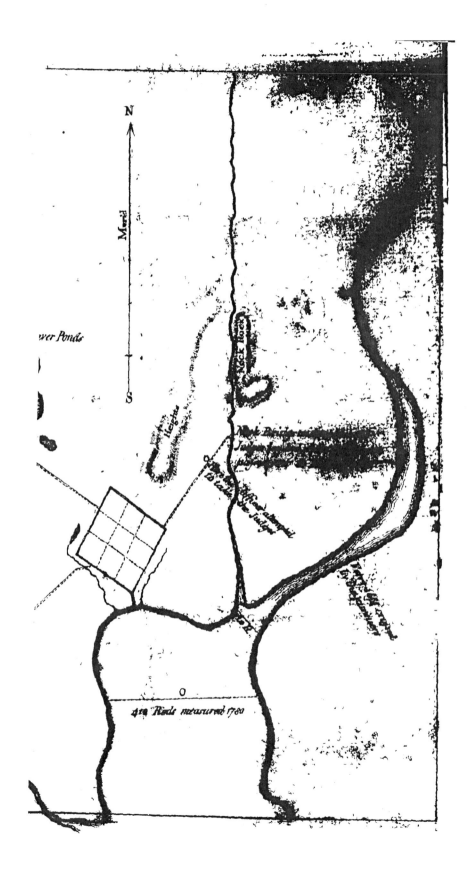

in the country, and refpect had been fhewn them by fome of the Magiftrates. I am loth to omit an anecdote handed down through Governor Leverett's family. I find Goffe takes notice in his journal of Leverett's being at Hadley. The town of Hadley was alarmed by the Indians in 1675, in the time of public worfhip, and the people were in the utmoft confufion.—Suddenly, a grave elderly perfon appeared in the midft of them.— In his mien and drefs he differed from the reft of the people.—He not only encouraged them to defend themfelves ; but put himfelf at their head, rallied, inftructed, and led them on to encounter the enemy, who by this means were repulfed.—As fuddenly the deliverer of Hadley difappeared.—The people were left in confternation, utterly unable to account for this ftrange phœnomenon. It is not probable they were ever able to explain it. If Goffe had been then difcovered, it muft have come to the knowledge of thofe perfons, who declare by their letters that they never knew what became of him."†

Thus far Governor Hutchinfon's narrative concerning thefe two perfons ; which is the more valuable, as being extracted from their journal, it muft contain the moft accurate information we can ever obtain. To this extract pofterity muft ever have recourfe, fince it is out of our power again to recur to the original journal, which with Goffe's other papers, in the Governor's hands, were irrecoverably loft when the Governor's houfe was demolifhed in the tumults of the Stamp Act, 1765. But that we may collect all he fays in other parts of his hiftory refpecting thefe Judges, I fhall fubjoin another extract.

In 1664, four commiffiones were appointed by the King, Colonel Richard Nichols, George Cartwright, Efq. Sir Robert Carr, and Samuel Maverick, Efq.— After the reduction of Manhados, they returned to Bofton, exhibited a number of articles to the General Af-

† Hutch. Hiſt. Maſſ. V. I. p. 218.

fembly of Maffachufetts, on which they were charged by the King to make inquiry; and to which the Af-fembly, in May 1665, make their anfwers. In an-fwer to the tenth inftruction, they fay, "That they knew of no perfons attainted of high treafon, who had arrived here, except Mr. Whalley and Mr. Goffe, and they before the act of Parliament, and they departed this jurifdiction the February following, and a procla-mation againft them coming foon after by way of Bar-badoes, the Court fent two gentleman, Mr. Kel-lond and Mr. Kirk, after them to Connecticut and New-Haven, to apprehend them."†

Hitherto we have proceeded upon accurate and au-thentic documents. I fhall now collect and exhibit other fcattered lights and traditionary information, pre-ferved partly in the public fame which fuch an event would be likely to produce at New-Haven and Hadley, and partly in families whofe anceftors were privy to the fecrets of thefe men, and concerned in their conceal-ments. Thefe anecdotes, together with the defcription and delineation of their places of abode, may illuftrate the hiftory of thefe fugitive pilgrims.

Among the traditionary anecdotes and ftories con-cerning the events, which took place at and about the time the purfuers were at New-Haven, are the follow-ing.

1. The day they were expected, the Judges walked out towards the neck bridge, the road the purfuers muft enter the town. At fome diftance, the Sheriff or Mar-fhal, who then was Mr. Kimberly, overtook them with a warrant to apprehend them, and endeavored to take them. But the Judges ftood upon their defence, and placing themfelves behind a tree, and being expert at fencing, defended themfelves with their cudgels, and repelled the officer; who went back to town to com-mand help, and returned with aid, but found the Judges

† *Hutch. Hift. Mass. p. 243.*

had efcaped, having abfconded into the woods, with which the town was then furrounded.

2. That immediately after this, on the fame day, the Judges hid themfelves under the bridge one mile from town ; and lay there concealed under the bridge, while the purfuivants rode over it and paffed into town : and that the Judges returned that night into town, and lodged at Mr. Jones's.   All this, tradition fays, was a preconcerted and contrived bufinefs, to fhew that the Magiftrates at New-Haven had ufed their endeavors to apprehend them before the arrival of the purfuers.

Under bridge.

3. That on a time when the purfuers were fearching the town, the Judges, in fhifting their fituations, happened, by accident or defign, at the houfe of a Mrs. Eyers, a refpectable and comely lady : fhe feeing the purfuivants coming, uthered her guefts out at the back door, who walking out a little ways, inftantly returned to the houfe, and were hid and concealed by her in her apartments.   The purfuers coming in, enquired whether the regicides were at her houfe ? She anfwered, they had been there, but were juft gone away, and pointed out the way they went into the fields and woods, and by her artful and polite addrefs, fhe diverted them, put them upon a falfe fcent, and fecured her friends. It is rather probable that this happened the next day after their coming to town : and that they then left the town, having fhewn themfelves not to be concealed in Mr. Davenport's, and went into the woods to the mill, two miles off, whither they had retired on the 11th of May.

Mrs Eyers.

4. The family of the Sperrys always tell this ftory : that while the Judges were at the houfe of their anceftor, Mr. Richard Sperry, they were furprized with an unexpected vifit from the purfuers, whom they efpied at a diftance coming up a long caufway to the houfe, lying through a morafs, and on each fide an impaffible fwamp, fo that they were feen perhaps fifty or fixty

Sperry

rods before they came up to the houfe.   But the'Judges efcaped into the woods and mountains, and eluded their fearch.   This ftory is current at New-Haven, and is always told, as what took place after the return of the purfuers from New-York, and fo was unexpected to Sperry and the Judges.   Governor Hutchinfon fays, the purfuivants returned from Manhados to Bofton by water ; but the conftant tradition at New-Haven is otherwife, and that they were here a fecond time, and that it was thought they got their information of their being at Sperry's, in confequence of the bribes they had fcattered here, at their former vifit, among fervants.

5. About the time the purfuers came to New-Haven, and perhaps a little before, and to prepare the minds of the people for their reception, the reverend Mr. Davenport preached publicly from this text, Ifai. xvi. 3. 4. *Take counfel, execute judgment, make thy fhadow as the night in the midft of the noon day ; hide the out-cafts, bewray not him that wandereth.   Let mine out-cafts dwell with thee ; Moab, be thou a covert to them from the face of the fpoiler.* This doubtlefs had its effect, and put the whole town upon their guard, and united them in caution and concealment.

As Kellond and Kirk, befides the royal mandate, received a warrant from Governor Endicot at Bofton, to make fearch through the colony of Maffachufetts : fo paffing out of that jurifdiction into the jurifdiction of Connecticut, they obtained a fimilar warrant from the Governor, Winthrop, at New-London, and upon entering into the colony of New-Haven, they applied to Governor Leet, at Guilford, for a like warrant to fearch this jurifdiction alfo.   They lodged at Guilford May 12th, and next day rode eighteen miles to New-Haven, and might enter the town about noon. The banks of the river at Neck-Bridge are low, and falt marfh on both fides, fo that the bridge is low, being only high enough to avoid high water, which is here fix to eight

feet tide ; fo there could be no hiding under the bridge
at high water. From the aftronomical or lunar tables
we find, that on the 13th May, 1661, the fun was in
the fecond degree of gemini, and the moon in the firft
of aries, or about fixty degrees apart, and fo about two
days and half after the laft quarter ; when it is always
high water at New-Haven about, or a little after fix
o'clock, and low water about noon, the only time when
they could have fecreted themfelves under the bridge,
agreeable to tradition.

6. To fhew the dexterity of the Judges at fencing,
this ftory is told : That while at Bofton, there appeared
a gallant perfon there, fome fay a fencing-mafter, who
on a ftage erected for the purpofe, walked it for feveral days, challenging and defying any to play with him
at fwords : at length one of the Judges, difguifed in a
ruftic drefs, holding in one hand a cheefe wrapped in a
napkin, for a fheild, with a broom-ftick, whofe mop
he had befmeared with dirty puddle water as he paffed
along : thus equipped, he mounted the ftage :—The
fencing-mafter railed at him for his impudence, afked
what bufinefs he had there, and bid him be gone.—
The Judge ftood his ground—upon which the gladiator
made a pafs at him with his fword, to drive him off—
a rencounter enfued—the Judge received the fword into
the cheefe, and held it till he drew the mop of the
broom over his mouth and gave the gentleman a pair
of whifkers—The gentleman made another pafs, and
plunging his fword a fecond time, it was caught and
held in the cheefe, till the broom was drawn over his
eyes—At a third lunge, the fword was caught again,
till the mop of the broom was rubbed gently all over his
face.—Upon this the gentleman let fall, or laid afide
his fmall fword, and took up the broad fword, and
came at him with that—Upon which the Judge faid,
ftop fir, hitherto you fee I have only played with you,
and not attempted to hurt you ; but if you come at me
now with the broad-fword, know, that I will certainly

take your life.   The firmnefs and determinatenefs with which he fpake, ftruck the gentleman, who defifting, exclaimed, who can you be?   You are either Goffe, Whalley, or the Devil, for there was no other man in England that could beat me.   And fo the difguifed Judge retired into obfcurity, leaving the fpectators to enjoy the diverfion of the fcene, and the vanquifhment of the boafting champion.   Hence it is proverbial in fome parts of New-England, in fpeaking of a champion at athletic and other exercifes, to fay that none can beat him but Goffe, Whalley, or the Devil.

I fay nothing on a few variations in narrating this ftory—as that fome fay the fcene was at New-York, where the fencer ftaked and offered a hat crown full of filver to the man that fhould beat him—The place certainly was Bofton, if any where, for they never were out of New-England, and that the fencer difcerned and recognized his mafter in the act of fencing, and defifted inftantly, faying, you are my mafter, Colonel Goffe, who taught me fencing—You, fir, and no other man can beat me.

I fhall now confider more particularly their critical fituation at New-Haven, during the dangerous period of the laft two months of their public appearance, and efpecially of the laft month previous to their final abdication.   But a fummary view of the polity and fpirit of the little republic of New-Haven colony, will be neceffary to throw light upon thefe tranfactions, and without it thefe events will not be perfectly intelligible.

The colony of New-Haven jurifdiction, was begun 1637 and 1638.   The fettlers came over from England together, chiefly from London and its vicinities.   They came three diftinct congregations with their minifters; from the beginning intending to fettle down in three diftinct and feparate townfhips, and to form and coalefce into one body politic, diftinct from Maffachufetts, Plymouth, and the other colonizations.   They planted down together at and about New-Haven, with thefe original views, which they carried into immediate execution. They therefore at their firft coming to Bofton, went beyond Maffachufetts, and Connecticut then juft fettling alfo, to Quinipioke, with the view of fettling, fomewhere by themfelves, within the Earl of Warwick's patent affigned to Lord Say and Seal, who held in truft for Puritan exiles. Here they pitched and fettled their towns, and formed into a feparate independent government ; and framed their polity for themfelves, one of the wifeft ever devifed by man. This embryo of a perfect republic was conceived by the concurrent wifdom of Governor Eaton, Goodyear, Newman, Leet, Defborough, and other fenfible and patriotic civilians, and the three learned minifters, Davenport, Whitfield and Prudden.

Samuel Defborough, Efq. afterwards Lord Keeper of Scotland, was related to Major-General John Defborough, one of Olivers Lords. He came over with the reverend Mr. Whitfield, was a magiftrate, and at the head of the fettlement of Guilford. He returned to England 1651, became " one of the commiffioners of the revenues ; the fame year reprefented the city of Edenburgh in Parliament : at a council held at Whitehall, May 4, 1655, he was appointed one of the nine counfellors for the kingdom of Scotland, and the fame year Keeper of the Great Seal of that nation, and alowed £2000. annually :—The year following he was returned a member of the Britifh Parliament for the Sheriffdom of Mid-Lothian, and was continued in all his employments under the Protector Richard.' †— This fhews him a man of political abilities to fuftain fo many and fuch high betruftments with the reputation and acceptance with which he difcharged them.

Upon amicable confultation, they devifed this little fyftem of policy, the miniature even of our prefent po-

† *Noble, Vol.* 2. 254.

licy, admitting an unfolding of itfelf into an enlarge-ment and application even to the efficacious dominion of the largeſt republic.   Their idea was to found and inſtitute a general aſſembly, or a court of general juriſ-diction, for legiſlation and dominion over all the towns, and a regulation of the ſubordinate interior local policy of the reſpective towns, left in this to themſelves.   Or, to invert the order of origination, the towns to govern themſelves abſolutely and independently as far as re-ſpected themſelves:—In as far as reſpected the common public intereſt of all the towns, to inſtitute an authori-tative governmental and judicial Council, to which all ſhould ſubmit and be ſubordinated, ſo far as reſpected the common intereſt of the republic.

The General Court was to be conſtituted and con-ſiſt of two branches ;   both elective in different modes by the people : The one to conſiſt of deputies of the towns, elected twice a year by each town reſpectively ; the other, by the name of Magiſtrates, conſiſting of a Governor, Deputy-Governor, and three or more others of abilities and patriotiſm, elected by the general voice of all the freemen annually.   The concurrence of theſe two branches made a public act or law.   The ſupreme adminiſtration, both civil and military, to be with the Governor or Deputy-Governor ;   the judiciary was in the Governor and Magiſtrates   The mode of election was thus : In April, preceding the election and ſeſſion of Aſſembly, which was the laſt week of May, annu-ally, the towns elected two deputies each ; and at the ſame time nominated in each town, one or more per-ſons fo. the Magiſtracy : but this was not election. In the firſt inſtance, each of the three towns nominated two perſons , and their names were ſent by the Go-vernor to all the towns , which, on the day of election, were limited and confined to make their choice of Ma-giſtrates (not Governor nor Deputy-Governor) out of theſe perhaps half a dozen nominated perſons, electing three uſually, ſometimes more, out of the whole, for

Magiſtrates   On the day of election a ſermon was preached by one of the Miniſters.   It was originally deſigned that, however Moſes and Aaron ſhould walk together in co-operative harmony, yet the Miniſters ſhould not be eligible into the Magiſtracy.   When all the freemen of all the towns were aſſembled on the day of election, they firſt choſe a Governor and Deputy-Governor, not herein confined to the nomination ; then out of the nomination a Magiſtrate for each town, not as a repreſentative for that town only, for they differed from the deputies, ſtood on general election, and were thereby become charged with the general intereſt of all the towns.   They at the ſame time choſe a Secretary, Treaſurer and Marſhal, out of a previous nomination of the towns as general officers.   The choice thus annually finiſhed upon the election day ; the general officers and town deputies formed themſelves into an organized Aſſembly, or General Court, for the Juriſdiction. This for the Legiſlature and General Government.

For the executive adminiſtration, whether judical or govermental, they eſtabliſhed this ſyſtem :   Each town annually choſe four deputies, or judges, for town Courts, diſtinct from deputies of the General Court : theſe ſat in their reſpective towns, and acted judicially in all civil matters and lower felonies, much like the Juſtices for keeping the peace, and local for the town, or rather ſimilar to our County Court Judges for the Counties. Theſe four deputies, choſen by the towns, were reported or preſented to the Aſſembly, who approved, empowered and eſtabliſhed them : ſo that they became within the town diſtricts, judiciary officers of the law, veſted with civil authority and legal juriſdiction.   There were then no Juſtices of peace in the colony.   In each town was a Marſhal ; and a military company whoſe chief officer was a Lieutenant, under the Governor, who was commander in chief.   The Supreme Judiciary was a Court of Magiſtrates, firſt at New-Haven, to which

D

the whole colony was amenable ; confifting of the Governor, Deputy-Governor, and the three or more Magiftrates.   Thefe had the cognizance and trial of all caufes civil and criminal, being held to proceed according to ftrict law and juftice, and according to the principles and fpirit of the laws of England.   It was a Court of original as well as appellate jurifdiction, but chiefly original, caufes ufually being brought before them in the firft inftance.   With them, alfo, was the probate of wills, and all teftamentary matters, and fettlement of inteftate eftates.   This Court adminiftered juftice with great firmnefs, impartiality, and dignity.   It was in the conftitution that this judiciary power fhould veft in the Magiftracy, and not be the effect of an annual inveftiture by the Affembly.   In the public records this judiciary Court was ftiled the Court of Magiftracy, and the meetings of the General Affembly, are ftiled General Courts, and were folely legiftatorial and governmental, while the former were only executive and judicial.   It belonged to the Governor in his double capacity of Governor of the colony, and chief judge or head of the Magiftrates or Supreme Judiciary, to take cognizance of treafon, and to execute the King's warrant for the apprehenfion of the Judges, had he received it in feafon, which he did not, and which as foon as he received it, he executed, fo as to fave himfelf and the colony from imputations.

Here we fee a diftinction between Deputies of the Town Courts, and Deputies of the General Court — The former were the civil authority of the town, and on occafion were frequently confulted by the Governor and Court of Magiftrates.   Thefe, not thofe of the General Affembly, were the Deputies which Governor Leet advifed to go and advife with, when he heard the Magiftrates meet at New-Haven, on the application of Kellond and Kirk for a warrant of fearch, which application they refufed, becaufe they had as yet received no orders from the King's majefty.

Thus have I given a general and summary idea of the initial polity, legiflatorial, judicial and govermental. Their laws and decifions were excellent, founded in juftice and wifdom. The hiftory of their laws and tranfactions, with a very few exceptions of undue, tho' confcientious rigidity, and yet far lefs oppreffive than any other policy on earth, ancient or modern, would do honor to any national councils. As to their initial jurifprudence, it was a fingular and judicious fimplication of law, and recovery and emancipation of it, from the confufed colluvies of European jurifprudence, involved and embarraffed with contradictory decifions in the accumulation of ages, a fimplification as honorable to the jural world, as to the republic of letters was the Newtonian difcovery of the fimple energetic laws of nature which operate with diffufive efficacy through the fyftem, the fimple principle of gravity, which commands the moon and the fatellites, governs the planets and comets in their vaft extended orbits, their lofty and magnificent revolutions. In 1656 they printed their little code of laws, and difperfed five hundred copies among all the freemen through the whole jurifdiction. If their laws and adjudications have been in fome inftances juftly ridiculed and condemned, let it be remembered that there is no ftate in which it may not be eafy for candid and liberal minds, and efpecially for a fatyrical and malicious Zoilus, to felect at leaft a few laws and adjudged cafes, which juftly merit contempt, even when the general dige t of their jurifprudence and law proceedings may be wife, juft and excellent. Befides taking care for civil policy; they took care of religion and learning. From the beginning they by law eftablifhed a miniftry in each town, to be fupported by the inhabitants, from the beginning, they by law eftablifhed fchools in each town for common education, the teaching of reading and writing, and arithmetic; and a colony grammar fchool to prepare youth for College. By 1654 Mr. Davenport brought forward the inftitution of a College, to which the town of New-Haven made a donation of lands and meadows, distinguished to this day by the name of College Land. Upon a donation to this College in New-Haven, of perhaps £400 or £500 sterling, by Governor Hopkins, who died in London 1656, which donation was procured by the correspondence of Governor Eaton and Mr. Davenport with Mr. Hopkins, the General Assembly erected the Colony School into a College for teaching " the three learned languages, Latin, Greek and Hebrew , ' and for " the education of youth in good literature, to fit them for public service in church and commonwealth , ' and settled £40 a year out of the Colony treasury upon the preceptor or rector, besides the salary from New-Haven school, with £100 for a library. Mr. Davenport took the care of the Colony School for several years, until the Trustees, with the Magistrates and Ministers, in 1660, established the reverend Mr. Peck in it, according to act of the Assembly , who undertook and proceeded in it, teaching the learned languages and the sciences. But the convulsions of the times, the dissolution of the colony in 1664, the discouragements Mr. Peck met with for want of proper support, and the removal of Mr. Davenport from New-Haven to Boston in 1667, broke up the college—and left this well begun literary institution to go out and terminate in a public grammar school, upheld in this town, and holding the Hopkins' funds, and the other endowments of college estate, to this day. Yale College is a different institution, and not at all built upon the foundation of this first college, which became extinct in 1664, and especially long before 1700, when the present college was founded at Saybrook, and before 1717, when it was removed and settled in New-Haven. By this it appears what early attention was paid to literature by New-Haven colony, from its foundation and first settlement. Our ancestors from the first paid an early attention to every thing that respected the well ordering of society, as to laws, government, religion and literature.

Never was dominion and government more justly and firmly administered than in the colony of New-Haven, during the first twenty-five years from the original plantation of the colony to its consolidation with the colony of Hartford, or Connecticut, 1664; when New-Haven colony terminated, and was absorbed in the joint union of the two colonies of New-Haven and Connecticut, under the polity of the charter procured by Governor Winthrop in 1662; a polity very similar to that which had obtained at New-Haven from its original.   Though it began with the three towns of New-Haven Milford and Guilford, as did Connecticut at the same time, with the three towns of Hartford, Windsor and Wethersfield; yet it was joined so early as 1642 by Stamford, while Stratford and Fairfield, about the same time, joined with Hartford: and 1648 New-Haven was joined by Southold, on the east end of Long-Island, and was in negociation to be joined by Oyster-Bay Before this, 1644, Totoket, or Branford, had sprung from New-Haven and Guilford, as had Paugasset, or Derby, from Milford and New-Haven, by 1658 or 1660, or about the time of the Judges, who sometimes, lodged there.   At first, as I said, only three towns consociated: from 1643 to 1653, they were five, by the union of Southold, in 1654, they became six: and so continued a confederacy of six towns to the time of the Judges, and to the dissolution of the colony in 1664.   So that here was the basis for a House of twelve deputies, which, with a Governor, Deputy-Governor, and three or four, and some times five Magistrates, formed the Senate of this little Sovereignty.

The state of the Magistracy was thus: Theophilus Eaton had been annually elected Governor, and Stephen Goodyear Deputy-Governor, from the beginning till 1657, when there was the magistracy.

Election, 27th 3d. m. 1657.

Theophilus Eaton, Governor.
Stephen Goodyear, Deputy-Governor.

Francis Newman,
Mr. Leet,   } Magiftrates.
Mr. Fenn,

Francis Newman, Secretary.
Mr. Wakeman, Treafurer.
Thomas Kimberly, Marfhal.

Governor Eaton died in New-Haven 1657; and Deputy-Governor Goodyear died in London the year 1658. At the election, May 1658, Mr. Newman came in Governor, and Mr. Leet Deputy-Governor. Matthew Gilbert. Benjamin Fenn, and Jafper Crane, Magiftrates : Wakeman Treafurer, William Gibbard, Secretary, and Kimberly Marfhal. In 1659, the fame, only Robert Treat, of Milford, inftead of Mr. Fenn. In 1660 the fame. Governor Newman died November 18, 1660 : and at the acceffion of the Judges, March 1661, they ftood thus :

William Leet, of Guilford, Deputy-Governor.

Matthew Gilbert, of New-Haven, }
Robert Treat, of Milford,   } Magiftrates.
Jafper Crane, of Branford,   }

John Wakeman, Treafurer,   }
William Gibbard, Secretary,   } All of N. Haven.
Thomas Kimberly, Marfhal,   }

Thefe, with the four deputies of New-Haven town court, were the principal men concerned in the tranf- actions about the Judges. At the election, May 29, 1661, the critical time, the freemen concluded to aug- ment the Magiftracy to five, though for feveral years they had but three, befides the two Governors ; and accordingly the election, 1661, ftood thus :

Court of Election, 29th *May*, 1661. †
William Leet was chosen Governor.
Matthew Gilbert, Deputy-Governor.

Benjamin Fenn
Robert Treat,
Jasper Crane,   } Chosen Magistrates
John Wakeman,
William Gibbard

All took the oath of office but Mr Wakeman and
Mr. Gibbard, who refigned. Mr. Fenn took the oath
" with this explanation (before the oath was adminiftered) that he would take the oath to act in his place according to the laws of this jurifdiction. But in cafe
any bufinefs from without fhould prefent, he conceived
he fhould give no offence if he did not attend it : who
defired that fo it might be underftood."

Roger Alling, Treafurer.
James Bifhop, Secretary.
Thomas Kimberly, Marfhal.—All for the year
enfuing.

General Court, May 29, 1661.
Prefent,
The Governor.
Deputy-Governor.
Mr. Fenn, Mr. Treat, Mr. Crane.
Deputies.

Lieutenant Nafh,
John Cooper,   } New-Haven.
John Fletcher,
Thomas Welch,   } Milford.
Mr. Robert Kitchell,
John Fowler,   } Guilford.
Richard Law,
Francis Bell,   } Stamford.
Barnabas Horton,
William Purrier,   } Southold.
Lieutenant Swaine,
Lawrence Ward,   } Branford."

† *New Haven College Records.*

Having exhibited this synoptical view of the polity and government, I shall next make a chronological statement of events and occurrencies to be afterwards verified and enlarged upon.

1660—1. *March* 7. The Judges arrived at New-Haven and appeared publicly, having in their way first called upon, and been hospitably received by Governor Winthrop , and been in like manner received by Governor Leet.

27. Went to Milford, as if departing for Manhados, or New-York ; but returned in the night, and were secreted at Mr. Davenport's till the 30th of April and at Mr. Jones's till 11th of May.

April. The King's warrant arrived at Boston ,—where they had previously, upon seeing the King's proclamation from Barbadoes, in March, made a fictitious search through Massachusetts.

May 11. Removed from Jones's to the Mills, two miles from town. On the same day Kellond and Kirk arrived at Governor Leet's, with only the copy of the King's order, sent by the Governor of Bolton , on which Governor Leet did not act decidedly : yet sent a letter to magistrate Gilbert, with advice of the town deputies, to search and apprehend. The Judges had notice, and left Jones's for the woods, yet designedly appeared twice afterwards, while the pursuivants were in town—First at the bridge, again at Mrs. Eyers's.

May 13. The pursuivants arrived in New-Haven. The Governor and Magistrates convene there the same day and under great pressure and perplexity, the pursuivant demanding a warrant in the King's name for a general search—which was refused. On this day it is supposed the singular and dangerous events happened, partly before the Governor arrived in town, by the Marshals attempting to take the Judges near the bridge, which must have been by a warrant from Mr. Gilbert, though not at firſt to be found—partly afterwards at Mrs. Eyers's. The Judges this day retired and went to Hatchet-Harbor, and thence to the Cave prepared by Sperry, conducted by Jones and Burral. After the purſuivants were gone, and before the ſeſſion of Aſſembly, a thorough but illuſory ſearch was made by order of the Magiſtrates. The preſſure ſo great and dangerous, that ſeveral declined ſerving in office the next Aſſembly and town court.

May 17. The Aſſembly convened ſpeedily in four days after the purſuivants arrived in town, and perhaps in two days after their departure. To whom the Governor ſtating, that upon receiving the King's real order, he had iſſued a warrant, and had cauſed ſearch to be made; every requiſite ſeemed to have been already done, and ſo the Aſſembly had nothing further to do in the caſe.

29. Came on the General Election; when the Court found no neceſſity of doing any thing further about the Judges. Yet as the Governor and Mr. Gilbert were in danger, it was concluded that the Judges ſhould ſurrender, which they ſtood ready to do.

June 11. The Judges left the Cave, and went over to Guilford to ſurrender themſelves to the Governor: who, though he never ſaw them, yet lodged them ſeveral nights in his ſtone cellar, and ſent them food, or they were fed from his table. Here and at Mr. Roſſeter's they ſpent above a week, while it was deliberated whether the ſurrendery could or could not be put off, or at leaſt deferred. Finally, their friends would not ſuffer them to ſurrender at this time, and it was concluded that they ſhould retire again to their concealment. Upon which they returned to New-Haven.

June 20. They appeared publicly at New-Haven; and though cautiouſly, yet deſignedly.

24. They retired into the woods to their Cave, and never more came into open life, or out of concealment.

But wandering about and shifting their several harbors, were some times at Hatchet-Harbor, some times at Totoket, some times at Paugasset, and at three different places or lodgments behind the West-Rock, until the 19th of August, 1661, when they removed and settled in secrecy at Milford for two years. At times the places of their lodgments were secretly made known to the Governor, to whom they ever stood ready to surrender themselves.

July 4. The Governor and Magistrates of Massachusetts colony were greatly agitated both for themselves and for New-Haven They wrote a fraternal but reprehensory letter to New-Haven. Upon which Governor Leet convened the General Assembly.

Aug. 1 The General Court met at New-Haven, and wrote an answer to Boston.

Sept 5. Declaration of the Commissioners of the United Colonies, that search had actually been made in all the Colonies without success, and enjoining and ordering further search and apprehension. Thus very much ended the business, and the Judges left at rest, at least no further molested.

The New-Haven politicians of that day judged more justly and with deeper discernment, and acted with more ultimate firmness, on this great and trying occasion, than their brethren at Boston. While Boston trembled for them ; they knew and felt themselves, from circumstances then unknown to Boston, to have conducted with safety and security in this dangerous situation. Having made this statement of facts, I proceed to adduce extracts from the public records, and traditionary elucidations upon them.

" *At a meeting of the General Court for the Jurisdiction, May* 17, 1661.

" The Deputy-Governor declared to the Court the cause of the meeting, viz. that he had received a copy of a letter from his Majesty with another letter from

the Governor of the Maffachufetts, for the apprehending of Colonel Whalley and Colonel Goffe, which letters he fhewed to the Court, acquainted them that
forthwith upon the receipt of them, granted his letters
to the Magiftrate of New-Haven, by the advice and
concurrence of the Deputies, there to make prefent and
diligent fearch throughout their town for the faid perfons accordingly , which letters the meffengers carried,
but found not the Magiftrate at home ; and that he
himfelf followed after the meffengers, and came into
New-Haven foon after them, the 13th May, 1661,
bringing with him Mr. Crane, Magiftrate at Branford,
who when they were come fent prefently for the Magiftrates of New-Haven and Milford, and the Deputies
of New-Haven Court.   The Magiftrates thus fent for
not being yet come, they advifed with the Deputies
about the matter, and after a fhort debate with the Deputies, was writing a warrant for fearch of the above
faid Colonels, but the Magiftrates before fpoken of
being come, upon further confideration (the cafe being
weighty) it was refolved to call the General Court, for
the effectual carrying on of the work.   The Deputy-
Governor further informed the Court, that himfelf and
the Magiftrates told the meffengers, that they were far
from hindering the fearch, and they were forry that it
fo fell out, and were refolved to purfue the matter, that
an anfwer fhould be prepared againft their return from
the Dutch.   The Court being met, when they heard
the matter declared, and had heard his Majefty's letter,
and the letter from the Governor of the Maffachufetts,
they all declared they did not know that they were in
the colony, or had been for divers weeks paft, and both
Magiftrates and Deputies wifhed a fearch had been
fooner made, and did now order that the Magiftrates
take care and fend forth the warrant, that a fpeedy diligent fearch be made throughout the Jurifdiction, in
purfuance of his Majefty's commands, according to the
letters received, and that from the feveral plantations a

return be made, and that it may be recorded. And whereas there have been rumors of their late being known at New-Haven, it hath been enquired into, and several persons examined, but could find no truth in those reports, and for any that doth appear, are but unjust suspicions, and groundless reports against the place, to raise ill surmises and reproaches."   [*N. H. Records.*

Those in administration at this critical time will appear by the following extracts from the public records.

"*At a General Court held at New-Haven for the Jurisdiction, August 1st,* 1661.

PRESENT,

The Governor,
Deputy-Governor,
Mr. Benjamin Sterne,
Mr. Bobert Treat,   } Magistrates.
Mr. Jasper Crane,

Deputies.

John Cooper,
James Bishop,   } New-Haven.
John Fletcher,
Thomas Welch,   } Milford.
Mr. Rober Kitchill,
George Hubbard,   } Guilford.
Richard Law, Stamford.
Lieut. Swane,
Lawrence Ward,   } Branford.

" The Governor informed the Court of the occasion of calling them together at this time, and among the rest, the main thing insisted upon was, to consider what application to make to the King in the case we now stood, being like to be rendered worse to the King than the other colonies, they seeing it an incumbent duty so to do.   The Governor informed the Court also, that he had received a letter from the Council in the bay, which was read, wherein was intimated of sundry complaints in England made against New-England,

and that the committee in England take notice of the neglect of the other colonies in their non application to the King.

Now the Court taking the matter into serious consideration, after much debate and advice, concluded that the writing should be sent to the Council in the Bay, the copy whereof is as follows :

Honorable Gentlemen,

" Yours, dated the 4th of July, (61) with a postcript of the 15th, we received July 30th, which was communicated to our General Court, August 1st. We have considered what you please to relate of those complaints made against New-England, and of what spirit they are represented to be of, upon occasion of that false report against Captain Leveret, who we believe to have more wisdom and honesty than so to report ; and we are assured that New-England is not of that spirit And as for the other colonies neglect in non application with yourselves, to his Majesty the last year, it hath not been forborne upon any such account, as we for ourselves profess and believe for our neighbors. But only in such new and accustomed matters, were in the dark to hit it in way of agreement, as to a former satisfaction that might be acceptable ; but since that of your colonies hath come to our view, it is much to our content, and we solemnly profess from our hearts to own and say the same to his Majesty , and do engage to him full subjection and allegiance with yourselves accordingly, with profession of the same ends in coming with like permission and combining with yourselves and the other neighboring colonies, as by the preface of our articles may appear, upon which grounds we both supplicate and hope to find a like protection, privileges, immunities and favors, from his Royal Majesty. And as for that you note of our not so diligent attention to his Majesty's warrant, we have given you an account of before, that it was not done out of any mind to slight

E

or difown his Majefty's authority, &c. in the leaft, nor out of favor to the Colonels, nor did it hinder the effect of their apprehending, they being gone before the warrant came into our colony, as is fince fully proved;— But only there was a gainfaying of the Gentlemen's earneftnefs who retarded their own bufinefs to wait upon ours without commiffion, and alfo out of fcruple of confcience and fear of non faithfulnefs to our people, who committed all our authority to us under oath by owning a general Governor, unto whom the warrant was directed, as fuch, implicitly, and that upon mifinformation to his Majefty given, though other Magiftrates were mentioned, yet (as fome thought) it was in or under him, which overfight (if fo it fhall be apprehended) we hope upon our humble acknowledgement his Majefty will pardon, as alfo that other and greater bewailed remiffion in one, in not fecuring them till we came and knew their place out of over much belief of their pretended reality to refume upon themfelves according to their promife to fave their country harmlefs, which failing is fo much the more to be lamented, by how much the more we had ufed all diligence to prefs for fuch a delivery upon fome of thofe that had fhewed them former kindnefs, as had been done other where, when as none of the Magiftrates could otherwife do any thing in it, they being altogether ignorant where they were, or how to come at them, nor truly do they now, nor can we believe that they are hid any where in this colony, fince that departure or defeatment. But however the confequence prove, we muft wholly rely on the mercy of God and the King, with promife to do our endeavor to regain them if opportunity ferve. Wherefore, in this our great entrels, we earneftly defire your aid to prefent us to his Majefty in our cordially owning and complying with your addrefs, as if it had been done and faid by our very felves, who had begun to draw up fome thing that way, but were difheartened through fenfe of feeblenefs and incapacity to procure a meet agent to prefent it in our difadvantaged ftate, by thefe providences occuring, hoping you will favor us in this latter and better pleafing manner of doing, which we fhall take thankfully from you, and be willing to join in the proportionate fhare of charge for a common agent to folicit New-England's affairs in England, which we think neceffary to procure the benefit of all acts of indemnity, grace, or favor, on all our behalfs, as well as in other refpects to prevent the mifchiefs of fuch as malign and feek to mifinform againft us, of which fort there be many to complot now-a-days with great fedulity. If you fhall defert us in this affliction to prefent us as before by the tranfcript of this our letter or otherwife, together with the petition and acknowledgement herewithall fent, we fhall yet look up to our God that deliverance may arife another way refting."

[*Extr. New-Haven Records.*

Thus far had I written, when I thought of looking into Governor Hutchinfon's Supplement, or Collection of Original Papers, edited by him, 1769, to fee if I could collect fome fcattered lights. Upon this I found what I had read many years ago, but which was out of my mind, the purfuivants' Report, in which there is an elucidation of fome dates and tranfactions already alluded to, and wherein there are fome omiffions, as refpecting Mr. Davenport and the thorough examination of his houfe, and the fearch of other houfes in town and the vicinity, the memoir of which is preferved in the uniform and conftant tradition in New-Haven.

I fhall proceed to give the copies of authentic documents, as well to illuftrate the hiftory, as to fhew the preffing danger in which thefe hunted exiles were involved, and alfo to fhew the diftreffes with which Mr. Davenport, and Governor Leet, and the Magiftrates of New-Haven colony were incompaffed, by their perfeverance in protecting and concealing thefe meritorious exiles—meritorious, if the cause in which they suffered was *it*.

Copy of a Reference made to Governor Endicott, by Thomas Kellond and Thomas Kirk.

" *Honorable Sir,*

" We according to your honor's order departed in search after Colonels Goffe and Whalley (persons declared traitors to His Majesty) from Boston May the 7th, 1661, about six o'clock at night, and arrived at Hartford the 10th day, and repaired to Governor Winthrop, and gave him your honor's letter and his Majesty's order for the apprehending of Colonels Whalley and Goffe, who gave us an account that they did not stay there, but went directly for New-Haven, but informed us that one Symon Lobden guided them to the town. The honorable Governor carried himself very nobly to us, and was very diligent to supply us with all manner of conveniencies for the prosecution of them, and promised all diligent search should be made after them in that jurisdiction, which was afterwards performed. The 11th day we arrived at Guilford, and repaired to the Deputy-Governor, William Leet, and delivered him your honor's letter and the copy of his Majesty's order for the apprehending of the aforesaid persons, with whom at that time were several persons. After the perusal of them, he began to read them audibly, whereupon we told him it was convenient to be more private in such concernments as that was, upon which withdrawing to a chamber, he told us he had not seen the two Colonels not in nine weeks. We acquainted him with the information we had received that they were at New-Haven since that time he mentioned, and thereupon desired him to furnish us with horses, &c. which was prepared with some delays, which we took notice of to him, and after our parting with him out of his house and in the way to the ordinary, came to us Dennis Scranton, and told us he would warrant that Colonels Goffe and Whalley at the time of his speaking were harbored at the house of one **Mr. Da**-venport, a minister at New-Haven, and that one Goodman Bishop, of the town of Guilford, was able to give us the like account, and that, without all question, Deputy Leet knew as much, and that Mr. Davenport had put in ten pounds worth of fresh provisions at one time into his house, and that it was imagined it was purposely for the entertainment of them.

And the said Scranton said further, that Goffe and Whalley should say, that if they had but two hundred friends that would stand by them, they would not care for Old or New-England: Whereupon we asked if he would depose to that: He replied he would, that it was openly spoken by them in the head of a company in the field a training. Which words were also confirmed by several others, as also information that Goffe and Whalley were seen very lately betwixt the houses of Mr. Davenport and one Jones, and it was imagined that one lay at one of their houses, and the other at the other's. Upon which we went back to the Deputy's and required our horses, with aid, and a power to search and apprehend them ; horses wree provided for us, but he refused to give us any power to apprehend them, nor order any other, and said he could do nothing until he had spoken with one Mr. Gilbert and the rest of the Magistrates : Upon which we told him we should go to New-Haven and stay till we heard from him, but before we took horse the aforesaid Dennis Scranton gave us information, there was an Indian of the town wanting, which he told us was to give notice of our coming. But to our certain knowledge one John Megges was sent a horse-back before us, and by his speedy and unexpected going so early before day was to give them an information, and the rather because by the delays was used it was break of day before we got to horse, so he got there before us ; upon our suspicion we re-

quired the Deputy that the said John Megges might be
examined what his businefs was that might occafion his
fo early going, to which the Deputy anfwered, that
he did not know any fuch thing, and refufed to examine him ; and being at New-Haven, which was the
thirteenth day, the Deputy arrived within two hours or
thereabouts after us, and came to us to the Court Chamber, where we again acquainted him with the information we had received, and that we had caufe to believe
they were concealed in New-Haven, and thereupon
we required his affiftance and aid for their apprehenfion :
To which he anfwered that he did not believe they
were there : Whereupon we defired him to empower
us, or order others for it. To which he gave us this
anfwer, That he could not, nor would not make us
Magiftrates : We replied, we ourfelves would perfonally adventure in the fearch and apprehenfion of them
in two houfes where we had reafon to imagine they lay
hid, if they would give way to it and enable us. To
which he replied, he neither would nor could not do
any thing until the freemen met together. To which
we fet before him the danger of that delay and their inevitable efcape, and how much the honor and fervice
of his Majefty was defpifed and trampled on by him,
and that we fuppofed by his unwillingnefs to affift in the
apprehenfion, he was willing they fhould efcape. After
which he left us and went to feveral of the Magiftrates
and were together five or fix hours in confultation, and
upon breaking up of their Council, they would not nor
could not do any thing until they had called a general
Court of the freemen. Whereupon we reprefented to
them your Honor's and Governor Wirthrop's warrants
as prefidents, whoupon the receipt of his Majefty's
pleafure and order concerning the faid perfons, ftood
not upon fuch niceties and formalities, but endeavored
to make all expedition in feizing on them, if to be
found in their government, and alfo how your honor
had recommended this grand affair to him, and how

much the honor and juftice of his Majefty was concerned, and how ill his facred Majefty would refent
fuch horrid and deteftable concealments and abettings of
fuch traitors and regicides as they were, and afked him
whether he would honor and obey the King or no in
this affair, and fet before him the danger which by
law is incurred by any one that conceals or abets traitors, to which the Deputy Leet anfwered, we honor
his Majefty, but we have tender confciences.

To which we replied, that we believed that he knew
where they were, and only pretended tendernefs of confcience for a refufal : upon which they drew into confultation again, and after two or three hours fpent, in
the evening the Deputy and Magiftrates came to us at
the head of the ftairs in the ordinary, and takes one of
us by the hand, and wifhed he had been a ploughman
and had never been in the office, fince he found it fo
weighty.

To which we told him, that for their refpect to two
traitors they would do themfelves injury and poffibly
ruin themfelves and the whole colony of New-Haven,
and ftill continuing to prefs them to their duty and loy-
alty to his Majefty, and whether they would own his
Majefty or no, it was anfwered, they would firft
know whether his Majefty would own them.

This was the fubftance of our proceedings, there
was other circumftantial expreffions which are too
tedious to trouble your honor withall, and which we
have given your honor a verbal account of, and conceive
it needlefs to infift any further, and fo finding them
obftinate and pertinacious in their contempt of his Majefty, we came away the next day in profecution after
them, according to inftructions, to the Governor of
Manhados, from whom we received civil refpects, and
a promife, if they were within his jurifdiction, we
fhould command what aid we pleafed, but for fending
of them according to your honors requeft, he could

not anfwer it to his Mafters at home, but if they came there he fhould give your honor timely notice : Whereupon we requefted his honor the Governor of Manhados to lay a reftraint upon all fhipping from tranfporting them, which he promifed fhould be done, and also to give order to his fifcal or chief officer to make private fearch in all veffels for them that were going thence.

Upon which we finding any other means would be ineffectual, we made our return hither by fea, to give your honor an account, and to which (when your honor fhall require it) are ready to depofe to the truth of it, and remain,

Sir,

Your honor's humble fervants,

THOMAS KELLOND,
THOMAS KIRK.

Bofton, May 29th, 1661.

30th May, 1661.

Mr. Thomas Kellond and Mr. Thomas Kirk having delivered this paper to the Governor as their return, in anfwer to what they were employed, depofed before the Governor and Magiftrates, that what is there expreffed is the truth, the whole truth, and nothing but the truth.

Per EDWARD RAWSON, Secretary."

Copy of a Letter from Secretary Rawfon to William Leet, Efq. Governor of New-Haven Jurifdiction.

" Honored Sir,

" The Council of our jurifdiction being affembled the 4th inftant at Bofton, ordered me to fignify to you what lately they have received from England by Captain Leverett, his letter being dated 12th April, 1661, who tells us that however our addrefs to his Majefty came feafonably, and had a gracious anfwer, yet many complaints and claims are multiplied againft us, and that we are like to hear from his Majefty's committee what thofe complaints are, and what is expected from us, that an oath was produced againft him for faying that rather than we fhould or would admit of appeals here, we would or fhould fell the country to the Spaniards: which though he abfolutely denied that ever he fo faid, and that if he fhould have fo faid he had wronged his country very much, fome of the faid committee faid the words if fpoken they were pardoned, but they looked at the words not fo much his as the fpirit of the country, and though again he defired that the country might not fuffer in their minds for what he knew was fo much and fo far from them, as to think ought in any fuch refpect, yet one of them proceeded to queftion him, whether if we dared we would not caft off our allegiance and fubjection to his Majefty : He anfwered, he did apprehend we were honeft men and had declared in our application to his Majefty the contrary, and therefore could not have fuch thoughts of us without the breach of charity, that it is no lefs than neceffary we had fome able perfon to appear for us, well furnifhed to carry on our bufinefs, which will not be without money : that the Council for plantations demanded of him whether we had proclaimed the King, and whether there was not much oppofition to the agreeing of our application.   He anfwered he knew not, only had heard Captain Bredan fay fo, but humbly fubmitted to their confideration, that neither we nor any other were to be concluded by debates, but by our conclufions, which were fent and prefented to his Majefty in our names.   They took notice, from enquiry, that it was only from one colony, namely, Maffachufetts, and have their confiderations of the other colonies neglects, to fpeak moft favorably thereof   Thus far as to the letter. Further, I am required to fignify to you as from them, that the non attendance with diligence to execute the King's warrant for the apprehending of Colonels Whalley and Goffe will much hazard the prefent ftate of thefe colonies and your own particularly, if not fome of your perfons, which is not a little afflictive to them. And that in their underftanding there remains no way to expiate the offence and preferve yourfelves from the danger and hazard but by apprehending the faid perfons, who as we are informed are yet remaining in the colony and not above a fortnight fince were feen there, all which will be againft you. Sir, your own welfare, the welfare of your neighbors, befpeak your unwearied pains to free yourfelf and neighbors. I fhall not add, having fo lately by a few lines from our Governor and myfelf looking much this way commuicated our fenfe and thoughts of your and our troubles, and have as yet received no return, but commend you to God, and his grace, for vour guidance and direction in matter of fuch moment, as his Majefty may receive full and juft fatisfaction, the mouths of all oppofers ftopped, and the profeffion of the truth that is in you and us may not in the leaft fuffer by youi acting, is the prayer of, Sir,

    Your affured loving friend,
      EDWARD RAWSON, Secretary.
  In the name and by order of the Council.
Bofton, 4th July, 1661.

  Sir, fince what I wrote, news and certain intelligence is come hither of the two Colonels being at New-Haven, from Saturday to Monday and publicly known, and however it is given out that they came to furrender themfelves and pretended by Mr. Gilbert that he looked when they would have come in and delivered up themfelves, never fetting a guard about the houfe nor endeavoring to fecure them, but when it was too late to fend to Totoket, &c. Sir how this will be taken is not difficult to imagine, to be fure not well, nay, will not all men condemn you as wanting to yourfelves, and that you have fomething to rely on, at leaft that you hope will anfwer your ends? I am not willing to meddle with your hopes, but if it be a duty to obey fuch lawful warrants, as I believe it is, the neglect thereof will prove uncomfortable. Pardon me, Sir, its my defire you may regain your peace (and if you pleafe to give me notice when you will fend the two Colonels) though Mr. Wood Greene is bound hence within a month, yet if you fhall give me affurance of their coming I fhall not only endeavor but do hereby engage to caufe his ftay a fortnight, nay three weeks, rather than they fhould not be fent, expecting your anfwer, remain,

Sir, your affured loving friend and fervant,

EDWARD RAWSON."

Copy of the Declaration of the Commiffioners of the United Colonies concerning Whalley and Goffe.

" Whereas it appeareth by his Majefty's order directed to John Endicott, Efq. Governor of the Maffachufetts, and to all other Governors and Magiftrates in New-England, and by him communicated to the refpective Governors of the United Colonies, for the apprehending of Edward Whalley and William Goffe, who ftand convicted of high treafon for the horrid murder of his royal Father, as is expreffed in the faid order, and exempted from pardon by the act of indemnity ; in obedience whereunto diligent fearch hath been made for the faid perfons in the feveral colonies (as we are informed) and whereas, notwithftanding, it is conceived probable that the faid perfons may remain hid in fome parts of New-England, thefe are therefore ferioufly to advife and forewarn all perfons whatfoever within the faid colonies, not to receive, harbor, conceal or fuccour the faid perfons fo attainted, or either of them, but that, as they may have any knowledge or information where the faid Whalley and Goffe are, that they forthwith make known the fame to fome of the Governors or Magiftrates next refiding, and in the mean time do their utmoft endeavor for their apprehending and fecuring, as they will anfwer the contrary at their utmost peril. And we do hereby further declare that all such person or persons, that since the publication of his Majesty's order have wittingly and willingly entertained or harbored the aforesaid Whalley and Goffe, or hereafter shall do the like, have and will incur his Majesty's highest displeasure, as is intimated in the said order, and will be accounted enemies to the public peace and welfare of the United Colonies, and may expect to be proceeded with accordingly.

By the Commissioners of the United Colonies, at their meeting at Hartford, Sept. 5, 1661.

JOHN MASON,
SAMUEL WILLIS,
WILLIAM LEET,
THOMAS PRINCE,
SYMON BRADSTREET,
DANIEL DENISON,
THOS. SOUTHWORTH."

The King's Commissioners, who were Colonel Nichols, Cartwright, Carr, and Maverick, in their narrative about New-England, 1667, speaking of these Judges, say, among other accusations, " Colonels Whalley and Goffe were entertained by the Magistrates with great solemnity and feasted in every place, after they were told they were traitors, and ought to be apprehended. they made their abode at Cambridge until they were furnished with horses and a guide and sent away to New-Haven. for their more security, Captain Daniel Gookin is reported to have brought over and to manage their estates, and the Commissioners being informed that he had many cattle at his farm in the King's province, which were supposed to be Whalley's or Goffe's, caused them to be seized for his Majesty's use, till further order, but Captian Gookin, standing upon the privilege of their charter, and refusing to answer before the Commissioners, as so there was no more done in it. Captain Pierce who transported Whalley and Goffe into New-England, may probably say something to their estate."

By the purfuivants report to Governor Endicot it appears, that they arrived at New-Haven 13th May; and it fhould feem that they left the town the next day, and this without any fearch at all; and particularly no mention is made of their interview with Mr. Davenport. But the conftant tradition in New-Haven is, that they diligently fearched the town, and particularly the houfe of Mr. Davenport, whom they treated with afperity and reprehenfion. Goffe's journal fays, the Judges left the town the 11th May and went to the Mills, and on the 13th went into the Woods to Sperry's. It fhould feem that they were not in town while the purfuivants were here. But although the nights of the 11th and 12th they lodged at the mills, and on the 13th at Sperry's, they might purpofely in the day time fhew themfelves at the bridge when the purfuivants paffed it, and at Mrs. Eyers's in town the fame or next day, in order to clear Mr. Davenport, and return at night to their concealment. The Sperrys are uniform in the family tradition that the furprizal of the Judges at their anceftor's houfe was by the purfuers from England, known and diftinguifhable, as they faid, from our own people by their red coats; which could not have been if they ftaid in town but one day. Perhaps "the next day" in the Report, might not be that immediately following the 13th, but the next day after they found they could do nothing to purpofe. On the one hand, it is improbable they would fpend but one day in a town where they did not doubt the regicides, they came three thoufand miles in queft of, were; and on the other hand, 'tis doubtful whether they would do much at actual fearching themfelves without the Governor's warrant, which was refufed. They might however go into a few houfes, as Mr. Davenport's, Mr. Jones's, and Mrs. Eyers's, and finding it in vain, give over further fearch. Governor Hutchinfon fays, "they made diligent fearch." And this has always been the tradition in New-Haven. But of this nothing is men-

F

tioned in the report, unlefs it may be alluded to in the
"verbal account' given to Governor Endicott. The
tradition is, that the purfuivants went to Sperry's houfe
after their return from Manhados ; but this could not
be if they went from thence by water to Bofton ; unlefs returning again through New-Haven to Governor
Winthrop at New-London, they might go from thence
to Bofton by water.   But of this they take no notice in
the report.

After the purfuivants were gone, and before 17th of
May, the Magiftrates caufed a thorough though fictitious fearch to be made through the jurifdiction.—
They fent to Totoket. or Branford   I have thought
thefe purfuits. and thefe purfuers, might be the bafis
of the tradition refpecting Mrs Eyers, the bridge, and
Sperrys.   But moft that tell the ftory from ancient tradition, perfift in it, that they were the purfuers from
Bofton, or the Kings purfuers, and not our own people, which vifited and fearched both Sperrys and Eyers.   But enough of this matter, which can never be
fatisfactorily cleared and afcertained : While it is certain the purfuivants came here, had an interview with
the Magiftrates to no purpofe : and that the Judges
ceafed to lodge in town on the 11th of May, two days
before they came. and fo Governor Leet might fay
very true on the 13th, that he did not believe they were
in town, and indeed might have every reafon to think
at that time, that they were abfconded into the environs
or the woods beyond the Weft-Rock.   All tradition
agree that they ftood ready to furrender rather than
that Mr. Davenport fhould come into trouble on their
account, and they doubtlefs came into town with this
intention about 26th June, and tarried in town from
Saturda, till Monday for this end, and Mr Gilbert expected their furrendery.   But in this trying time their
friends, for their fake, adventured to take the danger
upon themfelves, and iffue events.   A great, a noble,
a trying act of friendfhip ! For a good man, one would

even dare to die! Great was the peril especially of
Leet, Davenport, and Gilbert! Inveterate the resent-
ment of Kellond and Kirk! and pointed and pressing
the remonstrances of the Governor and Secretary of
Boston. The Magistrates of New-Haven colony were
truly brought into great straits---The fidelity of their
friendship heroic and glorious! Davenport's fortitude
saved them!

Here follows a collection of scattered information.

Mrs. Sherman, relict of Mr James Sherman, aged
86, a descendant from Governor Leet, whose daughter married a Trowbridge, from whom Mrs. Sherman.
She tells me she was born in Governor Jones's or in
Governor Eaton's house, which had nineteen fire-places, and many apartments; where Goffe and Whalley
used to reside, that Mr. Davenport's house also had
many apartments, and thirteen fire-places, which indeed I myself well remember, having frequently, when
a boy, been all over the house. She says she knew
John Dixwell, son of the regicide. She has the whole
family history of the three Judges as in the families of
Mansfield, Prout, and Trowbridge. She was, as I
said, of the Trowbridge family. She was intimately
acquainted with Mrs. Eyers, and is full of the story of
the Judges being secreted at her house, which was repeatedly searched for them. It is necessary to observe
that this house was twice searched, and the circumstances are a little blended in the different narratives. The
first was by the pursuivants, when the Judges went
out at the back door, and returned and were secreted
in the closet while the pursuivants were in the house.---
The other was immediately after the pursuivants left
the town, and between the 14th and 17th of May,
when the search was made by Governor Leet's orders:
when the doors were all set open, and Mrs. Eyers left
the house for the searchers to come in and examine every room this was by our people. In narrating these cir-

cumſtances they are ſometimes varied.   Mrs. Sherman
conſiders and ſpeaks of the ſearch, not as once only,
but at ſeveral or different times.   She ſays Mrs. Eyers
had on one ſide of the room a large wainſcotted cloſet,
which ſhe has often viewed and admired : it had cut
lights at top, full of pewter and braſs, and a wainſcot
door, which, when ſhut, could not be diſtinguiſhed
from the wainſcot, and all over the door, and on the
outſide of the cloſet, was hung braizery and elegant
kitchen furniture, that no one would think of entering
the cloſet on that breaſt-work. Here ſhe hid the Judges—It ſeems to be as if it was more than once.—That
they uſed to frequent the houſe on Saturdays afternoon,
when ſometimes ſhe ſhut them up, and then opened
all the doors, and walked abroad, leaving all open for
the purſuvants to ſearch.   In this connexion I aſked
her, whether the purſuers were foreigners or New-Haven people ? She ſaid, ſhe took it they were not foreigners, but our own officers.   Here ſhe ſeems a little to
blend the circumſtances.   Which may be eaſily ex-
plained, by conſidering the firſt ſearch, made by the
purſuvants, and the laſt two days after by our officers,
to whom ſhe might throw open all the doors but the
cloſet door.

She ſays Mrs. Eyers, and her ſon and daughter,
lived together all to great old age—that ſhe died about
the hard winter, November 1ᵗʰ, 1740, when ſhe muſt
have been above an hundred years old, and her ſon
and daughter were ſeventy or eighty als old at the old
lady's death.   Mother and children ſo remarkable for
longevity, that the reverend Mr. Cooke (Mrs. Sherman's father uſed familiarly to enquire, how the good
old folks of that houſe did, where death did not enter ?
So much has been ſaid of Mrs. Eyers, that I will add
this characteriſtic deſcription of her:

Mrs. Sherman deſcribed Mrs. Eyers, though not
without imperfections, yet an excellent perſon, as a

fmall woman, of a fweet 'and pleafant temper, and of the greateft propriety of manners, to ufe her expreſſions, very genteel and refpeftable, univerfally efteemed and beloved, never did any thing wrong, but always with propriety and gracefulneſs, was much of a gentlewoman, neat, elegant, beautiful, comely and graceful, admired by all gentlemen of Charaƈter, and her acquaintance from abroad, who coming to town, would get fome of the genteeleſt people in town to go with them to pay her a vifit—And every one, high or low, always profited by her, were improved, inſtruƈted, and edified by her converfation, and pleaſed when they could vifit and fpend an hour at her houfe.—That fhe was rather reduced the latter part of her life, yet had the richeſt of apparel and furniture—Ufed to keep fhop, but left off everal years.—That her intelleƈtual powers were clear to the laſt—An excellent chriſtian. I ufe Mrs Sherman's words in this defcription, writing them from her lips. She adds, that her father was Mr. Ifaac Allerton, of Boſton, a fea Captain, who came early and fettled in New-Haven, and built a grand houfe on the creek with four porches, and this with Governor Eaton's, Mr. Davenport's, and Mr Giegfon's, were the grandeſt houfes in town. The houfe highly finifhed he had a fine garden with all forts of flowers, and fruit-trees, and in the beſt cultivation. Mr. Eyers was alfo a fea Captain, purfuing foreign voyages up the Mediterranean and to the wine iflands, and always had his cellar ſtored with wines and good liquors, and ufed to bring home much produce and foreign manufaƈtures, and elegant Nuns' work. Both went long voyages, and both died abroad at fea near together, leaving her a young widow, who never married again. She poffeſſed her father's, brother's, and hufband's eſtates.—This refpeƈting Mrs. Eyers. It is the ſtrong and concurrent tradition that the judges were fecreted at her houfe, fome fay in a chamber, fome in a clofet, probably both true.

Mr. Joseph Howell, merchant, tells me his grandfather Howell died here about 1772, aged 88 —That he came from Long-Island to live at New-Haven, Æt 13.—That he has often heard him tell about the Judges, and that his grandfather used to say he knew two men that helped in laying out Dixwell, and he shewed this grandson Dixwell's grave. He told him the story of Goffe and Whalley's hiding themselves under the Neck Bridge, and being under it while the pursuivants rode over it, and that they were the pursuers from Boston. Mr. Howell was intimate with Mr. Prout, who married his sister.

Captain Willmot, aged 82, remembers the story of their being hid in Mrs. Eyers's house when the pursuers came there. He remembers the old house, that it was grand, like Mr. Davenport's, which he also knew, and all of oak and the best of joiners work. There was more work and better joine-work in these houses, he says, than in any house in the town. He is a joiner, and helped to pull down Mrs. Eyers's house.

Judge Bishop, now mayor of the city of New-Haven, told me, tells me he received from his aged grandfather Bishop, with whom he lived from his youth up, son of the Governor, and who died 1748, aged 82, the tradition concerning the Judges being hid under the bridge, and that the pursuivants were those who were sent from England. The Judge remembers Mrs. Eyers. She was a small, plump, round woman, a worthy character. He remembers her old house, which he says was one of the grandest in town, like Mr. Davenport's, and fit for a nobleman. She left three children, Simon, Lydia, and Benjamin. Simon was a considerable reader, and a great historian, and used often to spend the evening at his Grandfather's, and converse upon old affairs. He has listened to their conversation many an hour. Benjamin settled on Long-Island.

General Ward, of Guilford, tells me it is the conftant tradition at Guilford, that the two Judges, Goffe and Whalley, were fecreted three or four days, or more, in Governor Leet's ftone cellar, and that the Governor and all the family of the Leet's were refolute and courageous. The reverend Mr. Fowler, and Henry Hill, Efq. of Guilford, concur in this and the general hiftory of the Judges, and particularly the Angel ftory, that of hiding under the bridge, and the humorous ftory of playing with the fword, or the fencing ftory. The fame have been told me by Major Davenport, of Stamford, defcended from the venerable patriarch at New-Haven, by the reverend Mr. Whitney, of Brooklyn, in the eaftern part of the Government, and the reverend Mr Bray, and others, indeed thefe ftories are to be found fcattered and circulating all over New-England to this day.

Stephen Ball, Efq. tells me, that when the purfuers were here, one of the roures in which Whalley and Goffe abfconded was Mrs. Eyers's, who feeing them coming, fent the Judges out the back door towards the fields, who returning immediately, fhe hid them in her chamber. The leaft that can be made of all this is, that they were actually fecreted by Mrs. Eyers.

Upon having recourfe to the records, we have feen that in May, 1660, Francis Newman was elected Governor, and William Leet Deputy-Governor: That Governor Newman died November 18, 1660: whereupon the adminiftration devolved on Deputy-Governor Leet till May 29, 1661, when he was chofen Governor, and Matthew Gilbert Deputy-Governor; and Fenn, Treat and Crane, Magiftrates. But a fortnight before, when the purfuivants were here, thofe in office were, Leet, Deputy-Governor,—Gilbert, Treat and Crane, affiftants. The town government of New-Haven was in the hands of fix townfmen, or felect men, for the ordinary fecular affairs, and four Deputies or Judges for New-Haven Court, all annually elective in the spring by the town, and the four Judges confirmed and authorized by the Assembly. The six select men then in office were, Roger Alling, John Harriman, John Cooper, —— Andrews, Henry Glover, Nicholas Elsey, and William Gibbard. Thomas Kimberly was Marshal, who attempted with a warrant to take the Judges, towards the Neck Bridge, the morning of the arrival of the pursuivants. The matter however did not lie with these town officers, but with the officers of the general jurisdiction: These were, as I said, the Deputy-Governor and three Assistants Governor Leet, who followed the pursuivants, brought along with him Mr. Crane, from Branford, and then sent for and convened the Magistrates of Milford and New-Haven, and the four Judges of New-Haven Court, who at this time were John Wakeman, John Nash, William Gibbard, secretary, and John Davenport, jun. of whom Wakeman and Nash were also Deputies to the Jurisdiction Court, or Members of the Legislature. These eight persons were all that were in the consultative consultation, and that afternoon in great numbers, were for a few hours on the point of issuing the warrant, which was also now begun to be written, and which was fixed upon their concerning the expedient of referring it to the Assembly, which they instantly called, and actual convened within four days, or the 17th of May. In this deliberation on the trying 13th, besides these eight persons, the Governor, Assistants, and four Judges, who sat ostensibly in Council, it is not to be doubted, but that they advised with the select men, and particularly with the reverend Mr. Davenport, Mr. Bishop, Mr. Jones, and others, and that their opinions had fell weight, especially Mr. Davenport's and Mr. Jones's, who were most exposed, and most deeply concerned My idea of them is this, that the Governor, though naturally firm, was in this pressure staid; Gilbert was bold and courageous, and refolute for faving the Judges at all hazards, though a month after, upon the letters from Bofton, he rather gave up. He and Treat coming in at the time of drawing the warrant, ftopt it, Jones was enterprizing, and had it been known, had really and knowingly done what would have been affuredly adjudged treafon, which the others had not : Bifhop was firm, he with Jones ftood their ground · none were difpofed to give up the Judges at this time, if poffible to fave them ; all faw and felt the danger, but that it would come upon Leet, Gilbert and Davenport, whom they were equally en- gaged to fave. Jones's activity was unknown to the purfuivants. The preffure was fo great the afternoon of the confultation on 13th May, as that then, I be- lieve, they would all have unanimoufly concurred in furrendering Goffe and Whalley, as Bofton had done, had it not been for the wifdom, difcernment, and firm- nefs of Davenport If he had fhaken and failed, all would have been over and loft. It was Davenport's in- trepidity that faved the Judges.

Mr. Jones was a new comer, having married Gov- ernor Eaton's daughter, an heirefs, in London, 1659, he came over with his wife in the fall of 1660 to take poffeffion of Governor Eaton's eftate, and lived in his houfe oppofite Mr. Davenport's. I prefume it was his and Mr. Bifhop's diftinguifhing themfelves with firmnefs upon this occafion, that brought them imme- diately forward to civil improvement, and into the Ma- giftracy. Timidity feized the people of New-Haven on this occafion of the Judges, and made them cool to office. In lefs than ten days after the departure of the purfuivants, on May 23, 1661, John Nafh and John Cooper, being chofen Deputes to the General Court, declined and the fame day, at a fecond choice, John Davenport, jun and John Nafh, being elected, decli- ned ferving. They made no choice, fuch was the re- luctance in all to ferve at this critical conjuncture. At length, Auguft 1, 1661, John Cooper and James Bifhop were elected, and they dared to accept. Mr. Jones had not been an inhabitant a year. However, the year following, May 23, 1662, William Jones was admitted a freeman, and nominated for Magistrate, he soon came into the Magistracy, and both he and Mr. Bishop became Governors of Connecticut. They were well informed, firm and decided characters

Further consideration brought New-Haven almost to a conclusion of the necessity of surrendering the Judges. Even the courageous Mr. Gilbert seemed to judge this expedient. It was undoubtedly the perseverance of Davenport, and his fidelity and heroism, that decided at this crisis also. And the Judges retired to their cave. This was the last public appearance they ever made. From this time to their death they were buried in obscurity, neither was it safe for their numerous friends to know the places of their concealment and shifting residences. None wished to betray them, none wished to know where they were, all wished to be totally ignorant. A few however adventured to secure their retreat, and as guardians of a holy deposit to watch secure and protect them, although at the known risque of their lives, as protectors of traitors. Among these we may enumerate Mr. Jones, Mr Barril, and Mr. Sperry, at New-Haven, Mr. Tomkins, and others, at Milford, and Mr. Rudd and Mr. Tilton, at Hadley.— These perhaps were almost the only, at least the principal persons, with whom they had immediate communication, and through whose hands they received all their supplies. A few other persons might be knowing of their places of concealment, and might secretly and occasionally visit them, as Mr. Davenport and Mr. Bishop, at New-Haven, Mr. Treat, at Milford; and Mr. Richard Saltonstal and Governor Leverett, at Hadley. The rest of the country, it is probable, not only wished not to know any thing of them, but were ever in actual ignorance. Thus they were shut out and secluded from the world to their deaths.

SECTION II.

Their secreted pilgrimages after their final abdication and evanescence from the world, June 24, 1661, to the last notice of them, in 1679.

This section will necessarily involve some repetitions, which may however be an illustration of the preceding period. It may be best to deliver the traditionary information collectively and promiscuously, just as it is received, respecting either the whole or part of their residence in New-England Every one will be able to select what falls within one period or another.— When we shall have selected what applies to one, there will be much left to illustrate the other. It is difficult to separate from the promiscuous mass of information, what belongs only to one, without losing some of the force of probability as to each. We must take narratives as they come to us, with all their attendant circumstances, and make the proper use, selection and appropriation ourselves. Some relate one thing, some another; some more, some less; some of one period, some of another; most deliver scattered notices of both collectively. We can select and apply illucidations at our own discretion. In examining evidences or witnesses in a court of law, it is best to suffer them freely to narrate their testimony and knowledge, each in his own way, with the attendant circumstances, as they lie or arise in their own minds, though much may be repetitions and superfluous, that we may more accurately discern and select that which is in point or to purpose. Often the same thing narrated simply and without circumstances, will yield a different aspect and force or weight, with from what it would without the circumstances and superfluous matter. And we easily select that which we need, and find different matter applicable to different subjects, even unthought of in the course of enquiry, and which the narrators would not discern themselves, and if they did, would not dif-

close, or would be diffident and uncertain.   And this
may excuse and justify me, in bringing the same things
repeatedly up to view in the course of this history, under different references, and for different purposes, as
it may be with profitable retrospective application in
variation of subjects already considered.   Nor is it in
the power of an historian always to bring together in one
view the whole illustration of a subject, especially when
such illustration may arise from subsequent events;
which is peculiarly the case in developing secret history, which often requires a generation, or the period of
many years, for a full, intelligible, and satisfactory investigation, and wherein, after the most diligent and
assiduous search and enquiry, many things will remain
obscure and dubious, and many things remain to be lost
in irrecoverable oblivion.

Let us now trace out these exiled pilgrims in their
several retreats, migrations, and secret residences —
To begin at New-Haven where they first vanished
into obscurity and oblivion.   They retired from town
to the west side of a rock or mountain, about 300 feet
perpendicular, commonly called the West-Rock, to
distinguish it from the Neck-Rock, to the N. E. of the
town.   The southern extremity of West-Rock lies
about two and a half miles N. W. from the town.   Between this, westward, and a ridge of mountaineous
or rocky elevation, ranging N. and S. parrallel with the
West-Rock, lies an interjacent bottom, or plain, three
miles long, containing a thousand or twelve hundred
acres of excellent land, which Mr. Goodyear, a rich
settler, had bought of the town, and on which he had
planted his farmer, Richard Sperry, which farm Richard Sperry afterwards became possessed of, and now for
above a century it has gone by the name of Sperry's
Farm   In the records I find, April 23, 1660, " Mrs.
Goodyear and her farmer Sperry."   Mr. Goodyear
brought farmers with him out of England, being himself an oppulent Merchant, and always followed com-

merce. On this tract Mr. Goodyear had built Sperry an house; and in the woods about one mile S. W. from Sperry's, stood the house of Ralph Lines. These were the only two houses in 1661 westward from New-Haven, between this West Rock and Hudsons River, unless we except a few houses at Derby or Paugaslet. All was an immense wilderness. Indeed all the environs of New-Haven was wilderness, except the cleared tract about half a mile or a mile around the town, which was laid out and built with 100 or 120 houses on a square half mile, divided into nine squares. Behind the West Rock therefore was, in 1661, a very secure retreat and concealment. This Mr. Jones provided for these exiles. At and about this mountain they secreted themselves between three and four months. Three harbors, lodgments, or places, of their residence there, at different times, are known and shewn to this day. I have visited all three of them, being carried to and shewn them by the family of the Sperrys still dwelling on that tract. The description of them is as follows:

Let it be observed that at this time, about 3 or 400 acres westward of the town was cleared in a common field, called the ox pasture. This might extend near half a mile westward from the central square of the town. All beyond was woods and wilderness. At two miles N. W from the town was a mill.* To this mill the Judges repaired 11th of May, 1661, and here they lodged two nights. On the 13th, Jones, Burril and Sperry, came to them in the woods near the south end of the mountain, and conducted them to Sperrys, about three miles from town. They provided for them "a place called Hatchet Harbour, where they lay two nights, until a cave or hole in the side of a hill was prepared to conceal them. The hill they called Providence Hill: and there they continued from the 15th of May to the 11th of June, sometimes in the cave, and in very tempestuous weather in a house near it."— Hutch. from Goffe's Journal. It is somewhat difficult

[* See Plate II. No. 1.

to afcertain where Hatchet Harbour was.   I have taken much pains to inquire out this place from the Sperrys, and other inhabitants ; and for a long time without satisfaction.   Upon Gov. Hutchinſon's Hiſtory coming out in 1764, the Rev. Mr. Woodbridge, the Miniſter of that pariſh, made diligent inquiry for Hatchet Harbour : but he told me he could not ſatisfy himſelf.   Not but that upon enquiry he readily found that the people knew the ſtory, and uniformly pointed out the place to be that, which was alſo called the Lodge at the ſpring, back in the wildernefs, and three miles N. W. from Sperrys.   On this tract weſt of the mountain, there is now the large and well ſettled pariſh of Woodbridge, of 150 or 200 families, chiefly peopled from New-Haven and Milford, thoroughly transfuſed and impregnated with the ſtories of the Sperrys and Lines, concerning the Judges and the places of their concealments : So that any and all of them point out the places with as much facility and precifion as a New-Haven man will point out Dixwell's grave, or a Saybrook man point out Lady Butler's tomb now ſtanding.   Until Mr. W. expreſſed his doubts, they never were more at a lofs to point out Hatchet Harbour, than the cave or clump of rocks called the cow and calves ; and as uniformly make that and the lodge the ſame. And now aſk a Sperry or an Woodbridge man, where was Hatchet Harbour   and they conſtantly ſay, at the Spring or Lodge, to this day : and never heard of any other place   Mr Woodbridge's difficulty lay here: Governor Hutchinſon places it in the ſide of a hill, called Providence hill, which was doubtleſs the Weſt Rock , and ſays that their concealment here was only two nights   and this at the beginning of their exile from New-Haven.   Now tradition here makes it a place three miles off, of a longer, and for a time a ſettled reſidence, and their laſt abode before they went and ſettled at Milford.   Though during their more ordinary and ſettled reſidences at three different places for three months, they at times wandered about in the wildernefs, and made tranfient extemporaneous lodgments in the woods, at Mr. Riggs's and at George's cave. I have often obferved this to the inhabitants, and though they are not able to reconcile or account for it, yet they uniformly and unalterably perfift in their feeling and anceftorial tradition, that Hatchet Harbour is three or four miles off of the Weft Rock, on Mr. Newton's farm, and at a place called indifferently by them all, fometimes Hatchet Harbour, fometimes the Harbour only, fometimes the Lodge near a fpring. Within a few rods adjacent to which is an eminence, called by the Judges, the Fort or Lookout: as from thence they commanded the view of New-Haven, feven miles off. Forty years ago, and many years before the publifhing of Hutchinfon's Hiftory, the very boys of a certain family and neighborhood three miles off, which cultivated a farm there, when afked where they were going to work that day, would anfwer, to the Harbour, or to the Lodge indifferently, but rather more commonly, to the Harbour, meaning this very place. This I have from fome of the perfons themfelves now living.

This having been fo conftantly the underftanding and language of the inhabitants, of the Sperrys, and all the people to this day; and their never having heard of any other place for Hatchet Harbour, has led me to conceive—that the firft night Sperry led the exiles into the woods, determining to place them in abfolute fecurity and fafety for a few days, till the cave could be prepared, he carried them out into the wildernefs to this recefs, and carrying a hatchet with them, or as conftant tradition fays, finding one there at the fpring, loft there perhaps by fome hunters, they cut down boughs of trees, and made a temporary covertue, where they lodged a few nights only, and then went to the Cave on the fummit of the Weft Rock. And after perhaps a months refidence, being affrighted from the Cave by wild and ferocious animals, they fought another place a mile or two northward, on the Rivulet at the foot of the same Mountain : but being discovered by the Indian's dogs in hunting, they removed three miles further westward into the wilderness, to Hatchet Harbour, their first transient place ; which from becoming thenceforth their more settled residence, was called the Lodge. So that the same place goes by the name of the Lodge or Harbour, to this day.

To return : after lodging two nights at Hatchet Harbour, they went to the Cave. From Sperrys they ascended the west side of Providence Hill to this Cave. But why the Cave should be spoken of as being in " the side of the Hill, I cannot conceive, unless it might so appear to the Judges, for the Cave is high up the hill, even on the very summit , although being enveloped in woods, they might not especially at first consider it as on the summit. it is however on the very top of the West Rock, and about half or three quarters of a mile from the southern extremity. This Cave then I shall consider as their first station or harbor, as they called all their residences Lodges, Harbors, or Ebenezers, without accounting their short lodgments of two nights each at the Mill and at Hatchet Harbor.

In 1785 I visited aged Mr Joseph Sperry, then living, aged 50, a grandson of the first Richard, a son of Daniel Sperry, who died 1751, aged 86, from whom Joseph received the whole family tradition. Daniel was the sixth son of Richard, and built a house at the south end of Sperry's farm, in which Joseph now lives, not half a mile west from the Cave, which Joseph shewed me. There is a notch in the mountain against Joseph's house, through which I ascended along a very steep acclivity up to the Cave. From the south end of the mountain for three or four miles northward, there is no possible ascent or descent on the west side, but at this notch, so steep is the precipice of the rock I found the Cave to be formed, on a base of perhaps forty feet

Rangia cave on top of W. Island being a clump of 7
irregular Rocks, 25 feet high & 130 f. round, 50 f. base

Elevation or erect View on S.E. front.

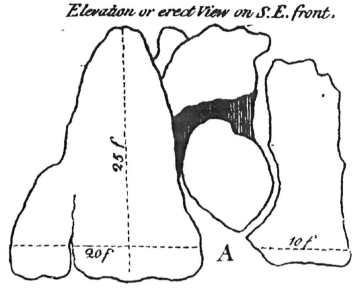

25 f

20 f

A

10 f

Horizontal Section or Base of the 7 Rocks, with the
Aperture of residence 2 to 3 feet wide & 4 to 6 f. high
A. the aperture or mouth of the Cave

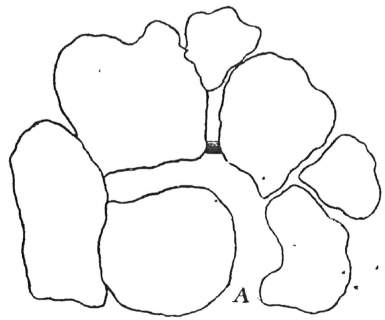

A

fquare, by an irregular clump or pile of rocks, or huge broad pillars of ftone, fifteen and twenty feet high, ftanding erect and elevated above the furrounding fuperficies of the mountain, and enveloped with trees and foreft. Thefe rocks coalefcing or contiguous at top, furnifhed hollows or vacuities below, big enough to contain bedding and two or three perfons. The apertures being clofed with boughs of trees or otherwife, there might be found a well covered and convenient lodgment. Here, Mr. Sperry told me, was the firft lodgment of the Judges, and it has ever fince gone and been known by the name of the Judges' Cave to this day. Goffe's Journal fays, they entered this Cave the 15th of May, and continued in it till the 11th of June following.— Richard Sperry daily fupplied them with victuals from his houfe, about a mile off; fometimes carrying it himfelf, at other times fending it by one of his boys, tied up in a cloth, ordering him to lay it on a certain ftump and leave it: and when the boy went for it at night he always found the bafons emptied of the provifions, and brought them home. The boy wondered at it, and ufed to afk his father the defign of it, and he faw no body. His father only told him there was fome body at work in the woods that wanted it. The fons always remembered it, and often told it to perfons now living, and to Mr. Jofeph Sperry particularply.

They continued here till 11th of June. Mr. Jofeph Sperry told me that the incident which broke them up from this Cave was this, that this mountain being a haunt for wild animals, one night as the Judges lay in bed, a panther, or catamount, putting his head into the door or aperture of the Cave, blazed his eye-balls in fuch a hideous manner upon them, as greatly affrighted them. One of them was fo terrified by this grim and ferocious monfter, her eyes and her fquawling, that he took to his heels, and fled down the mountain to Sperry's houfe for fafety. They thereupon confidered

G 2

this situation too dangerous, and quitted it. All the Sperry families have this tradition.

Mr. Joseph Sperry also told me another anecdote.—That one day the Judges being at Mr. Richard Sperry's house, some persons appeared riding up towards the house through a causey over the meadows, so that they could be seen fifty or sixty rods off; who by their apparel, and particularly their red coats, were by the famil. immediately taken to be, not our own people, but enemies. These were the English pursuivants unexpectedly returned from New-York, or Manhados.—Upon which the guests ascended into the woods of the adjoining hills, and concealed themselves behind Savin Rock, some rods west of Sperry's house. When the pursuivants came to the house, and enquired of the family for the two regicides, they said they knew not where they were, that they might have been there, but had gone into the woods. I have long ago often heard this story of the pursuivants' actually surprizing the Judges at Sperry's house, and that it was unexpectedly when they were off their guard, and upon their unexpected return from New-York. Yet by Hutchinson they returned to Boston by water. But it has always been a tradition at New-Haven that they remained here, and by corruption of servants learned this secret of the Sperrys, and made this sudden irruption to surprize and take them. That they came there, and unexpectedly, whether on 11th May, before they left the town, or afterwards upon a return, I think is without doubt.

I have described their first residence in the Cave on the Rock. Mr. Sperry told me of two others, one about two miles north, and the third at the Lodge and Fort, so called, about four miles north-west in the wilderness. These I afterwards visited.

This second residence is a little more dubious than the Cave and Lodge, which are unquestionably certain. It

was about two miles and a half north of the first, on
the west bank of a rivulet running along at the foot of
the west side of the West Rock, and about half a mile
north of the house of Thomas Darling, Esq.   This
gentleman was a man of literature and solid judgment,
and the most inapt to credulity, especially of fables, of
any man.   Retiring from town many years ago, he
settled on a paternal estate at the upper end of Sperry's
house.   He had been conversant with the Sperrys and
their traditions for many years, and was fully convinced
that this place was one of the residences of the Judges.
In August 1785, he went with me and shewed me the
spot of their little domicile, when some of the wall or
stone ruins were then remaining.   I examined it with
close attention, and made a drawing of it on the spot,
one of the Sperrys being with us, and affirming the
immemorial tradition, and herein concurring with Mr.
Joseph Sperry, who referred me to the same spot.

It was, as has been said, at the foot of the mountain
on the western bank of a small rivulet, which runs along
the west side of the West Rock, the spot just five miles
and a half from Yale College.   Descending a steep
bank, or brow of the hill of upland, sixteen feet, we
came to a bottom, or level, forty feet wide, four or
five feet above the water of the rivulet or brook, which
I measured thirty-four feet wide at that place.   This
bottom, or level, extended along the bank, on the
edge of the river, fifty-four rods, under the brow of the
hill, being two to three rods wide.   It was a beautiful,
shady and pleasant ambulacrum, or walk.   The upland on the west side is a level of twenty feet above the
river.   From under the western brow issues a perpetual spring about the middle of the ambulacrum, running in a perpetual pleasant brook or stream along under the western brow, and discharging into the rivulet.
The rest of the bottom is not wet and marshy, but dry
and salubrious.   The whole on both sides of the river

was, in 1785, inveloped in trees and foreſt, and yet the bottom was not ſo charged with trees as to be impaſſable, being only a pleaſant ſhady retreat, in which a philoſopher might walk with delight. Near the upper end of this walk, cloſed in at each end by the curve brow of the hill coming down to the very brink of the rivulet, was ſituate the hut of the Judges under the ſide or brow of the hill. Evident traces of it remained in 1785. It was partly dug out of the ſide of the hill, and built with ſtone wall, about eight feet one way and ſeven the other. The weſtern wall was yet ſtanding perhaps three feet high, and a remnant of the north wall. The ſcite, when I ſaw it, was filled with weeds and vegetables, and buſhes, in the manner of old cellars, for it ſeemed to have been dug out a little lower than the ſurrounding ſurface of the bottom. The remainder of the ſtone work evidently ſhewed that it had been built with deſign: and unvaried tradition ſay it was one of the abodes of the Judges. They could not have choſen a more ſecret, hidden, and pleaſant concealment. † They probably came to it next after they fled from the firſt Cave, which they left 11th of June. In the twelve days ſucceeding they were in great uncertainty whether to ſurrender or not. It is not improbable that in this ſpace of time they reſided in Sperry's houſe, or perhaps in the adjacent woods part of the time, and part of it ſhewing themſelves at New-Haven, as well as at Governer Leet's in Guilford. But concluding not to ſurrender as yet, they, on 24th of June, went into their wilderneſs retirement. Let us ſuppoſe they now went into this ſecond Cave lodgment, or reſidence by the rivulet. For ſome reaſon however they do not ſeem to have ſojourned here long: The Sperry's farm tradition ſays, becauſe the Indian dogs in hunting diſcovered them. They therefore ſought another lodgment. If Governor Hutchinſon had made more copious extracts from Goffe's Journal, we doubtleſs ſhould have had more particular deſcriptions. He ſpeaks of

† *See Plate* III.

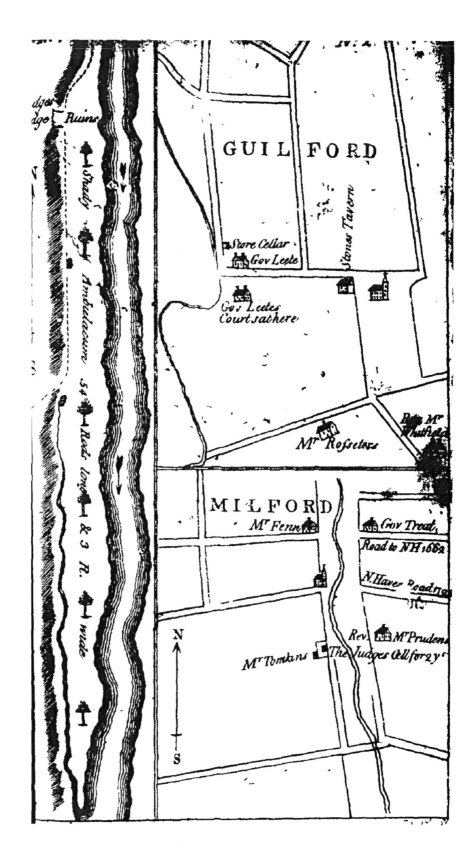

The boundary line between Milford and New-Haven passing here, its frequent perambulation has given notoriety and continued memorial of the names of several places on this territory ; names taken from the residence of the Judges there. And these are entered in the public records both of those towns and of the colony.

On the northern declivity of one of these hills issues a small perennial spring, between two trees, a walnut and chesnut, now three and four feet diameter, and judged to be two hundeed years old, standing twenty-two feet apart. This fountain is stonned as if with design, and probably remaining as the Judges left it.— Tradition says that when they came to this spring, one of them said, " Would to God we had a hatchet"— and immediately finding a hatchet, left there probably by the Indian hunters, they cut down boughs and built a temporary harbor, from this circumstance called Hatchet-Harbor to this day. Not indeed that all agree in indigitating this particular spring, though most do ; while all agree in placing Hatchet-Harbor some where on this mile square territory, to which they also universally give the name of " the Lodge," and " the Harbor," " the Spring,' " Hatchet-Harbor," "the Fort," " the Look Out," " Homes s Fort, 'and " Providence Hill." For different parts of this little territory go by these names, which are frequently used promiscuously and indifferently for any and all parts of it. But I believe that this spring was Hatchet-Harbor. On an eminence west of this, by the side of a ledge of rocks twenty feet high, was built a Cave, or convenient lodgment, ten feet long and seven feet wide, regularly stoned, I find the walls now remaining, though somewhat broken down. It was covered with trunks of trees, which remained, though much rotten and decayed, till within forty years ago : indeed I saw some of the rudera, rafters, or broken relics, limbs and trunks of trees, still lying in the cavity. This was undoubtedly their great and principal lodge, and in a very recluse and fecreted place. There is a beautiful fpring fix rods from it. A moft convenient and fecure fituation for exile and oblivion. This lodgment is fifty rods eaft of deacon Peck's, on whofe farm it is fituated, and about one hundred rods weft from Milford line : as Hatchet-Harbor, or fpring (at which I found an Indian ftone god) is fituate about as far eaft of that line, on Mr. Newton's farm. Between thefe two hills, and directly in this line, is a valley immemorially and to this day called " Hatchet-Valley," lying nearly in equal proximity to both fprings. The true fpot of Hatchet-Harbor is loft, while all agree in referring it to this fmall territory, and moft fpeak of Mr. Newton's fpring as the place.

Acrofs a valley, and fifty or fixty rods north of this fpring, lies a very rocky hill, called to this day "the Fort," and in the town patents 1675, " Homes's Fort" —perhaps a name acquired before the Judges' coming there. It was however a place they frequented, not for refidence, but for a look out and profpect into New-Haven town and harbor, feven miles off. From hence is was called indifferently " the Fort Rocks," " the Fort," " the Look Out,' " Homes's Fort."

Weft of this, and about one hundred rods north of the great or convenient lodgment, on deacon Peck's farm, lies another hillock or eminence, called to this day, and in the records fo early as 1675, " Providence Hill," between which and Fort Rocks hill is a valley and brook. Between thefe two hills runs the dividend line of the towns of Milford and New-Haven. Milford tradition is that it acquired that name thus : While the Judges refided at the lodge on the fouthern hill, they apprehended themfelves difcovered and purfued, while walking upon the tops of hills, and the Indians always burned rings or tracts on thofe fummits, to give a clear view for hunting deer . fuppofing themfelves difcovered they took to the bush, and to deceive their pursuers ranged a north course between the hills, and giving them a false scent, turned off to the westward, and came round the hill to their old place in security. On account of this deliverance they called this northwestern hill Providence Hill. It is said there are still the remains of another Cave at the south-east declivity of Fort Rocks, supposed and traditioned to have also been one of the Judges' burrows. However, all these several lodgments hereabouts, may be properly comprehended under the general name, " the Lodge.'

These, with one at Paugasset or Derby, and another in the woods half way between Derby and Milford, give, I believe, all their lodgments at and about New-Haven: and these inclusive of one at Totoket and Guilford, give all their lodgments in Connecticut, for three years and an half, and until their final removal and absorption in Hadley, where they ended their days.

Letter from Dr. Carrington.

" *Milford, September 1st*, 1794.

" Reverend and dear Sir,

" I find by examining the town records of Milford, that the place called the Lodge is the high lands a little to the westward of Captain Enoch Newton's house, the now farm of deacon Peck. near an hundred years ago this land is described to be at a place called the Lodge, above the head of Mill River, and is so described ever since in the deeds of transfer. To the northward of this about a mile, and on the north side of the road to Oxford, is an hill at this day called Providence Hill. 'Squire Strong, who is now above eighty years old, tells me that full sixty years ago he was on this hill in company with a Mr. George Clarke, then an old man, and who then lived a little east of the hill; he told them that was Providence Hill, and that it had its name from the Judges residing there. He adds, this Mr. Clarke was an intelligent man —And in a deed executed by this Mr. Clarke in 1716, of land on the hill below, to his fon, he defcribes it as being at a place called the Lodge, or Morocco. Betwixt thefe two hills there is a brook of water running weftward, called now Bladen's Brook, and was fo by the records, as early as 1700, but from what it had its name I cannot learn. A little caft of Providence Hill, on the New-Haven fide, is an hill which is commonly called the Fort, and I think ufed to be called the Lodge too, when I was a lad.— There is a tract of land lying on Milford fide, beginning as far north as Amity meeting-houfe, and running fouth three or four miles, which has always been called the Race. I find in the records, that in perambulating the lines betwixt New-Haven and Milford, early in Governor Law's day, they fay they fixed bounds on Homes's race: that they went northward and fet up another on the Lodge, and further on, and fixed another at Bladen's Brook, at the mouth of Station Brook, a fmall run of water coming out from Homes's Fort. Why thefe are called Homes's Race and Fort, cannot learn. 'Squire Strong fays he always fuppofed it was from the Judges affuming that name; but does not recollect he ever heard fo. There never was any perfon in this town of that name as I can find. I have enclofed you a plan reprefenting thofe places, which may make them more intelligible to you. The Lodge is juft twelve miles from Milford, and I judge about feven from New-Haven. Deacon Peck, who has lived on the Lodge about fifty years, and has heard many things from his anceftors on this fubject, particularly from the aforefaid Mr. Clarke, his father in law; but does not feem now to recollect much about them; but this he feems to fully recollect, that while the Judges lived here they had their provifions from one Sperry's houfe, in Sperry's farm, laft Richard Sperry's houfe, now Mr. Darling's land. Hutchinfon fays they left New-Haven, and lodged in a mill; this mill was pro-

H

bably at the Beaver Ponds , thence they went into the woods, met Sperry, &c. who conducted them to Hatchet-Harbor. This Hatchet-Harbor was, I believe, the same with the Lodge. I hear a Mr. Clarke, now 80 years old, son to George, and lives near the Lodge, says it was so called from the circumstance of their finding a hatchet there the first night they came there , but I have not seen him to make the enquiry myself.— Squire Strong tells me he has heard his mother tell of their living in Tomkins's stone cellar ; that a number of girls a spinning above, sung a royal song, counting on the regicides, not knowing they were below and heard them—the place called George's cellar. 'Squire Strong tells me the tradition is, that a person by the name of George Allop once lived there, but who he was, or from whence he came, there is none can give any account. The old people in this town have heard their ancestors tell about the Judges, but seem not to recollect any thing particular about them, except they all agree of their living at Tomkins's house. The first law book of New-Haven colony, you enquired of me about, published in Governor Eaton's day, 'Squire Strong tells me he has seen in Mr. Edward's library at Hartford. The Judges were probably known to Governor Treat, for he was at that time a man of great note in this town. He was born in 1622, came here from Hartford with the planters in 1639, was then seventeen years old He married the only daughter and child of Mr. Edward Tapp, one of the first and principal planters He intended to have returned to Hartford, but his wife's parents, and the planters, persuaded him to tarry in the plantation, and they made him grant of lands to induce him to tarry with them ; he lived with Mr. Tapp, at least his house was on Mr. Tapp's lot Mr. Tapp's great grand-son, and Governor Treat's grand-son, Mr. Edward Treat, now e ... ...y, lives on and owns the farm lot, together with ... ... pieces of land, that was Mr.

Tapp's and Governor Treat's.   The firft lands taken
up by the firft planters, are in many inftances yet in the
fame families, as the Pruddens, Clarkes, Fenns, Fow-
lers, &c. Governor Treat appears by the records to have
had the principal direction of the plantation very early,
as in building of the meeting-houfe, which was 30 feet
fquare, and ftood where the fteeple of the prefent ftands.
He is often mentioned in the records, and appears as
Deputy-Governor firft in 1678—as Governor in 1682,
and until 1699—from that time until 1708 he again
appears as Deputy-Governor.   Squire Strong tells me
that on the return of General Winthrop from England,
as agent, in 1698, Governor Treat requefted Mr.
Winthrop might have the chair, and he was accordingly chofen Governor, and Colonel Treat Deputy-Governor.   Mr. Winthrop died, it appears by our records, in 1707, and upon the 17th of December, 1707,
Deputy-Governor Treat convened the Affembly at
New-Haven, informed them of the death of the Governor, that he had convened them that they might make
choice of one, agreeable to charter.   Governor Treat
was at this time 86 years old, and probably declined
public bufinefs any more, for I do not find any further
mention of him after this in the records.   He died July
12th, 1710.   It is recorded alfo on his tomb-ftone,
that he ferved in the poft of Governor and Deputy-Governor nigh thirty years.   The Affembly, in 1707,
made choice of Governor Saltonftall, but as he was not
in the nomination, and by law they could not chufe any
one out of the nomination, before they gave him the
qualifying oaths, which was on the firft of January,
1708, they repealed the law fo far as refpects the
choice of Governor and Deputy-Governor, and left
them to the choice out of the freemen at large, which
has continued ever fince.   This tranfaction is on our
town records.

    "I am inclined to believe that Bladens Brook,
Homes's Fort and Race, the Lodge, or Morocco, all

had their names from the Judges, as well as Providence Hill; but at this day there is none can inform, Goffe's Diary, which Hutchinson mentions he had, might refer to these places, and point them out as it did Providence H., where they lodged. Hutchinson says their .... d... at places not known, to prevent their di..... .. Moreo.. I should suppose it likely for th.. to w.... them, as .benez.. When I found th... ... .. the .... I ...pe..ed to have got further in.. .. ..p.e, but they in general c. .. .. certainty to ..... fa... —Y... ... ...p... these records, or t.. may p... ... .p.. f..e matters you hav. ...ed of. There .. a .... Valentine Wilmot no. ... g in Be..a.., an o.. ..., ..hom I have not f.. ... v.. .ars, he knew a.. t.e anc.ent people at S.. .. .., was a great H..nter, and I believe from ..ha. I c.. ..... of the man, is likely to have heard a.. ... .. some an..d..es about the Judges.

I am, Sir,
With respect,
You.. m..t humble servant,
EDWARD CARRINGTON.

Re.... D.... S..bs.

"P. S. There is a tradition of a very curious fe- .... years ago, about two miles north- .. .. th.. t was in the ..de of some rocks, t.. ... . .s laid by ha.ds .n a very regu- ... . a.d w.. ..ened a ..... was found in i... .. ... e bones .. .. an f.pp...d to be f.x feet a .. .. It .. .. acc.dently ..und by removing i.. .. ..

... . in the woods the Judges re- ... . in the ..... of Mr. T.. .s, .n the c..... .. .. ..d, ... forty rods f..... t.. ...ting ... ... Gov..nor L.. afterwards

bought this houfe and lot, and built his feat within a
rod or two of it.   I have frequently been in this houfe
of Tomkins's in the Governor's life time, who died
1750, aged 73: it was ftanding fince 1750, and perhaps to 1770.   In this houfe the two Judges refided in
the moft abfolute concealment, not fo much as walking
out into the orchard for two years.   I have not learned
who were privy to the concealment here.   The minifter at this time was the reverend Roger Newton.   He
with Mr. Treat and Mr. Fenn, and a few others here
were in the fecret, and held interviews with them in
this fecret retirement.   But it is ftrange that the very
memory of their refidence there is almoft totally obliterated from Milford.   I do not find a fingle perfon of
Milford, or of Milford extract, except Judge Law,
now of New-London, born at Milford, the Governor's
fon, and Gideon Buckingham, Efq. of Milford,
now living, who is poffeffed of any idea or tradition of
the Judges having ever lived there at all.   Judge Law
is fully poffeffed of the matter, and corrects Governor
Hutchinfon's account, who places Tomkins's houfe
between New-Haven and Milford, whereas he informs
me it ftood in the very center of the town of Milford,
and on his father's home lot.   This houfe, it is faid,
was built for the Judges on Tomkins's lot, a few rods
from his houfe.   It was a building, fay twenty feet
fquare, and two ftories.   The lower room built with
ftone wall, and confidered as a ftore.   The room over
it with timber and wood, and ufed by Tomkins's family
as a work or fpinning room.   The family ufed to fpin
in the room above, ignorant of the Judges being below,
where they refided two years, without going abroad fo
much as into the orchard.   Judge Buckingham tells
me this ftory, the only anecdote or notice I could ever
learn from a Milford man now living.   While they fojourned at Milford, there came over from England a
ludicrous cavalier ballad, fatirizing Charles's Judges,
and Goffe and Whalley among the reft.   A fpinftrefs

Royalist ballad against regicides.

at Milford had learned to sing it, and used sometimes to sing it in the chamber over the Judges ; and the Judges used to get Tomkins to set the girls to singing that song for their diversion, being humoured and pleased with it, though at their own expence, as they were the subjects of the ridicule.   The girls knew nothing of the matter, being ignorant of the innocent device, and they thought that they were serenading angels.

But however the memory of the Judges is obliterated at Milford, not so at Guilford, New-Haven and Hadley.   Here I resume the situation before their final laceration.   It is a constant tradition at Guilford, not only that they actually were here, but were for some time, at least for several days, secreted at Governor Leets. They speak of two circumstances : 1st That the Governor, though a cordial friend to them, was filled with great anxiety and distress lest he should be brought into danger and trouble by their being there, and used certain precaution concerning their concealment, that he might be safe and secure from incurring danger. And to this end, 2d He would not suffer them to be lodged in his house, but made them lodge in his Stone cellar. * Now it is difficult to account for this tradition, on the supposition of only their transient friendly calling upon him, and even lodging with him, on their way from Governor Winthrop's in New-London, to New-Haven, which they certainly did on —— March for there really was no danger of impeachment for the harbouring and concealing traitors, till after Governor Leet, on 10th May, received a copy of the royal mandate. Governor Winthrop felt no danger, nor did Governor Leet, till the 10th of May. He might be courteous and solicitous for the regicides themselves, and for the matter he must be called to conduct himself, but not for his incurring any penalty by this action, even to travelling traitors, whom he had no public, nor by office as chief Magistrate was called, nor ordered to apprehend. Nor would he

at that time have lodged them in his cellar. But the
case was much altered after the 10th of May, and every
body was put into terror and caution after that. The
Judges certainly were not at Guilford after they went to
New-Haven, during the space of from 7th of March
to 10th of May, when the Governor told Kellond and
Kirk that he had not seen them for nine weeks. Although it is probable that he immediately, or in a few
days after 7th March, followed the Judges to New-
Haven, there to take counsel and concert measures how
to act concerning them, of which there is a flying tradition, yet if so, he saw them no more till after the
10th of May. After this, it became really dangerous
for the Governor to be concerned in the concealment.
From their first coming in March, to 11th June, they
certainly were not seen by the Governor. Between this
and 20th of June was the only space in which they
could be at the Governor's, for they were exposed three
days in New-Haven, and retired to their Cave June
24th. These eight or nine days it was in deliberation
to deliver them up, and Mr. Gilbert gave out that he
expected it. Let us conceive that they had concluded
to surrender, and went over with their friends, doubtless Jones, if not Davenport, to the Governor to surrender. Deliberating when they came there, they
might conclude that the only person in real danger was
Mr. Davenport, and if he would wave the matter,
the concealment might go on. The formal and actual
surrender they might hold in suspense. But this took
up time, and perhaps they must lodge in Guilford a
night or two. How should this be ordered so as to
save the Governor? Here might be room for the appearance of the Governor's timidity and caution;
which might terminate in a conclusion that it was not
best nor safest that they should lodge in the Governor's
house, and to avoid this they should, during these few
days secretion, take up their abode in the lone cellar,
and perhaps in Mr. Rossiter's house.

There is, as I have said, reason to think that they went over to Guilford with the bona fide and actual view of surrendering themselves to Governor Leet. The Governor's house was situated on the eastern bank of the rivulet that passes through Guilford. † He had a a store on the bank a few rods from his house, and under it a cellar remaining to this day, and which I lately (1793) visited and viewed with attention. It is, as I have said, still in the general and concurrent tradition at Guilford, that the Judges were concealed and lodged in this cellar several nights, most say three days and three nights, when the Governor was afraid to see them. A daughter of Governor Leet afterwards married in New-Haven to Mr Trowbridge. It is an anecdote still preserved in that family, that she used often to say that, when she was a little girl, these good men lay concealed some time in this cellar of her father's store; but that she did not know it till afterwards: that she well remembered that at the time of it, she and the rest of the children were strictly prohibited from going near that store for some days, and that she and the children wondered at it and could not conceive the reason of it at that time, though they knew it afterwards. Tradition says that they were however constantly supplied with victuals from the Governor's table, sent to them by the maid, who long after was wont to glory in it, that she had fed these holy men. Now, this caution could not be at the request in view with the Governor, at their coming at Governor Winthrop's from New-London to New-Haven, in March. On the 12th of May Leet told the pursuivants that he had not seen them in nine weeks, nor was it dangerous, as I have said, for any one to see them at that time, when he first received the King's proclamation. He doubtless studiously avoided seeing them ever after this.— This hiding in the cellar must therefore have been after 12th of May, and precedent to the 11th of June, and I conceive it to have been at the time when Mr Gilbert
— S. Pa...

gave out that he looked when they fhould have come in and furrendered, as he might fay with truth, if he knew they were gone to Guilford with the exprefs defign of furrendering. And as it would not have been proper for the governor to fee them until they actually furrendered, it was natural fo to contrive the matter, that they fhould be concealed in this cellar, during the two or three days' confultation and deliberation on what was neceffary and beft to be done. This therefore was a proper time, and here was fufficient reafon for all the caution and injunctions upon the family, to avoid and not go near that ftore, a thing long after remembered by the Governor's daughter, and narrated in her very old age, within the memory of perfons now living.— Perhaps Mr. Davenport himfelf was in this confultation, as being conceived to be the principal perfon in danger. Upon revolving and difcuffing the matter, they muft have perceived the folidity of Mr. Davenport's reafons, that both he and the Governor were fafe if they had never any thing more to do with the Judges after the recept of the King's proclamation and commands. For thefe or other reafons, it was concluded not to infift on their furrender, and accordingly they were left to retire from this concealment in the Governor's cellar, and returned to New-Haven; and after fhewing themfelves openly there from 20th to 24th of June, retired to their Cave at Providence Hill. This was undoubtedly the time, the dangerous time, when they were fo cautioufly concealed in the cellar.

Connected with this is another anecdote, which I extract from the records:

At a General Court at New-Haven, May 7, 1662.

Confidering the cafe of Mr. Brayton (Bryan) Roffeter, of Guilford, and his fon, John Roffeter: The Marfhal of Guilford had waited upon them for colony taxes, the father not at home. In converfation with the fon, the Marfhal " told him, his father fhould bring in an account of his charges about the COLONELS, &c."

Now at that day, that military office was not in being in New-England: there being only Majors and no Colonels in Maßachußetts, Connecticut, New-Haven, Plymouth or Rhode-Island. Were not theße Colonels Goffe and Whalley? and dont this concur in evidencing that they reßided ßome time at leaßt in Guilford in 1661? Doubtleßs they reßided in the Governor's cellar, and at Mr. Rosßeter s, from the 11th to 20th of June. Mr. Davenport ßtanding firm and the Governor now having demonßtration by the actual ßurrendery of the Judges, that they would at all times ßtand ready to ßurrender, and it being agreed that the places of their retreat ßhould always be known to him, ßo that they could be given up in caße of extremities, he felt himßelf ßafe, and could agree to poßtpone the actual acceptance of their ßurrendery to a future time, if it ßhould be abßolutely neceßßary.

Madam Dexter, of Dedham, originally of Boßton, whom I ßaw 1793, aged 92, tells me ßhe had formerly been acquainted with a pious woman at Dedham, who ußed often to glory that ßhe had lived with, ßerved and minißtered to theße holy men, but when aßked, would never ßay where it was.

An aged woman now living in New-Haven, of good intelligence, tells me, 1793, that her grand-mother Collins died about 1744, aged 87, when ßhe was aged 17 or 18. Mrs. Collins (formerly Mrs Trowbridge was Governor Leet's daughter. She has often heard her ßay, that ßhe remembered the children of the family were for a time forbid the ßtone cellar, but could not then conceive for what reaßon. But ßhe was afterwards informed, and ever after ßuppoßed the two Judges were concealed there. Mrs. Collins might be four or five years old in 1661. This is a dißtinct branch of traditionary information from the former, although of the ßame fact, and concurrent with other information.

It is difficult to conceive how any thing leßs than this ßhould be ßufficient for the tradition at Guilford.—

If this scene really took place, what commanded the ultimate determination ? Suppose it was this, that they should return to New-Haven, appear openly, and not only clear Mr †Davenport from then still concealing them, but confer with Mr. Davenport, the only man in danger, and if he felt his danger, then to surrender. And this would bring the whole matter upon Mr. Davenport. If he gave out, all was gone. Mr. Davenport was a great man in every respect, a great civilian, a great and deep politician, as well as divine, and of intrepid resolution and firmness ; and was a much deeper man, of greater discernment in public affairs, and every way superior in abilities to the Governor and all concerned. He saw they all gave up. He, like Mount Atlas, stood firm, and alone resolutely took the whole upon himself. Better than any of the Counsellors, he knew that the secreting he had done to the 30th of April, and whatever could have been done before the arrival of the royal mandate, could be vindicated by the laws of hospitality to unconvicted criminals, and could not in a court of law be construed into even a misposition of treason. It might subject him to some inconveniences, perhaps prosecutions, but could not be fatal. a thing which perhaps the others doubted. Supported by his good sense and deep discernment, he therefore felt himself secure, and stood firm , not out of obstinacy, which was indeed natural to him, but with an enlightened and judicious stability. What staggered Governor Endicott, a man of heroic fortitude, and other Hearts of Oak at Boston, never staggered Mr. Davenport. He alone was firm, unshaken, unawed Great minds display themselves on trying and great occasions He was the man for this trying occasion. Davenport's enlightened greatness, fidelity and intrepidity, saved the Judges.

They having shewn themselves three days at New-Haven, though doubtless cautiously, on the 24th of June, as I have said, retired to their Cave, and closed

their laſt open intercourſe with the world. Here they
continued about two months longer, and then, on the
19th of Auguſt, 1661, removed to the houſe of a Mr.
Tomkins in Milford. † Here they lived ſecreted two
years without going into the orchard. Afterwards their
religious meetings and exerciſes, as it is ſaid, gave them
too much notoriety to continue there any longer; and
they were obliged to meditate a removal to a more ſecreted aſylum. This was undoubtedly accelerated by
the news of the arrival of the Commiſſioners at Boſton,
1664, one of whoſe inſtructions from the King was,
to make enquiry for Colonel Whalley and Colonel
Goffe. They ſought for the moſt remote frontier ſettlement; and the friends provided for their reception at
the houſe of the reverend John Ruſſel, miniſter of the
new ſettled town of Hadley, one hundred miles off, upon Connecticut river, in Maſſachuſetts. They removed from Milford to Hadley on the 13th of October,
1664, after a reſidence and pilgrimage of three years
and ſeven months, at New-Haven and Milford. They
travelled only in the night, and lay by in the day time,
making little ſtations or arbors, which they called harbors, when in the woods on their journey. One of
the little reſts or harbors of theſe pilgrims, was near
the ford of a large brook or rivulet, which we paſs in the
way to Hartford, juſt twenty miles from New-Haven,
or half way to Hartford, and one mile weſt of Meriden
meeting-houſe: which circumſtance has given the
name of Pilgrims Harbor to this place or paſs, to this
day. From thence they proceeded to Hadley in 1664.

They kept a diary or journal of occurrences for the
firſt ſeven years of their exile, after they left London,
at Boſton, New-Haven, and Milford, and then at
Hadley. Theſe with their letters, and perhaps other
writings, were left in the hands of Mr. Ruſſel, of Hadley, till his death, 1692; and paſſed down to his ſon,
who died 1711, having removed them to Barnſtable,
and thence to his grand-ſon, the ſucceeding miniſter of

† See the Langd rts, Plate I. No II. and Plate III

Barnftable, where they were preferved to his death, 1758. About this time, or perhaps 1759, or 1760, Mrs. Otis, of Barnftable, an aged widow lady, removed from Barnftable, and came to live with her fon, Major Jonathan Otis of Newport, and became for many years a communicant in my church there. This brought me into an intimate acquaintance with her. She was a Ruffel, a grand-daughter of the reverend John Ruffel, of Hadley, daughter of the reverend Jonathan Ruffel, of Barnftable, and fifter of the reverend Jonathan Ruffel, fucceffor of his father in the paftoral charge of the church at Barnftable, who died 1758. She was every way a woman of merit and excellence. Of exceeding good natural abilities, very inquifitive, poffeffed a natural decency, dignity and refpectability, and was a perfon of confiderable reading, and extenfive obfervation. She had all along in life been much converfant among minifters, gentlemen of the Court, and perfons of the firft refpectability. She was ever learning and imbibing fomething profitable and improving, and took fingular delight in the converfation of inftructive characters. She was perfectly verfed in the Ruffel hiftory of the Judges, for whofe memory fhe had the family veneration. So much I think neceffary to obferve of her perfonal character. Among other converfations, fhe often brought up the ftory of the Judges. She confidered it an honor to have defcended from an anceftor who had concealed and protected them. She often told me of a trunk of Whalley's and Goffe's manufcripts which had come down to her brother, the fecond Mr. Ruffel, of Barnftable, and were preferved there in his library to his death. She faid fhe had fpent much time in reading them, and fpake much of what fhe found contained in them. What was given to the Mather library, was but a very fmall part of the collection of the Judges' manufcripts in this trunk, fome of which, though difperfed, may poffibly yet be found, and afford light and information.

When I read Governor Hutchinſon's hiſtory, publiſhed in 1764, and particularly his marginal notes
about the regicides, I inſtantly recollected this information of Mrs. Otis reſpecting this collection of manuſcripts, and at firſt judged that this was the ſource from
whence the Governor derived his documents. Lieu-
tenant-Governor Hutchinſon was then Chief Juſtice of
the Supreme Court of Maſſachuſetts. I at once conſidered, that in riding the circuit, when holding the
court in the county of Barnſtable, he came acroſs this
trunk of the Judges' manuſcripts, and ſelected from
thence the accurate and authentic information which he
publiſhed. But afterwards the Governor told me, that
he had never heard of this collection of manuſcripts in
the hands of Mr. Ruſſel, of Barnſtable; and that his
information was derived from original autographical
writings, which he had found among the papers and
manuſcripts preſerved in the Mather library, in Boſton,
and which the reverend Samuel Mather, of Boſton, had
obliged him with the peruſal of. The reverend Samuel Mather married Governor Hutchinſon's ſiſter. He
was the only ſon of the reverend Doctor Cotton Mather, author of the Magnalia Americana, who had been
long aſſiduous in collecting original information from
all parts of the country for that work. A moſt valuable
collection of Manuſcripts from the reverend Richard
Mather, of Dorcheſter, Doctor Increaſe Mather, and
Doctor Cotton Mather, deſcended and came into the
hands of Mr. Samuel Mather, brother-in-law to Governor Hutchinſon. This family connexion opened
all this treaſury of hiſtorical information to the Govern-
or. Here he found Goffe's original Diary, or Journal,
for ſeven years, written in ſeveral pocket volumes, and
alſo a number of Goffe's letters to his wife. But neither the Governor nor the poſſeſſor knew how they came
into the Mather library.

That they came from the Ruſſel family, and from
the Barnſtable collection, I do not doubt, as the libra-

ry of the Hadley Ruffel had been removed to his fon's at Barnftable, foon after 1692, before Doctor Cotton Mather began to write his hiftory, and ten years before the publication of the Magnalia. I do not believe the Hadley Ruffel would have fuffered them out of his hands in his life time. If Cotton Mather came acrofs them while writing, he for fome reafons never made ufe of them, as nothing of them appears in his works. Doctor Cotton Mather, as well as his father, Doctor Increafe Mather, was intimately acquainted with all the Ruffels, and doubtlefs from them received the manufcripts. But I am inclined to think that they never difclofed thefe manufcripts to Mather, till death had put every one out of danger. Probably Mr. Ruffel lent them to one of the Mathers, about 1715 or 1720, for Governor Hutchinfon fpeaks of them as of the collection of Doctor Increafe Mather, who died, 1724, as did Doctor Cotton in 1727, when they came into his fon Samuel's hands, and lay unnoticed till Hutchinfon delivered an extract from them to the public, 1764, But it feems they were but few, and a very fmall part of a larger collection, which may poffibly be yet remaining in the trunk at Barnftable Thofe which the Governor had, I have before obferved, were loft when his houfe was deftroyed at the time of the Stamp Act. Thus far the hiftory of the Judges' manufcripts I thought beft to infert.

When I once faw one of the pocket volumes of Goffe's Journal for 1662, which Hutchinfon fhewed me in 1766, I little thought of the ufe I could now have made of it. As the original is loft, I regret that I did not extract and copy more of it, while in my poffeffion, than this little relict. In the beginning of it was the following lift of names, which I then copied.

" Ifaac Ewre,   W. Purefoy,
S. F. Banners,   I. Blackftone,
S. T. Malevern,   S. W. Conftable,

R. Deane,
F. Alleyne,
P. Peckham,
J. Moore,
I. Alured,
H. Edwards,
S. G. Norton,
I. Venn,
T. Andrews,
A. Stapley,
T. Horton,
I. Fry,
T. Hammond,
S. I. Bourchier, *all deceased.*

———

O. Cromwell,
——— Ireton,
——— Bradshaw,
 * Pride.

———

Wm. Ld. Monson,
Ja. Challoner,
Sr. H. Mildmay,
S. J Harrington,
I. Phelps,
Robert Wale,
Sr A. Haslerig.—*I Chal-*
loner and S. A. Hasle-
rig, dead; the other five
are degraded, and when
taken to be drawn from
Tower to Tiburne with
robes, &c. and impri-
soned during life.

———

I. Lisle,
W. Say,
V. Walton,

E. W———,
J. Barks[d]. *
E. Ludlow,
M. Leusay,
J. Okey *
J. Hewson,
W. G———,
C. Holland,
T. Chattr.
M. Corbett, *
W. Cawley,
N. Love,
J. Dixwell,
D. Blagrave,
A. Brougton,
A. Dendy.—*Fled.*

———

J. Pennington,
R. Tichbourne,
O. Row,*
A. Garland,
E. Harvie,
H. Smith,
H. Martin,
H. Walter,
G. Fleetwood,
J. Temple,
P. Temple,
J Waite,
S. Mayne,
W. Henningham,
R. Lileburne,
G. Millington,
V. Potter,
T. Morgan,
J. Downes.—*Condemned,*
and in the Tower."

Here are given the name of sixty-nine persons; twenty-six of whom are dead; five degraded; nineteen fled, and nineteen in the Tower. Most of these were King Charles's Judges, as the following Ordinance and Warrant for his execution, with the signatures, will shew. In the above, probably *Peckham* should be *Pelham.*—Barks^d. Okey, and Corbet, were afterwards taken and executed, 1662. Morgan was not in the Tower.—*Phelps* is *Philips.*

Ordinance for trying the King, made January 6, 1649.

" WHEREAS it is notorious that CHARLES STUART, now King of England, not content with these many encroachments which his predecessors had made on the people in their rights and freedoms, has had a wicked design totally to subvert the ancient and fundamental laws and liberties of this nation, and in their stead to introduce an arbitrary and tyrannical government; and that besides all other evil ways and means to bring this design to pass, he has prosecuted it with fire and sword, levying and maintaining a cruel war against the Parliament and kingdom, whereby the country has been miserably wasted, the public treasure exhausted, trade decayed, thousands of people murdered, and infinite other mischiefs committed; for all which high and treasonable offences the said Charles Stuart might long since justly been brought to exemplary and condign punishment: whereas also the Parliament, well hoping that the imprisonment of his person, after it had pleased God to deliver him into their hands, would have quieted the distempers of the kingdom, forbore to proceed judicially against him; but found by sad experience that their remissness served only to encourage him and his accomplices in the continuance of their evil practices, and in raising new commotions, rebellions and invasions. For preventing therefore the like or greater inconveniences, and to the end no chief officer or magistrate whatever may hereafter presume

I 2

traitorously and maliciously to imagine or contrive the enslaving or destroying the English Nation, and to expect impunity for so doing; It is hereby ordained and enacted by the Commons in Parliament, that Thomas Ld. Fairfax, O. Cromwell, Henry Ireton, Esqrs. Sir H. Waller, Philip Skippon, Val Walton, Thomas Harrison, Edward Whalley, Thomas Pride, Isaac Ewer. R. Ingoldsby, Mildmay, Esqrs. Thomas Honeywood, Thomas Ld. Grey of Grooby, Philip Ld. Lisle, William Ld. Mounson, Sir John Danvers, Sir Thomas Maleverer, Bart. Sir John Bourcheir, Sir James Harrington, Sir William Alenson, Sir Henry Mildmay, Sir Thomas Wroth, Knts. Sir William Masham, Sir J. Barrington, Sir William Brereton, Barts. Robert Wallop, William Haveningham, Esqrs. Isaac Pennington, Thomas Atkins, Bowl Wilson, aldermen of London, Sir P. Wentworth, Knt. of the Bath, Henry Martin, William Purefoy, Godfrey Rosvil, John Trenchard, H. Morley, John Barkstead, Mat. Thomlinson, John Blackiston, Gilb. Millington, Esqrs. Sir William Constable, Bart. Edmond Ludlow, John Lambert, John Hutchinson, Esqrs. Sir A. Haslerig, Sir Michael Livesey, Bart. Richard Salway, H. Salway, Robert Titchburn, Owen Roe, Robert Manwaring, Robert Silburn, Adr. Scroop, Richard Dean, John Okey, Robert Overton, John Hewson, John Desborow, William Goffe, Robert Duckenfield, Cornelius Holland, John Careu, Esqrs. Sir William Armyn, Bart. John Jones, Miles Corbet, F. Allen, Thomas Lister, Benjamin Weston, P. Pelham, J Gourdon, Esqrs. Fr. Tharop, serjeant at law, John Nut, Thomas Chaloner, Algernon Sidney, John Anlaby, John Mare, R. Darley, William Say, John Alured, John Flagg, James Nelthorp, Esqrs Sir William Roberts, F Lassels, Alexander Rigby, Henry Smith, Edmund Wild, James Chaloner, Josias Berneis, D. Bond, Humphrey Edwards, Greg. Clement, John Fry, Thomas Wogan, Esq. Sir Greg. Norton, Bart. John Bradshaw, serjeant at law, Edm. Hervey, J. Dove, J. Ven, Efqrs. J. Fowles, Thomas. Andrews, aldermen of London; Thomas Scott, William Cawley, Abr. Burrel, Ant. Stapeley, Ro. Gratwick, J. Downs, Thomas Horton, Thomas Hammond, Geo. Fenwick, Efqrs. Robert Nicolas, ferj. at law, Robert Reynolds, John Lifle, Nic Love, Vinc. Potter, Efqrs. Sir Gilbert Pickering, Bart. John Weaver, Rog. Hill, John Lenthall, Efqrs. Sir Edward Bainton, John Corbet, Thomas Blunt, Thomas Boone, Aug. Garland, Aug. Skinner, John Dixwell, George Fleetwood, Sim. Mayne, James Temple, Peter Temple. Daniel Blagrove, Efqrs. Sir Peter Temple, Bart. Thomas Wayte, John Brown, John Lowry, Efqrs. are hereby appointed and required to be Commiffioners and Judges for hearing, trying, and adjudging the faid Charles Stuart. And the faid Commiffioners, or any twenty or more of them, are authorized and conftituted a High Court of Juftice, to meet and fit at fuch convenient time and place, as by the faid Commiffioners, or the major part of twenty or more of them, under their hands and feals fhall be notified by public proclamation in the Great Hall, or Palace Yard at Weftminfter, and to adjourn from time to time, and from place to place, as the faid High Court, or major part thereof, fhall hold fit : and to take order for charging him, the faid Charles Stuart, with the crimes and treafons above mentioned ; and for receiving his perfonal anfwer thereto ; and for examining witneffes upon oath, which the Court has hereby authority to adminifter, and taking any other evidence concerning the fame : and thereupon, or in default of fuch anfwer, to proceed to final fentence, according to juftice and the merit of the caufe, and fuch final fentence to execution, or caufe to be executed, fpeedily and impartially. And the faid Court is hereby authorized and required to appoint and dir all fuch officers, attendants, and other circumf as they, or the major part of them, fhall judge neceffary or ufeful for the orderly and good managing the premifes. And Thomas Ld. Fairfax, the General, and all officers and foldiers under his command, and all officers of juftice, and other well affected perfons, are hereby authorifed and required to be aiding and affifting to the faid Court, in the due execution of the truft hereby committed. Provided that this act, and the authority hereby granted, continue in force one month from the making hereof, and no longer."

[*Rufhworth's Collection. Vol. 6. 562.*]

At the High Court of Juftice for the trying of Charles Stuart, King of England, January 29th A. D. 1648.

Whereas Charles Stuart, King of England, is and ftandeth convicted, attainted, and condemned of high treafon and other high crimes, and fentence was pronounced againft him by this Court, to be put to death by the fevering of his head from his body, of which fentence execution yet remaineth to be done : Thefe are therefore to will and require you to fee the faid fentence executed, in the open ftreet before Whitehall, upon the morrow, being the thirtieth day of this inftant, month of January, between the hours of ten in the morning and five in the afternoon of the fame day, with full effect. And for fo doing, this fhall be your fufficient warrant. And thefe are to require all officers and foldiers, and other the good people of this nation of England to be affifting unto this fervice Given under our hands and feals.

To Colonel Francis Hacker, Colonel Huncks, and Lieutenant-Colonel Phayre, and to every of them.

John Bradfhaw,	(L.S.)	John Okey,	(L.S)
- Grey	(L.S.)	J. Dauers,	(L.S)
-ell,	(L S.)	John Bourchier,	(L.S)
'ley,	(L.S.)	H. Ireton,	(L.S.)
	(L.S.)	T. Mauleuerer,	(L.S.)

Har. Waller,	(L.S.)	William Cawley,	(L.S.)
John Blackiston,	(L.S.)	John Barkstead,	(L.S.)
John Hutchinson,	(L.S.)	Isaac Ewer,	(L.S.)
William Goffe,	(L.S.)	John Dixwell,	(L.S.)
Thomas Pride,	(L.S.)	Valentine Wauton,	(L.S.)
P. Temple,	(L.S.)	Symon Mayne,	(L.S.)
T. Harrison,	(L.S.)	Thomas Horton,	(L.S)
J. Hewson,	(L.S.)	J. Jones,	(L.S.)
Hen. Smyth,	(L.S.)	John Penne,	(L.S.)
Per. Pelham,	(L.S.)	Gilbert Millington,	(L.S.)
Ri. Deane,	(L.S.)	G. Fleetwood,	(L.S.)
Robert Tichborne,	(L.S.)	J. Alured,	(L.S.)
H. Edwards,	(L S.)	Robert Lileburne,	(L.S.)
Daniel Blagrace,	(L.S.)	William Say,	(L.S.)
Owen Rowe,	(L.S.)	Anthony Stapley,	(L.S.)
William Purefoy,	(L.S.)	Gre. Norton,	(L.S)
Ad. Scrope,	(L.S.)	Thomas Challoner,	(L.S.)
James Temple,	(L.S.)	Thomas Wogan,	(L.S)
A. Garland,	(L.S.)	John Downes,	(L.S.)
Edm. Ludlow,	(L.S.)	Thomas Wayte,	(L.S.)
Henry Marten,	(L.S.)	Thomas Scott,	(L.S.)
Vinct. Potter,	(L.S.)	John Careu,	(L.S.)
William Constable,	(L.S)	Miles Corbet.	(L.S.)
Richard Ingoldesby,	(L.S.)		

The original signatures are in seven columns: Bradshaw stands at the head of the first column; Linsey the second; Waller, Smith, Garland, Mayne, Wogan, at the head of the succeeding ones. Fifty-nine signed the warrant, out of seventy, who sat at the beginning of the trial, and afterwards withdrew before giving judgment. Some names in Goffe's list are not in this.— Others besides the Judges were comprehended under the accusation and title of regicides,—"the number of whom, including the officers of the Court, and others immediately concerned, amounted originally to four score. Of these, twenty-five were dead; twenty-nine or twenty-seven had escaped from the kingdom; seven were deemed proper objects of the King's mercy ; twenty-nine received sentence of death, but nineteen were reprieved during the King's pleasure, because they had surrendered themselves according to the proclamation. The ten devoted to immediate execution were, Harrison, Careu, Cook, Peters, Scott, Clement, Scrope, Jones, Hacker and Axtel."   [Smollet, V. 5. 350.

This was 1660. In 1662, Barkstead, Corbet and Okey, and a little afterwards Vane and Lambert, were also condemned and executed   This was the state of information at the time of Goffe's entries in his journal of 1662, which contain some others beside Judges signing the warrant, and not all those; as it contains Judges who sat during part of the trial, but did not sign, and some that were not Judges, but were accused and condemned, as Phelps and Wale. Goffe's list, however, shews that he had pretty just information, as to the number in 1662 dead; the number whose ashes were to be dishonored; those adjudged to perpetual imprisonment, who were fled, and in the Tower. Enough to shew Whalley and Goffe what would be their fate if taken. This information they received while at Milford. Of the first ten executed, six only were Judges, Coke was sollicitor at the trial, Peters a clergyman, Hacker and Axtel Colonels at the execution· neither were Vane or Lambert Judges. The bodies of Bradshaw, Cromwell, Ireton and Pride, were taken up at the Restoration, and hung and buried under the gallows.— These are in the second division. Of those in the third, two were dead; but the reason why separated from others dead is not obvious. It is to this day problematical, and can never be ascertained, whether the bodies of Bradshaw and Cromwell were actually taken up and dishonored at the Restoration. It is in secret tradition that Bradshaw was conveyed to Jamaica. His Epitaph is descriptive of him, and full of spirit. In a public print of 1775, it was said " The following inscription was made out three years ago on the cannon near

No.

Bradshaw-
Jamaia?

which the afhes of Prefident Bradfhaw were lodged, on the top of a high hill near Martha Bay in Jamaica, to avoid the rage againft the regicides exhibited at the Reftoration :

STRANGER,

Ere thou pafs, contemplate this Cannon.

Nor regardlefs be told!

That near its bafe lies depofited the duft of

JOHN BRADSHAW,

Who, nobly fuperior to all felfifh regards,

Defpifing alike the pageantry of courtly fplendor,

The blaft of calumny, & the terrors of royal vengeance,

Prefided in the illuftrious band of Heroes and Patriots,

Who fairly and openly adjudged

CHARLES STUART,

Tyrant of England,

To a public and exemplary death,

Thereby prefenting to the amazed world,

And tranfmitting down, through applauding ages,

The moft glorious example

Of unfkaken virtue, love of freedom, and Impartial Juftice,

Ever exhibited on the blood-ftained theatre of human action.

O, Reader,

Pafs not on till thou haft bleffed his memory :

And never, never forget

THAT REBELLION TO TYRANTS IS OBE-
DIENCE TO GOD.

There are no other anecdotes worthy of preservation concerning these two persons during their residence at New-Haven and Milford. We shall therefore now follow them in their pilgrimage to Hadley.

On the 13th of October, 1664, they left Milford, and proceeded in this excursion. I shall suppose that the first night they came over to New-Haven to their friend Jones, though of this there is no tradition, as there is of their making a lodgment at Pilgrims Harbor, so called from them, being twenty miles from New-Haven, at a place since called Meriden, half way between New-Haven and Hartford. Here they might rest and lodge one day, and the next night proceed to Hartford, and the night following at Springfield, and the succeeding night reach Hadley. But of this I find no tradition, saving only, that in their rout to Hadley they made one station at Pilgrims Harbor.

Being arrived at Hadley, they took up their abode at the House of the reverend Mr. Russel. At this house, and at the house of Peter Tilton, Esq. they spent the rest of their lives, for fourteen or sixteen years, in dreary solitude and seclusion from the society of the world. The almost only important anecdote that transpires concerning them in this secreted abode, was that of the angel appearance there, which is preserved to this day in the tradition at New-Haven and Hadley, as well as in Governor Leverett's family: and also that one or both died at Hadley, and that Whalley was buried in Mr. Russel's cellar, or lot adjoining his house, also as current at New-Haven as Hadley.

Angel of Hadley.

They came to Hadley October 1664, and Whalley died there about 1676, or 1678, and Goffe's last letter is April 2, 1679, and no more was heard of him after 1680. Soon after their arrival at Hadley, John Dixwell, Esq. another of Charles's Judges, came to them, in February 1664—5, and sojourned with them in their secrecy for some time.

Dixwell

Though told with some variation in different parts of
New-England, the true story of the Angel is this :—
During their abode at Hadley, the famous and most
memorable Indian war that ever was in New-England,
called King Philip's War, took place, and was attended with exciting an universal rising of the various
Indian tribes, not only of Narraganset and the Sachem-
eom of Philip, at Mount-Hope, or Bristol, but of the
Indians through New-England, except the Sachem-
dom of Uncas, at Mohegan, near New-London.—
Accordingly the Nipmug, Quanbaug, and northern
tribes were in agitation, and attacked the new frontier
towns along through New-England, and Hadley among
the rest, then an exposed frontier. That pious congregation were observing a Fast at Hadley on the occasion of this war : and being at public worship in the
meeting-house there on a Fast day, September 1, 1675,
were suddenly surrounded and surprized by a body of
Indians. It was the usage in the frontier towns, and
even at New-Haven, in those Indian wars, for a select
number of the congregation to go armed to public worship. It was so at Hadley at this time. The people
immediately took to their arms, but were thrown into
great consternation and confusion. Had Hadley been
taken, the discovery of the Judges had been inevitable.
Suddenly, and in the midst of the people there appeared a man of a very venerable aspect, and different from
the inhabitants in his apparel, who took the command,
arranged, and ordered them in the best military manner, and under his direction they repelled and routed the
Indians, and the town was saved. He immediately
vanished, and the inhabitants could not account for the
phœnomenon, but by considering that person as an
Angel sent of God upon that special occasion for their
deliverance ; and for some time after said and believed
that they had been delivered and saved by an Angel.—
Nor did they know or conceive otherwise till fifteen or
twenty years after, when it at length became known at

K

Goffe's military record in Civil War?

Hadley that the two Judges had been fecreted there; which probably they did not know till after Mr. Ruffel's death, in 1692. This ftory, however, of the Angel at Hadley, was before this univerfally diffufed thro' New-England by means of the memorable Indian war of 1675. The myftery was unriddled after the revolution, when it became not fo very dangerous to have it known that the Judges had received an afylum here, and that Goffe was actually in Hadley at that time.— The Angel was certainly General Goffe, for Whalley was fuperannuated in 1675.

Although they were fecreted at Hadley, yet while there, they were in jeopardy. Public enquiry was made after them particularly at two different times, one in 1665, and the other by Randolph, who probably gained fome fufpicious notice of them before their death, as being fecreted fomewhere in Maffachufetts. I have already fhewn that one of the inftructions from the Crown to Colonel Nichols and the other Commiffioners in May 1665, the year after the removal to Hadley, refpected the concealment of thefe regicides; to which the Affembly replied, that they had departed from their arild Ction before the proclamation arrived, and that they had fent Kehond and Kirk after them to New-Haven. Edward Randolph, Efq. was fent from England with the moft malicious purpofes againft the country, as preparatory to the refumption of charters, and the alteration of its whole civil and religious polity. He was a fubtil, fenfible and affiduous Inquifitor-General over New-England, and moft indefatigabl eand induftrious in procuring and collecting information of every thing in the public affairs here, which might be wrought up into a fyftem of accufation againft the colonies, as a ground and cafon to juftify the intended abolition of charters, and for fhewing the neceffity of erecting the arbitrary general government of Sir Edmund Androfs. Randolph undertook the dirty and invidious bufinefs of acting the fpy, and informer, upon all New-England—

Edward Randolph.

ind such was his indefatigable industry and researches, that it was next to impossible that any thing should 'scape his detection. Randolph was the messenger of death to New-England, being sent to Massachusetts with his Majesty's letter of March 10, 1675—6.

Randolph came over first in 1676. He went home repeatedly, carrying accusations, and returned to New-England in 1678, 1679, 1681, when he returned collector of the customs, surveyor and searcher for all New-England; and in 1683, when he came with instructions to inquire for Goffe and Whalley, not knowing that they were both dead at that time. In 1684. the Governor gave him such answer of his ignorance concerning them, and the probability of their having gone from Manhados to Holland, as silenced all further search and inquiry, especially as it may be probable the insidious Randolph now became well satisfied that both were dead. Thus the Judges were in imminent danger from Randolph during the two or three last years of their lives; and they had reason to suppose, could the places of their deaths be known, their ashes would be dishonoured, as were those of Bradshaw and others; for Whalley especially was considered as obnoxious as any of the Judges. It is true Whalley was past being affected with any such apprehensions, if alive at Randolph's accession, he was already superannuated in 1674, as appears by Goffe's letter of that date to his wife. But Goffe and Dixwell might justly entertain such apprehensions from the malevolence and virulence of Randolph, whose memory, with that of Sir Edmond Andross, has been accursed through New-England to this day.

The Judges led so recluse and concealed a life at Hadley, that we have but few anecdotes concerning them there. They were certainly well supplied with means of subsistence to the end; partly from Europe, and partly by secret friends here. Richard Saltonstall,

Efq. when he went to England, 1672, prefented them
with £.50. at his departure, and they received donations
from feveral others, but doubtlefs very confidentially.
Peter Tillton, Efq. was a member of Affembly from
Hadley, and a Magiftrate : he was often at Bofton during the feffions of Affembly, and through his hands donations might be fafely and fecretly made, as he was
all along in the fecret, and the Judges fometimes refided at his houfe.   His letter of 1672 will give fome
idea of his piety.   In 1680, Richard Saltonftall, Efq.
fon of Sir Richard, returned from England, and was
again chofen firft affiftant, and fo the two fucceeding
years.   He went back to England before 1683, and
died there 1694.   So that at the period of Randolph's
inquifition for the regicides, there were at leaft three in
the council who were privy to their fecretion, viz. Governor Leverett, Mr. Saltonftall, and Mr. Tilton, and
perhaps more.   Indeed Governor Leverett died 1678,
and Mr. Saltonftall was abfent in England 1672, but
Mr. Tillton was on the ground, and kept the fecret
from Randolph.   Indeed all New-England were their
friends, although they did not wifh to be too knowing
about them.   They did not view them as traitors, but
as unfortunate fufferers in the noble caufe of civil liberty, proftrated by the Reftoration, and again loft and
overwhelmed in a return and irrefiftible inundation of
tyranny.   They no more confidered themfelves as protectors of rebels, than England did in protecting the exiles from Germany at the Reformation, and the refu-
gees from France at the revocation of the Edict of
Nantz.

The Judges might have fome other fecret retreats and
temporary lodgments : I have heard of two more within ten miles round New-Haven, but not with fo perfect certainty.   The one about four miles from Milford,
on the road to Derby, where an old cellar remains to
this day, faid to have been one of their reclufes.   This
is called George's Cellar, from one George who after-

[margin note: Secret donations.]

wards lived there. The other at Derby, on the eastern bank of Neugitúck river, at a place then called,
Pawgafett, and near the church. Madam Humphreys,
confort of the reverend Daniel Humphreys, and mother
of the honorable Colonel Humphreys, the Ambaffador,
was a Riggs, and a defcendant of Mr. Edward Riggs,
one of the firft fettlers of Derby, between 1655 and
1660. She often ufed to fpeak of it as the family tradition, that the Judges who fometimes fecreted themfelves at the cave and in Sperry's farm, alfo for fome
time fecreted themfelves at Derby, in the houfe of her
grandfather, Mr. Edward Riggs, whofe houfe was
forted or pallifadoed in, to fecure it from the Indians;
there being, 1660, perhaps fewer than half a dozen
Englifh families there in the woods, ten or a dozen
miles from all other Englifh fettlements, and they all
lodged in this forted houfe. Certainly this was a good
and fafe reclufe. They might probably fhift their refi-
dences, efpecially in the dangerous fummer of 1661, to
difappoint and deceive purfuivants, and avoid difcovery.
This tradition is preferved in the Riggs and Humphrey
families to this day.

General Whalley died at Hadley certainly after 1674,
probably about 1678. And General Goffe is to be
heard of no more after 1679. Other circumftances
concerning them will occur in the 4th chapter. I
fhall therefore fubjoin here only Tillton's letter 1672,
and a long letter of Goffe's to his wife, by the name of
Mother Goldfmith, in 1674, and then proceed to the
hiftory of Judge Dixwell.

*Copy of a Letter from Mr. Peter Tillton to his Wife
at Hadley.*

Bofton, 18 3mo. 1672.

" Dear Wife,

" THIS opportunity gives occafion of thefe lines;
we have had a quiet and peacable election, no alteration or addition. O what a price doth Divine Patience

K 2

yet betruft us with, when he is drawing out the f
and arraying himself with the garments of vengeance
to other kingdoms, and when it is more than prob
many garments are tumbling in blood. As to the n
from England, all men, both wife and others of m
ordinary capacities, look on the effect or produce the
of will be as black a day in the world, as the wor
hath known. The late actions in England in commi
fioning their fleet to feize and fall on the Hollander
of which I wrote you in my laft, breaking their leagu
joining with the French, affifting them with foldie
out of England, and with their principal harbors to n
ceive a numerous army, and fhutting up the excheque
whereby many are outed of their eftates contrary to a
law, are things that both in England and here, by me
of all forts, are looked upon as ftrange, horrid, an
ominous. There is another fhip expected, one Jon
Clarke, if not ftopped by the embargo or otherwife,
which one Dr. Hoare, a minifter, is expected. Re
member me to mine and thine, with my love to all wit
you. I cannot forget you before the Father of Spir
night and day. The good will of Him that dwelt i
the bufh be with you, caufe his face to fhine upon you
all, and give you peace. So prayeth ftill

Yours unfeignedly to love,
PETER TILLTON."

Copy of a Letter from *William Goffe*, to his *Wife*.

" *Moft dear and honored Mother,*

" On the 23d July I received yours of the 29 Marc
1674, with the enclofed that fhould have come la
year, hoping you have alfo by this time received min
of the 21ft May laft, which informs you how it wa
then with myfelf and your old friend Mr R. [*Whalle*
and that I wrote largely to yourfelf and dear Mr
Janes, in October laft, which I perceive you have n
received, which I am very forry for ; but it hath be
a great mercy that all my former letters came fafely t

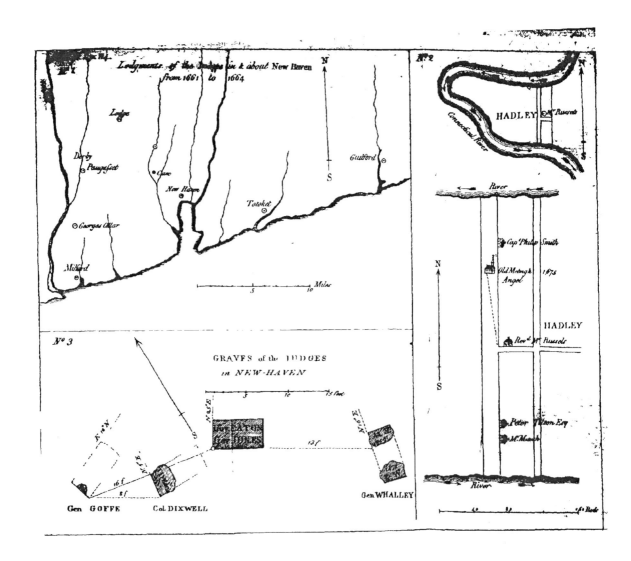

No 1.

Lodgments of the Judges in & about New Haven
from 1661 to 1664

N

Lodge

Derby
Paugasset
Cave
New Haven

Georges Ollar

Totoket

Guilford

S

Milford

Miles
5   10

No 3

GRAVES of the JUDGES
in NEW-HAVEN

Rods
5   10   15

13 f

Gen GOFFE   Col DIXWELL   Gen WHALLEY

No 2

Connecticut River

HADLEY   Mr Russels

N   S

River

Capt Philip Smith

Old Midnigh. 1675
Angel

HADLEY

Revd Mr Russels

N   S

Peter Tilton Esq

Mr Marsh

River

Rods
10   20   30

your hands, and as for those, knowing the hazard of
their miscarriage by reason of the wars, I kept the copies of them, and for your further satisfaction I have
again transcribed, that you may see I was not unmind-
ful in my duty in writing to you and answering your
desire of my advice concerning my sister Fr. [*his daughter Frances*] of whose disposal in marriage you have
now given me the account, so far as you conceive you
could, and I believe are longing to understand my
thoughts of it. Dear mother, you are pleased to say
well, that you gave me an account how it hath pleased
the Lord to dispose of her, &c. It is indeed the Lord
who is her heavenly father, that hath disposed of her
and provided this husband for her, and therefore, tho'
he be unknown to me, I do believe he is the fittest person in the world for her, and that she likewise is the
most meet help for him. I remember in a former letter to yourself, when you desired my thoughts in a matter concerning her, I told you I was confident the Lord
would take care of her and in due time provide a husband for her, and now he hath done it, shall I question
whether he hath done it well? No, I dare not do it.
It is a great satisfaction to me that you sought the Lord,
and took advice of our dear and christian friends, and
that my sister was guided in her choice by yourself and
them, and desire with you to bless the Lord that hath
provided so well for her, and shall not cease to pray
night and day on their behalf, that the Lord will be
pleased to make them great blessings to each other, and
that this new condition may be every way and always
comfortable to them both, for as you very truely say,
it will be as the Lord shall be pleased to make it. I
pray remember my most tender and affectionate love
to them both, and tell them that I greatly long to see
them, but since that cannot be at present, you may
assure them that whilst they shall make it their great
work to love the lord Jesus in sincerity, and love one
another dearly for Christ's sake, and to carry it with

tender love and dutiful respect to yourself, I shall esteem
it my duty to love and pray, and act faith for them as
if they were my own children, being not otherwise able
at this distance to be helpful to them. Dear mother,
that yourself and all friends did so well approve the
match gives much content to my heart, and I beseech
you not to give way to any recoilings that may arise in
your own spirit, do not say, as to the world, my sister
might have done much better, the Lord knows what is
best for us and ours, it may be that which we may
think would have been better might have proved much
worse. These are dying times, wherein the Lord hath
been and is breaking down what he hath built, and
plucking up what he hath planted, and therefore it is
not a time to be seeking great things for ourselves. Let
us read the 45th chapter of Jeremiah, and apply to our
selves what the Lords speaks to Baruch, and account it
a great mercy if he give us our lives for a prey, and
bring us again to see the faces one of another with comfort. The things that Baruch is dehorted from seeking
were worldly things. why then are they called great
things? Surely the Lord speaks it only according to the
esteem that we are too apt to have of them, for the
world's great things are indeed and in truth but poor little things, and the saints should look down upon them
with contempt, and shew themselves to be of high raised spirits, seeking things truly great, as our Lord himself doth exhort us, Mat. 6. 33. But seek you first the
kingdom of God and his righteousness, as if he said, for
they are great things, worthy your affectionate endeavors, and as for all these little things which Gentiles so
earnestly pursue, they shall be added unto you so far as
your heavenly Father knoweth that you have need of
them. My poor sister begins her housekeeping at a
time when trading is low, and all provisions dear, and
I cannot but pity her in that respect. I hope she will
not be discouraged nor her husband neither, but for prevention I desire them to consider seriously and to act faith

upon that most excellent counsel our Lord delivered with authority in his sermon on the mount, Mat. 6th, from the 24th ver. to the end of the chapter. I cannot but be full of longings to hear how the Lord hath dealt with her in her lying in, but I doubt not you will take the first opportunity to inform us of it, in the mean time I shall endeavor to stay myself upon the promise made to child-bearing women, 1 Tim. 2. 15.

Dear mother, I have been hitherto congratulating my new married sister, but I must now turn aside to drop a few tears upon the hearse of her that is deceased, whose loss I cannot choose but lament with tears, and so share with you in all the providences of God towards us, but my dear mother let me not be the occasion of renewing your grief, for I doubt not but you have grieved enough, if not too much already. Let us consider how graciously the Lord deals with us (as for our dear sister, she is got beyond our pity, we need not lament for her sake, but rather rejoice that she is at rest in the bosom of Christ) who whilst he is taking from us with one hand, gives double with the other. He hath added one to your family on whom I hope you may set that motherly affection as if he were your own son, and I hope hath before this time also made you to rejoice in the fruit of my sister's womb, and shall not we say with Job, the Lord hath given, and the Lord hath taken, blessed be the name of the Lord. But oh how apt are we to murmur, if the Lord do in any thing displease us, but what a shame it were that we should be displeased at any thing which God doth? Who are we, that we should set our corrupt wills in opposition to his most holy and blessed will. It is blessed counsel that a reverend minister of the gospel gives, who has been in the school of affliction, that I lately met with in a printed book of his, I pray you (saith he) drink in that notion, viz. That the will of God being pure, holy, perfect, yea God himself, should not only be submitted to, or rested in, but loved and chosen above all creatures, yea

Whalley mentally failing

above life itfelf, the beft of creatures. Would we but once learn this leffon (which the Lord is, I hope, teaching of us by all his dealings with us) and help us as you fay fweetly in your letter) to fee love in all his difpenfations, there could nothing come amifs to us.

Dear mother, I perceive, when you wrote laft, you were upon a remove from thofe dear friends with whom you then fojourned, I hope the Lord guided you to that motion, and fhall long to hear where you fettle · in the mean time it is my comfort that the Lord tells all your wanderings, and receives all your tears into his bottle, and will not fail to direct all your fteps, till he hath given you a fafe conduct through your wearifome pilgrimage, and at the end thereof open unto you an abundant entrance into thofe manfions that are prepared for you in our Father's houfe, where you fhall be at reft in the bofom of Chrift for ever.

Whalley

Your old friend, Mr. R. is yet living, but continues in that weak condition of which I formerly have given you account, and have not now much to add. He is fcarce capable of any rational difcourfe, his underftanding, memory and fpeech doth fo much fail him, and feems not to take much notice of any thing that is either done or faid, but patiently bears all things and never complains of any thing, though I fear it is fome trouble to him that he hath had no letter of a long time from *His life?* his coufin Rich, but fpeaks not one word concerning it, nor any thing you wrote of in your laft, only after I had read your letters to him, being afked whether it was not a great refrefhment to him to hear fuch a gracious fpirit breathing in your letters, he faid it was none of his leaft comforts, and indeed he fcarce ever fpeaks any thing but in anfwer to queftions when they are put to him, which are not of many kinds, becaufe he is not capable to anfwer them, the common and very frequent queftion is to know how he doth, and his anfwer, for the moft part, is, very well, I praife God, which he utters with a very low and weak voice ; but sometimes he saith, not very well, or very ill, and then if it be further said, do you feel any pain any where, to that he always answereth no , when he wants any thing he cannot well speak for it, because he forgets the name of it, and sometimes asks for one thing when he means another, so that his eye or his finger is oftentimes a better interpreter of his mind than his tongue , but his ordinary wants are so well known to us, that most of them are supplied without asking or making signs for them, and some help he stands in need of in every thing to which any motion is required, having not been able of a long time, to dress or undress himself, nor to feed, or ease nature either way, orderly, without help, and its a great mercy to him that he hath a friend that takes pleasure in being helpful to him, and I bless the Lord that gives me such a good measure of health and strength, and an opportunity and a heart to use it in so good and necessary a work ; for tho' my help be but poor and weak, yet that ancient servant of Christ could not well subsist without it, and I do believe, as you are pleased to say very well, that I do enjoy the more health for his sake. I have sometimes wondered much at this dispensation of the Lord towards him, and have some expectations of more than ordinary issue : the Lord help us to profit by all, and to wait with patience upon him, till we shall see what end he will make with us. Thus far I write of myself, I shall now ask him what he would have me to say to his friends concerning him. The question being asked, he saith, I am better than I was. And being asked what I should say more to his cousin R. or any other friends, after a long pause, he again said, the Lord hath visited me in much mercy, and hath answered his visitation upon me. (I give it you in his own words.) Being desirous to draw more from him, I proposed several questions, and the sum of his answers were, that he earnestly desires the continuance of the fervent prayers of all

his friends for him, and defires to be remembered to
his coufin Rich, and longs to receive a letter from her,
and defires her to exhort her fon and daughters, his dear
coufins, to fear God, and to be remembered to her
aunt at Chelfey, praying that the Lord will equite all
her great love, as alfo to be remembered to Mrs. James
and her good hufband, to whom he both as himfelf
greatly obliged for their g . . . . cular for
Mrs. James her care of p . N . . . . . . e, to continue the fame , as alfo to . . . . . . yourfelf,
and wifheth Frank much co . . . . ndition,
and faith he fhall not ceaf . . . . . . you and all
yours. This is written on . . . 6 . . . . . . , but I
know not when I fhall have . . . . to Bofton, it may be therefore bef . . I f . . . . . my letter
I may have fomething more to add . . . erning him.

Thus far I proceeded yefterday, t . night coming
on and having fomething elfe to do, I could proceed no
further, and fo laid afide my paper, intending this
morning to finifh (if the Lord pleafed) m, anfwer to
yours of the 29th March. But now my firft work
muft be to tell you that, through the great goodnefs of
God, I did alfo laft night, after fupper, receive your
welcome letter of the 8th of May (Franks birthday)
wherein you let me know that you have alfo received
mine of the 2d of October laft, at fuch a feafon, which
made it more refrefhing to you, which is a great fatisfaction and comfort to me, for which I defire to blefs
the Lord ; but it would have been the more full if you
had but faid, with the inclofed to dear Mrs. James,
which I have lately tranfcribed, together with your
own, from the originals, with a purpofe to have fent
them with this, but I fhall fend neither, for I have
good hopes that both were received, for I cannot but
think when you complained that the door of your houfe
was opened, if half of your goods had been taken away
you would have made mention of it , for your own letter was both the houfe and inventory of all the goods contained in it.

Dear mother, it is also a great comfort to me to hear that the Lord was graciously pleased to appear on my dear sister's behalf in the needful hour, and desire with you to bless the Lord for that great mercy, and I heartily thank you for giving me so quick a notice of it. Dear mother, it was likewise a great mercy that the Lord was pleased so far to satisfy your desire as to shew you the fruit of her womb, and to make you the joyful grandmother of a son, and though it hath pleased the Lord so soon to transplant him from the militant to the triumphant church, yet it may be a great comfort to yourself and my dear sister, that from your wombs hath proceeded the increase to the mystical body of Jesus Christ, and reckon it a mercy that the Lord being purposed to take him from you in his infancy, was pleased (that it might be the more easy to you) to do it before it had much time to take deep root in your affections, for I do believe the longer yourselves and his other relations had enjoyed him, the harder it would have been to us all to have parted with him: But what shall we say more? It may be such considerations as these are too selfish, it is enough to compose the hearts of the children of God under every providence, to say, it is the Lord that hath done it, our loving and tender hearted infinitely wise Father hath declared his royal pleasure, and it is our duty to submit to it, yea to rejoice in it (for it is most meet he should dispose of us and ours as shall seem good in his sight) and to apply ourselves to learn the lessons he would teach us thereby, and among the rest that is none of the least which you mention, to get our hearts weaned from creature comforts and to live upon himself as our all-sufficient soul-satisfying portion —and let my dear brother and sister remember what the H. G. saith, Lam. 3. 27. It is good for a man that he bear the yoke in his youth. Dear mother, I pray, in your next, speak a little more fully concerning his godliness, for you say nothing to that, except by the phrase of a very honest man, you mean a very godly man, as

L

I hope you do, for you give the fame epithet to that good man (whofe word you took concerning him) of whom another friend faith that he is a very godly man, aged and wife, &c. I pray, remember my dear love to fifter Judith, and tell her from me fhe muft now be a very good child, and labor to know the God of her father, and ferve him with a perfect heart and with a willing mind, 1 Chr. 18. 9. and leaving to grieve for her fifter and nephew that are at reft with God, ftrive with all her might to be a comfort to her poor afflicted mother, who is contefting with the difficulties and temtations of an evil world I humbly thank you for your motherly love and care for me, in your being fo defirous to fupply my wants, and becaufe you are pleafed to lay your commands upon me, I fhall make bold, when I need your help in that kind, to write to you for it.— There is yet a little meal in the barrel and oil in the cruife. The greateft thing I need is a heart to abide patiently in this condition until it be expended. I cannot but account it a great mercy that in thefe hard times you fhould be able to be fo helpful to your poor children, but I befeech you let not your love to them make you to forget yourfelf, in parting with what is neceffary for your own comfort in your old age. Dear mother, you fay you find nature greatly decaying in you, and therefore defire prayers that grace may be ftrengthened, &c. It cannot be otherwife expected but that as age comes on nature will decay, but I befeech you preferve it what you can, and take heed of immoderate griefs, or whatfoever elfe may be prejudicial to your health, which you are able to avoid, and when you have done all you can, if you ftill perceive the outward man perifhing, yet faint not, for I do believe, through the faithfulnefs of God, your inward man fhall be renewed day by day, 2 Cor. 4. 16. I blefs the Lord, though I cannot deny but I feel, with you, the decays of nature, yet I have and do enjoy a competent meafure of health and ftrength, and begging your pardon that I have been too flow in acquaint ing you with and giving you the comfort of it. I thank you for what you have written concerning those relations I desired to hear of, and the rather because you say you cannot write much, through the weakness of your eyes, and I fear it may hurt them to read these long letters, for I desire you first to read and then seal and deliver the enclosed to my honored and dear friend D. G. with my best respects to him and his dear wife. My dear mother, I recommend to you the counsel and promise given to the Philippians, chap. 4. 4, 5, 6, 7. and let me intreat you to rejoice in the Lord always, and again I say rejoice ; and I beseech you to remember that weak eyes are made weaker by too much weeping.   Pray take heed you do not hurt yourself thereby.

But alas, I see my paper is almost done, and must yet reserve a little room for a postscript, therefore (hoping I have not forgotten any material thing I should write of) I am forced here to break off abruptly, and with my most affectionate remembrance to all friends, as if I named them, desiring the continuance of your and their fervent prayers, I recommend you and my dear brother and sisters to the tender watchful care of Him who hath borne us from the belly and carried us from the womb, and will be our God and our guide unto death,   I am, dear mother,

Your most affectionate and dutiful son,

W. G.

Now, my dear mother, give me leave in a postscript to be a little merry with you, and yet serious too. There is one word in one of your letters that sounds so harshly, and looks so untowardly, that I cannot tell well how to read or look upon it, and I know not how to write it, and yet I must, though I cross it out again.   I suppose you do by this time sufficiently wonder what will follow, but the matter is this, after you had given me a loving account of a business wherein you have done your best, you were pleased to say, that if I should be *angry* you had many to bear with you, &c. Rash anger, I confess, is a burthen that needs more shoulders than one to bear it, for Solomon faith, a stone is heavy, and the sand weighty, but a fool's wrath is heavier than them both.   But oh, my dear mother, how could you fear such a thing from me? Yourself knoweth I never yet spake an angry word to you, nay I hope I may say (without taking the name of God in vain) the Lord knoweth I never conceived an angry thought towards you, nor do I now, nor I hope never shall, and in so saying I do not commend myself, for you never gave me the least cause, neither have you now, and I believe never will, therefore, dear mother, the whole praise belongs to yourself, or rather to the Lord, who, blessed be his name, hath so united our hearts together in love, that it is a thing scarce possible to be angry one with another.   But I shall now conclude with a request that you will not be angry with yourself for writing that word I have spoken so much against, for I suppose all your meaning was, if I should not altogether approve of what was done, &c. and I am abundantly satisfied that the root from which that fear sprung was tender love, and that you speak your heart when you say you love and honor me as much as ever, which may well increase my longings after you, for the exceeding grace of God in you.   Now thanks be unto God for his unspeakable gift. 2 Cor. 9. 14, 15."

2. Corinthians, Ch. 9, vv. 14 -15.

CHAP.

CHAP. III.

Of Colonel DIXWELL *and his Sepulture at New-Haven.*

COLONEL JOHN DIXWELL was another of King Charles's Judges. He was of the priory of Folkstone, in the county of Kent. He was a junior brother of Mark Dixwell of Broome, in the parish of Barham, in the county of Kent; who died 1643, leaving in the hands and in the care of Colonel Dixwell all his estate and children, all minors, and among the rest his eldest son and principal heir, Basil, afterwards Sir Basil Dixwell. He came to New-England a bachelor, then having neither brother nor sister living. The Colonel was a gentleman in good and easy circumstances, being possessed of a manor and sundry other estates in England. Engaging in the civil wars, he became an officer in the army under the Parliament and Protectorate; was nominated sheriff of the county of Kent, and became member of Parliament for Kent in 1654. He was one of the Judges that signed the warrant 1649. At the Restoration he abdicated his country in 1660: but when he first came to New-England is unknown. Very little can be recovered concerning him for the first ten or a dozen years of his abdication. The first notice we have of him is in Goffe's Journal, while the Judges were at Hadley, wherein it is entered that Colonel Dixwell came to them there February 10, 1664—5: but ever after they call him Mr. Davids; and afterwards he went by the name of James Davids, Esq. till his death. This name it is said he assumed, being his mother's name. Governor Hutchinson says he lived at Hadley some years: his grand-daughter, Mrs. Caruthers, says only six weeks. From thence, or after various wanderings and recluses, now unknown, he at length came to New-Haven, where, though covered with a borrowed name, he however was generally suppoſed to have been one of thoſe who were obnoxious in England. But he carefully concealed his true character from the public.

When he firſt came to New Haven is unknown — Stephen Ball, Eſq. of New-Haven, aged 67, a deſcendant of the original inhabitants, tells me the tradition is, that when Mr. Davids firſt came here, he put up and lived with an aged family, two ſedate old perſons, Mr. Ling and his wife, who had no children. Mr. Ling at his death requeſted him to aſſiſt and take care of his wife, and recommended it to her to be kind to him. He left his houſe and whole eſtate to his wife.— Mr. Davids aſſiſted in ſettling the eſtate. And afterwards he ſaid he did not know any better way to ſhew kindneſs and take care of her, than to marry her, and accordingly married her. She ſoon dying, he married another wife, and had children by her. Thus far deacon Ball. Mr. Ling's death was in 1673: his will and the inventory of his eſtate, £900. was then immediately entered and remain on the probate records to this day. So Mr. Davids muſt have been in New-Haven before 1672: and probably ſeveral years before, as a ſhort and tranſient acquaintance would not have been ſufficient to produce that truſt and confidence, which Mr. Ling repoſed in him at his death.

Mr. Ling's houſe was in a retired part of the town, at the north-weſt corner of what was afterwards called Mr. Pierpont's Square. * Here Mr. Davids lived in a retired indeed, but not ſecreted manner. For he conſtantly attended public worſhip, was openly converſant, though not very familiarly and intimately with the inhabitants, who conſidered him as a reſpectable and pious gentleman, who reſided among them in a quiet and peacable manner, without tranſacting any apparent buſineſs, and yet ſubſiſting with decency, leading rather a recluſe and private life. His countenance, but not his true name, was known to Mr. Jones at his firſt

* See Plate V.

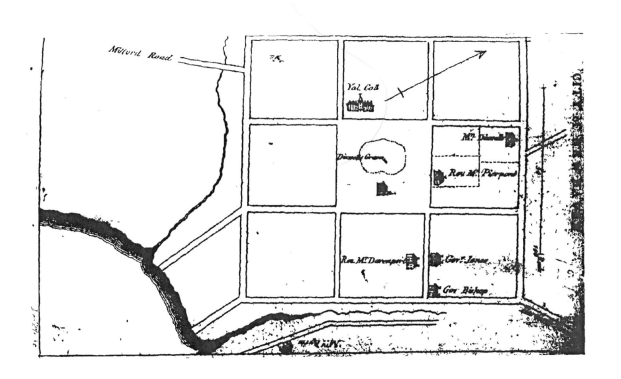

Milford Road

Yal. Coll

Davenport Green

Mr. Dixwell

Rev Mr Pierpont

Rev Mr Davenport

Gov. Jones

Gov. Bishop

coming, who probably was soon after possessed of his
true name and character, and proved his faithful friend
till death.   There is some reason to think he was early
known to a very few others in town, particularly to
Mr Street and Mr. Bishop, as he certainly was afterwards to Mr. Pierpont. The reverend Nicholas Street,
the minister of New-Haven, died 1674. In his will
dated April 14, 1674, he requests " his beloved friends,
Mr. James Davids and Mr. Nicholas Augur, to be
assistants" to his wife in the settlement of his estate.—
Doctor Augur was an eminent and learned physician of
the town, and opulent, and of early accession, and
long acquaintance with Mr Street , whose confidence
also reposed in Mr. Davids may seem to imply more
than a short acquaintance, not less probably than five
or six years intimacy.   Mr. Street was settled in New-
Haven a colleague minister with Mr. Davenport in
1658, and upon Mr. Davenport's removing to Boston,
1667, continued sole minister till his death, 1674.   I
believe Dixwell was unknown to Davenport, and probably did not come here till after his removal to Boston.
After all, I consider the first certainty of his actually
being here to be about 1672, and at least before Mr.
Ling's death in 1673 : while yet it is more than probable he was here still earlier.   From 1660 to 1665, we
know nothing of him, he was perfectly out of sight :
then he just appeared at Hadley and evanished, leaving
no certain trace of himself from 1665 to 1672, where
we must date the first certainty of his being at New-
Haven.   While here he always conducted himself like
a pious and exemplary christian.   One says, Mr. Dixwell was a very pious and religious man, and always
fasted on Friday of every week constantly."   Another
says, " he had the reputation of a worthy old gentleman,
a very pious and holy man, and lived very much by himself and retired."   Another, aged 83, speaking of Dixwell and all the Judges, says, that the good old people,
when he was a boy, used to speak of these men, " as

very good, and pious, and holy perfons, and they believed what they had done they did out of confcience,
and that they themfelves always thought they had done
right."

In New Haven records I find thefe entries :

" Mr. James Davids and Mrs. Joanna Ling were
married by Mr. James Bifhop the 3d of Nov. 1673."

"Mrs. Joanna Davids, wife of Mr. James Davids
died (between 15th and 26th in the entries) Nov. 1673."

" Mr. James Davids and Bathfhebeba How were
married the 23d of October, before James Bifhop, affiftant, 1677."

" Mary, daughter of Mr. James Davids, born 9th
June, 1679."

" John, the fon of Mr. James Davids and Bathfheba Davids, was born the 6th day of March, 1680—1."

" Elizabeth, the daughter of Mr. James and Bathfheba Davids, was born the 14th of July, in New-
Haven, 1682."

" Mr. John Dixwell and Mrs. Mary Prout were
married September 1, 1708."

From New-Haven church records, in the hand-
writing of the reverend James Pierpont, who was ordained Paftor of the church, July 1685, I extracted
this . " December 29, 1685, Mr. James Davids, alias
John Dixwell," admitted into church fellowfhip.

From hence it appears that Mr. Dixwell came to
New-Haven before 1672, that he was known here by
the name of James Davids, that by his firft wife he had
no children, that he married his fecond wife 1677, and
by her he had three children, one of which, his only
fon John, afterwards married Mifs Prout, and that he
was admitted a member in full communion with the
church of New-Haven in 1685, within half a year after Mr. Pierpont's ordination, and this by the name of

Timeline

Dixwell as well as Davids ; which fhews that his true
character was known to Mr. Pierpont at his firft coming to New-Haven, though the tradition here is that
Mr. Dixwell never revealed it till on his death bed,
and then to Mr. Pierpont.   In truth it was known to
Governor Jones, and Governor Bifhop, Mr Ling and
Mr. Street, from the beginning of his coming here,
fay 1672, and to Mr. Pierpont 1685, and to a few
others till his death, when it was promulgated to the
town.

During the feventeen years or more in which he lived in New-Haven, nothing extraordinary occurred
concerning him.   From 1674 to 1685, the church
had no fettled minifter, with whom he might affociate.
The reverend Nicholas Street, the minifter, at his firft
coming here, foon died.   For above eleven years the
church was deftitute of a paftor, and fupplied by occa-
fional and temporary preaching only, till Mr. Pierpont's
fettlement, 1685.   With him the Colonel entered immediately into an open and unreferved, but confidential
communication , but this was only for the fhort fpace
of the three or four laft years of his exile.   During this
fhort time there was the greateft intimacy and friendfhip ; which however feems for fome time to have been
concealed from even his wife   For tradition fays that
madam Pierpont obferving and remarking the fingular
intimacy, and wondering at it, ufed to afk him, what
could be the reafon of this intimacy, and what he faw
in that old man, who was fo fond of leading an obfcure
unnoticed life, that they fhould be fo very intimate and
take fuch pleafure in being often together : for their
houfe-lots being contiguous and cornering upon one
another, they had beaten a path in walking acrofs their
lots to meet and converfe together at the fence : and
fhe often wondered why he fhould be fo fond of meeting
and converfing with that old gentleman at the fence ?
To whom he replied, that he was a very knowing and
learned man , that he underftood more about religion

and other things than any other man in town, and that if she knew the worth and value of that old man, she would not wonder at it.

Among other traditionary anecdotes concerning him, this is one: The English, and perhaps Europeans in general, especially those who have been conversant in the variety of business and employments in large cities and populous towns, have a singular sagacity in judging from the external appearance and manner, a person's business and occupation in life. Sir Edmund Andross came to America, and became Governor of New-York in 16-5 to 1684; and of Massachusetts from 1686 till 1689. In one of his tours through the colony of Connecticut, perhaps about 1686, attending public worship at New-Haven, he observed a venerable old gentleman at meeting, and noticing him closely, discerned something singular in him, and suspected him. After meeting he inquired who that person was, and was told that he was a merchant who resided in town. Sir Edmund replied, that he knew he was not a merchant, and became particularly inquisitive about him. Probably Colonel Dixwell was notified of the inquisitiveness of this stranger concerning his person and character, for the Colonel was not seen at meeting in the afternoon.

In connexion with this, I may mention another tradition, which I received from Major Lyon and others, indicating how obnoxious Sir Edmund was at New-Haven, as well as through New England. Sir Edmund being at meeting here, and probably on the same Lord's day as the above, the deacon gave out the 52d Psalm to sing, in Sternhold and Hopkins's version, which begins thus :

Why dost thou, Tyrant, boast abroad,
   Thy wicked works to praise ?
Dost thou not know there is a God
   Whose mercies last always ?

Andross's Suspicion.

Why doth thy mind yet ſtill deviſe
  Such wicked wiles to warp ?
Thy tongue untrue, in forging lies
  Is like a razor ſharp.

Thou doſt delight in fraud and guile,
  In miſchief, blood and wrong ;
Thy lips have learn'd the flattering ſtile,
  O falſe deceitful tongue !

Governor Androſs felt it as an intended inſult upon himſelf, and after meeting reſented it as ſuch, and reprehended the deacon for it. But being told it was the uſage of this church to ſing the pſalmns in courſe, he excuſed the deacon, and let the matter paſs off. But it is not improbable that though this might be the general uſage, yet in this inſtance a pſalm was ſelected for Sir Edmund's contemplation.

Colonel Dixwell carried on no ſecular buſineſs, but employed his time in reading and rural walks into the neighboring fields, groves and woods, adjacent to his houſe. Mr. Pierpont had a large library, from whence as well as from his own collection, he could be ſupplied with a variety of books. He often ſpent his evenings at Mr. Pierpont's, and when they were by themſelves retired together in his ſtudy, they indulged themſelves with great familiarity and humour, reſpect and honor, and free and unreſtrained converſation upon all matters, whether of religion or politics. But otherwiſe when in company, Mr. Peirpont treated and behaved towards Colonel Dixwell with caution and reſerve. The Colonel ſpent much of his retirement in reading hiſtory. As a token and memorial of his friendſhip for Mr. Pierpont, he in his laſt will preſented him with Raleigh's Hiſtory of the World. This book is now before me, and in it I find inſcribed by Mr. Pierpont, in his own hand writing, with which I am well acquainted in the church records, " James Pierpont s book, 1689, èr Dono dom. John Dixwell, in teſta-

mento fuo noviffimo." What Raleigh wrote for the ufe of the learned world, as well as for his own amufement, during a fourteen years' imprifonment, under condemnation for treafon, became the entertainment of Dixwell, during his twenty-eight years' exile, under the fame high accufation and condemnation.

Whether Colonel Dixwell had any communication with Whalley and Goffe after he left them at Hadley, is not certainly known. But intelligence was probably kept up between them by means of Jones and Tillton. His fupplies for fubfiftence, and their channels, are alfo unknown. Befides the monies he doubtlefs brought over with him from England, he acquired eight or nine hundred pounds by his firft wife, befides his houfe.— His nephew, Sir Bafil Dixwell, totally neglected and abandoned him. And it does not appear that he received any thing from England, during his exile, from any but his niece, Mrs. Elizabeth Weftrow. And the tradition is, that in the latter part of his exile, though he was not needy, or in indigence, yet he was in ftraitened circumftances, for a gentleman formerly accuftomed to affluence.

After having three children born to him in New-Haven, he made a difpofition of his eftate in England, which he expected would be reftored. This he did in feveral indenture and writings in 1682, which he did fecretly, but left them to be recorded and ufed after his death. His wife procured them to be approved by the judges of the county court, in 1691, which had at that time the probate of wills, and the jurifdiction of all teftamentary matters, and fettlements of eftates.

There is no reafon to think that the three Judges were ever out of New-England after their arrival in America, though there were fome loofe flying ftories that they were at New-York. Suppofe Whalley and Goffe both died at Hadley, the former 1678, the latter 1680, then Dixwell was left alone. It does not appear that Dix-

Raleigh on
infpiration.

well's refidence in New-England was ever fufpected,
either in England by the Miniftry there, or by Randolph
in New-England. So that he who really lived the
moft openly of any of them, lived the moft fafely and
fecurely. He well knew, however, and fully felt the
danger that the regicides' afhes might be difturbed, as
he muft be well apprifed of the infidious vigilance of
Randolph. It is poffible alfo that the three Judges
might wifh that their graves might be together. What
has been before narrated is delivered upon fure documents. I fhall now narrate what is only conjectural,
and leave it with every one's judgment; only obferving
that if it ever did take place, no one will doubt but that
Dixwell was concerned in it. There is fomehow preferved, not in univerfal or general, but particular and
ftrong and lineal tradition, at New-Haven, which is
to be confidered more largely hereafter, that another of
the regicides befides Dixwell, lies buried in our burying
place, and that this other was Whalley. This is particularly preferved among the fextons, or grave-diggers,
who it feems for many years, and perhaps ever from
the time efpecially of Dixwell's death, have fhewn the
ftone marked E. W. for Whalley, as they have that
marked J. D. for Dixwell. I have not found the leaft
tradition or furmife of Goffe till I myfelf conjectured it,
January 1793, inferring in my own mind without a
doubt, that if Whalley, who certainly died at Hadley,
was afterwards removed here, Goffe would have been
alfo. But of this, I mean as to Goffe's being here alfo,
I can find no tradition, while yet I find it tenacioufly
adhered to by fome few, and particularly in the line of
grave-diggers, that Whalley is here. I have often examined the ftone marked E. W. but confider the matter without proof, yet poffible, not to fay a little probable, but by no means certain. Nor do I wifh, and leaft
of all attempt to gain any one's credulity to it, leaving
every mind perfectly free and unprejudiced. But as I
know that whoever takes the pains which I have done,

M

to trace out, and collect, and digeft the traditions in New-Haven, will find this among others, however it originated among us ; fo after this precaution and notification, I fhall proceed to what is of fome confequence in the life of Dixwell, if true ; and fhould it be indeed otherwife, will have no bad confequence, as not being adduced on the verity of hiftory.

It is then fuppofed by fome, that Whalley alfo lies buried in New-Haven. If fo, his corpfe muft have been taken up and fecretly conveyed here. For without repeating the proofs, it is certain he died in Hadley. Who will doubt this removal was at the procurement of his friend Dixwell, or at leaft that he was privy to it, and concerned in effecting it ? None. If done before 1685, none but Dixwell, Jones and Bifhop, in New-Haven, and Ruffel, Tillton, and perhaps Smith, at Hadley, were privy to it , and yet probably it was after Randolph's rage burned and became dangerous, which was after 1680, when Goffe was either dead or abdicated. At all events, the five or fix I have mentioned muft have been the principal perfons concerned in effecting this removal. If fo, Dixwell muft have been deeply concerned in the affair , and this event and tranfaction, however fecretly performed, muft become an important anecdote in his life, as being the laft care and office of furviving friendfhip to the memory and to the fecurity of the afhes of a venerable fellow exile and brother Judge. In this Governor Jones was unqueftionably the efficacious agent. He and Mr. Tillton muft have been the men, who procured the corpfe to have been conveyed from Hadley and interred in New-Haven, in fo private and fecret a manner as to have eluded even the fufpicion of Randolph. If Goffe died at Hadley, refo, as is probable the fame reafons which would induce the removal of one would induce the removal of the other, and perhaps from a fecret pre concerted plan that the three exiles fhould be depofited and flept in one fepulchre together, until they fhould arife together at the resurrection of the Just. Now if all this was true, which can never be fully ascertained, it would have been, as I have said, an important event in the life and transactions of Judge Dixwell. But the whole is submitted as only conjectural; though I shall attend further to it hereafter.

After a pilgrimage of twenty-nine years in exile from his native country, and banishment into oblivion from the world, of which seventeen years at least, probably more, were spent in New-Haven, by the name of James Davids, Esq. Colonel Dixwell died in New-Haven. He and all the other Judges lived and died in the firm expectation of a revolution in England. This had actually taken place the November before Dixwell's death, but the news not having then arrived, he died ignorant of it, about a month before the seizure of Sir Edmund Andross at Boston. At his death he discovered his true character to the people, and owned the name of John Dixwell, but requested that no monument should be erected at his grave, giving any account of his person, name and character, and alledged as a reason, "lest his enemies might dishonor his ashes"—requesting that only a plain stone might be set up at his grave, inscribed with his initials, J. D. Esq. with his age and time of his death. Accordingly a plain rough stone is erected at the head of his grave, close by the tombstone of Governor Eaton and Governor Jones, which stone is standing to this day, charged with this inscription, as at first put and engraved upon it by his friends.

"J. D. Esq.

DECEASED MARCH THE 18th,

IN THE 82d YEAR OF HIS AGE,

1688—9.'

He left a wife and two children. His will was afterwards exhibited and approved, and recorded in the probate office, from the records of which I have transcribed the following copy.

" The laft Will of James Davids, alias John

" I James Davids, of the town of New-H
ing in reafonable good health and perfect m
blefs the Lord for it, do make and ordain th
Will, and Teftament in manner and form follo
Imprimis I give unto my loving wife, my h
New-Haven aforefaid, with the home lot, the
and buildings, an   o my lands at the Beaver
ard one acre of a   land being in the quarter
Cooper's quarter, and likewife my land in the
with the woodlands, lving in two parcels: All w
give unto Bathfheba Davids, my wife, for and d
ter natural life, and after her deceafe, I give unto
fon John, my houfe and the lands aforefaid, unto
ard his heirs for ever. *Item* I give unto my fon
all fuch lards as fell to me by the laft divifion,
about four fcore acres, to him and his heirs for e
And if my fon John die without iffue of his body
fairly begotten, then my will is, that my daughter
ry fhall have the houfe with all the lands before
tioned, to her and her heirs for ever. *Item* I giv
honored friend, Mr. Pierpont, paftor of the ch
Chrift in New-Haven, Sir Walter Raleigh's Hi
of the Word *Item* I give unto my fon John all
reft of n books, and my filver ftandifh I ufed to w
with, and my treafers which is in a red tortoife-f
cafe, my fword and my gun, all which I defire
be carefully kept for him. *Item* I give unto my dau
ter Mary twelve pounds. *Item* I give unto my lo
wife, Bathfheba Davids, the reft of my perfonal e
here in New-England, and do make my faid wife
executrix of this my laft Will and Teftament. An
do hereby declare, that this will fhall not extend to
         enjoyed by me, or belonging to me in Old E
l   I do earneftly defire my loving friends,
W   Jones and Mrs Jones, his wife, of Ne
H   r my decafe before my friends,
E   and my children, unto whom I have co

Plate VI p 130

I. D. ESQ.R

DECEASED MARCH yᵉ

18ᵗʰ IN yᵉ 82ᵈ YEAR OF

HIS AGE 1688⁹

Two and a quarter feet high & broad
5 Inc thick, red stone Head stone.

Two feet wide & high, & 8 Inc. thick
Blue dark stone Head stone

80
M. G.

One foot broad ten Inc high
Head stone

Foot stone

mitted the care and education of them, that they would receive them into their family, and take care of them till my friends have opportunity to send for them, and what charge and expence they shall be at thereby, to be repaid to them. And I desire also my good friends aforesaid, that what belongs to my children here, they would take care that it may be preserved for them. In witness whereof I have hereunto set my hand and seal, dated the seventh day of May, one thousand six hundred eighty eight.

Signed and published } JAMES DAVIDS (L.S.)
in the presence of }
JAMES CLARKE,
JAMES HEATON.

I do also hereby signify my mind and will to be, that such of my books as have my daughter's name written upon them, belong to her, and that she shall enjoy them.

JAMES DAVIDS."

" An inventory of the estate of Mr. James Davids, late of New-Haven, deceased, taken and apprized by Captain Moses Mansfield and Thomas Tuttle, June 10th, 1689," amounting to £276 12 6. and among other articles, housing and homested, £65. By a cursory review of a number of inventories, about this time I should judge Mr. Dixwell's estate better than those of half the inhabitants of New-Haven, who were comfortable livers ; and consequently that he was not reduced to indigency. I have often been in his house, which was standing till twenty or twenty-five years ago. It was a comfortable, two story, old fashioned house.

Immediately after his death the news of the revolution and of the accession of King William and Queen Mary arrived here. Upon which things took a new turn, and assumed an aspect more favorable to civil and religious liberty. In a little time therefore, or in about two years after Dixwell's death, it became safe to bring forth the following indentures and writings, which I find recorded in the probate office at New-Haven; and which I have transcribed and copied from the records of that office, as they will illustrate the history of Colonel Dixwell.

Extracts from the New-Haven records.

" Here follows a record of several deeds and other writings, recorded at the desire of Mrs. Bathsheba Davids, and the allowance of the county court.

" Dixwell, John, Esq.

" This indenture, made the tenth of October, in the year of our Lord God one thousand six hundred eighty-two, between John Dixwell, alias James Davids, of the priory of Folkestone, in the county of Kent, Esq. of the one part, and Bathsheba Dixwell, his wife, on the other part, Witnesseth, That the said John Dixwill, alias James Davids, for the natural love and affection he beareth to his said wife, Hath given, granted and confirmed unto the said Bathsheba Dixwell, his wife, All that his farm lying in the parish of Hougham, in the county of Kent, with the houses and buildings, and all the lands, arable, and pasture, and meadows thereto belonging, formerly in the occupation of widow Vallier, To have and to hold, and enjoy, and also to take and receive the profits thereof during her natural life, with power also to lease out said farm and lands for a yearly rent, so that it be to the value of it, and her lease extend not for above eleven years at a time. In witness whereof the parties above named have interchanably set their hands and seals. Dated the day and year above named.

Sealed and delivered }
  in the presence of }
  Joseph Allsup,
  James Clarke,
  Joseph Allsup, jun.

    JOHN DIXWELL (L.S.)
        alias,
    JAMES DAVIDS.

This writing, as above is a true record of the original. Recorded and examined pt me,

JAMES BISHOP,
Clerk of New-Haven County."

" This indenture, made the twentieth of October, in the year of our Lord God, one thousand six hundred and eighty-two, between John Dixwell, alias James Davids, of the priory of Folkestone, in the county of Kent, Esq. of the one part, and John Dixwell, his son, of the other part, Witnesseth, That the said John Dixwell, alias James Davids, out of the natural love and affection he beareth unto said son John; Have given, granted and confirmed, and by these presents doth give, grant and confirm, unto the said John Dixwell, his son, All that his capital house, called the priory of Folkestone, with the pigeon-house, stables, barns, and all the lands thereunto belonging, called the Priory Lees, and also all that his farm called or known by the name of Sandgate Farm, with the buildings thereunto belonging, and all the lands, arable, pasture and meadow, thereunto belonging, formerly in the occupation of John Hill, or his assigns, and also all his marsh lands lying in Romney Marsh, formerly in the occupation of Basil Cloake, or his assigns ; and also all that his farm lying in the parish of Hougham, with all the houses and lands, arable, pasture and meadow, thereunto belonging, formerly in the occupation of widow Vallier, or her assigns ; and also all his manor and farm called Buckland, near unto Haversham, in the said county, with all the houses and buildings, lands arable and pasture, thereunto belonging : To have and to hold the said houses and lands, with the manor of Buckland aforesaid, after the death of the said John Dixwell, alias James Davids, unto his said son John and his heirs forever. And if my son John die without issue of his body lawfully begotten, if the Lord should give me another son, that then the brother of the said John shall enjoy all the houses and lands with the manor aforefaid, to him and to his heirs for ever. And if there be no iffue male to inherit the fame, then I give and grant all the houfes and lands beforefaid to my two daughters, Mary and Elizabeth, and to their heirs for ever. And if there be no iffue lawfully begotten from the children of the faid John Dixwell, alias James Davids, then I give and grant all the aforefaid manor and lands unto my dear and loving niece, Elizabeth Weftrow during her life, and after to Dixwell Weftrow, her fon, and his heirs for ever. And I do alfo hereby fignify and declare that all former fettlements of the lands before mentioned on any of the fons of my brother Mark Dixwell, deceafed, being upon revocation, either by indenture or by will, fhall be null and void. In witnefs whereof the parties above named have interchangably fet their hands and feals. Dated the day and year above named, 1682.

Signed, fealed and delivered in prefence of }   JOHN DIXWELL, (L.S.)
                  alias
   Jofeph Allfup,   JAMES DAVIDS.
   James Clarke,
   Jofeph Allfup, jun.

" This writing as above, is a true record of the original, recorded and examined pr me,

           JAMES BISHOP,
      Clerk of New-Haven County "

Mr Davids.

" Whereas my brother, Mark Dixwell, of Broome, in the parifh of Barham, in the county of Kent, Efq. deceafed, did by his deed of bargain and fale convey and fettle his whole eftate upon me for the confideration of thirteen thoufand pounds, to be paid to the beft of my remembrance in manner following, viz. To his two daughters, Elizabeth and Bennet, two thoufand pounds apiece at the time of marriage, or at the age of eighteen years, and to his fecond fon, Heardfon, three thoufand pounds, at his age of one and twenty years, and alfo to

his son William two thousand pounds, at his age of one
and twenty years, and likewise to his eldest son, Basil,
four thousand pounds, at his age of two and twenty
years : For the payment of which sums I entered into
several bonds. Now this sale of his estate was indeed
but in trust, my brother having that confidence in me I
would manage his estate for the benefit and advantage
of his eldest son, and pay those sums before mentioned
to his younger children, did leave his whole estate and
care of his children solely to me, he then casting after
three hundred pounds yearly being paid to his widow
for her jointure, and two hundred and fifty pounds
yearly being allowed for his five children's education,
allowing fifty pounds apiece for every one of them, did
suppose the sums aforesaid might be raised when his
eldest son came to the age of two and twenty years, not
considering of any taxes to be paid out of his estate nor
abatement of rents in regard to the great troubles that
was then in the nation. And this trust my brother committed to me I did with all the care and diligence I
could to the utmost of my power perform, in taking
care for his children as if they had been my own. My
brother died, as I remember, in February one thousand six hundred forty-three, and then I took upon me
that trust, and paid and laid out the sums following :
To his two daughters, Elizabeth and Bennet, when
they married, four thousand pounds, the taxes I paid
out of the estate could not be less than one thousand five
hundred pounds, for his estate was sessed to the full value · I laid out at least six thousand pounds in purcha-
sing the manor of Diggs and other lands for his eldest
son, and in buildings and other necessary expenses about
his chief house, and elsewhere one thousand pounds ;
and for the abatement of rents those troublesome times,
one thousand and twenty pounds, the sums before mentioned I do think, and rather more than less. Besides,
when I came away I left with my brother's widow five
hundred pounds, there being in the tenants' hands at

leaft one thoufand pounds, which with the profits of his eftate for two years more, would have gone near to have raifed the other fons portions, if their mother, that was entrufted with the fame had been as careful as I was. But the fums aforefaid could never have been difburfed, confidering the taxes which were paid out of the eftate, and the abatement of rents, and the necef-fary expenfes about building and reparation, and his eftate fo increafed, if I had made ufe of my own money, for what money I had, and what I faved out of my eftate for feventeen years, I made ufe of to improve my nephew's, the which I fuppofe to be between two or three thoufand pounds. And being confident of my nephew's ingenuity and honefty in paying the fame, did not make any provifion to fecure the fame when I fettled his father's eftate upon him ; but moft ungrate-fully and injurioufly he refufed to allow any thing to me for this confiderable fum, nor fhew any refpect for the care I had of him, by making fome provifion for me in my afflicted eftate. And that there was fuch a fum due to me from Bafil, my brother's eldeft fon, his mother, now the Lady of Oxinden, was fo perfua-ded of it fhe offered me two thoufand pounds for it, and if fhe be living can teftify to the truth of what I fay, and to the particulars before mentioned. Befides, for fe-venteen years I was at great expence and trouble in ma-naging this eftate and therefore in juftice there ought to be an allowance for the fame : And alfo for detaining such a fum from me, taking advantage of my condition, and fhewing unmercifulnefs in that they would allow me nothing for my prefent maintenance, that if the Lord had not extraordinarily provided for me, I had perifhed for want. Now being confident the Lord will appear for people and the good old caufe for which I fuffer, and that there will be thofe in power again that will relieve the injured and oppreffed, the Lord having given me opportunity to change my condition, and alfo given me children, I think I am bound to ufe the beft means I can whereby they may enjoy what is so injuriously kept from me.—Therefore, know all men by these presents, that I John Dixwell, alias James Davids, of the priory of Folkestone, in the county of Kent, Esq. do hereby constitute and appoint my dear and loving niece, Mrs. Elizabeth Westrow, and Thomas Westrow, her son, my true and lawful attornies to ask, demand and receive of the eldest son of my nephew, Sir Basil Dixwell, Knight and Barronet, deceased, or his executors, or any that may be justly liable thereto, the sum of two thousand five hundred pounds, and also allowance for the trouble, charge and expence, in managing the estate aforesaid for seventeen years, and likewise with allowance for detaining the sum of two thousand five hundred pounds for two and twenty years past : and if the executors of my said nephew, Sir Basil Dixwell, or his son, or any other that may be justly liable thereto, refuse to pay or give satisfaction for the same, then to sue, implead and use all other lawful means the law and justice will afford to recover the same : And I also empower my said attornies to compound with them upon just and reasonable terms, and also to give a full discharge from the same, by release, or by making any other legal discharge which may be according to law, and I do also hereby signify what my said attornies shall recover or receive for the same to be paid to my children according to a writing I have bearing date with this my letter of attorney. In witness whereof I have hereunto set my hand and seal.— Dated the two and twentieth of October, in the year of our Lord God, one thousand six hundred and eighty-two.

Sealed, signed and delivered in presence of }

Joseph Allsup,
James Clarke,
Joseph Allsup, jun.

JOHN DIXWELL, (L. S.)
alias
JAMES DAVIDS.

" The interlining of Thomas Weſtrow in this writing, and alſo the other interlining, is done by my own
hand, the reaſon being my dear niece Elizabeth Weſtrow being ſickly, I thought fit to join her ſon Thomas
Weſtrow with her in this truſt, and by reaſon of the
infirmities of my old age, being about eighty years old,
and not able to new write it, and not knowing any I
durſt to truſt to write it for me, I hope this will ſatiſfy
any that ſhall make any ſcruple thereof. And I do
hereby ſignify my mind to be, that if I die, it ſhall not
null the power I have given unto the ſaid Elizabeth and
Thomas Weſtrow, but this my letter of attorney ſhall
be of full force after my death as now. And I further
empower the ſaid Elizabeth and Thomas Weſtrow, if
they die before the monies mentioned to be recovered,
that they ſhall have power by writing under their hand
and ſeal, to empower ſuch as they ſhall think fit to recover the monies mentioned in this writing to be paid
as is expreſſed in another writing bearing date with this,
wherein my deſires are fully mentioned.

May the 7th, 1688.   JOHN DIXWELL.

" This writing as above, with that on the other
ſide, is a true record of the original. Recorded
and examined pr me,

JAMES BISHOP,
Clerk of New-Haven County."

Mr. Davids.

" Whereas I John Dixwell, alias James Davids, of
the priory of Folkeſtone, in the county of Kent, Eſq.
have conſtituted and appointed my dear and loving
niece, Mrs. Elizabeth Weſtrow, and Thomas her
ſon, my true and lawful attornies, to aſk and demand
and receive of the executors of my nephew, Sir Baſil
Dixwell, Knight and Baronet, deceaſed, or his ſon,
or any other that may be juſtly liable thereto, the ſum
of two thouſand and a hundred pounds, what I laid out for
the improving his eſtate, with allowance for the manag-

ing his estate at my own charge for seventeen years, and also for detaining the sum of two thousand five hundred pounds from me for these two and twenty years past, not affording me any thing for my subsistence the time of my affliction. Now I do hereby signify by these presents, that what shall be recovered concerning the two thousand five hundred pounds, owing to me, and also allowance for managing his estate for seventeen years, and likewise for detaining the said sum of two thousand five hundred pounds for two and twenty years, my said niece, Elizabeth Westrow, and Thomas Westrow aforesaid, in case my son John enjoy my estate which was taken from me in these times, that then they would pay to my daughter Mary one thousand pounds at the day of her marriage, or at her age of eighteen years, and if she die before she marry or attain to the age aforesaid, that then my son John shall have the same. And also my desire is, my said dear niece would take two hundred pounds for her own use, as a token of my love and respect to her, and also that they would pay to my loving wife, Bathsheba Dixwell, two hundred pounds, and what is remaining charges being allowed about recovering the same, they would pay it to my son John at his age of one and twenty years: But if my son John do not enjoy my estate, that then my said daughter Mary shall have but five hundred pounds. And I do hereby commit the education of my children and guardianship of them wholly to the said Elizabeth and Thomas Westrow, earnestly requesting, if the Lord take me out of this world, they would send for them and also my dear wife, if they please to come, for whom I have made some provision out of my estate I enjoyed, and I desire they would shew the same kindness to my wife they would shew to me. And I do make it my last and great request to my said dear niece and cousin Thomas Westrow, they would bring up my children in the knowledge and fear of God. And if any thing fall to my son in regard to my brother's estate,

Niece.

was intailed upon me for want of issue male, they would endeavor my son John or other children may enjoy the same. In witness whereof I have hereunto set my hand and seal. Dated the two and twentieth of October, in the year of our Lord God one thousand six hundred eighty two.

Sealed and delivered } JOHN DIXWELL, (L.S.)
   in presence of   }   alias
Joseph Allsup,   JAMES DAVIDS.
James Clarke,
Joseph Allsup, jun.

This writing as above is a true record of the original. Recorded and examined pr me,
           JAMES BISHOP,
   Clerk of New-Haven County.

" *Further instructions on the other side.*

" *Mr. Davids.*

" These are further to signify my request unto my dear niece, Elizabeth Westrow, and my cousin, Thomas Westrow, her son, That I do hereby declare my mind to be, that what my dear niece, Elizabeth Westrow, out of her tenderness hath furnished me with, or yet may if this condition continue, shall be allowed to her, or such as she shall assign it to, And I do also signify my mind to be, that my cousin Thomas Westrow aforesaid shall have for a token of my respect to him forty pounds. And my further request is, if I die before any thing be recovered, that then my dear friends aforesaid would allow unto my wife, for her and my childrens maintenance, twenty pounds yearly. And I do further declare my mind and will to be, that if my son John and daughter Mary die before the times mentioned in this writing for the payment of those monies to them, as is expressed, then I do hereby signify it to be my mind and will, that my dear niece, Elizabeth Westrow aforesaid, and the children she had by her late husband, Thomas Weſtrow, deceaſed, ſhall have all ſuch monies as remain due to me to be equally divided between her and them. In teſtimony hereof I have hereunto ſet my hand, May the 7th, 1688.

JOHN DIXWELL."

"Know all men by theſe preſents, that I James Davids of the town of New-Haven, in New-England, alias John Dixwell, of the priory of Folkeſtone, in the county of Kent, in Old England, Eſq. being under weakneſs of body, and uncertain what iſſue the Lord will pleaſe to make with me, do think fit hereby to declare that all the power and authority I have elſewhere given to my dear niece, Elizabeth Weſtrow, and her ſon, Thomas Weſtrow, ſhall after my death or deceaſe, continue, for the recovery of all that money mentioned in a letter of attorney already given or made unto the ſaid Elizabeth and Thomas, authoriſing them as above ſaid, unto the end and uſes expreſſed in the ſaid letter of attorney, and fully hereby declare, that the ſaid Elizabeth and Thomas, or either of them, ſhall have and exerciſe all the truſt, power and authority, expreſſed and conveyed in ſaid letter of attorney, as fully in all reſpects as if I were perſonally preſent and living. In witneſs whereof, and for a moſt full confirmation of theſe preſents, I have hereunto ſet my hand and ſeal, this fifteenth of March, in the year of our Lord God, one thouſand ſix hundred eighty-eight, or eighty-nine.

Signed, ſealed and } JAMES DAVIDS,
delivered in preſence of } alias
   James Heaton, JOHN DIXWELL.
   Enos Talmage,
   John Alling, tertius.

"Theſe two diſtinct writings as above are a true record of the originals. Recorded and examined pr me,

JAMES BISHOP.
Clerk of New-Haven County."
End of the Records.

These entries or records are indeed without date, but they were made 1691, in the hand writing of Governor Bishop, and among his last entries, as he died 24th June, 1691. They are between a record dated to have been recorded December 3, 1690, and the record of a deed acknowledged "before James Bishop, Deputy Governor," which acknowledgment is dated 31st of March, 1691, and the record " by James Bishop, clerk of the county," though without date. The entries in the next page of the records is in Governor Jones's hand writing. So this is the last recording of Governor Bishop.

From these papers it appears, that Mr. Dixwell had a handsome estate in England, that he received some supplies from Mrs. Westlow, but none from the rest of the family, though he had faithfully executed an important instrument for the benefit of his brother's children, and particularly Sir Basil Dixwell, who seems to have shown no gratitude to his uncle in his distress and impoverished case. It is probable that the estate he had by his friend the widow Ling, yielded him his principal income for the last years of his life, if not for the whole of his seventeen years residence in New-Haven. Besides what from his cousin, Elizabeth Westlow, and perhaps some private donations, as his brother Judges received at Hadley.

At his death he left a widow and two children, a son and a daughter. These children lived together eighteen or twenty years in New-Haven, immediately resuming the name of Dixwell. The son was put to a goldsmith, and through the faithful care of his friends received a good, virtuous, and respectable education, and became a pious and worthy man. The daughter, Mrs. Dixwell, married Mr. John Collins of Middletown, December 24, 1707, the year after the death of Governor Jones and his lady, to whose guardianship Judge Dixwell had recommended his two children, and

2 surviving children

who faithfully befriended them. The son soon married and settled in Boston. Hereupon the mother,, Mrs. Bathsheba Dixwell, the Judge's relict, removed and lived with her daughter Collins at Middletown, in Connecticut, where she died December 27, 1729, aged 85, on her grave-stone 86. Mrs. Collins's children were as follows :

Nathaniel Collins, born Nov. 17, 1708.
Mary Collins,   -   Sept. 23, 1710. living 1793*
John Collins,   -   Mar. 18, 1712. ob. May 6 '14
Twins—John Collins, ⎱ Nov. 13, 1714. ob. Oct 12 '14
One died in a few hours ⎰
Sibbel Collins   -   Aug. 16, 1716.
Abigail Collins,   -   Jan. 4, 1718—19.

This account was at my request extracted from the records of the city of Middletown in 1793, by the reverend Enoch Huntington, pastor of the first church in said city.

The Judge's only son, Mr. John Dixwell, settled as a goldsmith in Boston, about 1707, and afterwards went into trade, and became a merchant in good and flourishing circumstances. He was exemplary for amiableness of manners, and for strict integrity and religion—and became an elder in the new north church in Boston, and every way sustained a very worthy character, of which there is a respectable and affectionate testimony entered in the records of that church.

John Dixwell was among those who formed the new north church. The building was raised in 1714. In 1716, it is recorded, " That our worthy brother, Mr. John Dixwell, was unanimously chosen to the office of deacon.

1720—Sept. 7, " Voted to proceed to the choice of three ruling elders, and when the votes were brought in it appeared that our worthy brethren, John Baker, dea'

Mrs. Mary Caruthers of Bennington.

N 2

con Caleb Lyman, and deacon John Dixwell, wer chofen to faid office with great unanimity.

" 1725—April 2—On this day died that excellen elder, John Dixwell, in the 44th year of his age, greatl lamented by this church, and by all that knew his fin gular worth and abilities."

In 1710, he went to England to recover his father eftate, and was kindly received by Sir Bafil Dixwell. It is faid the eftate had not been confifcated. It wa doubtlefs fecured from confifcation by its being fhew that it was held, at leaft in part, by the Judge in tru for his brother's children. It appears by the indentur of 1682, that the Judge, before his leaving England had made a fettlement and transfer of all his eftates t his nephews, fubject however to " Revocation.' H made this revocation indeed in 1682, above twenty yea after: yet in 1660, or at the time of the feizure an confifcation of the eftates of the regicides, no fuch revo cation appearing, the eftate muft at that time have bee adjudged in law as vefting in the nephews, efpeciall confidering the truft and alfo that he being attaint of treafon, a fubfequent revocation by him muft be ba red. The truft as well as affignment, and efpeciall upon confirmeth, would have been fufficient to preve the confifcation in 1660 or 1661 ; and the fubfequer revocation, being perhaps a nullity in law, muft hav prevented a recovery in 1710. And it is probable tha Mr. John Dixwell, upon advifing with counfel learne in the law, might find it their opinion that the attain der and publication would be adjudged ever after to di fable the Judge from making a legal revocation. Whereupon the eftate muft be left to veft in the poffef fors. Whether for thefe or other reafons, yet it is cei tain that Mr. Dixwell returned without the recover of the eftate. And yet he does not feem to have given u the matter, for he afterwards intended another voyag of difcovery, after Sir Bafil's death, as he had pro

mifed or encouraged him *to* make a fon, whom he
fhould and did name Bafil, his heir. This may induce
us to give fome attention to a tradition narrated to me
by one perfon in New-Haven, whofe mother knew
Judge Dixwell, and who is from her poffeffed of much
of the Dixwell hiftory ; and which may fuggeft that the
reafons for the nullification of the revocation I have
mentioned, did not in fact operate fo ftrongly, even in
Queen Anne's time, as I have reprefented, but that
truely in 1710 the matter was fettled with Sir Bafil, in
fome good meafure to the fatisfaction of Mr. Dixwell,
though he did not then recover the full poffeffion of
the family eftate.   I fhall ftate the tradition as I received it from this perfon, as derived from Mr. Kilby—
That Dixwell's papers and all the documents were
committed to Mr. agent Kilby, who was empowered
to the purpofe.—That while in England he communicated them firft to a fon-in-law of Sir Bafil's, a lawyer
who had married Sir Bafil's daughter and only child,
who became convinced and fatisfied that the eftate was
recoverable.   But as the knight was aged and would
refent the motion, it was concluded the fon fhould firft
open the matter to Sir Bafil : Upon doing which, it is
faid, that the knight, as was expected, ftormed and
was in a great rage , afferting that he was the rightful
and lawful owner of the eftate.   Learned counfel in
the law were confulted, and the refult was that the right
heir was in New-England, and was recoverable efpecially in the more moderate days of the Hanoverian family. Upon which Sir Bafil was foftened, and acceded
to a compromife.   And that by an indenture or writing figned by Sir Bafil, it was agreed with Mr. Kilby,
that Sir Bafil fhould enjoy the eftate during his life, and
after his death it fhould come to the heirs in New-England   But that on Mr. Kilby's return to America, the
heir was dead,   This heir was Bafil Dixwell, fon of
elder Dixwell.   This is the tradition, perhaps miftaken in fome circumftances, and imperfect as to others.

If the matter was really brought to this crisis, it would not seem that the death of Basil in 1746, would prevent the descent and succession of the estate, but that it is open to this day, it not being confiscated : For although Basil died without issue, yet his brother John survived him.   This story was told by Mr agent Kilby himself, who resided sometime at New-Haven about 1760, and who then proposed erecting a monument over Dixwell's grave.

Elder Dixwell, who settled at Boston, married Miss Mary Prout of New-Haven, September 1, 1708, by whom he had the following children, born in Boston.

Basil Dixwell, born July 7, 1711.   Ob. 1764.
John Dixwell, born 1718.   Ob. 1749.
Elizabeth Dixwell, born 1716.   Living 1793.

Innoculation for the small pox was introduced at Boston for the first time in 1721, the same year that, through the recommendation of Lady Montague it was first introduced into England from Constantinople.   It is the tradition in the family of Prout here, that Mrs. Dixwell was in the first experiment, and died in innoculation.   Mr. Dixwell married again, and himself died 1724 leaving three orphans, all children by the Prout venter.   Thereupon their uncle, John Prout Esq. took those orphans home to New-Haven, and became their guardian   Madam Prout, his mother, took care of John , Mrs. Mansfield of New-Haven, his aunt, took care of Basil , and Elizabeth was taken into the family of Mrs. Christophers, his aunt, at New-London.

Mr. Basil was placed with a goldsmith at Boston ; settled at Providence , entered the army 1745 , and died unmarried and without issue, at Louisburg, 1746.

Mr. John Dixwell, his brother, was put to live with a brazier in Boston, where he settled in business, and entered into trade, and prospered.   He married Miss

Hunt of Watertown, and died in Boston 1749. Of three children, Mary only survived to maturity, and married Mr. Samuel Hunt, preceptor of the grammar school in Boston.

The daughter, Miss Elizabeth Dixwell, who was educated by her aunt Christophers at New-London, is now living there, 1793, aged 76, the widow relict of Mr. Joseph Lathrop, of New-London, married April 22, 1739, by whom she had four sons and three daughters.

Elizabeth Lathrop, born Jan. 23, 1740.
Joseph Lathrop, born Dec. 11, 1741. Died.
John Lathrop, born June 7, 1743. No issue.
Mary Lathrop, born Feb. 3, 1744.
Joseph Lathrop, born Sept. 16, 1747.
Sarah Lathrop, born Jan. 30, 1752.
Dixwell Lathrop, born July 29, 1753. Issue 8 chil.

Mrs. Lathrop tells me, that about 1745, or 48 years ago, upon a solicitation of some friends here, Sir Basil Dixwell sent over a gratuity in monies to the family of Dixwell here, of which she received £50 for her share, perhaps equal to £20 sterling.

I subjoin a letter of Mrs. Caruthers' an aged granddaughter of Judge Dixwell, now living at Bennington, 1793, aged 83, with three affidavits, and two other letters from the reverend Mr. Pierpont and the reverend Doctor Cotton Mather, procured for me by the reverend Doctor Belknap, of Boston, from Mr. Samuel Hunt, who married Mary, the last branch of the Dixwell family, in Boston. All which may confirm and illustrate the history of Judge Dixwell.

" *Bennington, April 26,* 1793.

" Sir,

" I received your letter of 16th February last, and have attended to all the matter of information which you have suggested. I find it is not in my power to

give you the certainty of information required.   I am
now 83 years of age, and not expecting to be interroga-
ted upon the subject you have mentioned, I have not
been particular in early life of refreshing my memory
with the history of my family.   I perfectly remember
my grandmother Dixwell, who after my grandfather's
death, lived with my mother until she died.   When
this event happened, I was eighteen years of age.

"I remember of hearing her mention that my grand-
father, when he came to America, was a single man,
and that he had neither brother nor sister living,   That
there were two perfons from England, who were his
friends (whether they came with him to Boston or after
him, I do not remember) that he staid with them at
Hadley, *about six weeks.*

" He communicated to my grandmother, long before his death his real name and character.   Mr. Pierpont was with him in his last sicknefs, and mentioned
to him, he was apprehenfive that he was struck with
death.   He obferved, that it did not surprize him, he
was prepared, and should meet death as a welcome
meffenger ;   and that after his death, if he would examine certain papers in his cheft, he would find his real
name and character.   This leads me to think Mr.
Pierpont was not acquainted with his real name, until
the death of my grandfather, * although my grandmother was well apprized of it.

" I can give no information of Goffe and Whalley, as
to their age or the time of their death , although I have
heard, as you mention in your letter, they died at
Hadley , but I cannot fay from whence I had this information.   What I have related as from my grand-
mother I have in perfect remembrance.

" My uncle John Dixwell went to England in the
reign of Queen Anne.   He did not obtain any thing
He intended going a fecond time, but did not.   One
* *Mr. Pierpont knew certainly who he was in 1685.*

Basil Dixwell, a relation of my grandfather, told my uncle, that if he ever had issue a son, and would call him Basil, he would make him his heir. He then had a daughter, Molly, who died very young; afterwards he had a son, whom he called Basil. He never went to England, but died unmarried in 1746.

"My uncle had all his grandfather's papers. It is very probable the papers are with some one of the family. His children are all dead, unless it be Elizabeth, who married a Lathrop, and lived at New-London.— She is a widow, and was living when I left Middletown, in 1778. Should you write to her, or her family, it is possible you may obtain the necessary papers.

"As to the property my grandfather may have left, I am apprehensive time has changed the lawful owners. I have no expectation of receiving any part of it for myself or children. But should you, sir, receive any information on this subject, or obtain any clue to the history of Judge Dixwell, that would enable me to give you any further information, you do me a kindness in communicating it to your aged, but

Very obedient and humble servant,

MARY CARUTHERS.

To Ezra Stiles."

New-Haven County Court, February 4, 1705—6.

" Upon the desire of Mrs. Bathsheba Dixwell, it is ordered by this Court that these following Depositions be entered, viz.

" *New-Haven, October 31, 1705.*

" Then personally appeared before me John Alling, the subscriber hereof, one of the Assistants of her Majesty's corporation of Connecticut, in New-England, and Justice of the Peace, William Jones, Esq. late Deputy-Governor of said Corporation, aged eighty and one, and made oath as followeth, viz.

" That the said William Jones, deponent, sundry

years, between sixteen hundred and forty, and sixteen
hundred and fifty, and in the time of the sitting of the
Long Parliament, as it was then called, was resident
at Westminster. And so had certain knowledge of many noblemen and gentlemen then conversant in court,
and particularly had certain knowledge of John Dixwell, Esq. and that the said Dixwell was a member of
the said Parliament sitting in Westminster, and had in
honorable esteem then. And afterwards the said deponent transporting himself and family to New-Haven,
in New-England, was minded of a gentleman or
manifest great education, who in one parts of the
country endeavored to lead a retired and obscure life,
who called himself James Davids. The deponent further affirms, that the Gentleman called James Davids,
removing from one place to another afterwards came
to sojourn in said New-Haven, whereby the deponent
had opportunity of personal acquaintance and frequent
conversation with him, and certainly knew well the
said James Davids to be the above named John Dixwell, whom he had often seen and known in Westminster, and that for some reasons he saw cause to abscond
in these remote parts, and under the name of James
Davids. This gentleman after some time married a
virtuous maiden, Mrs. Bathsheba How, by whom he
had three children, as inhabitants of and in said New-
Haven, one of which died in infancy, two, named
John and Mary, are now living, and of adult age, re-
puted and known relatives and reviewed to be the lawful
children of James Davids, alias John Dixwell.—
The deponent further more affirmed, that sometime
before the decease of said gentleman, which was in the
year of our Lord 1689, in his last and long sickness, he
discovered himself, and made it known to his friends that
his true and original name was John Dixwell; and
that he had been a member of said Long Parliament,
and that for those reasons he had concealed himself
under the name of James Davids. So that here-

upon his relict and children have paſſed ever ſince under the name of Dixwell. The ſaid deponent doth alſo affirm and teſtify, that the bearer hereof, Mr. John Dixwell, is the only ſurviving ſon of the aforeſaid James Davids, alias John Dixwell.

" The above affidavit taken the date firſt above mentioned. Pr me,

"JOHN ALLING, Aſſiſtant.

New-Haven, January 1ſt, 1705—6."

Then perſonally appeared before me, John Alling, ſubſcriber hereof, one of the Aſſiſtants of her Majeſt's Corporation of Connecticut in New-England, and Juſtice of the peace, the Rev. James Pierpont Paſtor of ſaid New-Haven, aged forty-ſix, and gave oath as followeth, viz.

That the ſaid James Pierpont, deponent, being in the year of our Lord God, ſixteen hundred eighty and four, called by the people of New-Haven to the Paſtoral work, obſerved among them an aged perſon of manifeſt great education, who called himſelf James Davids, but was generally ſuppoſed to be of another name ; whoſe obſervable wiſdom and great knowledge in the Engliſh Law, State policy and European affairs, made his converſation very valuable to ſaid Deponent, and rendered ſaid Gentleman honourable with all that knew him. Yet ſaid Deponent obſerved this Gentleman induſtriouſly to avoid public obſervation and employment. After many conjectures who this Gentleman ſhould be, the ſaid Deponent preſumed he was truly John Dixwell, which, on a fit occaſion, ſuggeſting to this Gentleman in private, he ſeemed conceeding thereto, but deſired ſecreſy in that matter. Having been married, ſaid Deponent was informed, to a virtuous Maiden, named Bathſhua How, this Gentleman had by her three Children, one ſon called John the bearer hereof, and two daughters, one of which called Mary is

O

now living : The said Deponent further affirmeth, that when Sir Edmund Androfs took the Government of Connecticut, the said Davids, alias Dixwell, brought sundry papers (as he said of importance) sealed up, which he requested the Deponent to take into safe custody and not to suffer the seals to be broken till after said Dixwell's deceafe, declaring it was not so safe under present changes those writings should be found in his hand. The Deponent also affirmeth, that the said Gentleman falling into a dropfy in the year sixteen hundred eighty and nine, whereof he at length died, sent after said Deponent, and sundry times fully declared himself to be John Dixwell of the Priory of Folkeftone, in Kent, Esq and brother to Mark Dixwell, Esq. of Broom, in the Parish of Oakham in Kent. whose relict was afterwards the Lady Oxinden, one of whose daughters was Mrs Elizabeth Wetrow, with whom said John Dixwell held correspondence until his death. He furthermore declared he had been a Member of the Long Parliament in the reign of Charles I. and for what reasons he had concealed himself under the name of James Davids, and that his proper name was John Dixwell, by which his relict and children are since called.

The above Affidavit taken the date first above mentioned. Pr me,

JOHN ALLING, Affist. & Justice of the Peace.

New-Haven, Jan. the 16, 1705—6.

Then perfonally appeared before me John Alling, the subscriber, one, &c. of the Affistants of her Majesty's Corporation of Connecticut, in New England, and Justice of the Peace, Mr. James Heaton of said New Haven, aged &c. &c., and made oath as followeth, viz.

"That the said James Heaton, deponent, living next door to one Mr. Davids, &c. &c. &c. said deponent afferted &c. &c. &c. &c. obscure place had &c. &c. &c. &c. and a long time gentleman called himself James Davids : his cloathing, deportment and manifest great education and accomplishments, in a little time caused many to conjecture the said gentleman was no ordinary person, but for some great reasons sought to conceal both his proper name and his character. But people could not be determined in their thoughts until said gentleman fell sick of a dropsy, whereof he died in the year of our Lord, sixteen hundred eighty and nine. In that long sickness having occasion, in preparation for his death, to sign and seal sundry writings, he was pleased to send for the said deponent among some others since deceased, to sign as witnesses to said writings, when he manifested himself to be by name John Dixwell, and so signed his said writings. This gentleman married with Mrs. Bathshua How, by whom he had three children, one son and two daughters, one of the daughters died in infancy, his son named John who is the bearer hereof, and his daughter Mary are now living, and pass under the name of Dixwell.

"The above Affidavit taken the date first above mentioned. Pr me,

"JOHN ALLING, Assist. and Justice of the Peace.

"Extracted from New-Haven County Court Records, b. 2, p. 208."

Copy of a letter from Mr. P—y to Sir Basil Dixwell.

"New-Haven, May 4, 1708.

"Honorable Sir,

"I have the honor of yours to Mr. Henry Newman of September 4, 1—, informed as of the 2d of that month, wherein your honor doth Col. John Dixwell the justice to declare him in the management of your father's Estate, a very honest gentleman and faithful friend to him, many papers of his in my hand manifest the truth of that character ; that he deserved the same and much honorable regard, his surviving observers cannot forget.   They were doubtless mistaken who informed your honor he died in Switzerland.   Anno Domini 168_, I was called to the pastoral work in New-Haven, in the colony of Connecticut, New-England, quickly professed an aged gentleman who called himself *James D— l*, his accomplishments and accurate gentility she led him to be no ordinary person.   People generally supposed there were great reasons of his retiredness.   I have enquired of, but could not find him out.   The late worthy William Jones, Deputy-Governor, I have enquired of at Westminster, but could not recover it ————, it was it certainly known this his death, which happened A D 168), and as near as I can learn Anno ætatis 84   His disease was a dropsy.   He had by the overthrew him.—During which time I constantly attended on me and fully declared his entire history and descent. Priory of Folk-stone in Kent, I ——and b—— to M— Dixwell, Esq. of Broom, in the parish of Barham in Kent, which estate was ———, I— the heir, the Lady Cynthia, the ————— was Madam Elizabeth W—— , who took the name of Elizabeth P———, ———— cis with him till his ———— he had been a Member of the ————— in the reign of King Charles —————— he had descended by ————— the name of James P—— . He ————— sealed, with order they should be opened after his death, which accordingly were, and entered in the Office of Probates, by which it appears, that he may be truly called the Just Judge, that he was not only a ———— as your honor most ———— acknowledges, but advanced great sums for the benefit of Sir Basil Dixwell's estate during his minority, which doubtless he would with suitable acknowledgments have reimbursed, had his kind and good uncle had not been unhappily necessitated to withdraw.

Much more on this head is left under his hand and feal. Your honor's grand-father died I fuppofe about 1643 ; left three fons, Bafil, Heardfon and William , the two younger fons died in adult. Elizabeth married with Thomas Weftrow, who died and left her with fix fmall children. Many other particulars I could offer for your honor's further affurance, that your honor's uncle died under our obfervation. He left two children, John and Mary Dixwell, whofe education hath been as good as our country and their fmall eftate would allow ; and truly their proficiency, honorable exemplary deportment, almoft fhews what root they fprang from, and declare them worthy of the name of Dixwell. At the requeft of Mrs. Dixwell and her fon Mr. John, with other gentlemen and friends, I have prefumed to give your honor the trouble of this long letter , but the fatisfaction of finding fome branches of your honorable family and name in New-England, who want little fave their father's eftate, or your honor's favorable regards to render them valuable in Old-England as they already be in New-England. If in any thing may contribute to your further fatisfaction, fhall ready receive your commands, and with utmoft truth and integrity worthy my own name and profeffion, fhall fhew that I am,

" Honorable Sir,

" Your honor's moft obedient humble fervant,

" JAMES PIERPONT.

" To Sir Bafil Dixwell."

Copy of a Letter from Doctor Cotton Mather to Sir Bafil Dixwell.

" *Bofton, New-England, Nov.* 13, 1710.

" S I R,

" From remote America there now waits upon you the only fon of one who was an uncle and a father to your honorable father. A word in which I perceive your honor already fenfible of a very moving and charming oratory. With an irrefiftable force, and a pathos

O 2

beyond any thing that we can fee in the oration for Ligarius, it pleads for a moſt affectionate notice to be taken of him. The ſon of ſuch a father!

"Sir Baſil has too wiſe and great a ſoul to let any old, forgotten, dubious, political conſideration extinguiſh his affection for the memory of ſo excellent an uncle. The temptations of that day, when he was on the ſtage, were ſuch on both ſides, that all generous and compaſſionate minds eaſily bury in a juſt oblivion the differences thereby occaſioned. Alas, how many changes and thwartings have you ſeen ſince that day! enough to cool the mutual reſentments of what was done in that day. Impartial poſterity will confeſs there were brave men on both ſides, braver than any which eſpouſed either Pompey's cauſe or Cæſar's. Our Dixwell was one of them. Ours in regard of his dying with us, and worthy to be is in regard of your kind aſpect on his offſpring. He had excellencies that render him worthy of eſteem, even from enemies. How much more from a kinſman of ſo poliſhed and ſublimed a character, that he perfectly underſtands how far the ties of nature are ſtrengthened by good quality and ſuperior education.

"Though your uncle be dead yet *Non totus receſſit Lorem in artibus . . .* Do but caſt an eye on this his only ſon. Look upon him, Sir, his perſonal merit will ſpeak for him. He is one of ingenuity. He has a genius cloſe elaborate the common level of the country, where he had his birth and breeding. There is in him, a modeſt but yet a ſprightly ſoul; thoughtful and cautious enough too; and a natural good ſenſe agreeable to the ſtock of which he comes. A little cultivation which the place of his nativity afforded him *not*, would have made him extraordinary.

"He had no ſhare in the confuſions which diſturbed the middle of the former century. And he is pure blank to all the modern diſturbances on your ſide the water. He forfeits nothing on those accounts. Yea, I will venture to say this of him, *though he has lived for near twice seven years in my neighborhood,* I never heard that he did one ill or base thing in his life.

" He comes not over because he is in any wants or straits, but Sir Basil is known in these parts of the world and well spoken of. It is known that as he is able so he is willing to do good unto many, much more to his *own kinsman !* He is esteemed a person of honor, figure and virtue. 'Tis believed it will particularly shine in his goodness to his *own kinsman !* People of the best fashion here have advised him to intermit his other business for half a year and wait upon his kinsman and see. 'Tis in obedience to their advice that he does what he does. His kinsman's reputation will be advanced in these distant colonies by doing for him.

" And among those who have encouraged him, from an high opinion we have of your generosity, be pleased, Sir, to allow him to number himself, who is your honor's unknown, but real and humble servant,

" COTTON MATHER."

Some account of the family of Dixwell, taken from sundry papers and fragments now in the possession of Mr Samuel Hunt, by JEREMY BELKNAP.

Boston, July 15, 1793.

The family of Dixwell was originally of Cotton in Warwickshire, where it was subsisting in 1733, in the person of Sir William Dixwell.

Colonel John Dixwell, a member of the Long Parliament, in the reign of Charles I. brother of Mark Dixwell, of Broom, in Kent, came into New-England at the restoration of Charles II. (suppose about 1660)—His style was, John Dixwell, of the priory of Foke tone, in Kent, Esq but for convenience assumed the name of James Davids. By this name he was married, October 23, 1677, to Bathshua How, at New-Haven, before James Bishop, assistant.

Under the assumed name of Davids he corresponded with his niece, Elizabeth Westrow, in London, who assumed the name of Elizabeth Boyse.

His other correspondents were Frances Prince, of Amsterdam, *Jo Du Bois*, London,* *Thomas Westmoe*, London,† Humphrie Davie, Boston.—From this last he received monies remitted by his friends in England. The following is a copy of one of the receipts :

" Received now and formerly of Mr. Hum. Davie, by the direction of Mr. Increase Mather, thirty pounds New-England money, by the order of Madam Elizabeth Westrow, in England. I have signed two receipts for this sum of this date, for fear of miscarriage.— 14 June, 1686.

The letters from his friends are directed sometimes to Mr. James Davids, *merchant*, in New-Haven— others omit this addition   They contain chiefly domestic and public news, intermixed with many pious reflections. One of them invites him to Holland, 1689, but it did not arrive till after his death.

John Dixwell, Esq. died at New-Haven, March 18, 1689, aged 82   *New-Haven records.*

Test, John Alling, recorder.

John Dixwell, son of John Dixwell, Esq. was born 1680—1. March 6, was married to Mary Prout, of New-Haven, 1708, removed to Boston, and was chosen a ruling elder of the New North Church, 1717, went to England in 1710, corresponded afterwards with Sir Basil Dixwell, died in 1724, intestate. It appears from the church records that he was a man of great worth, and highly esteemed.

* *Suppose the husband of Elizabeth Westrow.*
† *Suppose the son of Elizabeth Westrow.*

His children were, Basil Dixwell, born 1711, bred a filver-fmith, then went into trade, refided at Providence in Rhode-Ifland; never married; went as a Lieutenant in the expedition to Cape-Breton, and there died, 1746.—Elizabeth Dixwell, born 1716; married Jofeph Lathrop of New-Londer, mariner.—John Dixwell, born 1718, ferved an apprenticefhip with William Tyler, Efq. merchant of Bofton; married Mary Hunt of Bofton, died 1749 inteftate, left two children, and his wife pregnant. His fon John died in three weeks after him, as did his pofthumous child. His daughter Mary furvived, married Mr Samuel Hunt, preceptor of the grammar fchool in Bofton, died in 1793, leaving four children, three fons, Samuel, John and George, and a daughter, Sufanna, who are now living, 1793.'

It it fhould feem by Mr. Pierponts letter that Colonel Dixwell's true name was unknown to him and Governor Jones, till he was on his death bed, it may be obferved that it was in fact certainly known to them and more others years before this. To Mr. Pierpont in 1685, when he recorded his admiffion into the Church by his true name. To Clarke and the two Allfops, in 1682, witneffes of the indentures of that date, figned by Dixwell himfelf, his true as well as affumed name. To others alfo witneffes to other inftruments figned Dixwell. And the manner in which he fpeaks of Governor Jones and his lady, to whom he commended his children in his will, denotes an acquaintance and familiarity implying, that however at firft he could not recollect his name, though he did his perfon, yet that he was perfectly acquainted with both his name and character long before his death. In truth he knew long before Mr Pierpont came to New-Haven.

Both the names and characters of Dixwell and the other Judges, with their circumftances, were all along doubtlefs known to fome few perfons of confidence. The honorable Mr Secretary Wyllys, now living, venerable for age, and respectable for family and every personal merit, has often told me, and now while I am writing, tells me that *his father had seen Judge Dixwell.* His father, son of Governor George Wyllys, was the honorable Hezekiah Wyllys, an affistant, who after long improvement in public life, died 1741, aged 70. The Secretary has often heard him fay that *he knew Mr Dixwell*, that when a boy he waited upon his father, then an affistant alfo, from Hartford to the General Court at New-Haven (fay about 1682) when they lodged at Governor Jones's during the feffion of the Affembly and one morning the father in a walk took the fon and carried him with him to a houfe on the outfide of the town, when a grave old man received them at the door, to whom his father paid the greateft refpect and honor, at which he much wondered. His father lit him to play at the door while he went into the houfe with the aged perfon, and was gone fo long that the fon was tired with waiting. At length his father came out, and returning to his lodgings, as they walked along, he afked the fon, who he thought that old gentleman was? He faid he did not know. Upon which he further told him it was Mr Dixwell This was doubtlefs with defign that the fon might afterwards recollect that he had feen Mr Dixwell, when in future time he might hear him fpoken of. This muft have been feveral years before Dixwell's death In fact his true name and character were perfectly known to Mr. Wyllys and fome others long before it was *formally* publifhed by him on his death-bed, to Mr. Jones and Mr. Pierpont ; which Mr. Dixwell defignedly then did in *an open manner,* though among others to perfons who had been well acquainted with it years before in a *fecret manner.* It is not to be doubted but that at this interview he was benefitted by Mr. Wyllys's fecret liberality.

Thus I have finished the history of the Generals Whalley and Goffe, and Colonel Dixwell, who found an asylum in the city of New-Haven and at Hadley, and in other parts of New-England, during a pilgrimage and concealment of twenty-nine years. All three were of King Charles's Judges; all three of the Parliamentary and Oliverian army; all three members of Parliament, two of them of Oliver's most honorable House of Lords, and all three, like Joseph in the court of Pharaoh, Daniel and Nehemiah in the Court of Persia, of purity of morals, and eminent for piety and virtue.

CHAP. IV.

An inquiry into the foundation of the immemorial surmise of some, and of the belief of others, that Judge Whalley also lies buried near Judge Dixwell, in New-Haven.

THE certain interment of Dixwell here has been all along of public notoriety, and universally known by all the inhabitants of New-Haven to this day. Many of the inhabitants have seen and all along been acquainted with his grave and the stone set up at it—but all have heard the report, and all have believed it without a doubt. Not so with respect to Whalley's interment here. Few have heard of it to this day, and fewer still have believed it. But among a few there has been an immemorial tradition, however it originated, of two or three rough stones, marked E. W. and set up at Whalley's grave, near Dixwell's. Although I have been acquainted with New-Haven burying-place above half a century, yet I never heard of Whalley's grave, and it was entirely new to me, when a gentleman of intelligence, a native of the city, first informed of it in January 1793. At first I gave no credit to it because I well knew that he died and was buried a Mr. Richards in Hadley, and had entertained no idea that his corpse had been taken up and removed hither. But the confidence and assurance of this gentleman engaged me to make a thorough inquiry among all the aged people in New-Haven, to see if I could find any tradition of this kind; I also endeavored to search my own memory, whether among the numerous flying stories and transient information I had from time to time received concerning these persons, I could recollect any transient anecdotes concerning this matter, which through unbelief might have passed away without making any lasting impression. I have also reviewed all the scattered lights and traditions concerning the interment at Hadley, and laid them together that every one might form his own inductions, conjectures and judgment. In this deficiency of certain information some may be curious on this subject to see whether any thing can be made of fables and traditionary rumours, partially imperfectly retained by one and another. All will consider the fact of Whalley's burial here, as unevidenced, unproved; some will believe it, a few will consider it probable, in general it will be disbelieved, and none will think it certain. In discussing the subject I shall judge myself in going into more minutiæ than may be agreeable, or as to become tedious and burthen some to read, while yet others will perhaps be furnished with materials for more curious speculations, and inductions, on a subject which, since the death of the two persons in the secrets of the Judges, can never be satisfactorily investigated.

I shall narrate the matters very much in the order in which the information has come to me. Since I took up this enquiry, I have really conversed with almost all the oldest persons in town above 60, and find that none of them retain any thing of the matter, and never heard of it, while among a few I find it has been immemorially preferved. My firft information was from Mr. Ifaac Jones, a defcendant of Governor Jones, who fpeaking of it with a certainty that furprized me, I afked him from whom he received it, and what evidence there was for it. He faid he had always underftood it fo, that the ftone marked E. W. was Edward Whalley's, and that he had fo confidered it, whenever he looked on it, for many years paft, but could not name any perfons with certainty from whom he received it, as neither could he with refpect to Dixwell's ftone, but confidered both equally certain. - He however believed he was told it by Mr. James Pierpont, the eldeft fon of the reverend Mr. James Pierpont, which would certainly be a good line of information. I then examined the ftone myfelf with clofe attention, and made inquiry among all the families where I judged it moft probable fuch a tradition might be preferved, but with little fuccefs. If ever there was fuch a tradition or furmife is was now almoft obliterated and loft.—On the little, however, which I did collect, the patience of my readers muft fuffer me to be particular and prolix, as they can fave themfelves a further perufal, after being notified that all which follows, will prove as barren, unentertaining, and deficient of fatisfaction, as the difcuffions of hiftorians on the authenticity of certain letters of Mary Queen of Scots : as indeterminate as the hiftorical difcuffions of the queftion, whether Fauft, Guttemberg, or Cofter, was the inventor of the art of printing ? or whether Columbus, Huetra, or Behenira was the firft difcoverer of America, already before certainly difcovered and colonized by Modog and the Norwegian navigators of the eleventh century. Curiofity may fometimes innocently lead us into inquiries, even on fome fubjects on which we do not expect to obtain full fatisfaction

As I knew with certainty that Whalley died and was buried at Hadley, fo it occurred to me in walking to the burying-ground to look for this E. W. ftone, that the fame reafons which would induce Meffrs. Dixwell, Jones, Bifhop, Pierpont, Ruffel and Tillton (the only men in the world that could be privy to fuch a tranf-action) to effect the fecret removal of Whalley's corpfe, might induce them to remove Goffe's alfo, though of this I have never found the leaft furmife: I fay as I knew and confidered this, fo when I came into the ard, February 19, 1793, to fearch for the one, I ... hed alfo for the other, as fuppofing the three Judg-es might chufe to lie interred fecretly together around Governor Eaton's tomb-ftone. I went upon this fuppo-fition, whether it can be fupported or not, and found three graves, which for the fake of inveftigation, we will put down as Whalley's, Goffe's and Dixwell's.— When I firft vifited the E. W. ftone, the mofs of an-tiquity being yet upon it, both by infpection and feel-ing the lacunæ with my fingers, I read the date 1648, thinking it a miftake of the engraver, without once think-ing or perceiving that the inverted 4 might be 5. But afterwards revifiting it, I perceived that the 4 was alfo 5. The mofs being now thoroughly rubbed off, the 5 is more obvious than the 4.* Now if it read 1658, this was two years before the Judges came to New-Haven, and about twenty years before Whalley's death, which would decide the queftion, and fhew that the ftone was not Whalley's. The extenfion, however, of the line-al incurre in a ftrait or direct courfe beyond the curve of the 5, in the manner given in the drawing, feems rather too much for accident, and has the afpect of de-fign and artifice, for deception and concealment. The infcription upon the foot-ftone E W. and the three fig-ures 16-8, are plain and diftinct on both ftones, but the intermediate figure is obfcure and fomewhat dubi-ous on both. In the date of the foot-ftone, the curvili-near incifion 5 is pretty difcernible, as difcernible as the reft; more fo than a feemingly 7, and I think th

* See P. 172.

upper line of the 7 is also pretty obvious, with every allowance for the human mind under a certain kind of
possible prepossession, when, with Watts, we " guess
and spell out Scipio" upon antique defaced coins and
monuments. The whole seems to form this odd complex figure 57, which confuses one at first, and leaves
the date to be read either 1658 or 1678, more obviously
the former than the latter. There must have been some
reason for that intermediate figure being made obscure
and doubtful, in both stones. It seems to be too much
for accident in both cases. That it should be so is un-
accountable if perspicuity had not been designedly avoided and concealed, when the rest of the inscription is
rough indeed, but strong, clear and distinct. The
whole is represented in the Plate No. VI. wherein the
numeral figures particularly are given at full bigness:
which I took off by laying a sheet of paper over the
stones, and impressing my finger over it along the lacunæ or engraving, and thus with a pencil taking off
their shape and position. The E. W. as well as the
figures on the head-stone, are at full bigness and exact:
the figures only on the foot-stone. On which therefore
every one may form his own judgment. Under this
conjecture, that date it may be read indifferently 1658
and 1678, it may contain truth and error, error or deception if read 1658, and truth if 1678: as this might
have been the true year of Whalley's death, not otherwise certainly known. He was alive 1674, and dead
before 1679, according to Goffe's letter to his wife.

Upon the same principle of designed deception, it
may be suspected that the M on the little stone eight
feet west of Dixwell's, may be taken for an inverted W:
and thus W. G. be designed for William Goffe, and
the 80 over those initials may be 1680. And if Goffe
died also at Hadley, as Governor Hutchinson says, it
is likely his death was about 1680, for his last letter
was 1679, and it is said he was no more, or disappeared
soon after, and not long after Whalley's death.

If M G be William Goffe, the 80 at the top muſt be 1680, and not the age : for Goffe married Whalley's daughter, and entered the civil wars and army a young man about 1642: and ſo he muſt bave been born about 1618 or 1620, and conſequently could be but 60, or thereabouts, at his ſuppoſed death, 1680. The figures therefore of 80 muſt be 1680, if they referred to Goffe.

Upon this I repaired to the town records, and examined the book which contains the births, deaths and marriages in town, in which they are regularly entered from 1649 to the end of the century. At 1654, indeed I found the death of Mr. Edward Wigglefworth, anceſtor of the profeſſor. I found that in the year 1658, there was but one death in town, Thomas Naſh, who died May 12, 1658. But E. W. could not be the initials of his name. Such was the healthineſs of the firſt ſettlement, as is uſual in new countries, that the deaths were few and ſeldom, though probably 300 families now in town, for there were 208 freemen 1644, and 333 freemen in 1660; and ſo there is the more reaſon to think the entries would be accurate. I took out the number of deaths yearly for thirteen years, as follows :

1649—3.	1656—1.
1650—5.	1657—1. Gov. Eaton.
1651—5.	1658—1. Tho. Naſh.
1652—2.	1659—2.
1653—1.	1660—4.
1654—4.	1661—2.
1655—2.	

I then examined the year 1678, and found two deaths only, viz. Samuel Miles and Timothy Tuttle. Neither was E. W. the initials of their names. It ſeems then, if theſe records are accurate, that no perſon died at New-Haven either in 1658 or 1678, the initials of whoſe names were E. W. This favors the ſuppoſition of an interment from abroad, be the dubious figures 5 or 7. This as to the Whalley ſtone.

As to the conjectural Goffe ftone,' it is to be obferved that the engraving or incifion is plain and diftinct, with this fingular circumftance, that a deep ftrong line is drawn along under the M, thus <u>M</u>, moft evidently not by accident, but with defign. In the records of deaths 1680, I found the names ftand thus :

      Ephraim How,
      Jofiah, fon of John Paine,
      Elizabeth, wife of John Harriman,
      John Punderfon.

But neither of thefe names have their initials M. G. Nor do I find thefe initials in the deaths entered for feveral years hereabouts. Which indicates that if the 8● be taken for 1680, this corpfe muft alfo have come from abroad, which would accord with the conjecture that thefe two graves might have been Goffe's and Whalley's whofe names could not have been expected to be found in New-Haven town records of deaths.

Againft all this there are two very material objections: 1. The honorable Matthew Gilbert, of New-Haven, one of the Affiftants and Deputy-Governor of the Colony, died here 1679—80, fo this ftone might be his. 2. As his death is omitted in the records, fo this invalidates our confidence in the records. I am not able to folve this laft objection. I cannot account for this omiffion of fo diftinguifhed and refpectable a character. But of this I am fure that he was fo honored, acceptable and reverenced, that it was by no means defigned, but perfectly accidental. We know that omiffions fometimes take place undefignedly, and by an unintentional neglect in thofe public records which are moft faithfully kept. The records of New-Haven, efpecially the firft and moft ancient, appear to have been kept with great care and accuracy. I chufe to ftate this in the ftrongeft manner. So confpicuous a perfon no one would think of omitting defignedly. But as it was an immemorial ufage, and required from the

beginning by law, for the friends to procure the recording of births, deaths and marriages, and never was the
recorder obliged to do it *ex officis* until brought to him,
so this omission must have happened through family neglect. And though this might possibly take place in
other instances also, yet so established was the general
usage of that early day, that it is very unlikely this should
have happened often : so that there may be a general
reliance upon the veracity of the records, this notwithstanding. Whether this or any better reason for the
omission was the true one, must be submitted.

It is possible then that this M. W. stone may be
Matthew Gilbert, it is possible it might have been
Mary Goodyear, or some other person whose initials
were M. G. Let us consider the probability of its having been Matthew Gilbert's. Now the 80, if denoting
1680, agrees well with the time of his death. The
contemptible and despicable appearance of the stone is
against it. It will ever be difficult to persuade a New-
Haven man, and especially one of the family of Gilbert,
that so small and insignificant a stone was put up at the
grave of so honorable an ancestor, and so distinguished
a person in civil life as Governor Gilbert. Further,
although his grave and stone are not now to be found,
yet none of the family or friends think of his having been
buried in that spot. They shew a very different and
distant part of the burying yard as the original place of
the sepulchres of their ancestor and of the family of Gilbert, viz. at and about the S W. corner of the brick
meeting-house. Hereabout lie many of the Gilbert family, whose grave-stones remain to this day, and here
they tell me Governor Gilbert, their common ancestor,
was buried! But his stone is not now to be found.—
Captain John Gilbert was slain by the enemy at the
invasion of New-Haven, July 5, 1779. His friends
sought a place for his grave, and buried him in that part
of the yard where the Gilbert family lie buried. His
son, Mr. Jesse Gilbert, a man of enterprise, curiosity

and information, tells me that when ▮▮ ▮s fetting up
a ftone at his father's grave, he took ▮▮▮▮ to look for
that of his anceftor, the Governor.   Not being able to
find it, he enquired of a Mr. Jofeph Brown, the New-
Haven antiquarian, remarkable for embofoming in his
ftrong memory more of our antiquities than any man I
was ever acquainted with.   He was born 1701, and
lately died aged 90, in the full poffeffion of his mental
powers, his memory being good to the laft.   Mr. Brown
told him he well remembered Mr. Matthew Gilbert's
grave-ftone, and that it ftood in that part of the burial-
ground where the Gilbert family were generally buried
—that at the time of building the brick meeting-houfe,
which was about 1754, they encroached upon the eaftern fide of the cœmetery, and took down feveral grave-
ftones, and among others this of Mr. Matthew Gilbert,
the antient Affiftant and Deputy-Governor : and that
he fhould judge from his recollection, that this grave
was directly under the S. W. corner of the brick meeting-houfe.   Adjacent and quite contiguous to this S. W.
corner of the meeting-houfe, has been the immemorial
place of the Gilbert family.   This I confider as decifive proof that the M. G. ftone in queftion, ten rods
N. W. is not that of the honorable Matthew Gilbert,
Efq. though he died in the winter of 1679—80.   As to
which M. G. ftone there is no light either from the bill
of mortality or tradition.   It might be Goffe's ; it might
have been fome other perfon's ; but it certainly was not
Matthew Gilbert s.   And there being no perfon of
thofe innitials in the bill of mortality for 1680, leaves
room for a fufpicion or conjecture, that like E. W. it
might defignate an interment from abroad.

Madam Whittlefey, aged 60, relict of the late reverend Chauncy Whittlefey, tells me, fhe has often
heard Mr. Prout, the aged gentleman treafurer of the
college, whom I have heretofore mentioned, narrate
the ftory of the three Judges : and among other things
he faid, that Dixwell died here, and as to the other two,

one of them died and was buried at Hadley in Mr. Ruf
fel's celler, the other they knew not what became
of him ; but fome faid that he came off to the weftward
and fome, fays he, have fuppofed that he lies buried in
our burying-yard, but of this, fays he, no one know
any thing with certainty. However new and unthough
of this was to me when Mr. Jones firft told me of it
yet upon converfing with many, and hearing fo much
faid upon the matter, I fet myfelf to recollect whethe
I had ever come acrofs any thing of the like before.—
And I do recollect that fome time or other above fort
years ago, or 1750, when Mr. Prout firft fhewed m
Dixwell's grave, he added, "and fome have though
that another of thefe Judges lies buried fomewhere in
our burying-ground, but where is unknown." But
have no remembrance that it was he that furvived and
came off from Hadley. It made fo tranfient an impref
fion upon my entirely incredulous mind, that it ha
been for many years totally obliterated. And though
now clearly recollect the flying fable, yet I felt and con
fidered it as a vague rumour or furmife, wholly withou
foundation. I gave not the leaft heed or credit to the
furmife.

Some perfons are of a fingularly tenacious and reten
tive memory, and treafure up things in converfatior
which evanifh from others who hear them with curfor
inattention. Such is Mrs. Beers, confort of Ifaac Beers
Efq. born in this town 1746, and now aged 47 She
is well read, is an excellent hiftorian, and is verfed in
the family anecdotes and antiquities of New-Haven.—
She is of the Mansfield family, and a lineal defcendan
from Major Mofes Mansfield, her great grand-father
who died 1703, aged 63, and who was one of the ap
prifers of Dixwell's eftate, and made up his inventon
for the probate office, and was intimately acquainted
with the hiftory of Dixwell after his death, and I pre
fume with the hiftory of Whalley and Goffe. He
grand-mother was of the family of Alling, the affiftant

about the clofe of the laft century, alfo well acquainted
with the ftory of the Judges. The honorable John Alling, Efq. had three daughters, fenfible, very worthy,
and venerable, and fociable matrons, one of whom
was Mrs. Beers's grand-mother. They often met together on focial vifits at her grand-father, deacon Manf-
field's, fon of the Major, who was born 1684, or four
years before Dixwell's death, who was alfo full of the
ftory of the Judges. This vifiting circle and family
connection had the greateft efteem and veneration for
the Judges, and in their vifits together were often talking over the ftories about them. Mrs. Beers, when
young, was often among them at her grand-mother's,
and heard thefe good ladies converfe on thefe matters,
and tell all the anecdotes concerning them. She ufed
to fit and liften to them with attention, while the other
grand-children took little notice of the difcourfe. So
different are the taftes of children, that what ftrikes one's
curiofity will not touch another's. Mrs. Beers was
born an hiftoric genius, and curious narratives were
food and delight to her mind. I think this particularity
in defcribing characters neceffary, in this cafe, towards
making the moft or beft of what otherwife might be
deemed information too flight to have any weight.——
Mrs. Beers has from this fource as much of the interefting hiftory of the regicides, not only of Dixwell, but
Goffe and Whalley, as moft perfons, and narrates feveral anecdotes with fingular precifion and accuracy ;
but as they coincide with what I have gone over before,
from other more certain fources, I do not repeat them.
But what I principally aim to avail myfelf of from her,
is what refpects *more than one of the Judges* being buried
in New-Haven. From the converfation of her grand-
father, and thefe pious matrons among themfelves, fhe
was as indelibly impreffed with the idea that " *they all,*"
that is, all the other Judges, lay buried here, as that
Dixwell was here, and had no more doubt of the one
than the other. She cannot diftinctly remember fhe

heard this or the other of the women fay fo; but their repeated, long and uniform converfation left this impreffion on her mind. She always fuppofed that the reft of the Judges lay here. She had not, however, been fhewn the graves till fince fhe grew up and was married. But about the beginning of the war, or 1776, upon gentlemen's being engaged to vifit the Judge's grave, fhe had a curiofity to vifit not it, but them alfo, for hitherto fhe confidered all of them lying here. Accordingly walking with Mr. Beers into the yard, he fhewed her Dixwell's ftone, and after viewing and reading the infcription, fhe turned about and faid, " and where are the others? Upon being told there was no other, fhe could fcarcely believe it, as fhe had always conceived from the converfation before mentioned, that the others lay there alfo. She faid the others muft be there: but being affured there were no others, though fhe faid fhe felt difappointed, and knew not how to account for her miftaken idea, yet fhe gave it up as a miftake But to this day the impreffion made by the women and her guard ed or reflecting not only more than one, but on them lying there, is ftrong, and yield only to the hiftoric evidence, which fhe confiders certain, that the others died at Hadley. But her information lies to her to this day as if *all were buried here.* But how they fhould come here fhe has not the leaft trace of information, conceiving in her own mind that they had all died here. She never heard any thing about any removal of the corpfes from Hadley hither, and never was impreffed with any fuch thought, nor heard a fuggeftion of the kind: while yet till that time fhe had no doubt but all of them were here. This, however, fhews that twenty or thirty years ago it was in the idea of fome that more than Dixwell was here. A member of Congrefs, now living, when paffing through New-Haven to Congrefs in 1774, was fhewn Dixwell's and Whalley's ftones at the fame time, with fuch informatiom, that, in 1793, he faid he doubted not that both lay here.

It has always been in public fame that of the two Judges at Hadley, one died there and was buried in the minister's celler; but which this was, was never said; and that the other, to escape Randolph's dangerous searches, disappeared, and was supposed to have gone off to the west towards Virginia, and was heard of no more. This I perfectly remember to have been the current story in my youth. No one in conversation pretended to designate which was which, until 1764, when Governor Hutchinson first published his history. Ever since this, for now about thirty years past, the public rumour has sometimes spoken with more precision and accuracy, designating Whalley as the first that died at Hadley, and that he that fame considered as going off to the westward was Goffe. It is necessary to distinguish the two periods, that from 1680 to 1764, and that for the last thirty years, as the fame reports are spoken of with different information in the two periods. When therefore Mr. Prout and others used to speak of one going off to the westward, no one before 1764 thought of its being Goffe more than Whalley. Since 1764 every one might know it was Goffe if either, and certainly not Whalley. Hence the few here who have immemorially had the idea of Whalley's stone, had not the refutation at hand till since 1764, that it could not be his, because he was the one that died at Hadley. It seems to have been the idea of Mr. Prout and the few others, that the E. W. stone denoted him that went off from Hadley westward, and was overtaken by death at New-Haven, and secretly interred here by his friend Dixwell, who had the same reason for secreting E. W. as himself. And yet the information of Hutchinson does not seem to have been so accurately attended to, even by some few judicious persons, as to have abolished this traditionary confidence still to this day, that this is Whalley's stone and most of the people in New-Haven talk to this day only with the traditionary knowledge antecedent to 1764.

When I fay that the public did not diftinguifh till 1764, I would except the Ruffel family at leaft, and perhaps the Tillton family. But there is reafon to think, while accuracy was foon loft in other families, fome of which might be poffeffed of particular inform- ation, the truth was kept up the longeft in the Ruffel family, which was the depofitory of a trunk of manu- fcripts of Goffe's and Whalley's, which came down undifperfed till fince 1760, remaining and preferved at Barnftable from foon after the death of the Judges to that time. Mrs. Otis, of Barnftable, a grand-daugh- ter of Mr. Ruffel of Hadley, as I have before obferved, fpent much time in reading thefe manufcripts, as fhe has told me, and gave me much account about them, being thoroughly verfed in the hiftory of the Judges. I do conceive that Mr. Ruffel of Barnftable, and Mr. Ruffel of Branford, both minifters and fons of the Had- ley Ruffel, were perfectly acquainted with all the fecrets of this hiftory beyond any men. Others had it partially, thefe perfectly. I had it in my power thirty years ago to have become perfectly acquainted with the fubject, and now regret that my curiofity was not ftrong enough to have excited me to improve an opportunity now loft by death, which has buried much certain information in an oblivion from which it can never be recovered.

In this failure of *primary* and certain evidence, and while we are left to avail ourfelves only of *fecondary*, tra- ditionary and derivative information, I think not im- proper to ftate the dangers during the lives of thofe con- temporaries who were in the fecret of the Judges, with whom all certain information perifhed, and to fhew that fure and certain information has continued the longeft in the Ruffel family, from whom it is poffible the tradition of the burial of another or the other Judges in New-Haven may have derived. A repetition of fome circumftances and facts, may be pardoned, as fubferving different applications and ufes in the courfe of this hiftory.

I have already obferved the danger that arofe to the Judges and their protectors from Randolph, during the period of thirteen years, from 1676 to 1689. All which time he was an infidious fpy upon New-England, with Argos eyes, and with the zeal and acrimony of an inquifitor-general. By his crafty and inceffant fearches for mifdemeanors, he came acrofs fome lights concerning thefe Judges, long thought by the miniftry to have been dead in foreign lands. Whalley died foon after, or about the time of Randolph's firft arrival, fay 1678 or 1676, and Goffe evanifhed after 1679. In 1684 was Randolph's moft vigorous fearch, but it feems it was judged not prudent and fafe to inform him of their death, undoubtedly becaufe the perfons of their concealers were in danger of being called in queftion by his inveterate malice, or leaft violence fhould be done to their graves. It is probable he never had any notice or fufpicion that Dixwell was here. Whalley being under fuperannuation, might feel no alarm, if living, and he certainly was dead before Randolph's exertions. But Goffe and Dixwell, and their concealers, muft have been greatly alarmed. We may confider all the three Judges alive 1678, Goffe and Whalley dead by 1680, and all were dead by 1689.

Such was the vigilance, activity and malice of Randolph, that the two actually furviving Judges had reafon to think that both their perfons and afhes would not efcape his malicious vengeance, if difcovered. There was therefore a fufficient and very powerful inducement for the concealment both of their perfons and places of interment. And the danger of fome accidental difcovery might induce a removal of the bodies of Goffe and Whalley from Hadley to New-Haven, in the dangerous period about 1680 to 1684, while the ravenous Randolph was making inquifition. And although the ftorm was in fome meafure blown over foon upon the death of Dixwell, and the feizure of Sir Edmond Androfs one month after, or April 18, 1789; yet the con-

Q

cealers, who were liable to be profecuted and adjudged aiders, abettors, and acceffaries in treafon, would not feel eafy under the poffibility of detection, during their lives; and would have every motive to continue the concealment of as much of the affair as poffible. To fhew the danger of concealing traitors and obnoxious perfons, knowing them to be fuch, we need only advert to the execution of Lady Alicia Lifle, relict of one of the regicides who died abroad: a fact well known at the time by the accomplices concerned in the concealment of the Judges in New-England. This pious and venerable lady furviving her confort, and living in peace for many years, "was tried in 1685, by that difgrace to human nature, Judge Jeffries, for concealing a Mr. Hicks, a diffenting minifter, and Mr. Nelthorpe, who attended the Duke of Monmouth, when he made his expedition into England" " She was beheaded at Weftminfter univerfally pitied.——[*Noble's Memoirs of the Cromwell family.* V. 2. P. 471.

This came over to New-England, and though an event after the death of Whalley and Goffe, muft have excited terror in Dixwell, Ruffel and Tilton, and the gentlemen in New-Haven then living and concealing Dixwell, and confequently, if detected, more obnoxious than Lady Lifle. It muft have made them very cautious. Every thing therefore continued to be kept a profound fecret; nor do I think that Hadley itfelf had any knowledge that they had embofomed and entertained angels, till after the feizure of Androfs, and the news of the revolution, if indeed till after the death of their minifter, Mr. Ruffel, in 1692, or the recording of Dixwell's papers in 1691; after which the affairs of the Judges began to be more freely talked of.

After the revolution and extirpation of the Stuart family, 1688, and the halcyon days of the new charter of Maffachufetts, in 1692, from King William III. and efpecially after the public probate of Dixwell's will, 1689, and recording of his indentures, 1691, figned

James Davids, alias John Dixwell, and his avowal upon his death-bed of his being one of the Judges, it became impoffible to keep up an entire concealment of
their refidence and protection at Hadley and New-Haven. Yet even in thefe open times, and when fo much
of their hiftory was got abroad, fome reafons or other
operated both againft the full developement of the affair,
and of the perfons concerned in the protection, and
alfo for the continuance of the concealment of the places
of the interment of Goffe and Whalley.

The reverend Mr. Ruffel and Mr. Tillton knew with
certainty what was become of Whalley and Goffe: and
it is not to be doubted that Dixwell, Pierpont, Jones,
and Bifhop, knew the fame thing with a derivative certainty. They could have as eafily communicated the
certainty of the place of interment, as of their refidence
and death. There was a reafon of weight with them
why they did not, or if they did at all, that it fhould be
confidential, and not for the public. Should we miftake in conjecturing the reafon, it is of no moment.—
Enough for us to know that there was one, and that it
wrought too efficacioufly. Perhaps it was partly to preferve the bodies of the deceafed from violence, and principally to fecure the perfons of the protectors. This
laft endured till the death of Mr. Pierpont, at leaft 1714
—and yet the moft of the gentlemen active and in the
fecret, died before and about the revolution. Govern-
or Jones and Mr. Pierpont furvived the longeft. Let us
ftate the perfons in danger, and the times of their deaths.

The reverend Mr. John Davenport, ob. March 15,
1670, aged 72.
The reverend Mr. Ruffel, ob. December 10, 1692.
Honorable Peter Tillton, Efq. ob.
Governor Leveret, ob. 1678.
Governor Leete, ob. 1687.
Governor Jones, ob. October 17, 1706, aged 82.
His Lady, ob. April 4, 1707, aged 74.
Deputy-Governor Bifhop, ob. June 24, 1691.

Judge Dixwell, ob. March 18, 1688—9, aged 82.

Reverend Mr. Pierpont, ob. Nov. 22, 1714, Æ 55.

Mr. Richard Saltonſtall went to England 1672, re-turned 1680, went to England again 1683, and died there April 29, 1694.

The moſt of theſe were deceaſed by 1692. Certain information ſurvived into this century only with Jones and Pierpont, and the two brothers, Ruſſels, of Barn-ſtable and Branford, and poſſibly ſome few others un-known to me, and after 1731, only with him at Barn-ſtable, and expired with his death, 1758, unleſs it ſur-vived with his brother, honorable Judge Joſeph Ruſſel, of Briſtol, who died about 1775.

It may be proper to diſtinguiſh the degree and ſtate of information under three different periods : that from the acceſſion of the Judges to America, 1660, to 1690, or rather the death of Mr. Ruſſel, 1692 ; that from thence to the death of his ſon at Branford, 1731, and laſtly, the period from thence to the preſent day.

1. The firſt may be called the period of ſecrecy and public ignorance. For though within this ſpace of about the firſt thirty years there was a little open knowledge of them at the beginning, yet they ſoon ſo evaniſhed and buried themſelves from the public view, that except ſome little apprehenſions of them in 1664 and 1684, which ſoon paſſed off, they were ſo loſt that the body of the people, the magiſtrates and miniſters, thought and knew no more of them than if they had been in Swit-zerland, and really ſuppoſed they had abdicated the continent. They were willingly and really ignorant. All the knowledge there was of them was certain, but it was confined and ſhut up in the endangered boſoms of the few confidents immediately concerned in aiding in their concealment, and theſe few were ſome of the beſt and moſt excellent characters in the country, both civilians and miniſters. It may be ſaid therefore that the year 1690 found the country and world in total igno-

rance. Two had been now dead for ten or a dozen years, and the other was alfo then deceafed.

2. The fecond period opened with a certain portion of communication or degree of public difcovery, which fpread in a general, vague and blind manner through New-England, and has continued much the fame to this day, with only this difference, that the means of certain information, as far as the information was actually imparted, continued in being, and could at any time be appealed to, by fufficient numbers to fupport and eftablifh the public affurance, during that term.—— This expired with the death of the Ruffels. A part of their hiftory was communicated, and part ftill concealed to the end ; and this was done with thoroughly meditated defign and counfel. That they had all along lived, and that two of them died in the country, and the places of their concealed abodes, were difclofed and afcertained. But for fome reafon or other, the flight or death of Goffe, and the graves and places of interment of two of them were concealed, though equally known to the few in the fecret. The reft of their hiftory was fufficiently and defignedly communicated. I fay fufficiently, although with a cautious avoidance of a too particular account of the refpective agency of each particular perfon, and the fources, mode and inftruments, through which fupplies and comforts were adminiftered to perfons attainted and fubjected to the *Perduellionis & læfæ Majeftatis Pæna.*

It being determined to conceal the graves, it became neceffary to frame and adjuft a narrative accordingly, adhering to the truth as far as any thing was pofitively communicated, and leaving the public to their own deductions, inferences and conjectures for the reft, which fhould be fuppreffed. Thofe in the fecret were very willing to let the public bewilder and deceive themfelves on a matter as to which they had no right to information, en which information might induce danger to the bones of their deceafed friends, if not to fome furvivors. We may then diftinguifh the ftate of the *public* information during this period into what was *certain*, and what was *uncertain* ; and again the *fecret* knowledge preferved among a few at firft equally *certain*, but now *loft*. I have already faid that there was public certain information, 1. As to the places of the actual refidence of all three. 2. That one died at Hadley, and was buried in Mr Ruffel's cellar or garden. 3. The Angel ftory. 4. That the other one difappeared from Hadley foon after the death of the firft. 5. The time of Dixwell's death, and the place of his grave.

The information or conjectures which were left vague, undetermined and uncertain, and which were within the certain knowledge of a few during this period, were, 1 The remaining hiftory of Goffe, and the place and one of his death. 2. The removal of the bodies of Goffe and Whalley to New-Haven, if this was fact. Thefe things were once within the certain knowledge of Ruffel, Tillton, Dixwell, Pierpont and Jones. The reafons which induced them to withhold an eclaircifement upon thefe fubjects continued to their deaths, and with them all primary certain information terminated In truth there occurred no time during their lives in which the full development of the hiftory of the judges would not have endangered the difturbance of their bones, a thing frequently threatened even down to the prefent day, and which was probably the ultimate and commanding reafon for concealment. So late as the laft French war, 1760, fome Britifh officers paffing through New-Haven, and hearing of Dixwell's grave, vifited it, and declared with rancorous and malicious vengeance, that if the Britifh miniftry knew it, they would even then caufe their bodies to be dug up and exhibited. Often have we heard the Crown Officers afperfing and vilifying them, and fome fo late as 1775 vifited and treated the grave with marks of indignity too indecent to be mentioned. It was efpecially dangerou in Queen Anne's time, and even during the Hanoverian family, there has been no time in which this grave has not been threatened by numerous fycophantic crown dependants, with indignity and minifterial vengeance. All which will fhew that the reafon for concealment of the graves of Goffe and Whalley continued to the end of the lives of thofe who were poffeffed of primary certain knowledge. In confequence of which all that they left from them to the public, was with " it is faid," and " fome fay," and " fome have believed," and " fome have fuppofed"—that one was buried in **Mr.** Ruffel's cellar or garden ; that the other was buried in Mr Tillton's garden, or went off weftward towards New-Haven, Virginia, &c. This was what came from the really knowing ones, when preffed with the queftion, Where were Goffe and Whalley buried ?— They left the public perfectly uncertain ; although I believe they left or knew the public to conceive with one general confent that they were both buried privately in fome place unknown in Hadley. Nor had the public the leaft idea of their removal. If Randolph had found out their deaths, which took place in his time, and had been empowered to difturb their graves at Hadley, he might have been pointed to the places in which they had been truely buried, and reaked his malice upon earth then uncharged with fuch precious relicts.— The Judges were Oliverians, and might have placed an illufion of their enemies, as the Protector is faid to have done, by enclofing the decapitated Charles in a coffin infcribed with his own name, in the certain forefight of future indignity.

During this fecond period, or the period of *certainty*, the few perfons of *primary* certain information, might take effectual care to impregnate a felect few, with derivative and *fecondary* certain information, that it might be fecurely tranfmitted to the times of fafety. That is Mr Ruffel of Branford, Governor Jones and Governor Bifhop, perfons of primary certainty, might confidentially impart it to Major Mansfield, the Alling and Trowbridge families, with whom Governor Leete's family had become connected by marriage, and a few others at New-Haven, to continue the tradition. And if the bodies were in fact removed, these might be thus possessed of a *secondary* certain information of the fact, and of the place of their graves in our burying-yard.— And yet death might have overtaken them before the time of safety for public promulgation. In which case the next generations must be left to fable and the vague and unevidenced traditions of the present day. Thus I have gone through the state of information to 1731, or the death of Mr. Russel of Branford.

3 The third period may be that from 1731 to the present day. In the beginning of this period and down to 1748, the death of Samuel Bishop, Esq. aged 82, son of the Governor, there were still means of continuing certain and authoritative information from them who were first concerned. But whether the thing grew into desuetude, or whether they communicated it to persons of unawaked curiosity or heedless inattention, or from whatever cause, the thing is so gone from us, that from a very diligent inquiry at Hadley and New-Haven, I have not found a single person that can say, that whatever knowledge they now have, they received it from any of those ancient persons now dead, whom I know, or have reason to think, to have been possessed of the *secondary* certain information. I have reason to think indeed that such persons of a third descent in derivative evidence have been to be found here till 1775 And I believe about that time the line of authoritative information ceased. None now living can say that they were told by Mr. Samuel Bishop, son of the Governor, or by any other person possessed of *certain* derivative information where Goffe died, or whether the bodies of Whalley and Goffe were removed, or where finally deposited, either at Hadley or New-Haven. As to these things all authoritative information is at an end,

all terminates in immemorial tradition. I mean this with refpect to that fecreted information which was long preferved and tranfmitted among a few, but never left authenticated ; not with refpect to thofe *certain* facts before ftated, as given forth at the firft promulgation of the hiftory of the Judges, about 1692 ; of which authentic documents are preferved in Hutchinfon, as well as in unqueftionable tradition.

4. There remains however fome traditionary notitiæ, which after the failure of the line of certain information, fome may have the curiofity to attend to, and expend fome little pains in attempting to account for, or perhaps adventure fome deductions and inferences from them. I fhall therefore reprefent and ftate them at large, leaving every one to make their own improvement of them.

I have obferved, that though heretofore unknown to me, I have lately found, that there has been an immemorial tradition among fome very few perfons in New-Haven, that more of the Judges than Dixwell, and that particularly Whalley, lies buried in New-Haven. The moft of the inhabitants now living know nothing of it, nor have ever heard of fuch a furmife. I have converfed with almoft all the very aged inhabitants now living, and with above fifty aged 60 and upwards to 90 —and have not found above two or three who feem to have ever had the idea. I have converfed with numbers under this age, and have found but five now living who have had this idea , but thefe have it ftrongly and immoveably. The firft of thefe was Mr. Ifaac Jones ; and though a defcendant from Governor Jones, he does not pretend to derive it from the Jones but the Pierpont family, which is equally original. This is only as to the E W. ftone as Whalley's, but not a word of Goffe's being here. Two others I can trace to the Mansfield and Alling families, of derivative and fecondary certainty. One I trace to a direct and immediate derivation from Samuel Bifhop, Efq. fon of the Governor,

who was of primary information, and undoubtedly af-
fifted in the removal and interment of Whalley here,
if indeed he ever was interred here. The derivation
from Mr. Pierpont refpeɛts Whalley; that from Manf-
field, Alling and Bifhop, afferts that other and all the
Judges lie buried together here. But when I afked
how they came here, thefe informants knew nothing
of the matter, and not one of them feemed to have
turned it in their thoughts; and particularly upon my
affuring them that Whalley certainly died at Hadley,
and muft have been taken up and removed, they all
declare they never heard any thing about fuch removal,
nor could recollect the leaft furmife of the kind. Mr.
Jones is particular and confident as to Whalley being
here, but never heard of Goffe being here, nor of any
removal. The others never difcriminated the names of
either Goffe or Whalley, but only that all the other
Judges befides Dixwell lay here, as well as Dixwell.
Mr. Mofes Mansfield, now living, a great-grand-fon
of Major Mofes Mansfield, received information not
only in the Mansfield and Alling families, from both
of which he is defcended, but moft particularly from
Mr. Job Bifhop, fon of Samuel, and grand-fon of the
Governor. Mr. Job Bifhop was curious and of reten-
tive memory in thefe matters, and was full of the anecdotes and memoirs of the Judges, and ufed even to old
age to talk of them, and narrate the ftories about them
with a very feeling and interefting fenfibility. Their
fate and hiftory had made a deep and lafting impreffion
upon his mind. He died about 1786, aged 81. Often
has Mr Mansfield fat and heard him tell their hiftory.
And among other things, he perfectly remembers that
Mr. Bifhop ufed to fay that " they all lay buried here
with Dixwell." I wifhed him to reconfider: he did;
and remained certain that Mr. Bifhop faid, " they all
lay buried here." But he never thought how they came
here, nor did Mr. Bifhop fay any thing that he remembers about any removal. Nor did he ever turn it in his

mind, or advert to the circumftance that one at leaft
died at Hadley. This concurs with Mrs. Beers, in a
derivation from the Alling and Mansfield families, that
the other Judges lay here as well as Dixwell.

Walking the Green in this city one evening lately, I
met another perfon aged 75, who was born and lived
many years on the eaft fide of the Green, about twenty-
five or thirty rods from thefe graves; which graves, he
faid, he always knew from a boy, and that the Judges,
were buried there. I afked him if all three lay there?
he faid, no; there were but two there. I afked, if certainly more than Dixwell? Yes, two, I fay; there
were two, and only two. He was a frank, plain, blunt
fpoken ruftic. Who were they? Dixwell,—and I
don't remember the name of the other: but there was
another, and there was only two—I can't certainly remember his name—but I think it was one Doctor
Whalley. Did you never hear that three lay here?—
No, I tell you, there were only two; and go along with
me, and I will fhow you their graves. It was in the
dufk of the evening, between eight and nine o'clock, in
May, and I omitted it. When was your firft knowledge of thefe ftones and graves as the Judges'? I know
not—always—from a boy—I don't know when I did
not know it—I always knew it—I have known it all
my life long. This I confider as evidence that it is not
a modern or late furmife, but that it was fo rumoured
feventy or eighty years ago, when perhaps it was trite
among a great number of the inhabitants, and in many
families, though now loft in all but two or three; and
almoft extinct in them.

In connexion with and in addition to this, is the uniform tradition among the grave-diggers, particularly
of one family, not that all the Judges, but that one befides Dixwell, lies buried here, and that this one was
Whalley, and that the ftone E. W. was Whalley's—
This is efpecially to be found in one particular branch

of the family of Tuttle. All the Tuttles in and about this town have derived from Mr. William Tuttle, one of the first planters, and among the more wealthy settlers of New-Haven in 1637. It is in one subsequent branch that this tradition is to be found, that of Caleb and his descendants, as I cannot find it among any of the other descendants of the first William. Mr. Caleb Tuttle was the son of Thomas, son of the original ancestor, William. He was born about 1670, and died about 1750, so very aged, as to have been grown up, and perhaps aged 18 or 20 at Dixwell's death, and so must have personally known him. I formerly knew sundry aged persons here, who knew and were acquainted personally with Dixwell, and with his character from its first promulgation. This Caleb Tuttle was the first of the grave-diggers, or sextons, of this name. From one of the Tuttle family born in New-Haven, 1708, and now living, aged 85, as well as indeed from several other aged persons, I have learned the names of all the grave-diggers here during his life. When he was a boy, Nathaniel Tharp was the first he remembers, who died 1716 very aged, when he himself was aged 8. Since that there have been Dawson, Butler and others, while all along without interruption, to the present day, the principal of the business has been done by Caleb Tuttle and the branch descendant from him.— Caleb began before Tharp's death, and continued to within my memory, and as his sons and grand-sons grew up they took the business down to the present time. The succession in this family has been thus.

Grave-Diggers.

Old Mr. Caleb Tuttle, say from 1710 to 1742.
His son, James Tuttle, from about 1735, to 1770.
Abraham, brother of James, 1760, to 1780.
Richard Tuttle, son of Abraham, 1768 to 1792.
Richard tells me that he received the story of the E. W. stone, as well as Dixwell's stone, from his father and his uncle James, and they from his grand-father,

Caleb; a plain, good man, whom I well knew, a man of integrity, very intimate with Governor Jones's son, they having married sisters. But whence Caleb got it, Richard knows not. Caleb was acquainted with Governor Jones and Major Mansfield, was born and all his days lived a near neighbor to them both, and to the late Samuel Bishop, Esq. son of the Governor, which Mr. Bishop lived to 1748, when he died aged 82, and must have been aged 23 at Dixwell's death. Thus he was all his life cotemporary with Mr. Bishop, who was perfectly acquainted, partly of himself and partly from his father, with all the anecdotes respecting the Judges. Caleb, as I have said, was a son of Mr. Thomas Tuttle, who with Major Mansfield, was an appraiser of Dixwell's estate in 1689.— Thomas I have been told assisted in laying out Mr. Dixwell, and there is some reason to believe that he was the very person that privately dug Whalley's grave, and assisted at his secret interment here. If so, it is no wonder that his descendants should be charged and strongly impregnated with this family idea and designation of Whalley's grave. Thus Caleb from his father, and by his intimate connexion with Governor Jones's family, Mr. Bishop and Mr. Pierpont, was certainly on the way of secret information sufficient for the purpose of this impregnation, at least that Whalley as well as Dixwell was buried here, and for the designation of their graves. He was a zealous religionist, and warmly captivated and carried away with characters distinguished for holiness and piety : and according to my idea of the man, whom I well remember, he would, I should think, have listened to the anecdotes and history of these pious and heroic sufferers, with avidity and curious and feeling attention. I doubt not he knew more about the subject than all his posterity. And he is the source of the information concerning the Whalley stone.

The original knowing ones, might judge it one of the safest and surest means, besides oral tradition among

R

a few families, of transmitting and perpetuating the memorial of Whalley, by impregnating the grave-diggers in this line with the information. However they got it, they have immemorially had it, certainly for eighty or ninety years; and have often pointed it out to unbelieving spectators, for few ever believed or realized it to be the grave of the true Whalley. And hundreds doubtless considered it as only a fable : while the grave-diggers have, for no reason indeed which they can adduce, steadily believed it with the most confident assurance. They no more doubt Whalley's than Dixwell's —they are equally positive as to both.

Mr. Prout might, and doubtless often did, hear it from the grave-diggers : but I do not learn that he ever spake of it as derived from them. Indeed he derived elsewhere. His age and connexions enabled him to have recourse to much higher, even original authority. He was always in the Dixwell connexion from his youth up, he was personally acquainted with Mr. Pierpont, Mr. Russel, Major Mansfield, Mr. Alling and Mr Bishop, and indeed with Governor Jones himself, and indeed with all those few characters at the beginning of the present century, who were most intimately concerned in this affair. His sister Mansfield, consort of sheriff Marsfeld, son of the Major, was a warm admirer and great venerator of the Judges, and versed in their history. Her daughter, Madam Throope, aged 75, relict of the reverend William Throope, tells me, that once, when a girl, riding with her parents together in a chaise, or calash, they passed by Dixwell's house, her mother desired Mr. Mansfield to stop, and while sitting in the carriage she mourned over and lamented him, as a pious and holy man, and enlarged in his praises and commendation, saying many holy prayers had been made in that house. From her I was ascertained the place of Dixwell's house, which was standing till 1756. Her brother Prout had the same veneration for these good men. And to old age, and even forty years ago, he used in conversation with me to speak of the affair and history of these Judges, with the most engaged and interested feeling, beyond any man I have ever heard speak of it. He had almost their whole history familiar to him, and was full of it, and delighted to tell it, and to dwell upon it. He never said any thing about their removal. But in his frequent and verbose conversations with the reverend Mr. Chauncey Whittelsey, of this city, upon the subject of the Judges, after mentioning that one died and was buried in Mr. Russel's cellar, he spake with the same caution that the Russels and the other confidential cotemporaries must have been used to speak—"as to the other, it is not known what became of him, some said he went off from Hadley to the westward towards Virginia; some have supposed that he lies buried somewhere in our burying yard." This he said to Mr. Whittelsey and others. I do not find from sundry that have heard Mr. Prout speak of the matter, that he ever spake of more than one of the other Judges being supposed to be buried here besides Dixwell. Indeed though he was personally acquainted with originals, I should not judge that their discretion would have selected him for confidential and plenary secrets, while he was, on account of his social and communicative disposition, a very proper person through whom to transmit, preserve and diffuse important information. He was the gentleman and the christian. He was born in New-Haven November 19, 1689, and died here April 4, 1776, aged 87.

But supposing Whalley buried here, whence came it that tradition fixed upon the stone E. W. for Whalley's monument, with 1658 engraved over it, when the very date must refute it, being two years before the Judges came into this country? This is a question I leave every one to solve for himself: as well as to reconcile it with the archives of New-Haven, in whose obituary no such initials are to be found at that year; as neither are they at 1678, supposing the date to be so read. I

leave it alſo with every one to account for the dubiouſ-
neſs, to ſay the leaſt of that figure in both the head and
root ſtones, if in either it might be aſcribed to accident
and caſualty. How ſhould the caſualty happen to both,
eſpecially when the other figures are plain ? If any
ſhould rather aſcribe it to intentional and deſigned artifice for concealment, it might comport with that vi-
gilant, preconcerted and unremitted caution, which
has certainly been practiſed in this whole affair, by the
few who were certainly knowing, and even perfectly
knowing to the whole affair, and could have put the
matter out of all doubt, but deſignedly, and moſt induſ-
trioufly, and too efficaciouſly concealed it, ſo as even
to become totally loſt, as never to be inveſtigated, until
the reſurrection of the juſt   I leave it further for every
one to account in his own way for the uninterrupted
tradition of the grave-diggers in the line of the Tuttle
family.   How ſhould it originate ? For that it has ſub-
fifted ſeventy or eighty years at leaſt, and even from
the beginning, or immemorially, I conſider as proved.
Although new to me, I have upon inquiry found with
certainty that ſuch a ſurmiſe and tradition has all along
been to be found here among a few, while the main
body of the inhabitants now living, have all along heard
nothing of it, or at leaſt never noticed it.   Whence
could it originate ? Had it been ſaid in Hadley that
they were buried in this and the other place, we might
conſider it a conjecture of ignorance : After knowing
they died there it was natural to inquire the places of
their graves, and in their ignorance there was room and
occaſion for uncertain conjecture.   But when nobody
ever thought of their dying at New-Haven, nor of their
removal hither, what ſhould have given occaſion amidſt
their ignorance alſo at New-Haven, to even the ſurmiſe, much more to the poſitively fixing on the very
grave ? and on account of the date, one of the moſt
improbable graves in the yard ?

Till within twenty years paſt there have been perſons of intelligence alive in town who were derivatively poſſeſſed of all the Ruſſel information, and could have annulled the E. W. ſtone. Among the inhabitants of New-Háven were theſe : Mrs. M'Neil, a daughter of Mr. Ruſſel of Branford, a very ſenſible woman, and an adept in the hiſtory of Goffe and Whalley ; which ſhe ſaid ſhe learned from her father ; and as to the Judges lying here or not ſhe undoubtedly knew all that her father knew. Samuel Mansfield, A. M. and Samuel Cook, A. M. who married ſheriff Mansfield's ſiſter, were full of the family information. Mr. Cook had not only the Mansfield information, but that of his father, the reverend Samuel Cook, of Stratfield, who had lived many years in New-Haven the beginning of this century ; was an intimate acquaintance and connexion of Judge Dixwell's ſon, Mr. Pierpont and Mr. Ruſſel, and ardently intereſted in the fate of the Judges. Theſe, beſides other branches of the Mansſield and Alling families, who were perfectly acquainted with Mr. Ruſſel, ſurvived to within theſe fifteen or twenty years. In this circle the hiſtory of the Judges was frequently converſed upon. And among them all, there muſt have been knowledge enough to have refuted the miſtake. It is, I find, certain that they knew this E. W. ſtone was ſpoken of by ſome as Whalley's, and none ever heard them contradict it. They certainly entertained and ſuffered this idea at times to paſs from them, that other Judges beſides Dixwell lay buried here. I was formerly acquainted with all theſe perſons, and have often heard the moſt of them with great engagedneſs converſe on the fate and anecdotes of theſe Judges ; and I doubt not, if they were living, they could throw ſufficient light upon the ſubject. But their knowledge is buried with them. They were the laſt, and there remain no more preſent means of ſatisfactory information. I have been told much that theſe and other ancient perſons have ſaid and narrated about the Judges,

I have been told that sheriff Mansfield, a very respectable character, in the year 1774 shewed a member of Congress, of another state, Dixwell's stone, at the same time shewed him the E. W. stone, and assured him that this was Whalley's, so that this gentleman to this day remains equally impressed with the equal certainty of both, the one as well as the other. And sheriff Mansfield knew it, if Mr. Russel of Branford knew it.

Still therefore pursuing the supposition that Whalley lies buried here, though by no means considering it as a thing that can ever be proved : it must follow that, after his undoubted sepulture at Hadley, he was taken up and secretly removed to New-Haven. But, as I said, I can find no tradition at New-Haven or Hadley of such a removal. In this place. I think proper to insert a letter which I received from the reverend Samuel Hopkins, minister of Hadley, in answer to my letter of inquiry upon the subject of the Judges

Hadley, March 26, 1793.

" Reverend Sir,

" Since I received yours of 11th ult. I have taken pains to enquire of the oldest people among us, what they heard said, by the oldest persons in town since their remembrance, respecting Whalley and Goffe, their residence in this town. The tradition among all of them is, that both of them were secreted in the town ; that the inhabitants at that time knew very little of them, or where they were concealed, except those in whose houses they were. And the tradition among them in general is, that one of them died in this town (those who remember which, say Whalley)—that the other, Goffe, after the death of Whalley, left the town, and that it was not known where he went. With respect to the one who died in this town, the tradition in general is, that he was buried in Mr. Tillton's cellar.

" Most of whom I have enquired for tradition say, that while they were here the Indians made an assault upon

The Angel of Hadley,

the town : that on this occasion a person unknown appeared, animating and leading on the inhabitants against the enemy, and exciting them by his activity and ardour, that when the Indians were repulsed, the stranger disappeared—was gone—none ever knew where, or who he was. The above is the general tradition among us.

" I shall now notice some things which were in the tradition, as given by some, differing from the above, or adding somewhat to it.

" According to the tradition given by some, Whalley and Goffe were not concealed the whole of the time at Mr Ruffel's and Mr. Tillton's, but part of the time at one Smith's. This I find in the family of the Smiths.

" An old man among us says, he remembers to have heard the old people say, there was a fruitless search (by order of the government, as I understand it) of all the houses in Hadley, but that they (to use his words) searched as if they searched not. That after Whalley's death, Goffe went off, first to Hartford, afterwards to New-Haven, where he was suspected and in danger of being known, by his extraordinary dexterity with the sword, shewn (as he tells the story) on a particular occasion. And in apprehension of danger, he went off from New-Haven. Here tradition, according to him, ends with respect to Goffe.

Goffe = swordsman

" Another still older says, that he heard both his father and his grand-father say, that Whalley and Goffe were both secreted at Mr. Ruffel's at first, who for their security, in case of search, made a retreat for them betwen his chambers, and behind his chimney.—That one of them died at Mr. Tillton's, and was buried behind his barn. That after his death Goffe went off into the Narraganfett, was there set upon, and in danger of being taken ; went from thence to the southward, was heard of as far as Pennsylvania, or Virginia, and nothing heard further of him.

" The tradition among some, connected with the family of the Marshes, is, that Whalley and Goffe both died in Hadley.

" Not many years after my settlement in Hadley (1754) he, who was then quite an old man, told me, among other things, that the tradition of the one that died in town was, that he was buried in Mr. Tillton's garden, or in his cellar. With respect to the place of his burial, I am of opinion, that it was kept secret, and was unknown. It seems to have been a matter of conjecture among the inhabitants,—in Tillton's cellar,— in his garden—or behind his barn—as they imagined most probable. Of his being buried under a fence between two lots, I do not find any thing ;—nor of his being afterwards removed. I have searched for his monument, and do not as yet by any means find the time of Tillton's death. Should I hereafter, I will inform you.

" SAMUEL HOPKINS."

I was at Hadley May 21; 1792, making inquiries only for gratifying my own curiosity, and without a thought of compiling this history. The reverend Mr. Hopkins carried me to Mr. Russel's house, still standing. It is a double house, two stories and a kitchen. Although repaired with additions, yet the chamber of the Judges remains obviously in its original state unmutilated, as when these exiled Worthies inhabitted it. Adjoining to it behind, or at the north end of the large chimney, was a closet, in the floor of which I saw still remaining the trap door, through which they let themselves down into an under closet, and so thence descended into the cellar for concealment, in case of search or surprise. I examined all those places with attention, and with heart-felt sympathetic veneration for the memories of those long immured sufferers, thus shut up and secluded from the world for the tedious space of fourteen or sixteen years, in this voluntary Bastile.—

They muſt have been known to the family and domeſ-
tics; and muſt have been frequently expoſed to accidental diſcoveries, with all their care and circumſpec-
tion to live in ſtillneſs. That the whole ſhould have
been effectually concealed in the breaſts of the knowing
ones, is a ſcene of ſecrecy truly aſtoniſhing!

Mr. Hopkins and others gave me the ſame account
as in the preceding letter. He ſhewed me the place
where the old meeting houſe-ſtood, 1675, at the Indian
invaſion, about eighty rods north of Mr. Ruſſel's houſe.
I viewed alſo the poſition of Mr. Tillton's houſe, ſtill
ſtanding, about a quarter of a mile below Mr. Ruſſel's.†

On my return from Hadley, paſſing through We-
therſfield, on the 25th of May, I viſited Mrs. Porter,
a ſenſible and judicious woman, aged 77, in full poſſeſ-
ſion of good mental powers, and particularly of memory. She was a daughter of Mr Ebenezer Marſh, and
born at Hadley 1715, next door to Mr. Tillton's, one
of the temporary and interchanged reſidences of the
Judges. This houſe was in her day occupied by deacon
Eaſtman. She had the general ſtory of the Judges, but
ſaid ſhe knew nothing with certainty concerning them,
but only that it was ſaid they ſometimes lived at Mr.
Ruſſel's, and ſometimes where deacon Eaſtman lived.
There were many flying ſtories, ſhe ſaid, but ſo uncertain that nothing could be depended on—as among
others, that one was buried in Mr. Ruſſel's cellar, and
another in Mr Tillton's lot, in the dividing fence between Tillton's lot and her father's Her father died
1772, aged 85, and ſo born in Hadley 1686, at his
father Daniel Marſh's, a few rods N. W. from Tillton's, and always lived, as did his father, in that
neighborhood. As ſhe ſaid ſhe had nothing certain, I
preſſed her for fabulous anecdotes. She ſaid ſhe was
aſhamed to tell young people's whims and notions,
which had nothing in them. But in the courſe of con-

† See Plate IV.

verfation fhe faid, that when fhe was a girl, it was the
conftant belief among the neighbors, that an old man,
for fome reafon or other, had been buried in the fence
between deacon Eaftman's and her father's ; and that
the reafon why they buried him in the line of the fence
was, that the poffeffors or owners of both lots might
each be able to fay, he was not buried in his lot ; but why
he fhould be buried in the lot at all, and not in the public burying-place, fhe had never heard any reafon or
tradition. She faid the women and girls from their
houfe and deacon Eaftman's ufed to meet at the dividing fence, and while chatting and talking together for
amufement, one and another at times would fay, with
a fort of fkittifh fear and laughing, " who knows but
that we are now ftanding on the old man's grave ?" She
and other girls ufed to be fkittifh and fearful, even in
walking the ftreet, when they came againft the place
of that fuppofed grave, though it was never known
whereabouts in that line of fence it lay. She herfelf
imagined it lay a little beyord the barn, eight or ten
rods eaft from the great ftreet that runs through Hadley, and perhaps eight or ten rods from her father's
houfe. But fhe fuppofed the whole was only young
folks' foolifh notions, for fome were much concerned
left the old man's ghoft fhould appear at or about that
grave. But this lady was very reluctant at narrating
thefe circumftances and ftories, to which fhe gave no
heed herfelf, and which fhe confidered as trifling and
unimportant.

In repeatedly vifiting Hadley for many years paft,
and in converfation with perfons born and brought up
in Hadley, but fettled elfewhere, I have often perceived a concurrent tradition that both died there, and
were buried fomewhere in Hadley unknown, though
generally agreeing that one was buried at Ruffel's. And
two perfons born in Hadley tell me that, many years
ago, they were poffeffed of the idea and furmife, or of a
little glimmering of uncertain tradition, but how they

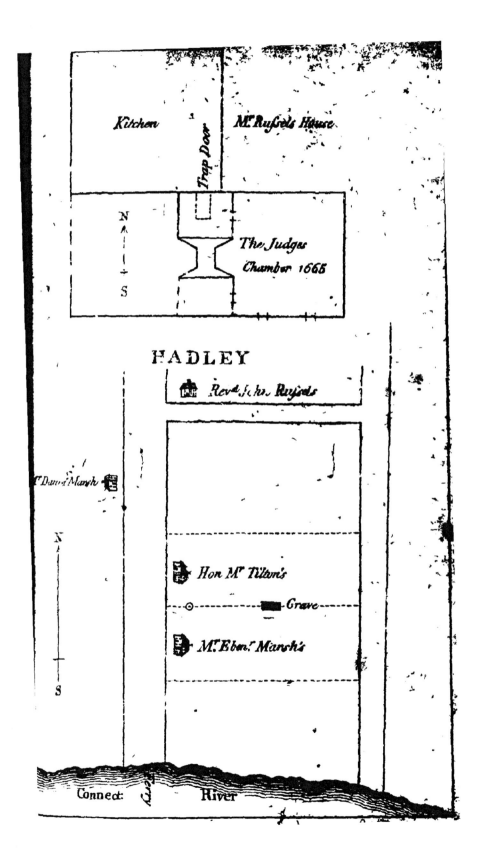

Kitchen

Trap Door

Mr Russels House

N

S

The Judges
Chamber 1665

HADLEY

Revd John Russels

Mr David Marsh

N

S

Hon Mr Tilton's

Grave

Mr Ebenr Marsh's

Connect. River

came by it they knew not, that though buried there, they ware afterward secretly taken up and removed, they knew not where. This is the only surmise of the kind that I ever came across: and the informers desired me not to rely upon it, as upon my requesting their re-attention and recollection, they said, it was so faint and transient an idea, that they felt at a loss, and could by no means be confident. Yet they assisted, that a faint idea or impression of such a report and surmise, imbibed in youth at Hadley, still remained on their minds.

One person in New-Haven, aged 70, is certain of having immortally heard that one of these good men, by his name Dixwell, lies buried here, and has the floating idea that this person was Goffe. Upon my asking if it was not Whalley? it was replied, No, but Goffe.— Upon asking whether he died here? it was replied, that he did not die here, but after living at a distance up the country secreted a long time, he came on a visit to Dixwell and wandered about and lived in secret places round about New-Haven, and died somewhere not far from New-Haven, and was secretly buried here. This was the floating idea, but of no certainty as to either the facts or derivation of information. This however seem-ed certain and without a doubt, that another besides Dixwell lay here, a little at a loss about the name, but inclined to adhere to Goffe, never heard of its being Whalley, nor of Whalley's stone, or if it had been here it was forgotten and lost. And yet this per-son has through life lived in the atmosphere of good traditionary and fabulous intelligence concerning the Judges, with however but slight and transient impres-sions, or with impressions now much confused and lost.

Possibly, upon General Goffe's danger increasing af-ter Whalley's death, he and his friends at Hadley might plan a delusion, for a foundation of saying truly, that after Whalley's death, Goffe went off to the westward towards Virginia. So Goffe might leave Hadley, and

Dixwell, wander about secretly and lose himself for a time in some of his old recesses round about New-Haven, and perhaps then concert with his friend Dixwell the removal of Whalley s corpse out of the reach and investigation of Randolph. During which time it might be truely said, "that after Whalley's death, the other went off to the westward towards Virginia, and that it was not known where he was, nor what became of him." When however he might, after a short excursion, return to Hadley, be there soon overtaken by death, and be buried first at the old man's grave, near Tillton s, and be afterwards with Whalley taken up and removed to New-Haven. This is but conjectural, and left in uncertainty, though it would have been good Oliverian generalship. The story of one going off to the westward, after the other's death at Hadley, is spread all over New-England, and is as trite at Rhode-Island, at this day, as at New-Haven and Hadley.

I think some use may be made of all these sparse, and unconnected traditionary lights, all perhaps alluding to truth, if rightly understood, towards supporting the conclusion of Governor Hutchinson, that both the Judges died at Hadley.

1. That Whalley died at Hadley, I consider as evidenced fully by Goffe's letters, that he was buried in Russel s cellar, or under his hearth, or in his garden, or about his house, is evidenced by almost universal tradition, by the uniform information in the Russel family, and the tradition which can be traced to them. Mrs. Otis and Mrs. M'Neil constantly affirmed this. If so, it was not Whalley that was buried at Tillton's.— Mr. Hopkins s recent inquiry, indeed, makes the one that died at Hadley to have been buried at Tillton's. But last spring, and heretofore, both Mr. Hopkins and others at Hadley, have told me, what I had always received before, that the first was buried at Mr. Russel's, although the traditionary idea at Hadley at this day may be that of Tilton s. This however I would consider as

verifying the idea that there was indeed a burial at Tillton's. And as I have no doubt but that one was buried at Ruffel's, this would conclude in both dying and being buried in Hadley. And this I believe was really the truth. It is to be obferved, that the uinverfal tradition at Bofton, Barnftable and New-Haven, has been, that one of the Judges died at Mr. Ruffel's, and was buried in his cellar, or under his hearth. We know from Goffe's letter that this was Whalley.

2. That another Judge, befides Whalley, died at Hadley, and was buried at Tillton's. There is a tradition, with fome variation, that one was buried in his garden, behind his barn, in the line of dividend fence : all confpiring to render it probable that one was buried there. And if Whalley was buried at Ruffel s, this muft have been Goffe. And fo both died and were buried at Hadley, agreeable to Governor Hutchinfon, which he perhaps received from the Leveret family, who were in the fecrets of the Judges. The leaving the manufcripts at Hadley in the Ruffel family, indicates both the Judges dying there, and finifhing their days at Hadley, fay about 1680, for we hear and trace nothing of them after this time, only that foon after the death of Whalley, the other went off to the weftward towards Virginia, and was no more heard of.— This might be true if he died at Tillton's, and by his friend Dixwell and others conveyed to New-Haven, which was weftward towards Virginia : which might have been done to elude the fearches of Randolph, who would doubtlefs have procured the execution of vengeance upon the relicts and graves of the perfons, could they have been found. If both died at Hadley, and Whalley was removed, will any one doubt that Goffe, u buried at Hadley, was removed alfo ? And thus, though in an oblivion, into which there remains now no traceable light, all the three Judges may he depofited together in the burying-yard at New-Haven. I

S

know thefe are ftrong and perhaps unfupported deductions, but in reference to fuch a conclufion, whether
decifive or not, thefe difconnected and feemingly fabulous accounts and furmifes, however trifling, may feem
to be not altogether inappofite.

I have indulged myfelf in an enlargement on this inquiry, not fo much for afcertaining the unfupported
conclufion that Whalley lies buried in New-Haven, as
for bringing together and exhibiting in one view thefe
fabulous narratives, and ftatement of circumftances,
with their inductive connexions; that fo whoever may
curforily and tranfiently hear of them at any time, may
reft fatisfied that he is poffeffed of all the fcattered information poffible to be obtained, and judge for himfelf
how much or how little weight and confidence may be
given to them; and alfo for giving opportunity to
others to purfue and trace thefe lights in different parts
of the country, together with any other circumftances,
which may verify or perfect thefe accounts, and contribute to any further elucidation of the pilgrimages and
hiftory of thefe Judges. On the whole, I confider it
by no means certain, yet rather probable that they all
three lie buried in New-Haven. Of this, however,
every one will form his own judgment, having before
him, I believe, all the light and information, that can
ever be poffibly obtained on the fubject.

CHAP. V.

Justification of the Judges, with reflections on the English Polity and government.

CONNECTED with the history of the Judges, will be an inquiry, immediately arising in every mind, whether the High Court of Justice, which passed sentence upon the King, is to be justified or condemned? And this question has been, and still will be determined by each one for himself, very much according to each one's decision and judgement upon the previous question, Whether a sovereign is amenable to the community which he governs? To those who are fixt and decided in the despotic principles, that Kings can do no wrong, that no tribunal can be authoritatively erected but by the King, who can never be supposed to consent to the erecting one for the trial of himself; and who of consequence believe and hold for law that no King can or ought to be tried at any earthly tribunal; and who finally hold that a King, however guilty of the *common Traditionis Reipublicæ*, cannot be justly punished by death,—To such I have nothing to say. Among those who have previously settled in their minds the responsibility of Kings to their subjects, some condemn this particular transaction in the case of Charles I. It is not to convince or make converts of any of these that I write. But that body of whigs in England, and their American offspring and descendants, who for a century and half have approved the act, and the Parliamentary war, have a right to adduce their reasons.— This body is increasing in the nation, and their principles are spreading in the world. Europe has another and the last conflict to sustain, in the present war of Kings; and it will be a vigorous, severe and bloody one. The English nation are so enlightened, so tenacious and understanding of their rights, so enthusiastically impregnated with the inextinguishable love of civil

liberty, that they will never fubmit, they will never
defpair. The conviction is already publicly eftablifhed
of the impoffibility of the coexiftence and cohabitation
of their rights and liberty with the permanency of an
hereditary ariftocracy and fovereignty, and that the perpetuity of the one muft be attended with the ultimate
downfall and extirpation of the other. In the conflict
of the patricians and plebeians at Rome, the former
yielded and faved themfelves. But the confidence and
tenacious firmnefs, even to blinded obftinacy, of the
prefent hereditary ariftocracies through Europe, and in
England among the other powers, will never give way.
They expect to ftand, but they will affuredly fall. The
pontiff and conclave at the Reformation had no doubt
but that they fhould infidioufly compafs and effect a
reunion and refubjugation of the Proteftants: but two
centuries and a half have elapfed without any other effect than a conviction now generated and diffufed through
Europe, and the Court of Rome itfelf, that the Hierarchy is ruined, and the Pontificate is no more. The
ethnical worfhip was ages in dying, nor did the Gen-
tile priefthood, nor the civil powers of the three firft centuries, believe that their opulent and pompous idolatry
was fatally ftruck with a death wound in the apoftolic
age, and yet it fell, not by arms, but before the convictions of chriftianity in the fifth and fucceeding centuries. When eftablifhed fyftems arrive at a certain
height of corruption, they become incurable, the experience of all ages fhews that they cannot be reformed,
and their fall and extirpation become inevitable, in the
natural courfe of events. In England, that delufory
fhadow of liberty, the femblance of a Parliament, once
a wife inftitution, is fo effectually fubdued to the irrefiftable influence of the Crown, and the omnipotence
of a Prime Minifter, who conftantly affigns to one of
the privy council the bufinefs of managing the Commons, that is corrupting and fecuring a venal majority
at his will and difclofure, that, fupported by an hered-

tary ariftocracy always at the will of the Crown, government bids defiance to every exertion for liberty, and
completely modifies and renders the dominion independent of the nation, who feem to enjoy fome liberty becaufe they elect their reprefentatives to be fent to mar-
ket for certain corruption to betray their rights and immunities. This every man in the nation believes, and
more, he knows it. This new modification of power
and crown dominion commenced at the happy revolution. It was a court device, after it was found and
eftablifhed that a King could not rule England without
a Parliament. But it as effectually fubjugates a nation
to the will of one, as did the former mode of exercifing
royalty under the Tudors and Stuarts. Now this cannot be broken up but by the diffolution of monarchy
and hereditary ariftocracy or nobility. They fee this,
will never yield, but will rifque the moft arbitrary and
defpotic exertions of power for their fupport. This has
all along been feen by many, and yet fcarcely believed
and realized by the nation at large to this day. However, the conviction is now growing and eftablifhing,
and the miniftry are undefignedly accelerating and pre-
cipitating the crifis of an univerfal conviction. The
crifis is near at hand, and it muft be a bloody one. The
prefent modified government can never recede. It cannot rectify itfelf: it has neither authority nor will to do
this It cannot be done but by the nation at large, it
having become now known to be abfurd for a legiflature, which ftands, or ought to ftand, on a conftitution, to make its own conftitution. And adminiftration dare not rifque the calling a national convention, to
amend the Commons' Houfe, leaft under the idea of
redreffing grievances and rectifying acknowleged defects,
they fhould endanger the fubverfion and overthrow of
the whole prefent polity. The prefent fyftem of polity
therefore muft ftand and remain, unamended, corrupt
and defpotic as it is. There is left to the nation then
no alternative between quiet and tame fubmiffion to the

prefent unqueftionable defpotifm, and a recourfe to the
old principles of 1641, the principles of Hampden and
Sidney; principles which purfued and acted out to their
full operation, would terminate in the juftification of
the Judges Thefe principles will rife into energetic
operation, and a burft of the public fpirit will fooner or
later effect the downfall of ariftocracy and monarchy;
and out of thefe ruins will arife an elective republic.—
In order to this, recourfe will be had, as I have faid, to
acknowledged principles of law and juftice, and to the
extraordinary precedents in the Englifh hiftory; and
among the reft to this of the Judges. The main body
of the whigs now lately anexing themfelves to a motly
miniftry and parliament, and through an unhappy miftake deferting the caufe of liberty for a feafon, will after finding themfelves duped, like their brethren at the
revolution, refume the principles which they fet up at
the Reftoration.   They will refume them not partially,
but wholly, and go all the lenghts of their operation
and confequences, as they have been all along avowed
in the Englifh nation and conftitution, though overwhelmed, fmothered and fubdued in their operation,
and even nullified by court artifice, intrigue and venality. This hoodwinked policy being overthrown, every
Englifhman will ever afterwards know and feel that de-
lufion no longer, but that law and liberty is his birth-
right.   The events in France have effected fuch a
change in the public fpirit in England, that the Epifcopal whigs have deferted the caufe, joined the miniftry
to the wifhes of toryifm, now as vigorous as ever in the
nation, and left the Diffenters to inherit and fuftain the
opprobrium of civil liberty, under the pretext and imputation of anarchy and the principles of rebellion. The
penal laws of Queen Elizabeth yet hung over them,
but I believe the miniftry, however they may threaten,
will hardly have the temerity to go fo far as to enforce
them, an enforcement, however, which I doubt not
they would fuftain with the exemplary and chriftian

fortitude of their anceftors. But in every other refpect the Diffenters have now to become the fcape-goat of civil as well as religious liberty. And they will endure till the eyes of the whigs are again opened to perceive that they a third time have been unhappily deceived and deluded to facrifice a caufe they by no means intended to furrender. But finding themfelves caught and enfnared, they will turn about, refume their old principles, and act with united energy in regenerating a public polity, in which liberty and the rights of citizenship fhall be effectually fecured. In the mean time, through every ftorm, a fucceffion will furvive of thofe who will fteadily approve, and advocate the juftice of the war of 1641, and the fentence upon Charles I. not from the principles of rebellion, with which they are afperfed and villified by the prefent Englifh Mountain, but from uncorrupted, enlightened and fober judgment. And as in the darkeft times they have uniformly perfifted in the avowal of their principles, though with an unavailing effect under overpowering corruption, or everpowering miftake of their fellow citizens; fo in this age of liberty, and in the prefent ftage and progrefs of the prevalence of truth, they ever ftand ready to ftate the reafons, which to them now, and perhaps in time may to the world extenfively appear fufficient to legitimate the tribunal which arraigned Charles I. and not only to exculpate, but intirely to juftify the Judges.

Nor are they deftitute of fupports by precedents.— Says a modern writer—" We read in Rapin how Edward II. when conquered and made prifoner by his wife, was tried by the Parliament, which decreed that he had done all poffible wrongs, and thereby forfeited his right to the crown. The Parliament tried and convicted Richard III. Thirty-one articles of impeachment were alledged againft him. The Parliament depofed Henry VI. declared Edward IV. a traitor, confifcated his effects, and afterwards reftored him in his profperity. In regard to Richard III. he certainly had committed more wrongs than all his predeceffors. He was another Nero, but a politic, courageous Nero; and hence the prudent Parliament did not declare the wrongs which he had done until after his death.

" In later times the Reprefentatives of the Englifh nation brought to trial and condemned Charles I. to lofe his head on the block—declared James II to have done the greateft wrongs, and in confequence dethroned him." All this has been done, though by the concurrence of both houfes of Parliament, except in the laft inftance, yet by tribunals not erected by the King.

A few inftances in ancient ages, multiplied in the two or three laft centuries, of Parliamentary controul on Kings, and of transferring the hereditary fucceffion of princes to other family branches, has at length eftablifhed a principle in the Englifh government, that a concurrence of parliament is neceffary, to ratify the hereditary fucceffion —which may fet it afide; and even proceed to the punifhment of criminal Majefty, as well as criminal nobles: while the fame principle purfued might lead to elections in all cafes, both of princes and nobles, in the room of thofe who violate the obligations of the hereditary character. And even the hereditary idea itfelf may be fet afide and abolifhed, when all the reafons for hereditary dominion fhall at length, in the public conviction appear to be futile and miftaken, as being in fact founded in a fubferviency to the aggrandifement of particular families, and oppreffion of the community, rather than in the public weal. But it requires a tract of ages for the truth to ftruggle into public reception and prevalence. and many facrifices lie in the road to the triumphs of truth,† While fome changes are fudden and rapid, others require a longer time, both to prepare the public mind, and to combine and draw forth the exertions of thofe popular powers in ftates,

† *W. Wiff, Savanarole, Hufs, Jerom, Whalley, Goffe.*

neceffary towards eftablifhing fome great principles of public right and utility. When the laft at length takes place, it excites a new retrofpective idea upon the former exertions and characters, few and rare at firft, and overwhelmed by prevailing powers not yet broken up. Witnefs the public fenfe on Wickliff, Hufs, and Jerome of Prague. The fubferviency of thefe rare though fpirited examples of facrifices, preparatory to the bringing on of the ultimate happy crifis, will then be feen and admired. An evil may be oppofed for ages, and many fall in the conflict and oppofition, without fuccefs, but a continued feries of vigorous exertions may at length bring on a united and vigorous burft of the public fpirit, terminating in the ultimate falvation of the public.

To return to the furvey of the laft century. The main body of the nation, wearied out by the ftruggles with tyranny, and being by the time of the revolution 1688, glad to recover fo much true liberty, or feeming liberty, as they did under the houfes of Orange and Hanover, rather chofe to leave thefe uncomfortable matters to go into oblivion, and having thus far fecured their liberty and rights, have ever fince filently permitted a court faction and crown intereft, mixt with defcendants of hereditary defpotic caviliers, the Filmers and vociferous advocates for high government and arbitrary power, to caft an odium and afperfion on the adjudication of Charles, and on the period of the Protectorate. In confequence of which the two or three laft generations have grown up even under the houfe of Hanover, rather impreffed with a doubt of the perfect legality of thofe tranfactions, and in a fort of fubmiffive and unconvinced acquiefcence, that they were not altogether nor radically juftifiable : even fo as to produce a prefent generation, who either generally difapprove and repudiate, or reluctantly fpeak of a tranfaction, which they rather think fhould be condemned. The national and annual afperfions of the Temple upon this period, have contributed to this filent, tame, and half convinced acquiefcence, even of the real and firm and uncorrupted friends of civil liberty. But afide from the compromife and acquiefcence of political parties, and their union in a fuppofed well controuled and limited monarchy, let it be fairly inquired, whether thofe principles, which the united body of the whigs in the nation, both thofe who approve and thofe who difapprove this act, have to this day uniformly avowed, and have never given up, and never will give up, will not involve the vindication and juftification of the Judges. They performed a great work, a dangerous work, a a work and enterprize in which they perifhed : was it a work of righteoufnefs, or unjuftifiable rebellion?

It is necefTary to look into the defects and perfection of the Englifh conftitution towards making a judgment on thefe matters. Let us fuppofe the practical, though not written conftitution of England, of a government by King, Lords, and Commons, to be excellent : and liberty to be fecure while the three branches acted feparately, and truly independently, and uninfluenced by one another, by any thing but the public weal. But let an undue influence of one over the other be introduced, and prevail to any confiderable height, freedom of difquifition, and freedom of acting, are at an end, and the conftitution violated. This was done by Charles I. acting independent of both houfes, and for twelve years without either houfe. England thought this was remedied at the revolution by an eftablifhment that the King fhould not rule, but with the concurrence of the two houfes. By the bill of rights they thought their rights and liberties were fafe. They were fo, while the houfes were really independent. But corruption has found a way, from one of the acknowledged and conceded prerogatives of the Crown, the appointment of all officers through the realm, and the crown appropriation of revenues granted to the King's difpofal for their fupport for fecret fervices and for penfions, to originate a new mode of influence, effectually subduing both houses to the King's will. It was not thought at the revolution, that this could have arisen to the present enormous and pernicious height. But so open is this transaction now, that it is become the direct object and business of one of the King's privy council, by the distribution of offices in the revenue, the army and civil departments, and by pensions, to manage, that is secure a majority in the house of Commons: the same for the Lords; so that both are securely held at the King's pleasure: tho' by the good providence of God, it has happened, that the succession of sovereigns since the revolution has been well affectioned to their subjects, and disposed to rule with wisdom, justice, and clemency. A clemency and facility however, which has permitted a Bute, a Hillsborough, a North, and even a Pitt to plunge the nation into the most unwise, sanguinary and despotic projects, which can bring odium and dishonor on regal government. Thus the excellent government and constitution of England, is by the avidity and folly of ministers under a lenient but yielding crown, again changed into indeed a new modelled but efficacious and real tyranny a tyranny which will not be long endured, but as assuredly hastens an awful crisis as did the despotism of Charles I. It must and will be rectified.

This evil might be rectified, but it will not be, by the efficary power being shared, for the appointment of the principal officers and pensionaries of all descriptions, between the Crown and the two Houses of Parliament, instead of a council of ministers of the King's sole appointment. And with this rectification the government of England would be excellent, even with the retention and continuance of the two other great defects of the constitution, an hereditary and useless aristocracy, and an unequal representation in the commons. both of which ought to be, and will be, by a future spontaneous national convention, rectified in a reform and amelioration of the constitution to an elective and perfect polity. Hereditation of dominion in Nobles and Princes is the first step to despotism. This ruined the republic of Venice. This modified and converted the feudal system into a complex tyranny. This was gradually and but partially introduced into England.— "Earl, *comes*, was not originally hereditary, nor a degree of dignity, but of office and judicature. They sat and judged with the Bishop. At length grew into government, but not hereditary. There was not at the entry of the Saxons a feudal and hereditary earldom in all Christendom." Even in Alfred's time A. D. 900, not yet hereditary in England, but supplied by appointments as officers in the army, or Judges of Courts.— See Spelman's Feuds and Tenures c. vi p. 13. The same appears in Montesquieu and Vattel. Their recovery back to their original officiary institution, would be a radical relief to the English constitution. The English constitution is not incurable, it contains principles which if suffered to operate and to be acted out would cure itself, but this operation will be obstructed, and it never will be cured. There is no alternative but its demolition.

After a vigorous and successful struggle with the Stuart family, a partial rescue of liberty has been obtained; and it has been settled ever since the glorious revolution that Kings shall not rule without law, nor without parliament. The sovereigns of the houses of Orange and Hanover having learned wisdom by the example of the preceeding house of Stuart, have given up the contest, and the old principles, the old energetic spirit, are in some degree gone to sleep and become dormant. Nor need they be awaked and called forth into energetic operation, but upon pressing and great occasions; while a general vigilance will be ever necessary and sufficient for the ordinary conservation of liberty. But whenever these great occasions offer, and one already begins to shew itself and will not be baffled, these principles will be recurred to, and this national spirit reawakened.—

In the mean time, as in the prefent period, three quarters of the nation fuffer the other quarter to talk and write licentioufly, and to broach defpotic and dangerous political doctrines with impunity, which the nation will never fuffer to be realized and carried into practice, and which they know they have power to controul. The femblance of a parliament has hitherto produced a national acquiefcence. But it will at length be found that a king ruling parlrament, or more truely the King being a cypher, and a minifter one of his fubjects ruling parliament and his fellow fubjects with the defultory defpotic and wild politics of the late rnnifters, who have foolifhly loft the King one third of his realm, and have plunged the kingdom into unmeaning wars, enormous, and oppreffive augmentations of the national debt ; I fay, at length it will be found that a King ruling parliament, and a King ruling without parliament, are one and the fame thing. And let the experiment be tried by any future King, that King Charles tried, and affuredly it will not fail to wake up the fpirit of 1641, and would as affuredly go the lengths of 1649, if tyranny could not be otherwife fuppreffed. Nothing but the certainty of its going thefe lengths, fecures England from the open unmodified defpotifm of monarchy. But Englifh Kings know where the matter would end, and fo their temerity is repreffed, and they are happily controuled. I appeal to all acquainted with the fpirit of Englifhmen from Alfred, and even from Cæfar to this day , I appeal to half the tories themfelves, for toryifm remains as vigorous in this as the laft century : I appeal to the united and collective body of the whigs, as well thofe who difapprove or approve of it—whether they have the leaft doubt of fuch an iffue in fuch a conflict, and on the fuppofed experiment repeated on the nation ? Such an experiment would not fail to bring the nation, though now quiefcent, to an explicit avowal and refumption of their old and never ddifcarded principles— principles, on which may be eftablifhed the juftification

T

of the Judges of Charles I. both as to the legality of the
court, and the juftice of their fentence.   Let fuch a
conflict and ftruggle, through the folly of princes, be
repeated a fecond and a third time, in diftant centuries,
and the point would at length be fettled as effectually, as
the demand of the commons kept up for ages; has at
length now for a long time fettled and finifhed the queftion of the equity and juftice, of their privilege, and right
to their place, power and importance in parliament.

How long was it contefted that the confuls fhould be
felected from the patrician order only, until at length
this honor was by the immortal Cicero opened to the
plebeians and became no more controverted? Other mutations of power have required long and diftant periods.
How long after the efficacious fettlement of the Saxons
in England before the coalefcence of the Saxon Heptanly
under Alfred? How long before the admiffion of the
commons as a diftinct order into the Wittena gemot?
How long before the Norman parliament fucceeded the
legiflature inftitued by Alfred? How long before the
immemorial principle of the Saxon government, that no
property fhould be taxed without the confent of its
Lord or owner, could be gotten to be extended to the
commons after that great property had fhifted into Plebeian poffeffion? The fame obfervation holds refpecting
the mutations in law and policy, many of which have
required ages for their eftablifhment, as is manifeft in
the effect which the act of parliament had *de donis con-
ditionalibus*.   It has taken ages to educe and fettle fome
points and principles of national juftice, which at length
ceafe to be controverted, are now acquiefced in by all,
and are become firmly eftablifhed principles in the public polity, though for a time condemned and reprobated.
And with how much difficulty have many long eftablifhed principles of jurifprudence as well as polity had to
ftruggle, and while many have been loft in Norman and
other infractions; with how fevere and long a conflict
have fome furvived, and after living through many at-

tacks and ftorms, at length gained a fixt eftablifhment ?
Grotius, Puffendorf, and Montefquieu, and Vattel,
inform us of a number of thefe in various parts of Europe :
and Spelman, Selden and Blackftone, with the writers
on the Feudal Tenures, inform us the fame thing for
England. The taxation of foreign nations is to this
day without confent of fubject : a vigorous ftruggle for
ages has deforced this power from the crown in England :
but was it poffible, there remains enough in the prefent
ariftocracy to refume it. The impoffibility is the only
fecurity. What ftruggles have juries had with arbitrary power and crown law, once primeval and almoft
univerfal in Europe, now for ages abolifhed every where
except in England and Sweden : but in England and
the United States too firmly eftablifhed ever again to be
overthrown, and probably may be refumed through
Europe. Abfolute monarchs formerly feized and imprifoned fubjects at pleafure. How long time did it
take in England to deforce the conceffion from Kings,
that no man fhould be arrefted and imprifoned at the
will of the Prince, nor be arrefted but by law ? How
long to eftablifh the habeas corpus act and the bill of
rights ? Even now that thefe principles are eftablifhed
into law, we ftill daily fee the operative influence of
crown and minifterial efforts to evade, elude and defeat
thefe laws. So many pillar principles however of public right and juftice are at length become eftablifhed in
England by the bill of rights, that any great attack, any
direct effort for their fubverfion would coft an Englifh
fovereign the price not of his crown only, but of his
life. Thus alfo the right of fubjects to judge their
King will at length be univerfally acknowledged or not
fuffered to be difputed, after the prefent war of Kings
fhall have had its full courfe and termination, and a
few more royal Tyrants have had their deferts. In
fuch an exigence however unprovided with a regular
tribunal, either by prefcription and ufage or conftitution, the Englifh nation would find a way to originate,

institute, authorise and legitimate a tribunal which would dare to judge and execute justice on so great an occasion. Every such transaction would inure to the justification of Charles's Judges. The nation, or the spirit of the nation did it in the instance of Charles I. and they will ever repeat it and do it again in every similar emergency. They will not only assuredly do it, but will be more convinced that herein they should do right, as the United States are that they did right in the declaration of independency. Liberty has endured too successful a struggle with tyranny, and too firmly fixt the pillar principles of the constitution in England, ever to permit again their submission and subjugation to the tyranny of the houses of Stuart or Tudor, or to the haughty despotism of any other reigning family or line of Princes.

But it is said in the given case of Charles now before us, that the majority of parliament in 1647 were ready to enter into a pacification with the King. It is true. and they certainly had a right, that is authority to do this ; but they might have made a mistaken use of this power, and Oliver might have seen this mistake. Had they seen it as he and some other patriots did they would not have listened to the King's delusory proposals, which he certainly never intended to fulfil. The question is, what was in reality safe and for the public good at that time : not what was deemed to be so, for the wisest legislators or councils may be undesignedly and honestly mistaken. Now to investigate this, let us suppose that providence had continued the lives of all the members of the long parliament, and that the same members had always been chosen till 1688, and seen and acceded to the reconciliation of the King and the accessions of Charles II. and James II. and that Charles I. would have ruled, as all have no doubt he would have ruled, had he been conciliated. Now would they not have found themselves to have been deceived ? Would they not have acquired a conviction that they had erred, or

were going to err, in 1647, in voting that the King's
terms were a proper foundation for a treaty which was
safe to the liberties of the nation ? I think it may be left
with the moſt prejudiced advocates for Charles to judge
what would have been the opinion of the parliament
both lords and commons, in conſequence of forty years
experience of Stuart infidelity and intractibility.   They
would at once ſay that they were unwiſe to have receed-
ed from their firſt voting for the abolition of Kings,
that Oliver's judgment was right, that there was no
ſafety in truſting the King, and therefore he ought to
have been diſcarded as James II. was : that is, that
the judgment of the deſpiſed parliament was wiſe and
juſt.   And if ſo, they would be at no difficulty in judging that the acts of this parliament and of the judges
which acted under their authority were right.   Eſpecially as the vote of the parliament about to be put, preci-
pitated and neceſſitated the King's deſtruction, who
otherwiſe perhaps might have been permitted to abdicate
and eſcape.   But this alternative would have been cut
off by a vote for negotiating with him.   All are now
convinced that had the nation then pardoned the tyrant,
the tyranny would have been re-eſtabliſhed.   Why was
it not time then, and why not juſt to cut him off?

In all ſovereignties judiciary tribunals have been immemorially provided for the trial of criminal ſubjects,
from the loweſt plebeians to the higheſt nobles, and
dependent feudatory princes.   But an High Court of
Juſtice for the trial of delinquent Majeſty, has hitherto
been excluded from the politics, conſtitutions and laws
of nations.   The hereditary indefeaſible rights of Kings,
their inviolability, " the right divine of Kings to govern wrong, and their being unamenable to the laws,
and accountable only to God, have ſo prevailed among
ſovereigns, and the hereditary ariſtocracies moſt generally combined with them, that Kings have been effectually ſcreened and ſecured from judiciary trials.—
Theſe doctrines and principles have gained the force of
T 2

laws, by the deliberate opinions of many of the ableſt civilians and writers on polity and government, and by the ſolemn deciſions of learned and upright, but miſtaken Judges, until the iniquity of thrones has been eſtabliſhed by law, and this without remedy. All other wrongs have, or ought to have, a remedy by law, but regal injury and wrong are without remedy. In the future ameliorations and perfection of the public policies throughout Europe and the world, proviſion will doubtleſs be made, and tribunals conſtitutionally defined and eſtabliſhed for the trial of royal criminals, of ſupreme magiſtrates, emperors, kings, and ſovoreign princes. This æra is now commenced.

In the middle ages the pontifical power had uſurped ſuch an aſcendency, in all the ſtates of Europe, that cardinals, biſhops, and the digniſied clergy, became exempt from civil juriſdiction. "There have been times, ſays Vattel, when an eccleſiaſtic could not be brought before a ſecular tribunal for any crime whatever." It was once dangerous for a civil judge "to puniſh an eccleſiaſtic with death, though a rebel or malefactor.'—"Hiſtory affords a thouſand examples of biſhops, that have remained unpuniſhed, for crimes which coſt the lives of the greateſt lords. John de Braganza, King of Portugal, cauſed thoſe lords, who had conſpired his deſtruction, to be juſtly puniſhed; but he did not dare to put to death the Archbiſhop of Braga, the author of that deteſtable plot.' †

Ages of conflict and ſtruggle, between the ſecular and eccleſiaſtical powers, among the nations, produced and exhibited, at firſt a few rare examples of eccleſiaſtics, in capital caſes, rendered amenable to civil judicatorie. Similar inſtances were repeated and multiplied, until this amenability is at length recovered and eſtabliſhed through Europe. But Kings have hitherto eſcaped, and held themſelves as exempt from criminal

† Vattel's Law Nat. B. 1 C. 12.

judiciaries, as formerly were archiepifcopal malefactors.

A few more inflances of adjudications upon criminal Kings, will bring on the fame eflablifhment for them. And then the preceding examples of thofe tribunals, which have poffeffed the refolution and fortitude to do juftice to a delinquent monarch, will be contemplated with approbation, reverence and honor. Then the heroic and high example of the High Court of Juftice, which fat and paffed fentence upon King Charles I. will be recurred to and contemplated with calm impartiality. And however it hath been overwhelmed with infamy for a century and a half, it will hereafter be approved, admired and imitated, and the memoirs of thefe fuffering exiles from royal vengeance be immortalized.

Much has been faid concerning the mode of inftituting this court, and the authority of it when inflituted: And it has been generally condemned as irregular and illegal. All concur that extraordinary public exigencies neceffitate and juftify extraordinary meafures. All will allow that thefe extraordinary meafures may be fometimes violent, injurious, and inconfiftent with the public good, and fometimes wifely adapted to fecure the public welfare.

Criminal judiciaries may be erected by law and conflitution fuch are thofe of the Englifh nation for fubjects Thefe may be *flanding and permanent* tribunals, like that of the Areopagus at Athens, or the Senate of Carthage, or the Courts of Weftminfter, or they may be *occafionally inflituted* by the authority tacitly fuppofed to be vefted in the King, as was that for the trial of the regicides, 1660. The King had the power to inflitute Star Chamber and other courts *pro re natâ* through the realm This as all other powers may be abufed, or may be exercifed wifely. But whence Kings derived this power is not to be found. No man can trace the Englifh conftitution to writing. An explicit confent

to certain fundamental principles, or rights, has bee
at different times deforced from unwilling Kings; bu
even magna charta is not a complete fyftem of
rights and liberties. In its jumbled compofition,
contains, however, principles, which purfued to thei
extent and juft comprehenfion, would eftablifh the fyf
tem of univerfal right. The criminal code in particu
lar, and the courfe of adjudications in felonies and al
kind of crimes, for the commons and unenobled fub
jects, has been for ages well fettled in England. A
well eftablifhed is the criminal and judiciary laws for
the trial of nobles, though in a different mode. For
while in civil matters and the lower felonies they are ame
nable with other fubjects to the ordinary courts of juftice,
and efpecially to the fupreme courts of Weftminfter,
in high crimes and mifdemeanors, and in accufations
for treafon, they are by impeachments to be brought
before their *pares*, that is, a court of nobles, or the
whole houfe of the barons of the realm There is indeed no written conftitution for this, but immemorial
ufage has eftablifhed this mode of judiciary for nobles.
Juftice we may fuppofe is as well done in this as in any
other mode. And it might have been as well done by
tribunals, or felected nobles, inftituted *pro re natâ* by
the fovereigns themfelves alone, or by them and the
Houfe of Lords conjunctly, had ufage and cuftom eftablifhed it. Anv of thefe modes had been equally legal,
regular and authoritative. Provifion is however made
for an efficacious profecution of criminal nobles. And
it is well. Happy had it been, had ufage alfo eftablifhed a judiciary for Kings.

There have been great variations in the judiciaries of
nations in a fucceffion of ages: moft of which, though
feemingly irregular at firft, have at length grown into
regularity, and obtained with full and legal force, till
fuperfeded and laid afide for a new change, which has
been found by experience fome times for the public benefit, and fometimes to public detriment. We fee this

in the republics of Grece, and in that of Rome, and the ftates which arofe all over Europe † upon the diffolution of the Roman empire.

In the Roman government, "the judiciary power was given to the people, to the fenate, to the magif-ftrates, to particular judges," under various, combined and often changing modifications of authority. " The confuls had the power of judging after the expulfion of the Kings, as the prætors were judged after the con-fuls." Afterwards the confuls were " fatisfied with naming the judges and with forming the feveral tribu-nals.' " The Kings referved to themfelves the judg-ment of criminal affairs, and in this they were fucceed-ed by the confuls.   It was in confequence of this au-thority that *Brutus*, the conful, put his children, and all thofe who were concerned in the Tarquinian con-fpiracy, to death.   This was an exorbitant power."— This produced a new change in the criminal judiciary ; it gave rife to the Valerian law, by which it was made lawful to appeal to the people from every ordinance of the confuls that endangered the life of a citizen.   The confuls after this had no longer a power of pronouncing fentence in capital cafes againft a Roman citizen, with-out the confent of the people." But this was doubtlefs judged by the confuls and fenate as irregular, as was the high court of juftice, in 1649, by the Parliament of 1660. " In the firft confpiracy for the reftoration of the Tarquins, the criminals were tried by Brutus, the conful, in the fecond the fenate and comitia were af-fembled to try them."*

The Judges were chofen from the order of the Sena-tors till the time of the Gracchi Tiberius Gracchus ef-fected the change that they fhould be taken from the equeftrian order.   Some of thefe changes were for the public good, efpecially for the fecurity of life, others were not fo, but all legal.   I might fhew the fame

† *Montef.* Sp. *Laws.* B 27 and 28.
* *Montefq.* Sp. *Laws.* B. 11. C. 18.

mutations in the criminal judiciaries of Athens and Sparta, and of all ancient and modern ftates, and particularly in the Norman judiciary in England. And unjuftifiable violences have attended almoft all of them, at firft even the changes which have proved the moft wife and falutary. What ftruggles and violences has the conflict of Englifh liberty, that political jewel, endured from Alfred to this day, in the mutation of the Witena Gemot, the reduction of the Meycle Gemote, and the fubftitution and introduction of the commons to an efficatious participation in the Englifh parliament, or national council and legiflature. For ages thefe perfevering exertions of the public fpirit were reprefented and treated as refractory tumultuous and rebellious, by the Kings and Barons, while at length victory has declared on the fide of liberty, and the opprobrium of ariftocrats is taken off, and fucceeded by the approbation of the wife and the admiration of the world.

With the candid and liberal ideas which arife from a large, full and comprehenfive view and comparifon of the criminal judiciaries of nations, and the caufes and reafons which might have neceffitated and certainly brought about their changes, we may be prepared to make up an hiftorical judgment on the legality and juftifiablenefs or expediency of any given inftance, example, or event, either antient or modern, which may come under our contemplation. We may contemplate the inftance, or fhall I fay the inftances in England the laft century, with calmnefs and juftice. Certainly great were the exigencies in the conflict of liberty with royal tyranny. For the warmeft advocates for the Stuart family and high government, admit their government was a tyranny. Few contend but that the Englifh monarchy is a government by laws ; and that it is herein diftinguifhed from defpotifm, which is the government of a monarch by *will without law*. † The monarch of England, and originally all monarchs by their coronation oaths, are to rule not by will, but by the *laws*

† *Mac'q* V. 1. B. II. C. 4.

of the land, the *lex scripta* and *non scripta.* It remains
then for him to investigate these, and by these to rule.
His coronation oath obliges him to this: and a wise
King would wish no greater power. If therefore in his
avidity for power, he should transcend the limits and
boundaries of the laws, and by high and overt acts
should violate the laws and shew himself aspiring to a government of insidiousness and absolute will, he becomes
dangerous, and is guilty of a high crime, and a violation of this solemn pact with the community of his subjects. And if the crimes of subjects ought to be judged
and condemned, no one can shew a reason why this
great *crimen regale* ought not somewhere to find a trial,
judgment and condemnation also. But though the coronation oath implies that the violation of it should be
judged in some tribunal or other, yet this judiciary is
said not to be provided for in the English constitution.——
Be it so, though this is questionable; yet shall the patience of subjects endure the oppression of Kings forever?
Shall the cause of liberty be given up as lost and irre-
sumable? Can no expedient be found to remedy this
evil of Kings? Are subjects, are millions made for
Kings, or Kings for subjects, for millions? Is there
not wisdom and power enough in every sovereign state
to devise and execute this emancipation? And shall
they be deterred from the exertion, or such exertion
condemned for want of precedents, or provision in the
constitution, if such a political constitution can be
conceived? What principle of political or moral right
forbids their even originating a precedent in this instance? And this may be by one united effort or burst-
ing forth of the national spirit—or—if the body of the
nation, by intimidation or intriguing delusion, or a
junction of aristocratical official and other interests,
should be prevailed upon to hug their chains and sit still
in slavery. In such an exigency should some spirited
phalanx arise and spontaneously assume upon them the
vindication of liberty, rush on the throne and seize the

despot, what could be said against it? Even should they light upon him like bees, and fall upon him till he died, as did the citizens upon Phalaris of Agrigentum—this might be well—it certainly would be just. But should they in this tumultuous and dangerous exigency, retain such noble and manly possession of themselves, such controul and restraint of the public passion, as to withhold them from this sudden though merited violence, and so as to give opportunity of a fair and open trial, that the condemnation should proceed on real justice: and thereupon by their own assumed authority institute and erect, and empower a court of trial sufficiently qualified and numerous let the judges be men of common integrity, and discernment adequate to the determination of a plain matter of fact upon evidence—for let it be remembered this trial of a King for the breach of a coronation oath by overt acts, is not a *quæstio juris* which might require profound law knowledge, but a *quæstio facti*, as to which all the *boni homines*, the very elders of the gate, are competent judges : If such a court thus established and authorized, after a fair and open examination of evidences, should pass upon a King, that he is guilty of treason—and he be executed accordingly :—If this procedure should be had by those who voluntarily assumed the salvation of their country upon themselves, would they not honor their intrepidity, justice and patriotism, in the history of nations? Would they not have done a glorious work? Should the nation however through any fatal versatility, be again duped into the re-admission of tyranny, and throw opprobrium on their spontaneous benefactors and deliverers : would not their uncharged posterity, upon regaining liberty in a subsequent period, contemplate their memories with veneration? and the long protracted reproach be wiped away and turned into lasting honor and applause?

Let us then see whether any thing like this has been

difplayed in the civil wars of 1641, and the decollation of Charles I. 1649.

After feven years war againft his parliament and fub-jects he was at length apprehended, and undoubtedly ought to be tried by fome high court. Had both houfes of parliament mutually and unanimoufly concurred in inftituting and erecting fuch a court, we fhould not at this day queftion its legality, though no fuch provifion is made in the Englifh conftitution. Yet this affump-tion of power would have been acqu efced in. But this was not the cafe. In the diffonance of the houfes, in this great exigence, every one fees the caufe was gone, had there been no other expedient.

A tribunal might have been, erected as I have faid, in the conftitution , in *magna charta* , in long ufage, in an antecedent act of parliament completed with the King's affent, if fuch affent could even be fuppofed to have been obtained ,—Had this provifional court for the trial of Majefty, been defined to have been both houfes of parliament, or a fingle houfe, either of the lords or the commons , or a felected number of judges, nobles and commons mixt ; it might have been equally well, and none could have juftly difputed or doubted its legality. But no fuch provifion is made , every et-fort for this has been baffled , it has been kept off by the Kings themfelves, ever delicate and jealous of their prerogative of inviolability. Indeed in the hiftory of England there have been cafes, as I have faid, wherein parliament have affumed upon themfelves, to judge Kings and transfer hereditary fucceffions. But this was an affumption of exigence and neceffity, and not by virtue of written and defined conftitution. And when, as in the inftance of Charles, the parliament themfelves were divided, the affumption muft be left to others, or a criminal King go unpunifhed.

If juftice ought not to be eluded : and Kings ought to be tried, as few doubt it, it became neceffary that the

U

patriots fhould come forth openly, and honorably originate a court without precedent.   The refolution taken,
it became proper that the judicial procedure affumed
not by parliament, but by the fubjects of the community
at large, or by any refpectable affociated body of them,
or as in the prefent inftance by the army in concurrence
with the houfe of commons.—it became proper that
the procedure fhould be conformable to the regular and
ufual forms of the trial of ftate criminals, or perhaps in
the fame manner as the whole body of fubjects duly enlightened would, if convened, have approved, directed
and authorized.   It ought to be, a civil, not a military,
nor ecclefiaftical tribunal.   One may conceive various
modes of forming fuch a court.   If the whole legiflative order fhou'd have affumed and confidered themfelves empowered, or one houfe, or fhould a commiffion of felected individuals be pitched upon ; it might
be well.   Any and all of thefe are but fo many *modes of*
*a   *, would be regular and fufficient to fecure the
great end of a formal, open, fair, and impartial trial
and adjudication.   Each of them are at an equal remove both from anarchy and defpotifm.   And the authority o Judges acting on either of thefe modes of appointment would be equally legal and right in the eye
of eternal juftice and reafon, provided their decifions and
adjudications were founded in proof and juftice. A national tribunal of feven hundred and fifty Judges fyftematically appointed by the voice of twenty-five million
people, is indeed another mode of judiciary, and equally
legal, and according to the original law of nature and
reafon applied to the national ftate of fociety, regularly
empowered and vefted with full authority to fit in judgment and pafs fentence on a King   A legal and juft
tribunal, even one filled with able and upright Judges,
may err, may judge wrong, may judge right.   The
high court which fat on Charles, I confider as legal in
that rational exigency.   There remains then only to
confider, whether their judgment was right ? Whether

it was that, which a suppofed unqueftionably legal court ought to have rendered ? This is all the queftion that is worth the attention of civilians and nations. However both the regularity of this high court, and the juftice of its fentence may be further confidered.

The public fenfe may be miftaken, it may alfo be right The judgment upon this muft be configned and demandated to pofterity and the calmer ages. There is however a right. The public councils may not always be poffeffed of this right : they may hold it a long time they may be perverted, corrupted, deluded to their ruin. Nations as well as factions have been deluded, and afterwards corrected themfelves. It took the nation forty years to learn by dear bought experience, that a treaty or compact with the Stuart family was nugatory. Inwrought in them and indelible were principles totally incompatible with the Saxon Englifh ideas of public right and national liberty.

Was the parliamentary war of 1641 right ? Few Englifhmen will dare to deny it. Let the caufe then, for which they fought, be confidered as juft and defenfible. By 1648 the fame national council, which had, with heroic fortitude purfued the vindication of liberty, partly by becoming tired out with war, partly by the impolitic divifions and alienations of contending fects, but principally by corrupting intrigue, became difheartened, and were going to give up the caufe, and return to their former vaffalage. They were hearkening to, and were daily ripening for a clofure with the infidious offers and promifes of a King, who, as all the world now believe, would have certainly deceived them, and have refumed his former tyranny, as did his fon at the reftoration. The army and a numerous body of the nation, probably an intereft equal to three quarters of the nation, or that united body confifting of the eftablifhed church and diffenters which afterwards became diftinguifhed by the appellation of the Whigs, the great faviours and vindicators of liberty at the revolution, and the fupporters of the Prince of Orange and the Hanoverian Family to this day, and the only prefent defenders of liberty in the Englifh nation : I fay they only and a numerous body of patriots both in and out of parliament faw the fnare, dreaded the lofs of liberty, and wifh'd an effort for the falvation of the nation from Stuart flavery. They boldly did that which was done at Rome in the inflance of Tarquin, at Agrigent in that of Phalaris, and what the parliament did at the revolution, and America and France have done in recent inflances. They adventured upon an extraordinary meafure, which preffing exigencies only juflified, and which, as of neceffity it muft have been, was devious from the ordinary courfe of redreffing evils, and according to the long ufage and the eftablifhed courfe of criminal procefs, illegal. Thus one people illegally deprived a King of Rome, another inftituted an illegal Congrefs, and the Englifh patriots illegally did that, which ought to have been done by the conftitution—they made a high court of juftice for the trial of a King, who was in the conviction of all men, by his folly and tyranny, the caufe of all their calamities.

The commons at this time might confift of three hundred bofides the fecluded members. The awfulnefs of the work they were going upon, not the army (which however defired but a few) fo intimidated them, that though a quorum yet fewer than fifty members were prefent at fall meeting, and nominating a high Court of Juftice, confifting of one hundred and thirty Judges. This act of the commons was non concurred by the reft of the Lords Houfe, which to defeat the work, adjourned to a different day. The commons deferted by the lords, did that in this exigency, which both lords and commons had done when deferted by the King, they took the matter upon themfelves, as did both lords and commons again without the King afterwards at the revolution 1688, when they invited the Prince of

Orange, approaching them alſo with an army. Both
according to uſual forms illegal and irregular, both legal and regular from the extreme preſſure of the occa-
ſions.

Inſtead of queſtioning then the legality of the high
court, inſtituted with this original deliberate formality,
reſolution and ſolemnity, the attention of poſterity and
the world ſhould be called only to two things, the *ability*
and qualifications of the Judges, and to the *juſtice* or
injuſtice of their ſentence. As to their abilities ; if
ſome were of as ſlender abilities as even the nobility of
all nations generally are, which they were not, the
moſt rigid and prejudiced muſt all own that there were
men in this commiſſion of capacities ſufficient to conduct a court-trial with jural dignity and impartiality,
ſufficient for an accurate examination of evidence and
judging on facts, and ſufficiently learned in the law to
judge on treaſon in ſo plain a cauſe, where fortitude was
more wanting than great abilities. Abilities however
they had. There was a Serjeant Bradſhaw, a Lord
Grey, a Harriſon, a Temple, a Haſlerigg, a Whalley, a Lord Say and Seal, a Blackiſton, a Ludlow, an
Ireton, a CROMWELL, and an ample ſufficiency of
others abundantly adequate to the work. Let not the
abilities of the Court then be doubted. I will ſay little
on the *juſtice* of their judgment or *ſentence*, but leave
every one to himſelf. Had it paſſed on a duke or a
marquis upon the ſame proofs of treaſon, it would have
been approved of by all men. A King of England,
that, diſſolving the Parliament, dares to rule the Kingdom without the Parliament, for twelve years, and
without their conſent deforce loans, levy ſhip money,
and be guilty of the other arbitrary and oppreſſive enor-
mities, which, by the united and uncontroverted teſtimony of all the hiſtories of thoſe times, King Charles I.
was guilty of : ſuch a King by an impartial and juſt
tribunal, ought to be judged guilty of treaſon, *tradiq*
libertatis juriumque reipublicæ. And if plebeian and na-

U 2

bility treafon merits death, royal treafon or fovereign ... ade again the ftate, moft juftly merits *tyrannic di-* ..., or the d... ... deaths. Charles might have been a faint ... for a ... canonization, and Garga... re ... ... that all ... are real faints, and fo was Thomas ... Becket, and if he was the author of the *Icon-Ba-filica*, ... to heaven, but he was an arbitrary, haughty and tyrannical monarch. But had he for his fuppofed though dubious piety, merited all the high eulogiums which have been annually lavifhed upon his memory, had his moral character been immaculate, ... fo fincerely principled in defpot... ... ... atrocious and arbitrary were the overt acts of an erroneous mind, fo enormous and intolerable the violences and oppreffions of his government, which was one continued tiffue of folly and tyranny, one incefant ufurpation in civil rights and religious liberty, that he loft and extinguifhed the confidence of his fub-ject, excited national hatred and horror, forfeited his crown, and ... ... merited his deplorable and exempla-ry ... ... However it required a fingular fortitude to ... forth, and refolutely do that great work of public juftice. It was done. And it was well done.

The ftate and fpirit of the parties in thefe times was ... ... The Diffenters, at leaft a fifth part of the realm of England, were indeed fomewhat divided, but collectively friends to civil and religious liberty. At the beginning of the war, the Parliament was generally Epifcopal, but difgufted with the tyranny of bifhops courts, the difputations which led them to vote out the bifhops from the houfe of lords, terminated inevitably in Independancy, not but that they would have preferred Epifcopacy or even Monarchy, had it been mode-rated ... ... to civil liberty, on which they were ... ... Rather than give up civil li-berty, they ... ... both Epifcopacy and Monarchy ... ... the Venetian Republic admitted ... ... retained in their ... ...

hearts to both. For a time, however, these ideas pervaded three-fourths of the inhabitants of England, who were thus united in republican ideas. Church and Dissenters thus coincided and coalesced in the defence of liberty. The rest of the nation were loyalists and high church, and never changed nor moderated; but they were a minority, though a brilliant, a powerful and invidious minority. The revolution broke up the union of church and dissenters, detached the church patriots into union with high church and loyalists, and left the dissenters alone. The body of the church were moderated and ordered from the high church, not only as to episcopacy, but as to high principles of civil government, and did not pretend to doubt the rights of mankind even to controul Kings. This produced a few writings in which a vigorous political controversy was raised on among themselves on the principles of civil and ecclesiastical government. Many of these masterly writers did honour to that age, and wrought up the fundamental great principles of liberty in a limited monarchy. Besides, this interest was uniformly Protestant. The high exertions of prerogative, and the dangerous Popery of James II. brought on again a coalescence of the friends of liberty, church and dissenters, loyalists, high church and patriots united by themselves, out of the body of whom sprung up that large coalescence, which at length received the malevolent appellation of Whigs, an invidious name given to the most reasonable body of the church of England, most of whom gave the name of Tories to the high church and loyalists, now united, and those royalists who, whatever their religion, were advocates for the divine right of Kings, their indefeasible hereditary right, and were lovers of, and agents in arbitrary measures, and for paying every obedience in common to the people and ...... the ...... a ...... the church were involved in ...... which of the reign, to their alliance.

And though they had been duped and solemnly deceive
at the restoration, yet upon the promise of redress the
joined the whigs, and this reconjoined force became a
impregnable bulwark for liberty, against papacy, an
the royal or crown interest of despotism, effected th
revolution. But the poor dissenters were again forgot
ten, and have been forgotten ever since, while in ever
exigency and party, again in Queen Anne's time, ar
the Hanoverian accession, they never failed to jo
in the cause of civil liberty. An unparalleled instanc
of persevering fidelity to the rights and liberties of Eng
land—while they themselves continue to this day, th
the most hearty and genuine protestants, deprived o
civil liberty, and disfranchised from all civil affairs thro
the realm. Now all this has grown out of the spirit o
1641. The body of the nation, the minority of tories
only excepted, have all along down to the present day
been, and still are such firm friends to civil liberty, that
they will never give it up. And the prerogative having
acquired strength in a new mode since 1688, by corrupting both houses of parliament by peerages, pensions, and distributions of a system of lucrative offices,
the nation is preparing and ripening for a new burst of
the spirit of liberty, and a rectification or purification of
the national parliament, which will assuredly take place—
The ... the houses, ... the con-
... leading the nation to
... privileges, will convince them that, however de-
..., it must sooner or later be done; and that the
... have no authority to make the constitution,
... part of it, on which they stand themselves,—
they will therefore see the necessity of a national convention, empowered by the people for the express purpose of receiving, altering and amending it. And
when they shall be assembled, who can say how far
they will go? They will go so far as to put an effectual stop to the possibility of the parliament being
bought up by the crown.—This will bring on not only

the modification of the commons, but of the lords, an exchange of hereditary for an elective aristocracy, and as tend to the touching of sovereignty itself; and as England is a mixt monarchy, controulable by law, magna charta and parliament, the King's power of appointing all officers, civil, military and ecclesiastical, must necessarily be restricted and modified, One cannot see how many changes may take place. Twenty years ago the parliament might have reformed themselves, and the people would have acquiesced This is now become impossible, or, if parliament should do it, it will only bring on those national agitations on the occasion of their power, which will terminate in a national convention A revolution in Britain is certain, and all the policy of the ministry cannot avoid it. All this is grown, and will grow, out of the parliamentary war, 1641.

It is necessary to trace out this state of the political parties in order to discern the mistake of the cardinal friends of civil liberty, and the temporary change this mistake produced in the time of the Protectorate, and in order to judge whether Oliver discerned and judged right or wrong, and also whether the execution of the King, even suppose it to have been contrary to the then mistaken sense of the nation, was what posterity ought to approve or disapprove. For certainly this event, with the subsequent violent dissolution of parliament, and elevation of Cromwell to the protectorate, with the apprehension that the nation was about to be ruled by a standing army, were among the principal causes that effected the discordance and alienation of the public sentiment, and reconciled the nation to a return to monarchy, and to concur in a general obloquy upon those times, as a period of the grand rebellion. We do not sufficiently distinguish between the general obloquy; both tories and whigs agreeing in obloquy, but meaning very different things. While both agreeing in general, though not univerfally, in anathematizing the execu-

tion of the King and the administration of the protecto
ate, the genuine whigs in all successions to this day
would never suffer or endure that the parliamentary re
sistance to Charles I. should be stigmatized or vilifie
with any aspersions. They to this day give the par
liament and patriot army co-operating with them, th
highest applauses, the firmest and most decided justifi
cation · not sufficiently yet adverting or considering tha
in reality, what will justify them, will justify the whole
course of procedure through the protectorate, until th
giving up the cause at the restoration. When the par
liament altered their minds, the army became formida
ble, not before.

Through the whole period from 1641 to 1660, the
army continued faithful and uniformly devoted to the
republican interest for which they took up arms, till
corrupted by Monk, the Dumouriei of Britain. The
parliament stood firm for the republican cause six years,
they began to waver in 1647, when there was no need
of it, and when they had already accomplished their
end, and thereby endangered the cause. The patriot
army stood firm, interposed, and gave the finishing
stroke to tyranny. But four years after, instead of establishing the liberty they had gained, by a certain fatality
attending the noblest cause, mistaken ideas of perpetuity became conspicuous in many truly sincere and patriotic characters in parliament, and manifested itself in
bringing forward a bill for filling up vacancies only, in
the commons or parliament, by the people, as they tell,
instead of dissolving themselves, and calling triennial
parliaments, or otherwise establishing a liberal constitution. Thus the national government would soon
have grown up, into a polity, not very dissimilar to the
Venetian aristocracy, and very abhorrent from that for
which the nation and army, and parliament itself, had
taken up arms and so vigorously contended What did
the public good require in this exigency ? This defection from the original grand cause of liberty first seized

the parliament, *not the army*, which perfevered, keeping the firft great object accurately in view. Without
any umbrage given by the *army, ever faithful to the
rational intereft*, and the caufe of liberty, for which they
had taken up arms, the *parliament firft conceived without reafon a jealoufy of the army*, the only or principal
obftacle to their afcending into this noxious ariftocracy.
This miftaken jealoufy began the alienation and oppofition between the army and, parliament. The army
had fhewn no difpofition either to perpetuate themfelves
or to fubjugate the parliament. They continued faithful fervants to the parliament till they perceived by the
overt act they were about to pafs, which tended to, and
inevitably would have terminated in perpetuating themfelves For themfelves, the army might have been
fecure under fuch perpetuation, but the caufe of liberty,
all muft fee, was gone. They faw it. How ought
they to act as a patriotic army ? They were not dangerous to the nation, nor to a polity ftanding on the election of the people. At the fame time ideas friendly to
monarchy were growing and prevailing in parliament :
all which was laying the foundation of that coalefcence
of republicans and loyalifts, which Oliver had the faga-
city to forefee would defeat all, and that the republicans
would be duped and deluded by the royalifts, finally
to bring in Majefty Both thefe parties now joined in
expreffing loudly their fears of the army, and by irri-
tating themfelvs with fanciful, with fhadowy, and ideal
dangers, rendered the great work of the confervation
of regained liberty exceedingly critical and difficult.

How miftaken thefe alarms were, are better judged
by pofterity and the world, than by the patriots themfelves, in the day of deception. The generality of
the nation faw it, even in that day, as appears from
their acquiefcing and rejoicing at the violent diffolution
of the long patriotic parliament , and we in this day
fee the miftake, in not calling a new parliament immediately upon the death of the King. To fuch a par-

liament, undoubtedly the army would have been faithful and obedient, in every thing but the recalling
King. But a perpetuating parliament must feel an a-
larm from an army originally raised against the continuance and perpetuation of any power, whether royal,
aristocratical or parlimentary, beyond a period necessary for redress of grievances, when the general public
object was a settlement of public liberty. But as I said
these alarms were without foundation : and were so seen
by . . . part, the minority of parlament, and
by . . . al. We can now more easily
. . . were suspicious without just foun-
da . . . could Nor would the
pa . . . which apprehensions, had they
not . . for . . rents charged I believe at
first w . . honest, but mistaken, judgment.
Th . . friends of liberty, even at this day,
c . . . apprehensions respecting the danger
. . . be permitted as patriot, to say,
. . . been freed from such terrors
and . . .

A army . . . probably be dangerous to an elective
repub . . . be supported by the electors or
people. The . . . by withholding pay and
supp es, . . . liberate and divide even the vet-
eran army . . . Casar . . . they, like his, turn
the arms . . . let it be remembered that the
English forces . . . composed of hereditary or
perpetual . . . was, or ought to have been
elective . . . Casar have succeeded, had the
patrician . . Iy elective, or had the people been . . . request election of
th . . . of the consuls Had
O . . . dear pai d sup-
p . . . on the com-
. . . commonshi in a single
. . . racy the po
. . . ds of England, either in the

or in freehold tenancies for life or lives, they would have met a warm reception, and would have begun a contest which would have assuredly terminated in their overthrow and dissolution. It will prove next to impossible for a standing army to establish conquest over an elective republic, or to overlay the liberties of a people among whom property is equally diffused.— Even in a monarchy this cannot be effected unless a great portion of the feudal system remains in its constitution. Indeed whatever be the policy, whether monarchical or republican, of a nation possessed of diffusive freehold property, it can never be lastingly subjugated either by a foreign or domestic army. The diffusion of property among so great a part of the people of France, by secularizing the church lands to the amount of one quarter of the whole territory of France, and the allodial distribution of it among the peasants or occupants, will engage so large a body to defend their possessions, as will effectually secure their liberties and republican independency. This policy will effectually and permanently furnish a spontaneous host of bold, courageous, and unconquerable defenders. Property has been so diffused among the commons of England, that it has not been in danger from armies for several ages. The commons will fight *pro agris* as well as *pro aris & focis.* The relict of a tenure of property somewhat similar to the feudal system, tenancies at will or for terms, retained a foundation of danger; but already is such an aggregate of property floated into the hands of substantial yeomanry as will prove an effectual barrier against the conquest by armies interior or exterior. Cromwell wisely filled his army with substantial and hardy yeomanry. And whenever the yeomanry are invaded, it may be assured they will stand on their defence.

The original reasons of the beautiful feudal system have ceased in Europe. It was excellently adapted to hold the dominion of a conquered country, but now the conquerors and conquered are become mixt and incorporated together, throughout Europe, the reason of the policy ceases ; and it would work no mischief or injustice to the holders of fiefs, or danger to the public, if the heirs were diffolved, and fales were permitted, which would foon alienate and diffuse the property, and render it allodial. Let the peafants of Poland be vefted with allodial property, and they may be trufted with Prufia, Aultria and Ruffia : and I fhould not doubt their refumption of liberty. See the effect of this allodial tenure of land in America. We have been witneffes that in thirty hours from the moment of fhedding the firft blood at Lexington, thirty thoufand fubitantial free-holders were fpontaneoufly in arms, and in full march from all parts of New-England. Let the experiment be tried all over the world, and the effect will be the fame. Freehold property has too much footing in England, after all the great aggregate of tenancies at will or for years, without reference to day-laborers, mechanics and manufacturers, of no property, to permit ultimate danger from armies.

It is among thefe that an army muft be fought for efficacious defence. Ten thoufand of thefe are worth three times the number raifed in the ufual manner of confcribing venal armies. This, much more than religion, was the fecret of the invincibility of Olivers and the American army. Thefe had a motive to fight for liberty and property. France has now got enough of thefe men to defend her republic. And they will do it effectually.

But the contemplation of the Alexandrine, Roman, Ottoman, and other national armies, has occafioned the ableft civilians, the moft firm and enlightened friends of liberty, to be greatly terrified with the danger and fear of armies, and to anticipate their exertion of conftitutions, as in foreign nations and ancient ages, not fufficiently perhaps, adverting to that which has rendered them dangerous, the impolicy of forming great divifions of landed property into fiefs, fo as to be occupied by the body of inhabitants in a very depend- ant tenure.   There needs no agrarian law, arbitarily to make a new divifion of territory, and give it away from the old poffeffors, and diftribute the property of great land holders among the people.   Let the Triuariots of Turkey, the Barons of Germany, the Staroftas of Po- land, be only permitted by law to fell and alienate, let there be a public law that entails fhall terminate, and fiefs and all hereditary property fhall veft in the prefent poffeffors in what the Englifh law calls fee fimple , and in lefs than a century fo much of the territorial property will become allodial, or transfered from the hereditary nobleffe and ariftocrats to the common people, or to the community at large, as will render them unconquera- ble, and beyond the danger of armies, efpecially if the citizens of the community be formed into militia, or even if the citizens are not prohibited arms.   The game act in England, in the time of James I and in France in the time of Henry IV. operated completely to dif- arm the common people.   The repeal of this, and the abolition of laws reftricting the people all over Europe from purfuing wild game, defigned by the God of na- ture to be untamed and unappropriated, and like the air or ocean free for the common ufe of all mankind, and the people would foon be armed.   An armed people are capable of being formed into a defenfibility which would preferve them from invafion.   Even Oliver's army would not be dangerous to a country whofe inha- bitants were poffeffed of diffufive property, and were regularly formed into a fyftematical militia.   I know indeed that many of the beft and wifeft patriots, and the firmeft friends of liberty are of a different opinion, and I muft therefore fubmit it.   I myfelf confider Oli- ver's army powerful and victorious, but not dangerous to liberty in England, though they were fo to Scotland and Ireland, in the unjuftifiable war he carried on in thofe two kingdoms.   And here I wifh to infit this, general apology. If there fhould be any miftakes in thefe hiftorical touches, and ftatements, they can be eafily corrected by referring to the authorities. To this correction I do and ought readily to fubmit, as I write more from the refult and recollection of former reading, than from recent reviews of the hiftories.

Oliver is generally confidered as a tyrant and an ufurper, full of religious enthufiafm, and of unexampled diffimulation in religion and politics. The time has been when I entertained fuch ideas, not from the Clarendons, the Sacheverels and Atterburys, but from the Hollifes, the Hales, the Barnets and the Lockes. And yet upon more thoroughly entering into the genius and fpirit of his character, I have altered my fentiments. With refpect to diffimulation, I never found a man freer from it. Indeed, like all difcerning and wife men, in different circumftances, upon new views and upon new evidences he altered his mind; but when he uttered himfelf he never diffembled, he fometimes concealed, but when he fpake, he ever fpake his mind, and no man more decifively and unequivocally. _ s my cc.r n ., underftood Oliver ; they dreaded him, but they knew what he meant, and what is more, without deception, they relied upon it that he intended to act, and ftill more that it would be done. He was ever clearly underftood. Unambiguous precifion, clearnefs and perfpicuity were apparent in all his public fpeeches. By his bold and mafterly generalfhip, by his fubtilty and difcernment, he eluded the intrigues and ftratagems of his numerous potent enemies. He could not have accomplifhed it by hypocrify. He did it by well concerted and deep policy. He was a match for the world, and efpecially for all the cabinets of Europe. He led others to deceive themfelves, but he never deceived them. Hypocrify was unnatural to him, it was fuperior to his own nature. He needed it not.— He was too decifive and open in religion to need hypo ... in grave ... the rel grounds. They

knew him well, and they had his heart, and he had
theirs · and he was too wife to expend a ufelefs hypocrify upon thofe who could never be brought into his
meafures. Away then with the ftupidity of charging
Oliver with hypocrify. He had too much courage to be
a hypocrite in religion or politics.

As to his religion he was a fincere Puritan. In his
youth, while at the univerfity, and until aged twenty-
five, he was thoroughly vicious and debauched, unprincipled in morals, of turbulent, of haughty and ferocious manners, and abandoned to all licentioufnefs.
He was then feized by the energy of Omnipotence, and
fo ftrongly impreffed with the awful folemnities of religion and eternity, as effectually changed his heart, gave
a new and decided direction to the purpofes of his life,
reformed his morals, and recovered him to exemplary
piety, in which he refolutely perfevered through life,
unfullied, unpolluted by vice, by the fplendor of courts,
or by the luxurious living ufually attendant upon the
elevation to which he afcended. Like a citizen of the
univerfe, he was ever feeking the Lord, as did King
David, and, the lord chief juftice Hale. If the ten
Kings of Europe had now a pious David among them,
who was always finging pfalms, praifing God, praying
and feeking the Lord, as that religious King ufed to do,
they might denounce him an enthufiaftic religious
hypocrite, with as much juftice as Oliver. ſ Ought
Daniel to be afhamed of worfhipping the God of heaven,
left he fhould incur the imputation of hypocrify, which
he certainly would have done in the licentious deiftical
age of Charles II. ? Shall Oliver be vilified for feeking wifdom at the Fountain of Wifdom ? At leaft is
not one hundred and fifty years long enough to caft reproach and derifion upon a man for afking counfel of
his God upon every important emergency ? Good God!
fhall it be a difgrace for mortals to fupplicate thy throne ?
Or do we find ourfelves in a part of the creation, where
it is infamy and reproach for a finite limited mind to

confult Infinite Wifdom and unerring rectitude? O Oliver! how I love thine open, thine unabafhed, thy undiffembled and undifguifed religion!

He believed in the moral government of the Moft High, regarded it, and reverenced it. He believed the grand leading principles of it were difplayed and developed in at leaft one fingle inftance, the feries of the divine treatment of the Hebrew nation, which he had felected as a fpecimen of his whole moral government of nations, and of the univerfe itfelf, and particularly as an example, in which all might look, and thence form a decided judgment of God's actual treatment of all nations, all fpontaneous fovereignties, however formed, that it fhould be, always had been, and always would be moft exactly according to their moral ftate for religion and virtue, or the reverfe. As he believed, fo he really faw God carrying on this government among all nations and that the rectification of the moral ftate of a people, and fuppreffing vice and irreligion, was co-operating with God, and ought to be the pole-ftar of political fovereigns. Hence he ftudied the law of the Lord, an antiquated work, very valuable it might be fuppofed as iffuing from Infinite Wifdom, a work however like the antient Digeft of Juftinian, grown obfolete and very little attended to by modern civilians and princes, but like the Pandects when found at Amalfi, greatly valued. The facred Pandects were deeply ftudied by Oliver, to learn from thence the principles by which the fovereign monarch would govern a nation, govern a univerfe, and as the great exemplar for his fubordinate imitation. Thus he ftudied the principles of the divine government in the BIBLE, which was the man of his counfel, as it was David's, rather than in the unprincipled deiftical views of the ftate of nations, in which he could learn little more than the corrupt and diabolical principles of a machiavelian policy. If at any time miftaken, he made it however his ultimate view and endeavor, to act his part under the God of heaven with integrity and fidelity, and with unawed refolution to profecute this, and at all events in his perfonal and governmental character to approve himfelf to his God. In great and numerous inftances he appears to have been the felf denying and difintereft-ed patriot He acted with a magnanimity, a purity and greatnefs of character, in many trying inftances, fcarcely to be equalized. He was a Phoenix of ages.—The more his character is examined, even with the feverity of the moft rigid, but difpaffionate juftice, the more will this idea force itfelf upon us, and evince that it will live and fhine with a permanent and abiding glory This for his *religion* and *hypocrify.*

Oliver is ridiculed for ftudying the fcriptures, and efpecially for modeling his laws and government by them. Unhappily this is too much confidered as abfurd and ridiculous by chriftian civilians and politicians, who fincerely take the Bible indeed for the directory to heaven, but not for civil life, and leaft of all for law and government. With avidity we feize the fcattered fcraps and reliquiæ of the antient legiflators, and the law codes of ftates and nations. With avidity we learn wifdom, we learn the principles of law and government, from the hiftories of nations, from the fragments of the XII tables, of the inftitutes of Numa Pompilius, of Lycurgus, Solon, Zoroafter, and Confucius, and even of the profoundly wife code of the Gentoo laws. All whofe inftitutes, however, alfo pretended to have been of divine original, yet by European civilians are now univerfally confidered as founded in the refearches and inveftigations of reafon, often fallible, various and contradictory

The Edda, Offian, any reliquiæ of the inftitutes of Odin, are read with admiration Could a book of the Druids be found, purporting to be two thoufand years old and written by a Druid, as the Penteteuch by Mofes, defcribing the facrifices and priefthood, the laws and history of the Druidical fyftem, a Burgoyn would lay hold of it with rapture, and would neither blufh nor difdain to learn from thence the office of priefthood, though defpifing the Mofaic and Chriftian priefthood. And even Hume, Gibbon, Voltaire and Roffeau would read it with avidity and admiration, and deduce from thence with triumph as from the Koran a contraft for the depreciation of chriftianity.

With entirely greater juftice might we admire and profit by the code of Bramin laws, as delivered by the Pundits and learned Jurifts of India, in which are to be found many excellent principles of law and equity as well as good government, worthy to be adopted into the jurifprudence of other nations. Could we find the code of Affred it would be read with valuable inftruction. If the reading and admiration of thefe antique compofitions, are applauded as indicating high tafte and difcernment, why fhould the reading of the facred code be reprehended. In the Mofaic code, if we except the ftatutes peculiar to the fucceffions in family inheritances, in the tribal divifions of territory, and the facrificature, there will be left a very valuable body of laws of contracts and commutative juftice, as well as of criminal law, having the advantage of being afcertained by God to be founded in eternal reafon, and the unerring immutable laws of nature. It muft therefore be worthy of the contemplation of political governors and judges who are fincerely defirous of invefligating and eftablifhing righteoufnefs and juftice in their adminiftration. To Deifts this would be of no moment, but to Revelationifts and Chriftians muft be of unfpeakable value and confolation. With peculiar profit and advantage might Kings and fovereign rulers look to the character of David and Jehofaphat, Vizirs and Prime Minifters to that of Daniel, and Judges to that of Samuel, and emulate the virtues of their examples, avoiding the vices and errors wherein they were difapposed of God ; and imitating their excellencies and virtues : with the singular heartfelt consolation of knowing with precision that herein they are so far acting to the approbation of the Most High, by whom Kings reign and Princes decree justice. Judge Hale was thus actuated. If a human system of national law, the principles of polity and govermental administration well digested, and compiled on the experiment and wisdom of ages, be thought worthy the study of a Judge, a Staesman and Legislator, or Politician, how infinitely more worthy of our study and contemplation a code of divine law and jurisprudence, could we find such an one infused by God for any nation on earth? Oliver found such an one, he saw this in that of the Hebrew nation. And under this view, deceived or not, how consistent and rational and just for him to study it with the greatest diligence? For besides that it ascertains, as he was weak enough to believe, the way to a better world, it gives innumerable important declarations and decisions in national law and equity, educes the principles of justice in numerous great law cases, with a divine attestation and ascertainment, thereby superadding a weight, of which the pandects and laws of all other nations are destitute. In the bible we are not only ascertained of laws, but *government*. Of what immense advantage is it that, in the general examples of Kings and rulers and statesmen, even under all the human corrupt mutilations of the original polity given by God, we may learn what Kings and Potentates may and may not, ought or ought not to do, what God has approved and what disapproved, in civil, military, and political administration, and what sovereigns and subordinate rulers, in what manner soever elevated to rule and dominion, ought to consult government, both for the welfare of society, and the acceptance of the Most High. I will not commit myself, nor surrender my discernment, I will not temporize so much in an excess of compliance to others, though on the first erudition, and higheſt literary and profeſſional abilities, as to make Revelation a queſtion. They well know, how much ſoever they may ſmile at our credulity, that we believe it with firmneſs, and that there are among believers men of equal abilities, and even of ſuperior, more profound, and more comprehenſive erudition: nor are they to conceive that they monopolize all the fair inquiry in the world. I ſhould as readily ſurrender the demonſtrations of the Newtonian philoſophy and aſtronomy, as the demonſtrations of revelation to fanciful philoſophic theoriſts and viſionaries. We have not followed cunningly deviſed fables in believing the ſyſtem of revelation. For a ſtate or civilian that believes it, ſhall it be turned to their reproach, that they attend to it and uſe it accordingly? that it ſhould become the daily uſe both of Princes and ſubjects? a uſe, which the diſciples of Confucius and Rouſſeau would themſelves applaud and announce worthy to be adopted and recommended, the moment they ſhould ſee it as we do, a divine Verity. Let Oliver then be no longer reviled for reverencing the law of his God, as a *legiſlator and politician*, as well as a *chriſtian.*

And as to his *tyranny*; let us once be determined, that the diſſolution of the long parliament was juſt and neceſſary; neceſſity will then require ſome character to do it, and that ſome ſuch head ſhould ariſe to do the work, and aſſume the government. Thus neceſſity required the American reſiſtance to parliament; neceſſity required a Congreſs, an Adams, a Hancock, a Randolph, a Jefferſon, a Rutledge, a pious Gadſden; neceſſity required, legitimated and juſtified the act of independency, and the diſmemberment of the United States from the Britiſh empire. Oliver was elevated to the ſovereignty of the commonwealth by a neceſſity, both as it reſpected himſelf perſonally, and the republic, which precludes and annihilates all ideas of uſurpation He enterprized, and by his fortitude united with heroic wiſdom, he did that, which, in a polity unviolated by its governors and administrators, would have been usurpation, but in this infracted and tumultuous period, was a glorious deliverance, rescue, and conservation of liberty. He seized the helm and saved the ship, when the course its pilots steered was to certain ruin and destruction. At one bold stroke he destroyed the perpetuation of the parliament, and left all open for a free republican establishment. And it was soon manifest that this dissolution was very grateful and acceptable to the great majority of the people. Thus he brought the nation to the very object of the parliamentary war. Every thing was now open and prepared for the nation to form its own constitution, founded on the rights and liberties of the people. But the nation was not ripe for deliverance. It was not ripe for the unnatural union and consolidation of the three kingdoms, on which, as to subjugation by force, Fairfax was right and Oliver erred. It was ripe for a republican polity for England, and no more at that time. But the necessary light and wisdom was withheld from them. The comprehensive views of Cromwel and the patriots grasped at too much, at more than was prepared then to hold together. Their uniting three kingdoms was a then impracticable and delusory object. Had the convention parliament of 1653 made England only the object of their republican polity, they might perhaps have succeeded. Scotland could not then bear to bury their sovereignty as an independent kingdom, in the commonwealth of England.

The principles of the constitution were good. The work was well begun, but never perfected. It was well done in part, that is for the elective protectorate, and a elective triennial and well apportioned house of commons, saving its object was too extensive, the consolidation of three kingdoms then impracticable: It also regulated as to the elective and succession of the senate, or house of Lords, making them in a certain degree dependent upon the house of commons.—

Upon this conftitution, which was regularly brought into ufe, the elevation of Oliver to the Protectorate was regular, and legal, and no ufurpation. He was no ufurper, but legally and conftitutionally invefted with the fupremacy in dominion.

However thefe happy beginnings were never firmly finifhed, and the whole fabric was overturned at the Reftoration, yet the great work, and the whole great enterprize of the Long Parliament and Protectorate, make an important and glorious period in the hiftory of England, by far the moft diftinguifhed and glorious in the Englifh hiftory from Alfred to the prefent time — This memorable confl ct and ftruggle has proved the means of the confervation of all the liberty remaining in the Englifh conftitution, and furnifhed an example for the contemplation of ages, and to which the Englifh nation will ever have recourfe, until in fome future period, animated by the examples of thefe patriots, and refuming their principles, they will act them out to their full extent, reform and perfect their policy, and work out the falvation of liberty And fo great will be the future benefit of the example of this period, it will abundantly repay all the blood and treafure expend- ed in the glorious conteft with tyranny, from 1641 to 1660, inclufive of the twenty or thirty regicides who were ingloriouʃly facrificed at the Reftoration. Had it not been for the parliamentary oppofition to Charles I. no man doubts but his tyranny would have been in- creafed, till the parliament would have been no more, or reduced to a cypher, and the government become as arbitrary and defpotic as that of France or Spain. This glorious ftruggle gave a check to it, and though abor- tive by the return of defpotifm, will be revived again and again in the nation, with redoubled and redoubling force, until it fhall at length eftablifh an enlightened and happy polity There will the meritorious characters which fhone and difplayed themfelves in the antecedent periods, of efforts leading on to this great and glorious event, receive the lasting tribute of perpetual estimation and honor

No more will the immortal Oliver then be considered as a tyrant and usurper, but as one who was legally and regularly invested with the protectorate, and as one executing that high betrustment with integrity and ability, and with an unexampled equity and benevolence. Being installed in office, " he proceeded to the exercise of his authority, which he used at home with great moderation and equity, but so effectually asserted at all foreign courts, that he soon made the greatest figure in Europe, and received marks of respect from all the sovereigns in Christendom, who trembled at his power, and courted his friendship, at the same time that they hated his person."† He reformed the laws, and for this end joined and availed himself of the assistance of persons of the greatest integrity and ability, to consider how the laws might be made plain, short and easy. He took care to put into seats of justice men of the most known integrity and ability, he reformed the chancery, he was of great discernment in characters, and filled all the offices of every department, civil, military and naval, with the best set of officers ever known in the nation. And when he had done this, he awed them into fidelity. He set them to work, and he saw that the work was done. They knew he would not be trifled with, they all knew it must be done, and it was done. Never was the whole system of interior government carried on with more firmness, justice and order, or freer from corruption, oppression and injustice. He was a terror to evil doers, and a praise to them that did well. He established liberty of conscience. His government was impartial, peaceable, mild and moderate, but energetic and efficacious, and firm as the mountains. It was excellent. He appointed Major-Generals to superintend the inferior magistrates in every

† *The Life O. C. by a Gent. Mid. Tem.* P. 167.

W

county. "It was hardly poffible for any governor to fhew more regard than Cromwell did for the rights and properties of private men. He fupplied the benches at Wellminfter with the ableft lawyers, whom he had invited to the public fervice. Maynard, Twifden, Newdigate, Windham, and other gentlemen of great integrity and learning, were made by him Sergeants at Law, and Mr. Matthew Hale, afterwards the famous lord Chief Juftice Sir Matthew, was advanced to be a juftice of the common pleas. Milton, the great Milton, was Latin Secretary, a man that would have done honor to the righteft monarch, to the moft polite and learned court in the beft ages.—" Nor can we better fum up the character of the civil government at this time, than in the following extract, which is chiefly taken from Echard, a moft virulent enemy of the Protector and his friends.—

"Cromwell, though he proceeded in an arbitrary manner againft thofe who contefted his authority, yet in the affairs, where the life of his jurifdiction was not concerned, feemed to have a great reverence for the law and the courts of law, rarely interpofing between party and party: and to do him juftice, there appeared in his government many things that were truly great and magnificent. Juftice, as well diftributive as commutative, was by him reftored almoft to its antient grace and fplendor, the judges executed their office without exceptions, according to law and equity, and the laws, except fome few, where much was immediately concerned, being permitted to have their full force upon all; vice of all prohibited forts, mens manners, outwardly at leaft, became much reformed, either by removing the incentives to luxury, or by means of the feverer laws made, and put in execution. There was a ftrict difcipline kept in his court, where drunkennefs, whoredom and extortion were either banifhed, or feverely rebuked. Trade began to flourifh and

* From Dr. Page.

profper, and moft things to put on a happy and pro-
mifing afpect.   The Protector alfo fhewed a great regard to the advancement of learning, and was a great
encourager of it.   The Univerfity of Oxford in particular, acknowledged his Highnefs's refpect to them in
continuing their chancellor, and beftowing on the public library the twenty-four Greek manufcripts, and mu-
nificently allowing one hundred pounds a year to a divinity reader   He alfo ordered a fcheme to be drawn
up for founding and endowing a college at Durham,
for the convenience of the northern ftudents.   Towards
all who complied with his pleafure, and courted his protection, he manifefted great civility, generofity and
courtefy   No man feemed to be more tender of the
clergy than himfelf, though he would not lift himfelf in
any particular fect, faying " it was his only wifh to fee
the church in peace, and that all would gather into one
fheep old, under one fhepherd, Jefus Chrift, and mutually love one another."   Though the public ufe of
the common prayer was denied to the Epifcopal party,
yet he allowed the ufe of their rites in private houfes:
and milder courfes were then taken than under the tyranny of others."   Ideas, how juft, liberal and noble!
fo, becoming the dignity and benevolence of the head
and rather of a republic !   An example how worthy the
emulation, the imitation of all fovereigns !

The purity of his principles are called in queftion,
or rather now with one confent reprobated by all.—
Shall we fay it is impoffible for a man to be ultimately
fituated by the views of patriotifm and public weal ?
Had any other man done half the good and excellent
things for the regulation of the public welfare, he would
have left his character for real patriotifm unproblema-
tical   Not only were his actions the moft wifely
adapted and efficacious for the public good, but he appears uniformly actuated by a fixt regard to public
peace and right, as it appears poffible for a character
whofe aggrandizement arofe out of the aggrandizement

and true glory of the state he governed. It is insidious to ascribe all to sinister and separate personal views in a character of so much public usefulness. But it is said he once put the question to Whitelock, "What if a man should take upon him to be King?"—letting out the secret that ambition and lust of dominion was his ruling passion and ultimate view. He saw further than Whitelock: he knew the nation and parliament were ripening into ideas of the necessity of Kingship, and knew that it would be fatal to republicanism, his great idol. And what if sounding the public sentiment, and being too knowing for Whitelock, he took him in with this subtil question, and by it unlocked all Whitelocks heart, without disclosing his own. Very instructive and useful was this conversation to Cromwell, who left his friend to deceive himself and the world, as if he aspired to the crown, when nothing was more abhorrent to him. The experiment was made upon him: the crown and title, with all it flattering glories were offered to him, and with the greatest importunity pressed upon him, by the unanimous voice of a misjudging parliament, joined with the first law characters in the nation. He was wiser and saw farther than all the parliament. He saw that by accepting the title the object for which he and the nation had been contending, a free state, would be given up, and this was as dear to him as to a Washington. The national object would be now changed into a family personal contest, whether Cromwell or Stuart should be King. Cromwell could have been King, but his idol liberty and the commonwealth must be given up. Not the gratification of ambition, but faithfulness to his country's cause operated, and he nobly declined the proffered, the delusory, the ruinous glory. In this, as well as in the uniform tenor of all his conduct, when critically, justly and candidly examined, he ever appears, to a distinguished degree of fidelity and perseverance, to have been decidedly actuated by pure and patriotic motives. Nor was it becaufe, under the name of Protector he had got the fubftance, and was poffeffed of equal power with a King, which was not the truth ; it was becaufe he faw that hereby the caufe would be given up, and the government return to a tyranny. And his ideas were verified at the Reftoration. Let republican liberty and the eftablifhment of the collective body of the people in the poffeffion of their laws and rights, be confidered as Oliver's ruling motives, and all his conduct may be refolved, without having recourfe to corruption, venality, ambition He would thereby be prompted to all the daring, the great and heroic actions which adorn and immortalize his character. The more thoroughly this character is examined, even with a rigidly juft, but unacrimonious feverity, the more will it approve itfelf as an high example of purity in governmental and political life

I have faid that Oliver was tried with the title of a King, and declined it. Many of the true patriots fincerely, as well as others from enfnaring views to reconcile the nation to a return to monarchy and revocation of the royal family, were fond that Oliver fhould have affumed the name of a king. But he faw beyond them all, that it was time to lay the name, as well as the thing afide. Such and fo various, fo complicated, perplext and indefinite had become the affociation of ideas connected with that name, that its further ufe was dangerous, under the moft exprefsly defined and well limited redemptions. No man knows the prerogatives of the crown with precifion, in any ftate in Europe to this day —All is loft in clouds and incomprehenfible myftery.— Like the title of Bifhop, which has become, in the notorious confeffion of all men, a very different thing from the original fcripture bifhop. All the world knows that the fcripture bifhop differs from the titular bifhop of the middle and fubfequent ages, by the additions paffed on him of civil, political and ecclefiaftical powers, and even in fome inftances of fecular fovereignty in civil dominion, as Mentz, Cologne, and Ofnaburg, as well as in the twenty-fix English bifhops, and in moſt of the epifcopacy of the Latin, and in fome inſtances of the Greek chuɩch particularly in Ruſſia. While al along through every age have been to be found all over Chriſtendom, amidſt the general ſhip-wreck and proſ titution of the Apoſtolic inſtitution, the ſcattered re. mains of the primœval ſcripture epifcopacy, in the paſtorate, or primacy in the coequal elderſhip of a fin gle congregatɩoral church Papa, or pope, was the common and univerfal appellation of the clergy, both bɩſhops and preſbyters, throughout Chriſtendom, in the ſecond and third centuries, and continues to be ſo to this day in the Ruſſian Greek church. But though originally figniſying only *Father*, it has acquired ſuch odium and infamy in Weſtern Europe, that there is not a proteſtant bɩſhop but wou'd now abhor and diſ da n it. After the preſent war of Kings, the very name King will become equally odious and infamous.

Suppoſing Chriſtendom at a given time, as the prefent, ſhould coɩſiſt of 130 millions of nominal chriſ-
t.ans; and theſe reſolved into 130 thouſand churches,
or congregations, of a thouſand ſouls each, and that
each of theſe congregations were furniſhed and organized with a preſbytery, and each a biſhop or paſtor at
ɩs head, that no biſhop, prieſts and deacons for each
congregation ſhould be the ſcripture model and
poſture of the church, and thus per diſtɩnɩs. Now for
the purpoſe of mutual communication both of the
miniſters and churches, what kind of artificial polity
they might need for prudential and wiſe reaſons to
throw theſe churches into, whether into an hierarchy conſiſting of various claſſes and ſubordinations under one
pontiff, or ɩnterchſſes unɩer different pon-
tiffs, or independent ſeparate heads, or however they
ſhould meaſure them into preſbyteries, claſſes or
after aɩɩ this it muſt be conſidered as only human
aɩɩaɩɩs, and not at all divine aɩɩaɩɩs. In the candor of

every mind they muſt be ſtript of all this, towards diſ-
cerning the true ſcripture biſhop. It ſurely is not a
little ſingular, that neither the omniſcient Jeſus, who
certainly foreſaw the growth and multiplication of his
churches, nor the inſpired apoſtles, ſhould ever have
ſuggeſted, nor have left any directions for the arrangement and formation of any ſyſtematical hierarchies, or
indeed of any combinations or polity at all, out of a
particular congregation, if they had ſeen it neceſſary or
expedient, for the well being of the Catholic or univerſal church. The preſumption is ſtrong, that Chriſt did
not ſee it to be neceſſary ; and from the apoſtolic pre-
dictions of an eccleſiaſtical apoſtacy, he certainly foreſaw, as Clement informs us, that it would be dangerous, as it has proved in hiſtory. In reviewing the ſtate
of the church, we ought carefully to diſtinguiſh what
is of divine and what of human wiſdom We do this
with reſpect to the inſpired books, and the uninſpired,
with clear and certain preciſion. With ſuch a diſtinc-
tion and analyſis we may eaſily diſcover the ſcripture
biſhops, which when ſtript of all additions paraphierna-
lia, will all become fratres brethren, and ſcarcely diſ-
tinguiſhable from the humble paſtors, the untitled
common miniſters of the churches. But if any ſect or
body of chriſtians are pleaſed with a ſacerdotal hierarchy, aſcending through various gradations, dignities
and eminencies, " from the dirt to the ſkies,' † yet let
them all ceaſe to think, there is any *jus divinum* in ſuch
a polity

In like manner, we are not to infer the primœval
meaning of a King, or title of the chief ruler of a ſovereignty among the nations, from the meaning to
which it has long grown up by uſe in the ages of tyranny and uſurpation. Kings, *Melakim*, leaders, rulers
were prevailed in all nations and countries around the
terraqueous globe, and muſt have been from the ſpontaneous voice of univerſal ſociety. The firſt ſeventy-

two nations immediately after Babel had them. But what were these primeval Kings? Not despots, rulers by their own will, but actors forth of the counsel and will of the people, in what for the public weal was by the people confided to their execution, as *primi inter pares consiliarios*, the first or chief baron in the teutonic policies, of a presidential, not autocratical authority, the organ of the supreme council, but of no separate and disjoined power. Early indeed among the Oriental nations sprung up a few Nimrods, while in general for ages, particularly in Europe, they were what they ought to be. If we recede back into early antiquity, and descend thence even late into the martial ages, we shall find the *reliquiæ* of the original policies, especially in Hesperia, Gaul, Belgium and Britain, and plainly discern the Duces, the Reges, the heads of nations, by whatever appellation designated, still the *patres patriæ*. The additions powers annexed to their titles afterwards, caused them to grow up to *tyranni*, governors of will. Not so in the beginning, when they were like the Sachems of Indian nations. And perhaps the primæval polities may have subsisted and survived with purity in the Indian sachemdoms, which however hereditary, are so in a mode unknown to the rest of the world, though perfectly understood by themselves; nor is any man able with our present ignorance to even pretend the genius of their polity or laws, which I am persuaded are wise, beautiful and excellent, rightly and fully understood, however hitherto despised by Europeans and Americans. We think of a Sachem as an European King in his little tribe, and reciprociate with him under our taken transatlantic ideas. And so are frequently rendering them cyphers to certain purposes without the collective council or warriors, who are all the men of the nation, whose subordination is settled and as far as it in the feudal system. At times we see a Sachem dictating with the seeming authority of a despot, and he is obeyed because of the united sense of

the nation—never otherwife   On their views of fociety
their policy is perfect wifdom.   So antient Kingfhip
and council monarchy in Afia and Europe, was like
that of Melchifedek, lenient, wife and efficacious.—
This ftill lives in Africa and among fome of the hordes
of Tartars, as it did in Montezuma and Mango Capac.
But thefe *primi inter pares* foon grew up to beafts of
prey, until ages ago government has been configned
to the will of monarchs, and this even with the confent
of the people, deluded by the idea that a father of his
people could not rule but with affection and wifdom.
Thefe in Greece and Sicily were called Tyranni, to
diftinguifh from Archons, Princes and other rulers by
council.   All government was left to will, hoped and
expected to have been a wife will.   But the experiment
raifed fuch horror and deteftation, and this official
title has for ages become fo difguftful and obnoxious,
that Kings themfelves cannot endure it.   Never will a
King hereafter affume the name of a tyrant, nor give
the name of Baftile to a national or ftate prifon.   The
brazen bull of Phalaris was ufed once, has been difufed
two thoufand years, and will never be ufed again.   So
the name of a King now excites horror, and is become
as odious in Europe, as that of Tyrannus at Athens,
Syracufe and Arigentum.   The name and title of
King will foon become as difguftful to fupreme magiftrates, in every polity, as that of tyrant, to which it is
become fynonimous and equipollent.   It may take a
century or two yet to accomplifh this extirpation of
title, but the die is caft, Kingfhip is at an end, like a
girdled tree in the foreft, it may take a little time to
wither and die—but it is dying—and in dying, die it
muft.   Slaying the monfter was happily begun by Oliver but the people fpared its life, judicially given up by
them to be whipt, fcourged and tormented with it
two or three centuries more, unlefs it may be now in
its laft gafps.   Now there muft be a fupreme and chief
ruler in every fociety, in every polity, and was it not

for the complex aſſociation of inſidious ideas, ideas of dread and horror connected with the appellation King, or could it be purged and reſtored to the purity of antiquity, it might ſtill be ſafely uſed in a republic. But this can not be done :—It muſt therefore be relegated into contemptuous neglect. And a new appellation muſt be taken up—very immaterial what it is, ſo it be defined to be but *primus inter pares, conſiliaries*, ſtand on frequent election, and hereditation for ever repudiated and baniſhed. The charm and unintelligible myſteries wrapt up in the name of a King being done away, the way would be open for all nations to a rational government and policy, on ſuch plain and obvious general principles, as would be intelligible to the plaineſt ruſtic, to the ſubſtantial yeomanry, or men of landed eſtates, which ought to be the body of the population. Every one could underſtand it as plain as a Locke or a Camden. And whatever the Filmers and Acherlys may ſay, the common people are abundantly capable and ſuſceptible of ſuch a polity. It is greatly wiſe therefore to reject the very name of a King. Many of the enlightened civilians of the Long Parliament and Protectorate ſaw this. Oliver ſaw it. And who ſhall ſay, this was not the governing reaſon of his rejecting it.— From reading his ſenſible and maſterly anſwer to Parliament, I believe it was his true and only reaſon. If acting on ſuch a motive is ever poſſible to the efforts of humanity, Oliver, of all men, was the man to do it. Certainly he could have exerciſed more power under the title of a King, then under that of a Protector, which was far, very far more limited, beſides the certain hereditation of the crown in his family. It is impoſſible juſtly to aſcribe his refuſal to avidity for power or family honor.

In the courſe of this diſquiſition, and eſpecially in this chapter, it will be remembered, that I am not to be conſidered, as a ſimple hiſtorian, but as profeſſedly advocating the cauſe of the Judges and the general cauſe of liberty, and as adducing hiftorical teftimonies and ftatements, to be applied in illuftrating and eftablifhing fuch a defence. To this erd a review of the principles of the long parliament and protectotate becomes neceffary, in every mind, for with them the caufe of the Judges ftands or falls.

I proceed then and fay, that Oliver was again tried in a fecond capital inftance. Connected with the ambition for royalty, would naturally be that of an ambition for heriditating this honour in his family. The protectorate was by the conftitution for life indeed, but elective It was doub'lefs in Oliver s power to have made it hereditary. Through the whole courfe of his adminiftration, does he ever difcover any intrigues and movements this way ? Do we ever hear of his negociations this way ? Yes, it is faid, that, at his death, he confented that his fon Richard fhould be proclaimed as his fucceffor This was true And this is all, and perhaps this was after death had invaded his mental powers. Had Oliver felt his wifh, and had he perceived a general fcale of the nation for it, and had he feen that fuch an eftablifhment would have received national fupport, we will for the prefent fay, that he would have hefitated, if not clofed in with the meafure. he would have been corrupted, if in fuch a ftatement it would have been corruption. But we in vain conjecture, what he wou'd then have done : he might heroically difplayed a frefh proof of his difinterefted and incorruptable patriotifm, and have rejected it.— It is in vain however to amufe ourfelves with conjecture upon fo fagacious a character, as Oliver's. Let us rather fubftitute ourfelves in his cafe, and judge how fo difcerning and wife a man as Oliver would have acted in the then prefent circumftances He plainly faw a growing, and fpreading inclination in the nation to the return of monarchy, and even of the Stuart family, that however he might have hoped to have warded it off in 1653, yet by 1658 he as clearly and fatisfactorily forefaw the inevitable deftruction of the caufe, and the reftoration of Charles II. by the union of the monarchical members and open royalifts, as if he had received it by prophecy. He faw the tide was turning and would overwhelm all. In this to me indubitable defpair of a good out loft caufe, what heart would he have, had he been as ambitious as Cæfar, for concerting and enteprizing plans for the hereditation of the protectorate? Add to this, that had fuch a thing been his wifh, he too well difcerned and judged of characters, even thofe of his own family, not to know, that the pacific, mild and inoffenfive Richard, had neither a fortitude nor wifdom, nor fpirit of enterprize equal to fuch a crifis. Indeed his family fituation was very peculiar and trying. He had four daughters and two fons. He was fo effectually deferted by them, that he could not poffibly have entertained any hereditary hopes or profpects.

Bridget—was againft monarchy and the protectorate, even in her father.

Elizabeth—againft her father's religion—a pious epifcopalian, a friend and partizan for both Charlefes.

Mary—for monarchy and the reftoration.

Frances—willing to have married King Charles II : to which her mother confented with earneftnefs, and was for having Oliver fign the *charte blanche.*

So the protector and his caufe, given up and deferted by his wife, and all his daughters. Nor were the two fons very tenacious of the caufe. He therefore never had a ferious thought that Richard could poffibly fucceed. And could he have forefeen the continuance and perpetuity of his beloved commonwealth, to which hereditation he knew was a poifon, I believe from the tenor and firmnefs of his former conduct, he would have given a new and further proof of his patriotifm, and have effectually renounced or rejected the election of his own fon, lea ft it fhould be led on to this baneful preditation. But, as I said, he knew that the restoration would soon take place, and therefore discovered no fruitless intrigues against it. He well knew that whatever might be done, nothing could prevent it. His council and parliament were perfectly at a loss, what were his wishes, and he never disclosed to any man this despair, which it is not to be doubted he felt to the heart. The election of a protector was with the lords of the council: they judged or conjectured that it would be agreeable to him, to be succeeded by his son: and as he was expiring, and had done with the world, they simply asked him his pleasure, whether Richard should be proclaimed? and without the least comment or directions, he as simply just answered, yes, on what his sagacity knew, if he had any sagacity left, would be perfectly nugatory. Had they asked him, even in his senses, whether say, Desborough, Whalley or Fleetwood, should have been proclaimed, his answer might have been the same. He had heroically fought through and sustained the cause, but he knew it terminated with his death. Oliver, if any man, ought to be credited in his declarations of sincerity, necessity and obedience to the calls *only of God and his country*. for I believe he was so thoroughly sick of the world, even before he ascended to the protectorate, that it had no charms for him, and that he would gladly, if possible, have escaped the burdensome and dangerous honor, and retired from public life into retirement and obscurity. And especially long before he left the world, he was subdued and brought to feel this humility and self annihilation. For certainly such a state of mind, and especially of a sagacious, circumspective and experienced mind, may be generated, and has in some instances been generated, witness Belisarius, by a comparative and even anticipated view of the goods and evils of office, that neither honour nor riches, nothing but *duty God and man* would be left the really influential motive of an office even of the highest power, dignity and

X

preeminence, I will not say, to wish and defire it, bi
even to *submit to its burdens* and dangers. God is abl
to make this poffible even to man, and I doubt not
has fometimes been the fact. That men are generall
thus affected, I will by no means affert. But amon
the few inftances wherein men have been thus difinter
eftly influenced, I do not hefitate to place Oliver, ful
ly I think evinced in his fenfible, intelligent and mof
mafterly anfwer to the committee of the houfe of com
mons in 1657, who waited upon him with the addref
of parliament, requefting him to affume the office an
title of KING "I hope, fays he, that the honefty o
my intentions, and the purity of my heart, will not b(
miftaken. I hope that neither hypocrify nor artifice
will be imputed to my open declarations, and fincere
profeffions, declarations and profeffions, which I make
not haftily and negligently, but with care and reflexion
and deliberate caution, in the prefence of Almighty
power, by whofe providence I have been guided, and
in whofe prefence I ftand I hope it will not be imagined, that I reject the title of KING from fondnefs for
that of Protector, a name and office, to which I wa
far from afpiring, and which I only did not refufe when
it was offered me.—The only motive by which I wa
induced to engage in fo arduous and invidious an employment, was the defire of obviating thofe evils which
I faw impending over the nation. I therefore could
not but accept, what the fame time I could not ardently
defire For nothing can deferve to be purfued wi a
eagernefs and affiduity but the power of doing good, of
conferring real and folid benefits upon mankind. And
furely while the only end for which greatnefs and authority are defired, is public good, thofe defires are at
leaft lawful, and perhaps worthy of applaufe, they are
certainly lawful, if he that entertains them, has, by a
long and diligent examination of his own heart, an examination ferious and fincere, without any of thofe fallacious arts, by which the confcience is too frequently

deceived, satisfied himself that his ultimate views are
not his own honor or interest, but the welfare of mankind, and the promotion of virtue, and that his advancement will contribute to them." If it be possible for a
man in Oliver's situation to be sincere, he might have
been that man.   We certainly may have sufficient reason to believe it, even though it should never in fact be
believed by prejudiced mortals, till the revelation of the
secrets of all hearts : when it is possible that Oliver,
may be found in this class of undissembled sincerity. To
us on this side the vale, it cannot, it ought not to be
wondered at, that amidst such high proofs of integrity,
there should be found some approvers and admirers
even of a character very generally despised and treated
with infamy and contempt.   There are those who tra-
cing the life of Oliver through its whole career, are convinced that the public welfare generally governed him,
that the cause he was in was righteous ; that the principles which actuated his general conduct, and that of
his compatriots, were justifiable and glorious , and that
the *purity of his intentions* was conspicuous to the last.
On the same principles we may vindicate and justify the
Judges, and others concerned in that abortive work, in
the great and memorable events of that day.

Oliver Cromwell once saved the nation ; and upon
deliberate consultation with both the army and parliament, and with the concurrent hearts of certainly a
very large and respectable body, even the main body of
the divided nation, devised and provided a very excellent constitution, in the form and spirit of it very nearly
resembling that afterwards adopted or conceived by the
United States.   The constitution by 1654, and especially by 1657, was ripened to this, that the government
be a commonwealth , the national legislature to consist
of a protector, and two houses , all elective and none
hereditary.

This constitution, it is said, was the production of
three days, and conceived and fabricated by the officers

of the army. Be it fo. This redounds to the honour of the army. It has been conceived that the ideas and ufages of defpotifm in military life, ill qualify for juft, equitable, civil dominion, and free government. But this inftance is in point to the contrary, fhewing the moft equitable and liberal polity conceived by men inured to command, and to the arbitrary domination of military life. An affembly of Barons or hereditary nobility would never have devifed a civil polity fo liberal and rational, fo lenient, juft and friendly to all, fo well adapted to promote the order, felicity and good government of a commonwealth, or republican fovereignty. It is worthy of inquiry, how this fingular phænomenon of wifdom arofe.

An army confcribed, like the European armies of modern ages, of " the gleanings of the loweft rank of people, ferving men difcarded, and mechanics without employments, *men ufed to infults and fervility from their cradles*, without principle or honor, or inducements to overbalance the fenfe of immediate danger, * though officered with men of military fkill indeed, and well verfed in every branch of tactics and in the whole art of war—officers taken from the nobility or their fubmiffive connexions, principled in tyranny : fuch officers, inured to arbitrary and defpotic command of flaves, might govern and difcipline an army well, but would give a dangerous tinge to civil polity. But let us choofe men, fays Oliver, " warm with regard to religion, men who think it a high degree of impiety to fly before the wicked and profane, to forfake the caufe of heaven, and prefer fafety to truth , and our enemies will quickly be fubdued." Accordingly he confcribed an army of men of different defcription, freemen above the meral feelings and fervility of vaffals, men of allodial and other property, fubftantial yeomenry, and intelligent gentry, officered with men of information and principle, and poffeffed of the feelings of liberty and

* O. Crom. Speech.

rational freedom. And when "thefe men were lead to the field, no veterans could ftand before them, no obftructions could retard, or danger affright them : and to thefe men, fays Cromwell, are to be attributed the victories that we have gained, and the peace we enjoy." Such men did the American army furnifh, men great in the field, and great in the fenate. Such men feel and fpeak the fenfe of a free community. Such were the men that formed Oliver's policy, and inftrument of government. Such an army as Olivers furnifhed men of intelligence, ability and political knowledge, of high-ly improved and fcientific characters, who rufhed to arms for the defence of liberty, of infeparable fidelity to the public weal, whofe interefts were effentially inter-woven with that of the body of the people, fo that they were, we find, abundantly qualified for an extempora-neous production of a policy, which however came pre-pared to their hands by fourteen years previous digef-tion, a policy, which will hereafter become the admira-tion, the adoption and imitation of ages. But whoever inveftigated the Oliverian polity, honored their coun-cils abilities and patriotifm to contemplative pofterity. For in the regeneration of policies, throughout Europe, all will find themfelves infenfibly led to an affumption of the leading and commanding principles of this policy, efpecially in elective, and unhereditary reprefentation.

Very different indeed would be the policies devifed by the different and feparate defcriptions of men, into which fociety in thefe ages has become artificially divi-ded, fhould any one or few of them hear the formation of a polity, it would be very different from one devifed by the people or population at large. But very uniform and almoft identical would be that which would iffue from indivifibility, equality and the united fenfe of foci-ety at large, in every independent community and fove-reignty on earth. Human nature and the rights of man would every where, if permitted, fpeak the fame lan-guage, the fame policy, all around the terraqueous globe. All nations would agree in the downfall of he reditary government, and in the substitution of electiv government. But if particularities should institute po licies, they would be different. Let a convention of bashaws and West-India negro-drivers devise a policy and how different it would be from one devised by th Dixwells, the Hampdens, the Sidneys, the Whalleys the Desboroughs, and the Fairfaxes? Commit th formation to a diet of Polish nobles, familiarized to sell and transfer their peasants, their stock of men, a their stock of cattle and horses, with the leasing of their grounds, or sale of their 22,000 estates, charged wit a population of eight or nine millions, of whom all but their nobles, devoid of allodial property, and like the inhabitants of the Hebrides or the north of Scotland, tied down and restricted to the territorial domains of their lords, who absorb and devour the fruits of their laborious industry. In a word, let a Congress of Eu ropean or Asiatic princes and nobles, looking down with sovereign contempt upon their subjects, the nu merous depauperated indigent populace, let them, I say, make a policy for dependent millions—How di ferent would it be from one devised by their equals and brethren in general, by those taken, either from the various orders and classes, into which society happens to have become artificially and unfortunately divided, or from feeling, substantial and enlightened characters among them, with here and there a William Tell, a Muir and a Palmer, intermixt among them no one can doubt the different polity they would institute, no one doubt whose polity would be most friendly to the general rights and liberties of society, to the welfare of nine-tenths of any and every community Nor indeed need it be doubted which polity would prove the most firm and durable, as well as extensively equitable and just. It would undoubtedly be elective in the one case, and hereditary in the other The firmness and dura bility of the former, would infinitely surpass the suppo

fed firmnefs and durability of dominion from the permanency and perpetuity of hereditary fuperiorities. It
would be a government of laws, which would gain, not
the deforced acquiefcence, but cheerful concurrence of
the collective body of the citizens, and combine them
into a union of force fufficient to fupport and render it
efficacious, and internally fortify the union againft
everfion, from interior or exterior aggreffion.

It is eafy to try all political characters : Thofe particularly who have the formation of a polity ; and from
thence either to predict the complexion of a polity, or
in one new formed, difcern the force and defign of certain traits interfperfed in it   What are the characters
and events in hiftory, which they approve or difapprove, or which are to the tafte of individuals,
or to the collective body of the framers? Select
the hiftories or anecdotes of defpotifm, and contraft
thefe with thofe of liberty. The admirers of the one
will inftantly be perceived to deteft the other, and refpectively give different complexions to the conceived
polity. Their refpective ideas will be refpectively
ftamped upon it   Try all kings and nobles with Cato,
Cicero, Brutus and Caffius, in the Roman, and fimilar characters in the Grecian hiftory, try them with
the events in France, Poland, and the United States ;
try them with the hiftory of Holland, Venice, Switzerland—They will uniformly deteft thefe—while the patriots throughout the world will ftrike unifon with all
the great characters, and heroic examples of emancipation into civil liberty, and unite in detefting tyranny.
Cicero has been obnoxious to nobles, kings and emperor, ever fince he boldly forced the way for plebeians
through the patricians up to the confulate. They have
never been reconciled to fuch a precedent or example of
fuccefsful oppofition to defpotifm and privileged orders.
They contemplate with an evil eye, with abhorrence,
every inftance of this kind in univerfal hiftory. In
favor of kings, eloquence perhaps more than republican

fentiments, has procured immortality to the works of Tully, which live in the univerfal reception of claffic reading. But eighteen ages have not fufficed to deforce from princes and hereditary nobles the eftimation due to the patriotic merit of the immortal orator; becaufe he cannot live without furviving an opprobium to patrician tyranny, and a friend to liberty.

So again monarchs contemplate Jacobin Societies with horror and dread, and this with great reafon — They need not be fo viewed by republics. The Jacobin Societies have proved the falvation of France. They have been the bulwark of liberty. Their exceffes are to be coerced by government, but their fuppreffion and extinction is unneceffary and impoffible. "The popular focieties are the columns of the revolution.— They fhall not be fhaken,' faid prefident Cambeceres. Violent and unjuft in many things they may be, and fo fometimes are congreffes, affemblies, parliaments, not therefore to be diffolved, for they may be generally right. Would it be wife to wifh the extinction of the winds, which are falutary and beneficial for navigation and for clarifying the atmofphere, becaufe fometimes attended with hurricanes? They may be fet up againft a good government indeed, but their efforts againft it muft ultimately be inefficacious and harmlefs. Becaufe they fometimes fucceed in overturning a tyranny, will it follow that there is even a poffibility of their fucceeding againft a good policy? The experiment is yet to be made Hitherto there has exifted no good polity to try them upon. In the nature of things they will become felf-correctors of their own irregularities and exceffes; and harmonization of the public fentiment muft refult from their diffufive deliberations. Nay, the ftrength of a general and uniform fupport to the adminiftration of a good policy muft arife. Their difcuffions, circulation of intelligence, and communication of light, muft eventually fix, digeft and unify the national judgment. None but tyrants need fear them. The

national convention has not feared them, but rejoined
in their support   Congrefs in 1775 did not fear the
body of the people in America, though fometimes wild
and anarchical.   A policy which fhall have fuftained
their ventilation and difcuffion, will be firm.   The end
being anfwered, and the care of the public configned
into the hands of conftitutional government, thefe focieties will fpontaneoufly difappear ;   nor rife again unlefs called forth on great occafions worthy their attention

I faid that men would judge of hiftorical events according as they are principled in politics.   Monarchies
of all modes are contemplated with a fufpicious eye, by
communities at large , which in their turn contemplate
republics, of any and almoft every form, with attention and pleafure.   There once was a time, and it is
not yet paft, when the fovereigns of Europe could not
contemplate but with horror and difguft, the Prince of
Orange, and Holland, diffolving their feudal fubmiffion
to their lord paramount, the revolt of the houfe of Braganza from Spain, the more recent erection of the felf-
created kingdom of Pruffia, or the felf-created republics
of Switzerland, and the United States.   But all thefe
examples come up into operative and efficacious view
in the prefent age , and are contemplated with fympathetic confolation by ftates ftruggling with the tyranny
of kings.

Self-erected fovereignties, whether monarchical or
republican bid fair for confiderable duration , while
popular focieties, are either defeated, or go to reft of
courfe, when their end is accomplifhed.   Their coerced extinction would prove as fatal to liberty and the
rights of man, as the forceable fuppreffion or extinction of letters or the liberty of the prefs.   Both ever
have done, and ever will do much mifchief , both do
ultimately more good   both are the combined conferva-
to e of the public liberty, in philofophy, religion, po-

litics. They are excellently adapted to frame the public mind to wifdom, and to an acquiefcence founded in
diffufive conviction and information of that wherein
confifts the public intereft, the general welfare of fociety. There is no alternative between their right to affemble, and the abolition of liberty. Extinguifh this
right in England and in every fovereignty, and the
people are flaves. It at any time extravagant, a prudent infertion of counfel, and circulation of it through
the popular focieties may generally correct and rectify
thefe extravagances, exceffes into which they are ufually betrayed by falfe brethren or enemies mafqued. It is
their unalienable right to meet and deliberate, even for
the purpofe of fyftematically altering the policy, provided they peaceably fubmit to obey the policy and laws
in being, until regularly altered by public confent. If
affembling even for this open and direct purpofe is to
be adjudged treafon, the change and rectification of the
moft tyrannous polity can never be effected, but by
fpontaneous recourfe to the tremendous alternative of
arms. If the popular focieties fometimes err, it is not
always, it is not ufually from malicious and inimical
views, but from, defective and partial information
among thofe the beft difpofed for the public good, or, as
I faid, from tories, which covertly, infidioufly and unawares infert themfelves as marplots. If well informed,
it is impoffible the community at large can be inimical
to the public good Enough of this general difpofition
for the public good may be fcund in every community
at large, to counteract and nullify the injuries of factions. And the common people will generally judge
right, when duly informed The general liberty is fafe
and fecure in their hands. It is not from deficiency of
abilities to judge, but from want of information, if
they at any time as a body go wrong. Upon information from an abundance of enlightened characters always intermixt among them, they will ultimately always judge right, and be in the end the faithful guardi-

ans and support and security of government. Nothing will kill a faction, like the body of a people if consulted. A faction may beat a faction, at a pretty fair and even conflict, but in a fair and full contest, it can never beat the people. The great art of factions is to keep the decision from the body of the people. But let a matter be fairly brought before the people, and they will not only determine it, but will judge and determine right. It is the insidious art of parties and politicians to keep things concealed from the people, or if they are alarmed and assemble, to excite parties, sow dissentions, and prevent as much as possible the question from coming up fairly before them, instead of harmoniously endeavoring in a fair, open and candid manner, to lay things clearly before them, and thus honestly endeavoring to form and obtain the public mind. And thus they ever attempt, and are too successful in deceiving, instead of a frank and open appeal to the people. But shall this cunning prevail forever? Politicians, with too much reason, say it will. I, who am no politician, but a prophet, say it will not. Almost all the civil polities on earth are become so corrupt and oppressive, as that they cannot stand before a well formed system of revolutionary societies. Those of the United States and France will sustain them without injury or exertion. The reformation of all others, must commence in associations, which by government will be considered and treated as factionary and treasonable, but will enlarge and spread into a system of revolutionary societies. In all states these will be frowned upon, and suppressed as treasonable. Their suppression and persecution will pour oil on the flame. They will burst out again and again, till they will carry all before them, till real treason shall be accurately defined not to the leak of aristocrats or the present usurped reigning powers, but to the general sense of the community. And such a law of treason will be infallibly supported by the community. This done every association will know

what it may, and what it may not do, with impunity.
Till this is done, the fpirit of enlightened liberty is become fo great, and ready to burft forth under oppreffive
and intolerable irritations, that it will rifque all confequences, until all the prefent policies fhall be fairly
brought to the tribunal of the public fenfe. Then no
one can doubt the refult Factionary focieties begun
even with the primary and direct defign of overturning
government, if the governme t or polity be fupported
by the general fenfe, will fall : otherwife they will
bring on and adduce at length extenfive difcuffions which
enlighten the public, defeat infidious and partial cunning, and bring forward an open and firm fupport of
good and acceptable government. Should they at any
time furrender, or duped and outwitted by counter factions, be prevailed upon to betray the public liberty,
the community will deferve flavery a little longer, until again aroufed to energy, unity, wifdom. Thus
England has now for a century been fuffering a national punifhment or chaftifement, brought upon them by
their own folly, for being duped by the infidious cavalier faction, which overturned the happy conftitution of
Oliver s republican polity. When at length brought to
their fenfes, and a conviction of their national folly, they
will break out and burft forth with united and irrefiftable
vigour, and recover and rectify themfelves. The French
have for ages been duped by court factions, but have at
length recovered their national rights and liberties, by
a voluntary, united, bold and daring exertion, by an
effort which makes all Europe to tremble. So it will
be in England. The forcible fuppreffion of focieties
there will only accelerate their revolution and political
regeneration More muft be done for the fatisfaction
of the national mind and fpirit of liberty, than parliament ever can, or ever will do, unlefs they fhall call a
national convention, which they never will do. The
national fpirit tired out with defpair of redrefs, will
become defperate confidence in parliament loft :

then to your tents, O Ifrael ! The national interest and welfare will take care of itfelf; and this with an unconquerable violence and impetuofity !

The Englifh nation flattered themfelves at the Reftoration—revolution—acceffion of the Houfe of Hanover.—Have been deceived and difappointed at each epoch, and find themfelves as before, or rather more clofely enchained and baftiled. The fame conviction feizes the patriots of the prefent as of the laft century. Never has the nation really defpaired of all poffibility of redrefs till now. Now at length *nationally defpairing* of the prefent polity, they will be filled with very energetic feelings. They feel anew what was felt of old. New wine put into old bottles, may poffibly burft the bottles.

In every ftate, good or bad, there will always be a number of reftlefs, fubtil, crafty, turbulent and ungovernable fpirits; who by writings and intrigues, will be exciting difcontent and ftirring up mifchief: and will moleft and embarrafs the beft as well as the worft adminiftration. Society will always have to encounter fuch characters. But calm difcuffion, and giving time for infidious projections to take their courfe and run their race, they may be wifely managed, contravened and defeated, efpecially after the public have felt and tafted fome of the ill confequences into which they are plunged by fuch artifices and delufory ftratagems. And perhaps voluntary affociations, without noticing them as feditious, are as proper theatres for them to difplay and fpend themfelves upon as any other. Faction may be turbulent and fuccefsful, applied to monarchy and ariftocracy—felf-defeated, when applied to community at large. Experiments in the old governments, in the Grecian and Roman, in antient and modern hiftory, will be no precedent to count upon, in judging their effect on the new republican polities.—The public will not be ultimately duped by factions or

Y

factionary focieties, though affembling with the great-eft freedom. They will be harmlefs, till they arm, and then they become amenable to the laws, which if made by the public, the public will effectually fupport, even finally by military coercion.

Abfolute monarchs have in all ages permitted indi-viduals, fubjects and flaves, to petition their King — Even the Dey of Algiers, the Sultan of Conftantinople, the Sophi of Perfia, will receive the petition of flaves. The fame thing is permitted in England ; where it has hitherto been alfo permitted, efpecially fince the fup-preffion of villainage, for fubjects affembled in popular, and even fyftematical focieties, to petition the King or Parliament for redrefs of grievances, for or againft bills depending in parliament, for or againft the repeal of laws already enacted. So far they may go with impu-nity, and without liability to criminal proceffes for fedi-tion or treafon. This is a conceded right in England. But to affemble for the direct purpofe of altering the conftitution of King, Lords and Commons, is by fta-tute, fedition, and arming in confequence, treafon.— Thus it follows that reformation by the people is im-poffible Let the conftitution become corrupt into the moft abfolute and conjuct tyranny, it is however invi-olable. There then exifts a cafe, in which tyranny ought not, cannot be *juftly* and legally corrected and abolifhed by the people. Will not the fame reafoning apply for the perpetuity and irreformablenefs of any the moft defpotic governments ? Will not thefe principles terminate in the univerfal everfion of liberty, in the univerfal eftablifhment of univerfal tyranny ? And is there no juftifiable expedient, no public meafure of re-drefs, whofe affumption and adoption may be juftified upon the high, tranfcendant and paramount principles of public juftice, right, liberty ? If there is, it will lead to and terminate in the juftification of voluntary focie-ties, affembled to confult the public good, augmenting, multiplying and dividing themfelves into a fyftem of

popular affemblies, for enlightening, forming, digeft-
ing, and collecting the general fenfe of the community,
whofe polity needs amendment. It fhould feem therefore, that however iniquitious and pernicious fome
may be, yet *all* affemblies for the exprefs purpofe of
altering and changing the polity, are *not* to be reprobated, as unjuftifiable, feditious and traitorous. It remains to fettle this point for all nations, that it is as
juftifiable to affemble for altering the polity, as for petitioning a national council, whofe polity and conftitution the whole nation approve, without the leaft defire
of fubverting or altering it. When this fhall have become the univerfal conviction, national affemblies will
become univerfal · and fuch polities as will not fuftain
their revifion and difcuffion muft fall. Thus it may be
feen all the prefent corrupt polities are gone. But it is
faid, by parity, popular affemblies may be inftituted
againft the new conceived polities, in endlefs progrefs,
ad infinitum. Very true : and let them be fo. If upon
revifion, they find the polity found and good, one to
fatisfaction, as fooner or later, after a few revifions,
they will find, they will of courfe leave it untouched,
return home, report and diffufe and generate univerfal
acquiefcence, fatisfaction and fubmiffion ; and thus
ftrengthen the whole community into one firm and
united bulwark for its fupport and defence. Afterwards they will feel no occafion for popular affemblies,
unlefs upon agitated bills, and very feldom for this end,
all readily acquiefcing in the determination and enact-
ment of the national council, if frequently elected,
which can have no other intereft but that of the people.
The very notion of petitioning parliaments, national
councils, or kings, for rights and liberties, is a badge
of flavery, founded on the fuppofition that they have both
the power and difpofition to counteract the intereft of
the governed. This abolifhed, petitioning dies of courfe ;
and will be fecurely confined to the wifdom and fidelity
of the council. They are empowered, entrufted and

confided in for this very purpofe. A good policy will generally enact wife and good laws, to which obedience ought to be exacted, if neceffary among turbulent fpirits, by the united military force of the citizens, not foreign force. Yet former good legiflators have erred, and thofe of a beft policy may err again, and enact laws which ought to be difobeyed and refifted. What muft be done in this cafe? Agreeable to the cuftom of all the kings and nobility throughout Europe in the middle ages, Evenus, a King of Scotland, caufed a law to pafs, by which all the wives and daughters of noble-men were fubjected to his luft, and thofe of the plebe-ians to the luft of his nobility. "*Tulit legem Evanus* *rex tertius, ut qui liceret, pro opibus quot alere poffet, uxores du-cere; ut rex nuptias fponfarum nobilium, nobiles plebei-rum prælibaret pudicitiam, ut plebeiorum uxores cum nobilitate communes effent.*" Could it be fuppofed pof-fible that Congrefs fhould re-enact fuch a licentious law in favor of privileged orders, of any defcription of men, it would exafperate and unite fo many plebeian hufbands, and in the United States even wives too, in refiftance, and even arming for defence, as that it would be wife to reverfe it. Here refiftance would be juftifia-ble, even to arming and civil war. In this cafe, whe-ther fuccefsful or unfuccefsful, the refiftance would be juft. But from a few fuch fuppofed cafes and ex-traordinary inftances of error, we are not to infer that we are juftifiable in refifting any and every law which we think and feel to be oppreffive. In elective repub-lics there is another way always open, which will al-ways be effectual for the redrefs of even real grievances. Defer and endure till the next election, and then fend up men that fhall abolifh the law. They will either do it, or bring back reafons which will convince their conftituents. Numerous have been the inftances of this in the New-England republics the laft and prefent century —and the public have been fatisfied. There is no need to alter the polity for this end. In an elective republic

factionary refiftance and infurrection ought to be repreffed by military coercion, not by foreign troops, but
by citizens, who will cheerfully lend their aid, in the
fupport of an act agreeable to the general fenfe of the
community.   If not agreeable to the general fenfe, it
ought to be repealed, till by becoming convinced of its
expediency they fha'l re-enact it.   But it is next to
impoffible that fuch a thing can be enacted by a national
council ftanding on biennial, or triennial, or fhort
elections.   Diffatisfactions may and will arife, will be
manifefted ; and if general, yet there is no need of
arming for refiftance, which would be and muft necef-
farily be treated as fedition and treafon.   If general
among the conftituents, and they cannot be enlightened
to fee the reafon and juftice of the law, the obnoxious
act will be reverfed, even by the exifting fenate.   If
not, the next election will return members who will
cancel and rectify the error, if there is one.   It is therefore next to impoffible to fuppofe a cafe in an elective
republic, wherein refiftance can be juftifiable.   Becaufe
redrefs may be at all times effected in another and more
peacable and fatisfactory way, without endangering the
public tranquility, or difturbing the public order of the
general government, and efpecially without everfion of
the conftitution.

But although infurrection and refiftance may perhaps
never be juft in an elective government , it will not follow but that they may be fometimes juftifiable in a defpotic government, and efpecially when the polities and
conftitutions are fo radically corrupt, as that the very
polity itfelf ought to be changed and rectified.   And
here refiftance is juftifiable, whether fuccefsful or not.
Whether the attempt and enterprize fhall be prudent
and wife, may be a queftion, when we confer with
flefh and blood, but whether juft in the view of right
reafon, need not to be queftioned.   The polities of all
the European nations are become fo radically corrupt
and oppreffive, that the welfare of mankind requires

that they fhould all be renovated. This would be beft for human fociety. Why fhould defpotifm and oppref-fion be entailed to fubfequent generations ? Why is it not juft that the ages of tyranny fhould be fucceeded by the ages of liberty ? Under the obftinate and perfevering oppofition of the reigning powers this emancipation cannot be made but by the people This muft com-mence, as I have faid, in popular focieties, connected, fpreading and growing up into a general popular exer-tion. If oppreffion occafions their rife, they muft take their fate. The enterprize is arduous, but combined national enthufiafm in the caufe of liberty is of great and awful force. All Europe is ripening with celerity for a great revolution, the æra is commencing of a *gene-ral revolution*. The amelioration of human fociety muft and will take place. It will be a conflict between Kings and their fubjects. This war of Kings, like that of Gog and Magog, will be terrible. It will, for there is no other way, it will commence and originate in voluntary affociations among fubjects in all kingdoms. Eluded fupplications and petitions for liberty, will be followed by armaments for the vindication of the rights of human nature. The public ardor will be kindled, and a national fpirit and exertion roufed, which undif-couraged, unfubdued by many defeats, will ultimately carry away all before it. So that popular focieties will be attended with very different effects, when directed againft an unjuft and tyrannous polity, from thofe which will attend them when directed againft a found and well conftructed one. In the one cafe they will prove in-noxious and harmlefs ; in the other alarming and terri-ble. In popular governments they may fometimes proceed to ofcitate on elections, reverfe wife and excel-lent laws for a time, and lay afide excellent characters, fome of their beft and moft ufeful friends, and reward their merits with public ingratitude, but they will fub-ftitute others in their room, who collectively will do well, and the public will go on, and the government proceed

regularly, though in new hands. But they will generally preferve a fucceffion of worthy characters. In the
other cafe they will demolifh polities, overturn thrones,
eject ariftocrats, and inftitute new elective governments
—differently policied perhaps, but uniformly elective.

When popular focieties are fet on foot, if the polity
be fo well fettled to the general fenfe, as that they fhall
turn out but a minority, and yet this minority fhould
be fo confiderable and daring as to arm againft the
conftitution, civil war or a war of citizens enfues, and
there remains no umpire, until victory declares it. In
that exigency it becomes of neceffity that the law of the
ftate fhould declare fuch affociations feditious, traiterous
and rebellious. And the fame muft take place, be the
polity juft or unjuft, provided the majority of the community concur in it. But it remains to be experi-
mented by future ages, whether there will often if
ever exift fuch a minority combination againft a polity
once, and efpecially repeatedly fettled with fatisfactory
revifions, by the collective body of the people, efpecially where frequent revifions are appointed and provided
in the conftitution , and whether an infurrection generally difcountenanced, will not give way and be eafily
fuppreffed with or without force, and perhaps only by
light and the fraternal perfuafions of fellow-citizens.—
Againft a generally acceptable polity, every popular
effort of minority affociations will die away and come
to nothing, terminating in the confirmation and ftrength-
ening the polity to an impregnable inviolability. A-
gainft fuch a bulwark of the united people, the efforts of
a clufter of popular focieties will prove but *bruta fulmi-
na*, harmlefs, and felf-defeated as well as felf-created.
But if the polity be a bad one, fuch a clufter may be
fubdued, may poffibly increafe, acquire irrefiftible
ftrength and carry all before it The little quarrel of
the Marfh brought on the *bellum fociale*. Not all the
Baftiles nor Botany Bays, no enforcement of the exifting laws againft fedition, can prevent the fpread and

progreſs of this conviction of the poſſible right, utility and neceſſity of popular aſſemblies at leaſt to contemplate the public ſtate, and in given caſes even to regenerate the policy.   And when this ſhall have become a little more the general conviction of nations, they wil burſt forth, and originate and deviſe modes of public exertion, adequate to the accompliſhment of a complete revolution in any polity.   Nor will the preſent age of light and liberty reſt in any thing ſhort of this. The nations will never ſit down content with this, that a defective conſtitution is irremediable.   They will not deſpair ; they will find a remedy ſomewhere, an efficacious remedy not to be defeated by aulic manœuvres and circumventions either of policy or force.   No meaſures of any actual exiſting government can ultimately defeat this.   Every Botany Bay deciſion in England will contribute to the acceleration and inſurance of ſuch an event.   And perhaps England will be the next to try the political experiment, after France ; even in the ſure foreſeen road to liberty, being marked with horror and blood.   Exaſperated deſpair will be fruitful in expedients, and bold, adventurous, and ſucceſsful in enterprize.   The public ſenſe on the preſent ſtate of the Engliſh conſtitution muſt ſooner or later be tried.   It can be tried only in theſe aſſemblies in the nature of things   Theſe might for this end be called by the exiſting ruling powers.   But the ruling powers certainly never will do it.   It can then never be done but by ſpontaneous origination.   This is the only alternative.   This cloſed, liberty is gone, tyranny is inviolable.   Will the world ſit down quiet and ſubmiſſive under this laſt gloomy, ſolitary, ſwiniſh concluſion : In the ſpirit of prophecy, I ſay, nay !

Should the expreſs, real, true and only object of the voluntary ſocieties in England, or the recovery of *annual parliaments* and *univerſal ſuffrage,* they would be guilty of no crime againſt the laws or the ſtate.   But ſhould they arm, that moment it becomes ſedition—

and punifhable as fuch—if the exifting powers fhall prove able to fubdue an armed minority, which may at length become an armed people   In this event all is reduced to hoftility and civil war : a conflict enfues till victory declares itfelf.   " Univerfal fuffrage and annual parliaments are legitimate and conftitutional objects of purfuit. '

A reform in parliament is neceffary in the public conviction, even of the parliament itfelf as well as the nation at large.   How far it fhould proceed is a doubt, whether by an equitable appointment of the reprefentation to the one hundred and fifty thoufand electors of fhires, cities, and boroughs ; or by univerfal fuffrage ? Mr Pitt, as well as Burke, Fox, and others were once for a reform in the commons , and Pitt publicly avowed in parliament, annual parliaments, and univerfal fuffrage, the very principles avowed in the Britifh convention at Edinburgh.   But the French revolutionaries changed their minds, or rather, affected that now was not the proper time, or that it ought to be procraftinated to a time, which he now forefees can never be found, which is in effect convincing him, that what he once advocated ought never to be done, becaufe he now forefees it never can be done, without the fure danger of the demolition of royalty and nobility.   The haughtinefs of high dominion can never give up, until it is too late.   It is intended by court politicians that the diffonance of opinion as to the mode of reform fhall nullify the whole.   They are content to have the queftion moft liberally agitated, but never to be fettled and determined : that the partizans fhould difcufs themfelves out of breath, as in a chancery fuit, and in defpair to leave all to an *uti poffidetis.*   Circulating this *ultimatum* among all the partizans of the miniftry, it is purpofed and affuredly expected to worry out the public fpirit, and go on with the prefent fyftem, until all fhall feel it incurable, and tamely acquiefce.

The national debt is confidered as combining and holding all together. It is fuppofed to be fatally endangered by a revolution, and efpecially by the change of a monarchy into a republic. But it is as eafy to fecure a national credit in the one as the other. Holland, Venice, America, and I believe France will fhew that national credit, ftocks and funds may be as fecure in a republic as in a monarchy. If in a revolution it fhall be provided that the public debt fhall be taken upon the new polity, all would be fecure, unlefs the debt, as it may be, fhould be fo heavy as to be impoffible to be fupported. But how powerful foever a public debt may be towards confolidating and holding the polity together, there are great exigencies, in which it will lofe this force. A debt of three hundred millions fterling did not withhold the Roman empire from diffolution, when its fate was expired. There are certain political tempefts which carry away all before them. The national debt of England will not repel a revolution, when the body of the people are brought to exert their force, which they certainly will do, when thoroughly fick of their polity : a crifis very faft approaching.

But if a reform, contrary to all court intention and expectation, muft come on ; the queftion will arife, fhall the parliament do this, or the people ? The parliament may feem to attempt, think to amufe the nation, but dare not to adventure a reform even of one houfe, and much lefs of both. And therefore from a concurrence of various motives, both houfes feeling themfelves to ftand or fall together, will unite in the moft firm and decided oppofition to it, and rifque the moft fanguinary meafures to defeat every attempt, and prevent, obftruct, and fupprefs every movement efficacioufly tending to a real reform , unlefs it may be they may propofe fo trifling and fo ineffectual a reform, as will rather mock and irritate, than give national fatisfaction. Add to this, that though they allow the people to fancy and conceive that they have rights and liber-

ties, and fuffer them to boaft of them, declaim upon
them and glory in them, as long as the politicians fee
them chained and fettered ; yet really in their hearts
and fecret counfels, they at bottom moft cordially hold,
that the herd cannot govern themfelves ; and as to participation in government the fwinifh multitude have no
rights and liberties, or which is the fame thing, none
originally and independently, none but what are held at
the conceffion of the King and parliament. And the
few afcending from the plebeians into parliament, foon
lofe their plebeian principles and become affimilated to
the ariftocracy. The two hundred and fifty nobles
therefore and five hundred and fifty commons, or their
venal majorities, become a combined Phalanx againft
the people, fet and firmly united againft any ultimate
and real alteration or reform of the polity. There remains therefore that the ftruggle muft be given up. It
will not be given up. The feelings of ariftocracy are
totally different from the feelings of the people. The
prepofterous conduct of the miniftry and parliament for
now almoft half a century have fo involved and oppreffed the nation, as to precipitate a revolution, A national inquiry is unavoidable. It has taken place in
France, it will take place in every fovereignty in Europe, it will take place in England fooner or later.—
The mode cannot be predicted, faving only that it will
be a popular one. A real Saxon meycle-gemot muft
be refumed.

The Englifh parliament is fuch a mockery on reprefentation, that the nation will never reft in its prefent
ftate. And it muft fooner or later be altered. The agitations for effecting this inevitable alteration will bring
on and advance other political difcuffions, terminating
in a republican renovation. So abfurd and difpropor-
tionate is the reprefentation in parliament, that it ftrikes
all with difguft, as an infult on the majefty of the people. Of the five hundred and fifty members, it appears that in England, two thoufank fix hundred and

eleven perfons elect and return three hundred and twenty feven members; and in Scotland, of the forty-five
members to reprefent two millions of people, ninety
eight perfons elect one third, and the other thirty are
elected by about one thoufand four hundred.

When the prefent national ftorm is a little over, parliament will attempt to appeafe the public fpirit by ap
portioning the reprefentation. So far it will be well.—
But they will fee that this will not fatisfy. They will
enlarge the election, but will not proceed to univerfal
or general fuffrage. This may reft the national fpirit
for the prefent, and refpite further popular exertions,
perhaps for another generation, perhaps not. However they will by both thefe meafures give the precedent
of a principle, on which the public will prefcribe for
further enlargements and amendments. Liberty muft
be difputed and gained by inches. The cure of the national diforder is not yet effected. The defignation of
all public offices is to be regulated. If left in the hands
of the monarch, fole appointment will ever give him
power to command and fubject both houfes to his will.
The poffibility of this autocratical controul in the crown
remains to be extinguifhed. The nobility will be with
the King. All this will ultimately fooner or later bring
on a ftruggle with ariftocracy, which muft be fought
out with blood, and then the nation will become a republic. Half a century will complete this. Or at
leaft it will be accomplifhed in fome given time.

Politicians fhould look upon irritated human nature,
and confider the extent of paffive national endurance.
They may view it in the Roman empire, in the hiftory of the reformation from the pontificate, in the Englifh hiftory from king John to this time, in the Barons
wars, in the endurance of the Duke of Alva, in fhort
in a thoufand fimilar inftances in the hiftories of nations. Look at the French revolution, look at the
American revolution; inftead of looking to Cæfar, to
the vanquifhments of tyranny, to the invafion of the

Gauls by the Franks, the Saxon, Danish, and Norman conquests, the English illegitimate conquest of Ireland, and the other successful conflicts of tyranny: and in numerous other examples, they may find that tyranny, however adventurous, is not always successful. But they will be taught by none of these. They will find, however, that the temerity of incensed Englishmen will, as in the last century, risque blood and every consequence. The conflict once begun, though none can foresee the means, yet it requires no spirit of prophecy to foresee the event. The end will be accomplished, as sure as the downfall of the Roman empire. The road however to this end must be strewed with blood. But will any madly adventure this? They will. And there must and will arise more Cromwells, Kosciuskos, Whalleys, Fairfaxes, more Warrens, Muirs, Palmers, and Geralds, must suffer martyrdom. Three or four more hereditary monarchies and aristocracies must be fought and hunted down, before the rest will submit to the empire of liberty, law and reason. Oh Parliament! O English Nation! you have before you to fight out, not whether a Stuart, Nassau, or Brunswick, this or that family, shall reign, no longer a war among Kings, a conflict between interfering and claiming sovereigns—but a more interesting, real and solemn conflict awaits you—a conflict between the people and sovereigns and hereditary aristocrats, and in connexion with them in England, a plebeian assembly or deputed show of fictitious, popular, unreal representative, called on fallaciously to support them. But let us be assured the conflict will be severe and bloody—it will however assuredly take place—and its end will be glorious! During the arduous trial, we of the United States, shall contemplate this struggle with heart-feeling solicitude, and share with the same estate, from which we ourselves gloriously emerged—in the pains and exultations of the final triumphs of liberty. We sprang from England, and hail that land of liberty, takes as much attention and fympathetic feeling, as our brethren, from whom we have been cruelly difmembered. And our reflexions are made and uttered here, with the moft liberal, unembarraffed and unbounded freedom, a freedom unknown even in England, that land, of all the tranfatlantic regions, the land of free difcuffion and liberty.

It is not alien or foreign from our purpofe, but directly in point to adduce thefe ftrictures and obfervations, or to attend to the prefent ftate of things in England and Europe, becaufe they have iffued from 1641, and are but the progrefs of the conflict of ages, and becaufe in their ftruggles with tyranny, the nation find themfelves obliged to recur to the principles of the laft century, and refume the work, which Oliver and the Judges once atchieved before them, and put into the hands of the nation, and which they were foolifhly duped to give back and furrender to the flattering and ever delufory promifes of tyranny. If the exifting polities will not reform themfelves, as they certainly will not, all muft come to the conclufion of the enlightened patriots of paft ages, + and efpecially of the laft century, who were more deeply ftudied in the principles of polity and dominion, than the civilians that any other age ever produced. After every the moft profound difcuffion of the fubject, every one muft finally come to a conclufion, which their progenitors clearly difcerned and fo announced, that in fuch an exigence, there remains the only alternative of fubmiffion or rebellion. And though every other rebellion is unjuftifiable, yet fuch an exigence may be adjudged to neceffitate and juftify rebellion—for it is faid, "rebellion to tyrants is obedience to God."

+ Some of the moft profound and learned productions of human nature are anonymous treatife, D [...] M [...] n f b [...] & [...] f [...] in that years, 15-6, in which the limits of obedience, and those in cafes of juftifiable irritation are [...]

But to return —Oliver Cromwell once faved the nation ; and, as I have faid, upon deliberate confultation both of the army and parliament, and with the concurrent hearts of certainly a very large and refpectable body of the divided nation, devifed a very excellent conftitution, in the force and fpirit of it very nearly refembling that afterwards conceived and adopted by the United States :—" *O fortunatos nimium fua fi bona norint!* " The conftitution by 1657 was ripened to this, that the government be a commonwealth, and the national legiflature confift of a Protector and two houfes, all elective and none hereditary. Herein it is provided, 1 That the Protector be for life. The fucceffion to be kept up by the election of the upper houfe. 2 That this confift of forty to fifty members, to be alfo for life, amoveable however for mifdemeanor. The fucceffion, either, by the houfe of commons electing fix, out of which the other houfe felect two , from which the Protector to elect one , or, if the commons omitted their nomination for twenty days, the lords to proceed, nominate and choofe three, out of whom the Protector to take one. 3 That the houfe of commons confift of 460, triennially elected by the people, in a judicious and proportionate manner. 4. A concurrence of the two houfes, by their refpective majorities, to make an act of Parliament , not fubjected to the veto or negative of the Protector. This is the outline of the polity.

But like Ifrael, the nation wifhed for a King , wifhed to return to Egypt. They returned, and God fent them a King in his anger , they returned, and went into flavery , felt themfelves caught and difappointed, and in twenty years became fo wearied out, that the public mind again changed, and became prepared for the partial expulfion of tyranny in 1688. They might have faved themfelves thirty years lofs of liberty, had they banifhed hereditation out of the Englifh government —had they perfevered in the republican form devifed by the difcerning enlightened Protector, and thofe of his

...patriots, ever faithful to their country's welfare.— Had his wisdom directed him to have left his other house elective by parliament, or by the people in almost eve... ... he had made the house of commons to ... ... elective, he would have left a policy so ... adapted to universal human nature, but ... ... making the ... ... Necker's allowances for ... fees, labors, and various distributions of pro... ... ... to be ... into new constitutions, ... should never have ... to have revised and ... ... But even his new ... ... although in the ... ... elective but ... at ... ... whose succession was left too indefinite, ... operation, a power ... controlling ... ... the power of the supreme legislature. and ... ... formed, and did in fact embosom, ... as well as patriotism, than Heaven usu... ... ... to an hereditary nobility, ever ignorant, ... and devoid of understanding, or ... ... and overlaying the really great and ... ... wisdom of the lower number, a small scattering of feeble and meritorious characters, always to be found among the lords or nobility of every nation. Thus liberty would be constantly ascending and streaming up ... to the national council. This with an elective Protector at its head, had been nearly a perfect policy. Had the Protector lived twenty or thirty years longer, or had the nation been possessed of patience and stability, Oliver's policy might have grown up into this firm and beautiful perfection. May I be indulged with stating my idea of a perfect polity?

Conspectus of a perfect Polity.

We may assume a territory of five hundred miles square, populated with five, ten, or twenty millions of inhabitants, universally free, according to their various industry possessing allodial property. On this field of dominion a polity is to be erected, which they will never ... ... It may be ... the national council confifting of a double reprefentative with a head, all ftanding upon the election of the community at large; and fo modified as that every member fhall efficaciuflv feel his dependance upon the people at large. Let thefe branches receive any appellation at pleafure. For the prefent theory, let them be denominated the Protecto, and the upper and lower houfes : the one to confift of about five hundred, more or lefs, the other of fifty or one hundred, more or lefs. In this council collectively fhall refide, under prefcribed and defined modifications, not only legiflation, but dominion and fupreme government. For this double reprefentation, the populated field of dominion may receive a double partition into five hundred and into fifty diftricts, confifting as near as may be of about an equal number of inhabitants, fubject to revifion according to the variation, increafe or diminution of population. Each of the five hundred local diftricts to elect a fingle reprefentative, for forming the lower houfe, or a houfe of reprefentatives of local diftricts. Thefe will bring up into the rational council a perfect information of the local diftricts. The election of this branch to be triennial.

For the upper houfe of reprefentatives ftanding, not on local, but univerfal election, the fifty larger diftricts to elect one for each; but fo that each member ftands, not on the election of that diftrict only, but on univerfal election—and that in this manner :—Although the citizens vote in diftricts, yet they fhall vote each for but one member in his own diftrict, and for one in each of the other diftricts . all the citizens in every diftrict fhall vote for fifty members, but they fhall be taken one in each diftrict, fo that by thefe means all the fifty fhall feel themfelves to ftand on univerfal election. Let the Protector alfo ftand on univerfal election. A certificate from each diftrict fhall be fufficient to afcertain the election of the diftrict, both for the Protector and both houfes The plurality of votes, not majority of all the votes, to determine all thefe elections. The Protector to be elected once in seven years : the upper house once in six years, with a rotation as in the Senate in Congress ; and the lower house once in three years. The public good, and permanency or stability of dominion, requires that there should not be a possibility of a total change of the national council at any given time ;— while the citizens will have power and opportunity to make a thorough change, if they think best, within a sufficiently short period for the prevention of public mischief and the security and perpetuation of liberty. The national council thus elected, are to form themselves, and stand completely and constitutionally invested with all the powers of dominion and government.— In them resides the ordinary and active sovereignty of the republic. Except in the rotation in the upper house, none to be excluded from re-elections into either house, as long as he can approve himself to his fellow-citizens. Should it be judged more convenient that the President, or Protector, should stand on the election of both houses, instead of the people at large, it will be perfectly safe, as even in this mode he must feel his dependence not on a part, but the whole people, and can of nation itself for the tender father of the republic at large. A rotation in the lower house is not equally necessary as in the upper house. Death and human casualty will make sufficient rotations in the lower house ; besides that the interests of a single local district is but of subordinate importance compared with the universal interest. Changes in this will not be equally dangerous with too great and frequent changes in an house that comes on universal election.

In this frame of government, this polity of the two houses, the one will primarily feel the local interests, and secondly the general interest, the other must irresistibly feel primarily and all the interests, not separately, but collectively, and their primary and only motive must be the public good, the universal interest of the whole, or majority of the community. The one

will be the faithful confervators of the local intereft, as
well as attend well to the general intereft alfo, and in
the moft cafes when his own diftrict is out of the quef_
tion, which will be the cafe in moft inftances, will
judge impartially and faithfully for the public good
the other detached from all particularity, can have no
object but the univerfal, or at leaft the general good,
with which his own perfonal intereft is infeparably connected.

The powers of the houfes are not mixed, but feparate and concurrent. Thefe with the quorum of each
to be defined and fettled in the conftitution. They fit
and deliberate feparately, and their votes are of independent and feparate import. The concurrence of the
two houfes in their votes to conftitute an act, and there
can be no public act of the national council without
this concurrence. A few other declarations regulating
the exercifing their powers and authority in tranfacting
bufinefs, may be defined in the conftitution, the reft
may be fafely confided to their united wifdom. But in
cafe the two houfes fhould ever hereafter concur in any
one for the hereditation of any offices or their perpetu-
ty in any family line, or for the hereditation and perpetuity of the Protector and upper houfe, the conftitution fhould be thereby *ipfo facto* diffolved. In which
cafe it fhould be provided and eftablifhed in the conftitution, that the republic reverts to a ftate of nature ;
when any of the 500 diftricts may affume upon themfelves to circulate a communication among themfelves,
and originate by fpontaneous delegation from the diftricts, a *republican convention*, for the exprefs purpofe
of regenerating the policy and conftituting a new republic, and if neceffary may arm for the purpofe without
criminal rebellion.

Before we define the powers of the Protector, and in
order to difcern what portion of authority fhould be affigned and entrufted to the fupreme executive, we may

make an experiment of this policy, from whence we may discern the utility of these balances, and the obvious preference of the double to a single representation, or instead of vesting the whole government in one house, or a senate or council of one order only of local representatives, and indeed its preferableness to a single order standing on universal election, modified as above, both in point of ample and accurate information of every part, and diffusing the knowledge of characters among their constituents, for future elections, through the community. At the same time that conjoined with perfect local information, there is provided a natural and unfailing security of fidelity to the public and general welfare. To proceed with the experiment,—Let a bill be brought into the lower house—upon reading it, each member will run home in his own mind, and think how it will affect his own district, his immediate constituents, and he will be faithful to his district, this will be his first care. If it does not affect that otherwise than as it is involved in the universal interest, then the public good becomes equally his care, and indeed sole object. Again in this house will unavoidably be room for faction or junction of district or vicinity interests, and clubbing with districts in different parts towards carrying votes. This cannot so easily take place in the other house. The great advantage of local representations, is for obtaining perfect information, and for having the district satisfied that they have a faithful advocate in the national council, for its particular interest. Both these are matters of great moment. But it may be possible, and often happens, that a bill passes in this house rather from a junction of particular local interests, the interests of a part of the community, than from the public good. It needs then to be contemplated and acted upon by a house whose only or primary and governing object must be the public welfare, because it stands not on local, ubiquitarian election — Let the bill be read here, and instead of the members

running to a local or a few local interefts, they feel themfelves irefiftibly conftrained to contemplate the whole
head of dominion, the public weltare. A bill then
having had this confideration and review, and thereupon
having the concurrence of the local and univerfal reprefentatives, may be confided in as having received a
well informed and thorough difquifition, and as faithful a decifion as can be had from erring man.

And now as the Head or Protector, by the fuperemi-
nency of his ftation, may be juftly fuppofed to have a
circumfpective view of the public intereft, efpecially
furnifhed with all the lights of both houfes, and
his dependence on univerfal election alfo himfelf,
equally fecured from partiality, every one will fee
the fafety and utility of another revifion by the father of
the republic: not indeed to his final negative or veto,
which might be embarraffing and dangerous, though
not of lafting and irremediable mifchief, as he cannot
ceafe to feel a reference to a future election. It will
therefore be for the perfection of the polity, that he
fhould have the power of a temporary negative with a
limited time, and a reference to a reconfideration with
his reafons. He may have difcerned fomething of moment which may have efcaped both houfes, at leaft he
will have his feelings upon it, and the feelings of a character fo fituated may not be unworthy the attention of
the wifeft and moft enlightened affembly. His reafons
and obfervations in a revifion of the whole, may be
found beneficial, and may occafion amendments, or
falutary alterations, or even abolitions. But if after
this the views of the two houfes fhall continue the fame,
and they adhere to their former opinion and judgment
after revifion, it may be juftly confided in, that they
are right, the bill having had a due courfe, and as complete a deliberation and decifion as human wifdom admits, before it paffes into a public law. Thus thefe
fources in the polity are demonftrably wife, and I
aik conftitute perfection.

By confidering the juftly elevated fituation of the Protector, his connexion with the national council, his relation to the whole community, his being the political head of a diftinct fovereignty among the fovereignties of the world, and the communications and intercourfe with other ftates in peace and war, we may be enabled to judge with what power he ought to be invested, without laying a foundation of his becoming a defpot — thefe powers I fhall not detail. Thofe who frame the conftitution will do it with careful attention I mean only to fuggeft the outline of the political conftitution. He muft be the organ of the republic, through which all common affairs muft be had with furrounding ftates, which Vattel confiders as fo many moral perfons fufceptible of a variety of national relations, from whence arife thofe fitneffes, propriety of treatment, and focial obligations which, with the treaties and compacts among thefe political moral perfons, become the law of nations, founded in principles of moral right, according to Grotius and Puffendorf, and of a rectitude and conformity immutable as the eternal laws of nature The whole national affembly will be called to confider thefe things, and none more than the head of the republic. The command of the navy, army and militia, muft and muft be likewife confided to him, while the national council hold the appropriation of the revenues in their hands The making of war and peace are both matters of too great moment to be left in the hands of a fingle individual perfon It is undoubted in the conftitution of the United States, that great republic the Prefident cannot act alone, but muft have the advice and concurrence of the Senate — The defignation of appointment of officers, civil, military, judicial, and the revenue, would be dangerous in his hands. With this power, like the King of England, he would foon fail to corrupt a majority of both houfes, and reduce them to a dependance on him, or the diftribution of honour The profufion of power

and unlucrative offices may be left to his direction with
[...] But an ample selection should be made of all
the great offices, especially of high emoluments, and in
general of offices in every department, to the amount at
least of three quarters of the aggregate value of all the
[...] in the republic should be guarded, by the nomi-
[...] of the Protector and concurrence of both houses.
This is a matter of vast moment. It will thus become
[...] for the supreme magistrate to corrupt both
[...] Other regulations respecting the powers, au-
[...] and necessary prerogatives of the protectorate,
[...] be of importance to define and limit in the consti-
[...] while others and perhaps more temporary pow-
[...] adapted to exigencies, may be safely left to the na-
[...] council, which by the facts may from time to time
[...] part to him the necessary powers, and revoke them.
[...] a guarded vigilance should be held that so im-
[...], and necessary a character should not
[...] to usurp an independence and controul,
[...] to overturn and prostrate the liberties of the
[...]

It has become fashionable to call the national coun-
[...] but entitle a LEGISLATURE,
[...] this with their name and principal duties. If a
[...] legislation
[...] The [...] the M[...]
[...] needed a[...]
[...] G[...] has from the[...]
[...] Z[...] H[...]
[...]
[...]
[...]
[...]
[...]
[...]
[...]
[...]

tions of laws according to the exigencies of society will in some degree be always taking place, yet after a while in a well settled government legislation will employ but a small part of its attention and labors and a national assembly. The other transactions in *government*, and of the other society, will soon become far more voluminous than the acconct of laws or statutes. When the nation is not cmployed in law-making they are properly .... er transactions ... .

....
....
....
....
....
....
....
....
....
....
....
....
....
....
....
....
....
....

....
....
....
....
....
....
....
....
....
....
....

and great law learning, and of uncorrupted integrity, limited to judge not according to their discretion, but according to the laws of the land, and that they hold their offices *quamdiu se bene gesserint :* that treason in the protector and corruption in the judges be punished with death. A high court should be provided and authorized, not by the legislature, but by the constitution, for the regular trial of such high delinquents. All other courts for the distribution of justice through the land may be instituted by the legislature.

This is the general idea of a perfect policy. The title or appellation of this public body may be, *Congress, Senate, General Council,* or *National Assembly.* The name is very indifferent, and will have no efficacy on their public acts and operations. The etymologies of the three last do not primarily lead to power and authority. The *congressus apt maturi* brings up with it both power and council united : and seems the most natural for a republican, unhereditary, elective aristocracy.— The whole national assembly is an aristocracy, while in office, not hereditary but elective. They continue in this elevation and superiority to their brethren, while by them entrusted with the high authority, and until, having run their race, and discharged their great and useful appointment, they revert back into the order of common fellow-citizens. This august body during their elevation are to receive all honor and respect, submission and free obedience from the whole union. While in office let them be treated with the honors of their office. There is a weighty objection to this policy. The unity of election will be objected, but a single Protector and one material branch, as impolitic and impracticable, and the like. To this it may be replied, that personal —— is not necessary. In —— on will be —— with respect —— —— is cha—— Experience has shewn —— the people at —— the —— —— —— ——

or one hundred characters, or more, all over the states, among which they are able to make a wife and judicious choice, or election. The men who are qualified for such high stations will soon be extensively known.— They should be those, who either by having been long in the national service, or by some distinguished atchievement of public utility, have approved themselves qualified with wisdom, experience, and a perfect acquaintance with public affairs, by which their abilities and fidelity will become extensively known to all the tribes through the union and community. This will supply an ample sufficiency of worthy, patriotic and excellent personages, characters of ability and public confidence, of diffused reputation, and universal notoriety, from which the community in general, will be enabled with good discernment and judgment, to elect those superior and universal members.

Finally, let that inestimable jewel and preservative be inserted in the constitution, the power of R E V I S I O N, alteration and amendment, after certain stated periods, until the polity become so perfectly satisfactory, as that to the feelings and sense of the community, it needs no further amendment : when the use of the revisionary powers would go into desuetude of course , unless called up at distant periods to rectify and reform corruptions, which may in time be insinuated into the administration of the best polity.

This is the view of an utopian polity, which, whether right or wrong, will always rest in harmless idea. Its refutation and absurdity will never appear by an actual experiment, for such an experiment will never be made. Not that it is impossible · for notwithstanding the ingenious ideas of the great patriot Neckar, that republics must be differently policied according to the existing diversities of national society on which they shall be formed, as to customs, laws, usages and manners, ranks and orders, yet this polity may be success-

fully applied to all the kingdoms, empires and fovereignties on earth, under all their exifting diverfities—
leaving otherwife all the diftinctions and tenures of property, dignities, titles, honours, orders and inequalities, comprehended and untouched, even the hereditary
honors, if they have not power combined with them :
only adopting *liberty* and *equality* to their extent, that
the accefs up into the fupreme national council be open
to all the *inequalities* of fociety, fo that upon conftitutional election princes and nobles, dukes, marquiffes,
earls, vifcounts, barons, governors, generals, ecclefiaftics, civilians, merchants, gentlemen, yeomen,
profeffional characters, and the literati, are all equally
eligible, and all meet and fit and act together as equals,
with a " *Nos hic una sedemus uti Barones..*"   As all
grades of nobility are *pares* in the houfe of nobles, fo
nobles and plebeians *pares* in national council.   The
houfe of commons in England, and the national affembly in France have exhibited and realized this equality
amidft inequality.   Adopting this commanding idea,
this polity might be readily and with facility applied to
all the diverfified kingdoms on earth.   As eafily might
a republic be formed out of the intricate and confufed
hotch potch of the Germanic empire, and the empires
of Turkey, Perfia, or Indoftan, as out of the plain co-
equal yeomanry, freeholders and citizens of the United
States.   All the diverfified nations are fufceptible of a
regeneration into the fame uniform republican policies,
with a fuperfedure indeed, but not deftruction of orders.   But all this will be treated and rejected as only
the impracticable theories and fpeculations of the ftudy,
the fanciful reveries of reclufe and unexperienced life.
Indeed fo many exifting circumftances muft and will be
attended to in the reformation of the old, corrupt and
worn out governments, and in the forming of new ones,
or in the regeneration of the fovereignties of the world
now already begun, that my idea will not, and in effect cannot be realized.   But perhaps an approximation

to the leading features and capital principles of it, especially as to election, banishing *hereditation of power*, and
providing reason, already begun and arisen among the
nations, begun in the unsuccessful efforts of 1641, and
successfully realized in 1796, may restore the present
places to a good degree of amelioration, effect the
ends of the efficacious, just and happy government,
and secure the reign, the dominion of law, rights and
liberties, as far as can be expected in the present state
of man. But this perfect idea will never be realized.
The neatest resemblance to it, which I have found,
among all the policies that have existed since the first
dispersion of the nations, was in the most beautiful and
well organized republic of Ireland, spontaneously formed by the emigration from Norway, and flourishing in
the tenth century.

Undoubtedly in the future structure of policies, there
will be a great variety; while most probably hereafter
they will all agree in the rejection of monarchy, and in
a government by a national council, or senate of one or
more orders, concluded in some mode or other. The
less complicated the more simple, systematical and intelligible to the body of the people, the better. It remains to be verified by experiment, whether a republic
ruled by one order of co-equal senators, and this elective, can be permanent and lasting. At present the
speculation is that it cannot. But, the tumultuous, self-
defeating confusion of the whole republics in Italy notwithstanding, I believe future trial will exhibit a proof
that its durability is possible, and that it may well answer the ends of liberty and permanent government,
and yet be by no means equal in excellency to the balances of two orders in the national senate. The policies of permanent republics may be as various, as those
have been of permanent monarchies. The ten existing
kingdoms of Europe are all differently policied, no two
similar, least of all exactly alike, unless in monarchy.

Of the half a dozen republics in Europe, no two are alike, all are of diverfified policies.

A republic fafe for liberty, laws, and energetic government, may be formed upon different modifications. It may be formed of elective or hereditary ariftocracies, for while in office and cloathed with power and authority, they are an ariftocracy, whether an elective or hereditary, and the conftitution may be equally permanent. The fenate may confift of unelective hereditary patricians, as Venice, which has fubfifted for ages, with great firmnefs and wifdom. Or it may be formed of one order elected from the people or citizens of the community at large, and this for life, the fucceffion in cafe of vacancies by death to be filled by election of the people. Or this fenate of one order may conftitutionally ftand on triennial, feptennial, or frequent elections, the elections to be made out of citizens of all orders and defcriptions promifcuoufly, or all to be indifferently eligible into the national fenate of one order. Perhaps fomething like this may be that which will in fact take place. Or a policy may be formed in another mode. The whole body of the citizens may be refolved into centuries and claffes, as among the Romans,† and balancing one another : that is, there may be one clafs of hereditary nobility, another of citizens of high opulence, a clafs of merchants, and claffes of other defcriptions, and poffibly in fome ftates the clergy and univerfities may make another clafs : and all thefe to be reprefented by election in their refpective claffes, and form a national fenate of two, three or more negatives, or vetos, as once in Sweden ; or form one co-ordinate body, or otherwife be differently modified, as circumftances and prevailing coalefcences may indigitate and point out, or as may arife on contingence and compact and fubmiffive acquiefcence But an elective fenate of two balancing orders, ftanding on *local* and *general* elections, would be the moft fimple, intelligible, and perfect. Howe-

† *Livy* A a 2

ver a republic, and even a monarchical republic might, in some or any of these modes be constructed, in which liberty and the public weal might be to a very good degree secured, and established with a very durable satisfaction. We all have our feelings, and national and perhaps speculative preferences. Among those who are sincerely principled and disposed to liberty in general, one from education or judgment will feel a lift to monarchical and aristocratical ideas, another to mixt and balancing republican ideas of equality as to eligibility. The future formation of policies may possibly exhibit several of these diversified forms. Which will really approve itself the most friendly to right, liberty, and the public weal, must be left to the experiment of two or three ages, when upon a comparison and history of all these liberty policies, it may appear which is best. I that have been educated in republican ideas, as was Vattel, and at a distance from nobility eminencies, feel very well satisfied with equality in the national council, and think it bids fair to succeed the best. Montesquieu, educated in high monarchical and aristocratical ideas, could not enter into the spirit of a republic. A genuine Englishman will ever think differently on the subject of rights and liberties from the rest of the world. There is no umpire in this matter but the experiment of ages, after various politics have been tried. Monarchical politics in all their variety have been abundantly tried, republican politics remain to be tried.

Far am I from thinking that the wisest and best policy can efface the impressions of corruption. Let us not expect but that it will break in with a constantly dreading influence. We have only to find which is susceptible of the least. Wherever the policy be, wherever the power rests, whether in a monarchy, aristocracy, or the people, let us count upon it, let us be assured corruption will apply itself with an insidious and equal dexterity. My only hope is, that it may be enervated by having a large and diffusive object to spend itself upon, and by the frequency of elections. Even in a republic universally elective, great will be the corruption, in defiance of all laws. Nobles and men of opulence, as well as indigent popularity, by money and intrigue, and disposition of offices through union of factions, will have full and overbearing weight, to render into the national council men whose personal interests will not coincide with those of the public. One opulent man will corrupt or influence a thousand plebeian electors. We see it in the English parliament, where popular corruption constantly renders a very great number of nobles into the house of commons, as well as that of the lords. Already of five hundred and fifty members, two hundred and fifty, perhaps two thirds, are noblemen, and of enobled blood. And it may possibly come to pass, that no longer shall the commons be represented by commons according to the original intention of that house, but the commons be wholly represented by nobles, English, Scotch, or Irish, so both become a double house of nobles, one hereditary the other elective. A similar corruption is taking place to at least in a small degree in the elections of the United States. Our only safety is in diffusing light and knowledge through the common people and body of the citizens at large, to guard them from being bribed or influenced against their own interest, for each citizen has an interest in the public interest; and by making the object, on which corruption is to operate, as diffusive as possible. On the whole, we seem to stand the best chance of gathering the greatest quantity of wisdom and public spirit into the council, by *election*, with all its corruptions, than by *hereditary* ignorance and folly. And under all the popular mutabilities, a succession and permanency of wisdom and patriotism is far more secure and certain in an elective, than hereditary aristocracy.

I have hitherto said nothing concerning religion, which seems to be agreed to be shut out of modern po-

licies. The mischiefs of sectarian tests, the injustice
of the elevation of any one sect in particular, to the ex-
clusion, disfranchisement, or destruction, or even mo-
lestation of the rest, as in England, Poland and Holland, have inclined all to a growing concurrence in
leaving them out of civil society. And some enlightened minds have proceeded the lengths of so daring a
liberty, as even to expunge the existence of a God out
of his own creation. A very liberal Catholicism ought
certainly to be cultivated among all sects of christians,
upon the principles of policy as well as of our holy religion, our common christianity. But I do not see
that a christian republic ought either to renounce christianity, on the one hand, or on the other hand, to extend charity to the equality, indifference and nullification of all religions. I am in decided opposition to the
deistical ideas, which have usurped too much influence
in the reformation of polities at this day, as if to put heaven to another trial, whether it can maintain christianity,
as it did the three first centuries. Christianity will up-
hold itself, be the policies of states as they may But a
christian state ought expressly to acknowledge and embosom in its civil constitution, the public avowal of the
being of a GOD, that Most High and Holy Sovereign,
upon whom all depends, and the avowal of christianity.
In this period, of taking great liberties with the person
and religion of Jesus, of conceited wisdom, of bold and
illiberal invectives against revelation, during the present rage and enthusiastic mania of deism, I fear not to
risque the offence and vociferous repudiations of the dis-
ciples of the open Voltaire and Rousseau, or the covert
deistical Gibbon, notwithstanding their public honors
in the recent apotheoses of the newly resumed ethnical
idolatry, and their repositation among the collection of
Gods in the motly pantheon of the Temple of Reason.
The blaze of this little political diaspora of extravagant
and self-opinionated philosophers (a fraternity bringing
that honorable name into contempt, as it did in the

fourth century) will, like other momentary lamps of error, burn down, go out and evanifh , and the world, inftead, of public conviction or general converfion, will foon write upon it, *mene, tekel.* Thefe men of eafy virtue, and generally of eafy morals, from infidioufly inferting themfelves into the various departments of the political adminiftration of ftates, will foon find it expedient in a chriftian community to bend and mafk their principles, under the pretext of becoming favorable to chriftian morals, and perhaps to become hypocritical advocates for the caufe of the Redeemer. Much better however for a chriftian republic, to take care in their elections, that they are ruled, not by covert deifts, but by real chriftians, rather than by dubious characters, characters whofe covert duplicity cannot but often break out and difcover themfelves on a thoufand occafions

I am the more open and explicit upon this fubject ; for it would ill become me, who, by the grace of God, have been fnatched and refcued from deifm, by the weighty, the prevailing force, the omnipotent convictions of truth, to apologize to men of half finifhed difquifitions, to the ignorance of my brother finners, or even to the moft enlightened philofophers of deified reafon, for moft freely and openly avowing and advocating the caufe of revelation. I make no apology · I temporize not in conceffions to the learned or unlearned.— After having been by heaven carried through the whole inquiry, through the feries and train of proofs, up to conclufive and certain demonftration, I fubmit not to the fuppofition of uncertainty, or of the poffibility of miftake, in a matter of fuch fuperlatively HIGH PROOF, and of as certain evidence, as that for the exiftence of a God. I could as eafily apologize for believing there is a God, as for the belief of chriftianity. Under demonftrative conviction of both, my mind, my confcious intelligence, efpecially at certain times of intenfe contemplation, ftruck and overcome with the powerful impreſſions of evidence, could as eaſily and readily give up the one as the other. I could ſay as truly under full perception of its truth, that the pythagoric problem, or the higheſt demonſtrations in Euclid, were dubious and falſe, as that chriſtianity is a dubious and erroneous illuſion ; when the conſcious perception of my mind ſees and knows, that it came down from the God of infallible truth. That great juriſt and civilian, Minutius Fœlix, could tell theſe men of light and reaſon, a Tertullian, that learned juriſperite of Carthage, who reſigned the toga of the forum for the ſacerdotal pallium, could tell them, that greater juriſt than both, I mean Father Paul of Venice, and a greater civilian and hiſtorian than theſe, the immenſely learned Selden, characters which, for comprehenſive collocation of evidence, deep diſcernment, ſolidity and accuracy of judgment, would weigh down a thouſand Gibbons and Monteſquieus, and others of ſuperficial and curſory diſcuſſion of the ſubject, a ſubject however whoſe evidence Lies equally level to the capacities of the vulgar and learned, in this as well as the apoſtolic age :—theſe, I ſay, can tell us, that the evidences of chriſtianity have blazed conviction into their minds, with as clear and irreſiſtible a force, as thoſe for the being of a God. The ſingle fact of the reſurrection and aſcenſion of Jeſus ſupports the whole . and this is as highly proved as his crucifixion, and is as indubitable as the exiſtence of a God. The reſurrection of Jeſus being eſtabliſhed, the whole fabric of revelation is ſupported thus —None can doubt but that Chriſt and his apoſtles believed the inſpiration of the whole old teſtament. If God ſhould raiſe up an holy prophet from among men, which deiſts will allow poſſible, and inſpired with documents and authority from on high , ſhould he lay his hand on Moſes and the Prophets (it would be believed ſhould I ſay, on the writings of Roſſeau and Voltaire) and in the name of God announce them inſpired, their inſpiration would at once be authoritatively ſettled, and even deifts would candidly renounce and give up the conteft. Now Jefus was that holy prophet, evidenced by the miracles of his life, paffion and refurrection. He and the difciples have declared this of Mofes and the prophets. Both their antiquity, authenticity, and real infpiration, are thus at once fettled and afcertained.— Thofe who have got fo far as to believe this, will have no difficulty as to the infpiration of the New Teftament. They will eafily find a way to get rid of all their fcruples and cavils at the bible. I will freely and cheerfully truft them with themfelves, only admitting the refurrection of Chrift with all its circumftances and connexions, knowing affuredly what will be the refult, even nothing lefs than a firm and indubitable belief of revelation. But at bottom, none of the deifts believe the fact of the revelation of Chrift. This is the great difficulty with them.

If they receive a profufion of fmiling indulgence, and even the moft cordial and rapturous applaufes, for perpetually interlarding their writings on policy, law, and government, on fecular and political hiftory, with foreign matter, with humourous invectives and farcaftical percuffions of revelation, they can have no juft objection at receiving in return the far more weighty, vigorous and repulfory reprehenfions of revelationifts. *Hanc veniam damus petimusque vicissim.* I have read moft of the deiftical authors, or at leaft fo many of the principal ones, that from thence. and my own fpeculations and feelings, I conceive myfelf poffeffed of all their arguments, and of the whole force of deifm : and I never found one that I thought had digefted the fubject, any more than Cofmas that of the fphericity of the earth, on which he wrote fo zealoufly, learnedly and voluminoufly, to no other effect than to difplay erroneous literature, and a pious but intemperate ardour on a miftaken fubject, of which he was finally ignorant. The fame with deifm.

If chriftians or deifts fhould believe the refurrection of Lazarus, they would not therefore believe him to be a prophet Hence it is faid that miracles, if facts, do not prove revelation. I attempt not the refutation of this confequence, which however admits of conclufive refutation : but fay that, this notwithftanding, if de-ifts bel eved the refurrection of Jefus (and efpecially if in con un on with this they alfo believed the reality of the thre years and a half miracles afcribed to him) there sp n en would hefitate to *believe* and k w m t be a prophet Never was there a believer of the r C n t Chrift, who doubted the hiftory of his mi nd s With fuch an one all the critical r on the th ty and conclufivenefs of mira-cles, would e an th They would confider, not the *nuda miracula,* but t e connexions and purpofes with wh ch they were operated, and become abundantly fa-tisfied. I never read of but one man, R Becai, who b eved the reality of Chrifts refurrection, that did not at the fame time believe even the Meffiahfhip, and he was convinced by it that JESUS was a *holy prophet.* If therefore his refurrection proves him a prophet, it eftablifhes the whole f per fructure and fyftem of reve-lation. Without being neceffitated to it, I however reft the whole fupport of revelation upon this fingle and moft momentous fact.

The rife of deiftical characters into fupremacy in European and American politics, t gives them an eclat, which is improved towards exciting a general defpair of the chriftian caufe, and towards a popular perfuafion that deifm is fpeedily becoming, if not already become generally prevalent throughout Chriftendom. But with-out obferving the providence and promife of God is againft it, as foon might we abolifh printing, letters, or the Newtonian aftronomy Indeed the recent tranf-actions which have been fuffered to pafs in the national councils of France, have countenanced this idea, and are confidered as a proof that they have generally
T

abandoned religion there, as well as in England and Germany. But is this implication just? Though they suffer atheists and deists, and unprincipled characters to join in the fighting their martial and political battles, in supporting what they are all concerned in as a common cause; and the nation may have gone too far, as they certainly have gone too far in gratifying and indulging this licentious description of men, in some of the measures they have brought forward, for the insidious abolition of religion, and the re-establishment of ethnicism; yet I make no doubt, they deceive themselves and the public in representing a general defection from religion.

Perhaps the picture which the Abbe Barruel has given of Paris, may apply to London, and the other capital cities of Europe. "The nobility of Paris too generally supported the doctrine of these sects," meaning the atheistical and deistical sects of the philosophers, "because they had long adopted the dissolution of their manners. They abandoned the churches to the people, instead of encouraging them by their example to frequent them: servants mimicked the vices of their masters, and the contagion soon spread to the humble cottage of the peasant. The citizen, the merchant, and his clerk, all affected to be witty on religious subjects. The magistrates, who were themselves not free from infection, winked at the infraction of the laws, and suffered the poison to spread through all ranks of the people. France was sinking into an abyss of impiety and corruption

"The clergy strove in vain to stem the torrent.— They were not all exempt from the vices of the age — This order of men may be ranked in two classes: the one little acquainted with the duties of the priesthood, but re the name and part of the ecclesiastical dress· too dissipated to be confined to the service of the altar, they were not inactive in soliciting the favor of courtiers who had the nomination to church preferment. They were a scandal to religion, and dishonored the cause instead of supporting t.

" The other class still more numerous, was composed of priests employed in the care of souls and of ecclesiastical functions. This was properly speaking, the body of the clergy. They were generally well informed of their duties. If some of them panted after the reins of the church, the greater number were seriously attached to the faith, and very few seemed disposed to betray it. The generality had not been wearied with religion Sophistry and impiety had infected a great number in every class of citizens, but still the French people in general were sincerely attached to the catholic religion. Nothing could reconcile them to the political revolution, but the strongest assurances, that no changes should be made in its doctrine or worship."*— This is agreeable to an account given me by M. Marbois, secretary to the Chevalier de Luzerne in 1779 — In a conversation with him, I asked him whether Deism was so prevalent in France as that the body of the nation had become impregnated and carried away with it ? He then replied that many of the nobility and dignified clergy indeed, with others of the higher and lower orders freely and openly went into it ; but that the most of the bishops, and the body of the ecclesiastics, with the main body of the people, were not only not deistical or disbelievers of revelation, but were even, as he expressed it, superstitiously devoted to religion. Accordingly of one hundred and thirty-eight bishops and sixty-four thousand curates or parochial clergy, only five prelates, and perhaps not a sixth of the clergy, took the civic oath, the rest refusing a conformity to the new civil and ecclesiastical regulations ; which would scarcely be credible had they been effected with the pliable indifferentism which a general deism would have generated. And the very general aversion of the people

* Barruel's Hist. French clergy, p. 6. 22.

at the thoughts of parting with the parochial religion throughout the realm, and the immediate neceffity which the politicians faw of fupplying the dereliAt parifhes with a new clergy, and leaving the people to en-joy their old religion, evince that the body of the nation were not become deifts.

Many data are neceffary towards *judicioufly* forming general eftimates. Let the matter be fairly and accurately explored, let it be brought to the trial, let there be a perfeAt liberty of declaring for and againft chriftianity, without incurring penalties or the lofs of immunities, place the mind in the moft perfeAt equilibrium and deliberate freedom, and examine hearts ; it would foon be found that the collecAtive aggregate of this learned, this philofophic and licentious defcription, would prove a fmall and inglorious, though brilliant minority : and that fo ftrong and fo general an adherence to the gofpel would appear, that of twenty-five millions in France, above twenty-four millions, and perhaps nine tenths of the other million, would now be found chriftians. From the unhappy omiffion of the exiftence of a God, and of chriftianity, in the conftitution of the United States, through deiftical influence, and that the road might be kept open for deifts to afcend into Congrefs, though to do the Convention juftice this was not the principle that aAtuated them : but from this omiffion however effeAted or occafioned, as well might it be inferred that the inhabitants of the United States were generally heathen, generally atheifts and deifts, when nine hundred and ninety-nine out of a thoufand would fhudder at the thoughts of renouncing their Redeemer. So they are generally tenacious of chriftianity in France, both from the habit of ages, and from the proofs and convicAtions tranfmitted with chriftianity.— And if the fubjeAt was examined with attention, I doubt not the fame would be found to be the faAt thro'-out Europe and chriftian America. Be affured that chriftianity will ever, and every where find able, learned, potent, weighty, and in the conflict irresistible advocates and defenders. The ultimate decision must be referred to futurity. For a long time during the present æra of conflict, as in that for establishing the republics of Poland and France, and as among the combatants in the pontifical controversy, the trumpet of victory which continue to be sounded *ex utraque phalange*, on both sides. In the mean time the defenders of revelation have no reason to be ashamed of the proof of their armour, or of the goodness of their cause: and may confide in it, that among all the defections, this of renouncing the gospel will be the last to become general in Europe or America. Would to God, we all lived it better. Sufflated bubbles of science and conceited wisdom, some balloon geniusses attack, impinge upon it, and fall one after another. The more christianity is attacked, the more firmly it stands, with an increasing and growing strength, not on power, not on the support of temporalities, or civil government, generally more fatal than beneficial, but on the calm, and weighty, and irresistible convictions of truth. Deism, like the Serpede, will spread and die, will blaze its day, overspread Europe and the world, spend itself, flit away and evanish from the globe, like the ethnicism of antient, or the tyrannies of modern ages. And its great and shining advocates will, in the future histories of nations, rank with the Democrituses and Pyrrhos, and other philosophical flambeaux of the luminous Grecian ages. These, with the other eminencies of fallacious delusion, will be given up in the ages of light and reason; which will marvel that preceding erring ages should be caught with those flimsy delusions, which by the weighty blast of truth, will eventually, like the thin gossamer, be dissipated and puffed into their great and unimportant nothings.

Let us be assured that the christian states are not going to give up religion. Nay, it will be, it cannot but be, that literature, justice and moral rectitude, patronized by the civil powers themselves. Let the deiftical politicians bring the matter to a crifis; let them adventure the trial, and affuredly they will not fail of receiving ample fatisfaction on the fubject. *N'en doutez pas, Quintius, la Religion a ses Heros. Polignac l'Anti-Lucrece.* **L. 1.**

I have finifhed my idea of a perfect republic. This I believe to be the arrangement of the grand monarchical republic of the univerfe: with this difference, that in the one immenfe, all-comprehenfive government of the Omnipotent, the power emanates, defcends and fpreads abroad, from the INDEPENDENT UNITY, and underived fource of all power and authority; in the other, in our little minutefimal polities, the power is left and ordained by the God of nature to derive from God, and to afcend through the people, up to the fovereign council, and from thence, in its beneficial influences and operations to be diffufed through the community. Other important matters here omitted, will fall in as auxiliary and fupplemental, and perhaps with confiderable admiffible variety, in conftructing and conftituting this polity, this edifice of public liberty. But it is conceived thefe are the effential, and I believe, all-comprehenfive outlines of one, which would approve itfelf a government, not of will, but of laws, wherein the liberties and rights of mankind, both perfonal and focial, would become too firmly eftablifhed, ever to be overthrown: for confident I am, that upon experiment, it would gain the univerfal acquiefcence and confidence of all embofomed and comprehended in it.

Comparing with this the Belgic, the Hœlvetic, the Venetian republics, or the antient republics of Greece and Rome, or the modern ones of France and Poland, and Egypt, with the monarchical republic of England, for according to Sir Thomas Smith this is a republic, and efpecially that of the United States of America; every one will eafily perceive, what ideas I muft have with refpect to their different approximations to this fyftem of perfection. And what I had principally in view, they will eafily perceive and fee the reafon why I fhould entertain fo high an opinion of the fafety and perfection of Oliver's republic, which I muft think will more and more approve itfelf to contemplative pof-terity, to have been excellent, and worthy the great, comprehenfive and deep difcernment, the noble efforts and exertions of fo great a genius as Cromwell's.— No wonder he was enamoured of it, idolized it, and rejected a crown for its fake. No wonder he was, with Cato, grieved, when he forefaw the certain ruin of fo noble a fabric, fo glorious a caufe. Examined in this view, we fhall perceive the neceffity of the bold, ad-venturous and heroic meafures, of firft bringing the King to juftice, and afterwards of diffolving the long and felf-perpetuating parliament. And in a word, the juftice and rectitude of moft of the infractions and viola-tions of the corrupt order of a defpotic policy, that on its ruins fo beautiful a frabric of liberty might be erected. And when in the fame light we examine the caufe of the Judges in the high court of juftice, we may at length fee them vindicated, and completely juftified.

We may fault the tribunal of Charles I. and fault the judgment: while there are and will be thofe, who will believe of both, that they were authoritative, juft and right. The republic of France is fuffering the fame public obloquy at prefent, but they may hereaf-ter be judged to have fet forth and exhibited an heroic inftance of public juftice, for the terror of Kings, which may learn them to tranfact in future with their fubjects with fidelity and finccrity. If two things appear proved of Louis Capet, a fovereign juftly efteemed and loved by America, his fate was juft. If he fecretly coinci-ded, negociated and intrigued with foreign cabinets, excited, abetted and promoted the coalition of foreign powers, for the exprefs purpofe of bringing a combined arm of 80,000 men, againft his own republic, with the direct objective purpose of its everſion : and if he paid 3000 forces, or the Swiſs guards at Coblentz, in that army *while in actual invaſion*, he was guilty of treaſon, *Traditionis Reipublicæ reus*. Now the national convention of 750, was aſſembled from the 83 communities, into which France had been regularly and conſtitutionally partitioned, and by them expreſsly and intentionally charged and empowered to three important works.—1. To form a conſtitution for the public reception and ratification. 2. In the mean time, upon the voluntary diſſolution of the national aſſembly, to take the whole government, the national defence, the whole adminiſtration, civil and military, into their hands.—And, 3. To judge the King. They were a new tribunal indeed, and very differently modified from any before erected on earth, but certainly, if twenty million people could regularly elect, legitimate, authorize and empower one, this was juſtly and legitimately veſted with this auguſt power and authority. Its regularity and authority cannot be diſputed. It was doubted but by few of the members themſelves. The only remaining queſtion then is, whether they judged right, whether they did juſtice ? All the world pitied and compaſſionated the mild and clement, the misguided, the unhappy Louis. But what ſaith, not compaſſion, in the ears of Judges, but juſtice ? Did he, or did he not, thus betray his people ? Seven hundred men examined the evidences, and paſſed ſentence upon him. Perhaps thirty or forty were intimidated and awed by the populace, or the Mountain, but 700 were unawed, they freely coincided with the very general ſenſe of the nation. Can we ſuppoſe they were all devoid of wiſdom, or ſo blinded with paſſion, as to be unable to judge on the evidences of facts ? No profound law erudition was requiſite ; but if ſo, they had it : they emboſomed a treaſury of law, wiſdom, and criminal juriſprudence, in that illuſtrious aſſembly. It is impoſſible to conceive 700 men, upon deliberative enquiry, unanimous in judging a fact, unlefs they faw the evidence. The inftance is not to be found in the hiftory of man ; it is impoffible. Nor did the King's defence deny the FACTS, but *eluded* them by afcribing them to his miniftry, though his own fignatures were fufficient. Could he have fhewn he had not been privy and knowing, and by his own overt and real acts confenting to and approving his minifters, he would have ftood acquitted, approved and vindicated, by that affembly, and they, and the fympathizing republican world would have rejoiced. But after a folemn enquiry and deliberation, the queftion was put, " Is Louis guilty, or not guilty of high treafon, or in other words, of confpiracy againft the liberty of the nation, and of attempts againft the general fafety of the ftate ?" Of 735 voters, of which 42 were abfent, 693 voted for the affirmative, and fentence was accordingly announced, " guilty." Such a concurrence I think impoffible on deficient evidence. " I know, faid Offelin, that Louis paid his guards at Coblentz ; I do therefore pronounce him guilty." Said Lafource, " Louis muft either reign, or be put to death. I vote for death." Said Anacrarfis Cloots, " In the name of the human race, I vote for the death of Louis." Thomas Paine, " I vote for the provifional confinement of Louis, and for his expulfion after the war." This was humane and compaffionate, the other juft, though ftrict and rigid juftice. It would have been humane and compaffionate, it would have been magnanimous and fafe, to have found him guilty, dethroned, and pardoned him, and out of refpect for a family they had honored for ages, and in pity to the mis-ftep of an embarraffed, and otherwife clement and juft King, to have fettled upon him a penfion of £.50,000 a year, turned him loofe among his brother Kings, and left him at liberty to dwell in France, Germany, or any other part of Europe , and rifque his ftirring up princes, who could have done no more with their united ftrength or impotence, than they have done, and that moft direct-

ly, to this only good purpofe, of accelerating the emancipation of nations, the humiliation of Kings, and the
downfall of Kingfhip, throughout Europe.

After the almoft unanimous vote of "guilty," the
queftion of punifhment arofe: and after a difcuffion in
an affembly of 722 voters prefent, befides others who
voted varioufly, 319 voted for imprifonment and ban-
ifhment, and 366 for death , and of the other 34, all
but two for death with delay. Finally, of 748 members, befides thofe who were abfent, and thofe who
did not vote, 310 voted for delaying execution, and
380 againft delaying it. The fentence was executed,
and the King was decapitated January 21, 1793.

We ought to view things in a juft and candid light.
It is a great thing to fee through an enterprize, and to
anticipate confequences. The truth is, that Louis was of
Lenient principles in government, and was difpofed to
yield to his fubjects a rational and lefs defpotic government than that of his predeceffors, and to come into a
plan and meafures which would give fatisfaction to his
fubjects. Whether this was owing to his contemplation of the abftract principles of government, fo liberally difcuffed in the prefent age, to his view of the com-
paratively happy government of England in his vicinity,
or to the principles of the American revolution, or to
all thefe collectively, fo it was, that he wifhed to be an
Antoninus, and to govern with lenity and wifdom.—
There was a time when Louis XVI. and the Emperor
really had thefe beneficent ideas, and were endeavoring
to carry them into execution in the happy amelioration
of their refpective governments. The difficulty of en-
forcing the regiftering of royal edicts in the parliaments
of France, and converting thefe, like the antient im-
peratorial edicts, into laws, ufurping upon and fuper-
feding the antient *jus civile*, and giving efficacy to laws
dictated by the will of the prince, appeared to him fo
arbitrary, as to induce him to adopt a method in which

the laws fhould in fact be founded in deliberate wifdom
and confultation of the minds of the public, and that in
effect the public fhould have an efficacious fhare in the
general polity. This by the advice of patriots he thought
might be accomplifhed by convoking the old affembly
of notables, or more confpicuous and influential perfon-
ages of the third eftate of the commons, as well as of
the nobility and dignified clergy. Neckar perfuaded
him that with refpect to finance, taxes, revenues, and
the principal general laws and rules of adminiftration,
this would give fatisfaction ; though herein he mifjudg-
ed. Thereupon the King affembled the notables, and
conftituted a national council of the efficacy of three
eftates, the King, the ariftocrats, or nobles, and dignified clergy, and the tiers etat, or third eftate of the
commons. Immediately they were difpofed, inftead
of an amicable confultation, in the firft inftance, to
throw themfelves into true balancing bodies, the nobility, the clergy and tiers etat. If they fat in three chambers, the nobles and clergy would always out vote or
controul, and the others become fubfervient and over-
ruled cyphers. Here the feparation of the nobles and
plebeians began. Both divifions contained ecclefiaftics
and civilians , moft of the dignified ecclefiaftics took
fide with the nobility ; fome of the nobility laid down
their honors, and in equality took fide with the third
eftate.

Before I proceed, I will collect and throw together
feveral difconnected extracts from the hiftory of the
French revolution by Rabaut, and its continuation
which, under different afpects and applications may
caft light on the feveral events in the great political phænomenon of France at the prefent day.

" In fact, what an aftonifhing combination would
a minifter, nay a monarch, have had to encounter.—
Sixty thoufand nobles, poffeffed of all the connexions of
the feudal fyftem, and that *hoft of dependents* which was

fed by them : thofe of the *military profeffion, all noble,* or what is ftill worfe, pretending to nobility : *a hundred thoufand privileged* perfons all leagued to fupport their prerogative of not paying fuch or fuch an impoft : *Two hundred thoufand priefts,* unequal indeed as to income, but all uniting in one common fyftem, forming out one whole" :—"*fixty thoufand* perfons leading a *monaftic* life . "—the *farmers general,* all the agents of the revenue, with their army of fifty thoufand men"—" finally all thofe belonging to the *long robe,* thofe parliaments, rivals of kings":—" the inferior courts, which were in fubordination to the parliaments , and that fwarm of practitioners, who all taken together, levied a tax upon the kingdom which imagination is afraid to calculate. This formidable mafs of men was in the poffeffion of all France : they held her by a thoufand chains , they formed, in a body, what was termed *la haute nation,* all the reft was the people. Thefe are the perfons whom we have fince feen uniting their voices and their clamours againft the national affembly ; becaufe with a refolution unexampled, it hath fuppreffed all the abufes on which they depended for their exiftence."†

The people, the nation, demanded ftates general, which fhould not be vain and illufive, like thofe of which hiftory made mention. This whole hoft of ariftocratic and crown connexions, wifhed no fuch thing, but if it muft be convoked they " were defirous of ftates general fimilar to thofe which had fit in 1614."

" But the third eftate, that immenfe portion of an enlightened and celebrated nation—took fire at being affimilated to the commons, newly enfranchifed in the reign of Philip le Bed, and at the attempt to reftrict them in 1788 to forms eftablifhed for the clowns and demi-flaves of 1302."

" A confiderable number of military officers, who

† *Rabaut's Hift. Revol. p.* 43. *Amer Edt.*

had assisted at the revolution of the United States, had brought home with them an indelible remembrance of the charms of equality and liberty, which they had beheld in a nation of brothers. These men who were all nobles, had learned to judge of the vanity of such a title, when compared with that of citizens."

" The notables were for the most part, either princes or nobles, or persons in high office. '

The council decreed " that the deputies of the states general should amount to at least, the number of one thousand.—and that the number of the third estate, should be equal to that of the two other orders taken together. These decisions formed the basis of the convocations." " The coalition of the two first orders with the court was well known. It was the determination of these, at the first meeting of the states general, that they should sit and act in three different chambers, and that the crown, with the two superior chambers of the nobility and clergy, should control the whole, and thus reduce the third estate to a cypher or tame and submissive acquiescence. The third estate, resolved against infringement, immediately insisted on equality. At a reconciliating scene, when Necker wished to have avoided, hoping that all might acquiesce in some modifications, were immaterial to him, provided in some manner or other their united wisdom could bring them to amicable agreement in the object of their convocation, a reformed, amended, or new old laws, agreeable to the general sense of the nation collectively. But this he could not effect. And as the two superior orders persisted in their sentiments, the commons or third estate, deeming themselves the true and real representatives of the people, and the true body of the nation, came to an almost unanimous resolution, to erect themselves into the national council, and to declare themselves, instead of states general the national assembly. This was in June 1789. Thus France in one _____ and the third

eftate became the " national affembly." Immediately
the chamber of the clergy, by a majority of one hundred and forty-nine voices againft one hundred and
twenty-fix determined to join the affembly as equals,
and a union of the orders feemed probable. The King
affected to favor it , but affembled troops. "On the
20th of June three days after the national affembly had
been conftituted, the members of the clergy were to
join it." Court meafures were taken to prevent and
elude this : and on the 12th July about three weeks
after the formation of the affembly, Neckar, not fufficiently coming into the idea of the two fuperior orders,
was difmiffed and retired to Switzerland. He forefaw
the fanguinary meafure refolved on at court in which he
would not be concerned. · The affemblage of the military force at Verfailles by the King, alarmed Verfailles,
the national affembly, and Paris. It was intended to
difpatch a number of the patriots to the Baftile, and to
difperfe the national affembly. This was the court
politics. Sixty thoufand Parifians deftroyed the Baftile,
and the national affembly was in fafety. The affembly
framed the conftitution, made the diftribution of the
realm into eighty-three communities, abolifhed the
feudal tenures, and the whole was ratified by the King's
acceptance on the 4th of Auguft.

The policy of one or three orders was difcuffed.—
Whether the national affembly fhould confift of two orders or one, was the queftion. " The equilibrium of
three powers, which balance one another, and prevent
the encroachment of any one upon the reft, became the
object of admiration But thofe who favored the idea
of an undivided affembly, confidered this equilibrium
in the conftitution of England, no otherwife than as a
treaty of peace between three exifting powers. " The
dignified clergy were inclined to two chambers"—" A
large party of the nobles was likewife for the two chambers : but the queftion concerning the peerage prefented

itself, and they became divided , for the provincial nobility underftood that the whole order fhould freely appoint its reprefentatives, while the nobles of the court,
were fecretly indulging the notion, that the dignity of
the peerage ought to be appropriated to themfelves."
" The majority of the deputies of the commons could
fee nothing in the upper chamber but a conftitutional
refuge for ariftocracy, and the prefervation of the feudal fyftem. ' A major ty of the clergy, and forty-feven
of the nobility had joined the commons in undivided
unity and equality " Neither did any fufficiently
comprehend the fyftem of a fenate for life, compofed of
perfons taken from every clafs of citizens ,—nor of a
fenate appointed for a ftated time, and felected from the
whole affembly." In fine, the affembly decreed, by a
majority of nine hundred and eleven voices againft eighty nine, that there fhould be no more than one chamber. It decreed moreover that the legiflative body
fhould be renewed every two years by elections." Thus
much for the conftitution.

Among other regulations, was that refpecting the
fecularizing of the ecclefiaftical eftates. It was " decreed that the ecclefiaftical eftates were all at the difpofal of the nation, fubject however, to the charge of
providing in a proper manner for the expences of public
worfhip, for the maintenance of minifters, and for the
relief of the poor. It was ordered that no parifh minifter fhould have lefs than twelve hundred livres a year,
exclufive of the houfe and gardens annexed to that par-
fonage. This celebrated decree paffed on the 2d of
November 1789." " The ecclefiaftics accufed the
national affembly of an intention to deftroy religion."—
" The affembly difconcerted this confpiracy, by making conftant proteftation of its union with the pope, as
head of the chriftian church, with regard to fpiritual
concerns, and of its fidelity to the religion of our fore-
fathers." " The affembly at length decreed that its
attachment to the catholic religion of Rome could not be

called in queſtion, at a time when that worſhip was
placed by the aſſembly at the head of various articles of
public expence, and that the majeſty of religion, and
the profound reſpect due to it, did not allow of its becoming a ſubject of debate, ſince the aſſembly had no
power over conſciences." "It had ſuſpended the mo-
naſtic vows, it finiſhed with ſuppreſſing them, and fixed the mode of treatment to be obſerved with reſpect to
thoſe who had belonged to any of the religious communities," by providing penſions for life. Thus far from
St. Etienne.

Extracts from the Continuation of the Hiſt. Revolution.
V. 2. P. 111.

" The extreme point on which the two parties differed, was that of pure democracy on the one part,
and the inſtitution of an upper chamber, ſimilar to the
Britiſh houſe of peers, on the other. Such an inſtitution, as a remnant of ariſtocracy, was regarded by the
French, with almoſt as much abhorrence as abſolute
monarchy itſelf ; while the eſtabliſhment of it was conſidered as the great object with the court, as a prelimi-
nary ſtep to the annihilation of liberty. The middle
party was ſtill numerous ; and it was judged that there
were many who might ſecretly incline either to the
court or the republicans, who would be well diſpoſed to
ſacrifice ſomething of their prejudices to the preſervation
of peace and order " In this ſtate of minds in the national aſſembly, Lamourette, the patriotic biſhop of
Lyons, by an inſtantaneous impulſe and without concert, ſuddenly propoſed to the aſſembly, " Let all who
hold in equal deteſtation, a republic and two chambers,
and who wiſh to maintain the conſtitution as it is, riſe !"
The whole aſſembly roſe from their ſeats. This ſhews
two things on which they were as yet equally unanimous :
1. In having a King. 2. In rejecting a ſecond chamber
—adhering to an elective aſſembly of one order only,
with a limited monarch at its head. All were recon-

ciled ; and had the King continued faithful to this experiment of the public mind, all had been well. This
was the beginning or 7th of July, 1792. Yet in the
courfe of this month, the public, either with or without
reafon, became extenfively impreffed with the idea of
the infincerity and duplicity of the King, and that he
was in fact in concert with the combined fovereigns,
whofe object was nothing lefs than the reftoration of the
King and former government. This was heightened
by the tranfaction of Fayette. And burft forth from
the national people in the bold declaration of Petion,
mayor of Paris, on the 3d of Auguft, at the bar of the
affembly demanding the depofition of the King The
die was caft. This was followed and fupported by fuch
numerous petitions from every part of the nation, as to
leave it without a doubt that the body of the nation were
heartily weaned from not only Louis XVI. but the very
idea of a King, and that the general voice was that their
policy fhould be a national affembly of one order only,
whofe head fhould be temporary Prefidents, but without a King and without a nobility. This was the mind
of France, and has continued fo to this day.

The following decree thereupon immediately paffed.
" The national affembly, confidering that the want of
confidence in the executive power, is the caufe of all
our evils, and that this want of confidence has called
forth from all parts of the kingdom, a wifh that *the authority entrufted by the conftitution to Louis fhould be re-
voked,* and that the only means of reconciling what they
owe to the fafety of the people, with their own oath,
of not increafing their own power, are to fubmit to the
fovereign will of the nation, decree (among other things)
" 1. The people are invited to form a national convention. 2. The executive power is provifionally *fufpended.*"
And Auguft 13, " The national affembly declares, that
the King is fufpended ; and that both himfelf and family remain as hoftages " And on the fame day the
national affembly proclaimed the convocation of " a

national convention, formed of representatives, invested
by them (the people) with unlimited powers." On the
21st of September, 1792, the national assembly dissol-
ved, and the same day the national convention assembled from the 83 communities into which France was
divided, convened, the monarchy ceased, and the republic commenced. This from the continuation.

Returning and assuming the subject we were upon
before we inserted these extracts, the first political
convocation of the states general consisted of 1200 members The nobility 300, the clergy 300, the tiers état
600. It was the immediate and original intention of
the two first, that the states general should sit and act
in three separate chambers, and that the concurrence
of two should be the act of the whole, subjected however to the veto of the monarch. It was from the beginning the intention and resolution of the last and most
nemerous, that all should sit, deliberate and act together
as pares or equals; and that the majority of votes in
this coalesced body, should be the public act. This reduction of the nobility and dignified and ennobled clergy
to an equality with the commons, was displeasing.—
And an altercation immediately arose on the question
whether they should sit in three or perhaps two chambers, or be consolidated into one coequal and fraternal
body? At length above half the ecclesiastics, and a part
of the nobles renounced their claims of superiority,
came over and joined the third estate as coequals. And
thus the national assembly was formed.

The contest had arisen, which Neckar could not
compose, though he wished to have avoided it; and
the commons were determined to proceed by themselves,
and not to be lost in balancing commixtures. The nobles, both secular and ecclesiastical, were divided. The
king had not foreseen this state of things. It was now
too late. There was no alternative between a very
new and potent influence in government, and breaking

up of the commons, now already joined by Fayette and
a number of the nobles and bifhops, and other ecclefiaftics, who with refpect to the national council openly
declared for an equality ef nobles and commons, an
equality as to eligibility into the national council, was
the only equality ever aimed at by France. The Baftile was deftined to have decided and determined this
alternative. For this purpofe the King, whofe otherwife benevolent and well intentioned heart, now re-
pented him to have convoked the ftates general, now
terminating in a national affembly, acceded to a cruel
idea: and as he was not prepared for thefe lengths, he
adopted the idea of a diffolution of the affembly by force,
and of refuming the old government, doubtlefs determining ftill to adminifter it with the utmoft lenity and
juftice. This miftake led the King fecretly to call
around him and collect the Swifs guards and a military
force at Verfailles, and to accede to the fevere difcipline of the Baftile for a number of the patriots in the
affembly, fufficient to break up and difperfe it. Rather
than go to the Baftile, to which they perceived they
were deftined, the patriot leaders in the affembly, with
the vociferous concurrence of the citizens and populace
of Paris, refolved upon feizing the perfon of the King.
The people flew to arms, and led by the illuftrious and
hitherto patriotic Fayette, who had voluntarily facrificed
his nobility, they, under his leading, feized the King,
brought him to Paris, and immured him and the royal
family in the Thuilleries. The national affembly formed a conftitution, which was eftablifhed. It was prefented to the King, and his confent deforced or gained,
henceforth to rule the realm by a King, with ftill very
great powers, though much abridged, and an elective
national affembly of one order only, in which nobles
and commons reduced to equality, fhould fit in the legiflature as pares or equals, and the whole realm in future, as one great republic, be governed by laws proceeding from this affembly. This was perfectly the

idea and idol of the Marquis de la Fayette. But the body of the nobleffe and the royal princes and connexions, endeavored to counteract and break up this fyftem, and prevent its taking effect , and immediately applied to the emperor and furrounding Kings to bring on a combined army, with a view of reftoring the original government, and replacing the King on the throne with his former authority, or perhaps with a national affembly of two houfes, that of the nobles and that of the tiers etat. England would have rejoiced in this, becaufe it fo nearly refembled their own conftitution ; and the emperor would not have been averfe to having fuch an example fet before Auftria and Europe, for there was a time when he was really friendly to the liberties of the people and the rights of fubjects. But the burying and overwhelming the nobility and ariftocrats in an affembly of one order, they could not endure. And at all events the King determined upon the everfion and ruin of the Gallic republic.

In this the King concurred in heart, wifhed to get from confinement, while it was accomplifhed, faw a profpect of its being accomplifhed by the combined army, attempted to efcape and abdicate ; but was taken, and in effect pardoned and reftored, although by the conftitution, this attempt to efcape was a forfeiture of his crown. Being reftored to his former ftate, here he might have refted. But a powerful army flattering and cherifhing his hopes of ultimate fuccefs, he fuffered himfelf to be afterwards guilty of betraying the caufe by the overt acts of concerting with the Kings and foreign cabinets, and the cidevant princes, and by paying a corps in the army of actual invafion. This being detected, what could fave him ? This was his error, and it was fatal to a King who wifhed to rule with clemency and juftice, but whofe abilities, difcernment and wifdom, were unequal to fo critical and momentuous a fituation.

Fayette and other patriots, feeing the nation aliena-
ted from the King, and ripening for a government without a King, found their views of liberty were tranf-
cended: and fixt in the impoffibility of a polity without
a King, now turned about, and in effect united with
the ci devant princes and foreign Kings in the project
of fupporting a King at all events ; but with very different views.   The ariftocrats were for recovering the old
government ; Fayette and the patriots for keeping indeed the King, and believing they could modify the polity, and accomplifh the acquiefcence of the nation in
a royal republic of one order, with a King at its head ;
while others were for a tripartite divifion of the realm
into three republics, confederated under a national affembly ftill with a King , among thofe for an indivifible republic, fome were for a balance of nobles, either
hereditary or elective, perhaps compofed of both, between the King and third eftate.   Thefe various ideas
feem to have been among thofe which agitated and divided excellent patriots, as well thofe who were not for
a King, as thofe who were for one.   Thefe are faid to
have been among the ideas of Condorcet, Autun, Bo-
veau, and other genuine patriots, as concurring in a
republic without monarchy, though differing on the
form of a republic   In this diverfity of views, fome
muft give way to that any one polity which fhould in
fact prevail and gain the afcendency. No wonder Fayette and other excellent patriots fhould take miftaken
and involving fteps.   To fave the King, he entered
deeply into the fecret councils of the King and the royal
family, and fo far acted in concert with them, as to
become obnoxious and really dangerous to the prevailing counfels of the exifting affembly , tenacious of a republic one and indivifible.   His attempts to fecure the
King's fecond efcape, with fpeeches and conduct offen-
five to the Jacobin Societes, which he at firft fet up,
a fyftem of fraternities now diffufed through the realm,
the great confervators of liberty, and affuming great

liberties in announcing and dictating to a national affembly, very willing to be dictated and fupported by them, brought on a crifis dangerous to Fayette, who himfelf efcaped and was unfortunately taken. His ideas for monarchy, which I once learned from his own lips in a perfonal though tranfcient acquaintance and converfation with him, were fo fixt, that, although as fixt for a republic of one order and equality, and elective, he could not proceed and go on with his compatriots, he muft counteract them ; and until he could get over his miftaken idea about a King, he muft become totally ufelefs and unfit to take a part in meafures which muft unavoidably be profecuted by a body weaned from Kings. Fayette was loft to the caufe of liberty, which he adored, and died a martyr to the whim of a King.

The ftate of the King's mind was fuch, and fuch his active fecret views and coincidences with the enemies of the republic, that he became unfit for the monarchy; they would have all acquiefced in, could the nation have depended upon the King's fincerity. But all confidence in him was loft. This gave birth to thoughts and devices how he fhould be difpofed of, and laid afide, as he was now ufelefs and dangerous. The nation were by this time poffeffed of evidence of his not only premeditated but overt treafon. They did not want to take the King's life, could they have avoided the danger of his intriguing with the combined powers without it. But this they thought could not be done. And as there was not clearly a provifion in the conftitution, except in the cafe of an abdicated King, they refolved to call a national convention to decide the queftion of the King, perfect the conftitution, and take the government upon them. To this convention as foon as formed the national affembly furrendered the whole, and diffolved themfelves. The convention, vefted with all the authority twenty million of people can give, have adjudged the King, and the juftice of their fentence is now committed to pofterity and to the world.

It may affift us towards conceiving aright, and with fairnefs and candor upon great political tranfactions and events, to contemplate fimilar events in different ftates, and the operation of human nature under fimilar circumftances. Such are the fellow feelings, fuch the fraternal fympathy of republics in diftrefs and in the conflict for liberty, and fuch the inftruction and confolation, which arife in contemplating the meafures which preffing neceffity dictates, that thefe reflexions on the French revolution feem not inappofite to the eafe of the Judges. And it may ftill furnifh light, to look a little further back upon the origin and progrefs of regal defpotifm in France, as that has had its operation on the crown of England, and brought on the parliamentary ftruggle of 1641.

The Kings of France difcontinued the national affemblies of the ftates generals fo long ago as the beginning of the laft century, and ruled without convoking them for one hundred and feventy years ; with a growing encroachment on the parliaments, to the total abolition of liberty, and the eftablifhment of rule by royal edicts, regiftered in the parliaments by royal violence, and enforced by banifhments and the omnipotence of the Baftile ; until at length the endurance of the public was exhaufted, came to a crifis, and burft forth even in the reign of an otherwife beneficent King, and obliged him, as we have feen, to convoke an affembly of notables, for the purpofe of affenting to taxes and revenue laws, and fome general regulations for the public good, and no more ; and then to be diffolved. But the affembly of notables, like that of the long parliament, inftead of voting taxes and doing no more, went upon other matters than the King or his miniftry intended. The King faw his error, and meditated their diffolution. But it was too late. He had fhewn the people or nation how to affemble by reprefentation.— Thefe reprefentatives refolving not to be configned to the Baftile intended for them, commenced the unconftitutional, but juftifiable exertions which have terminated in a republic.

The Kings of France had difcontinued the national affemblies from 1614. It is proper to remark this date or epoch. This example had not been fet before the houfe of Tudor : but it was recent and in full view of the houfe of Stuart. James I. felt it, and difcovered his longing after the fame boon. Charles I. emulating and avidous of the abfolute power and defpotifm of the houfe of Bourbon, firft adventured in imitation of France, and but fifteen years after the houfe of Bourbon had fet the example, to difcontinue parliaments, and had the temerity to adventure to rule without them for twelve years : and could he have diffolved and broken up the newly convoked parliament of 1641, England would have loft the ufe of parliaments forever, as France had loft the affemblies, and Spain the ufe of the cortes : unlefs refumed and wrefted out of royal hands at the expence of a violent and bloody revolution. The then recent examples of France and Spain, in their Kings getting rid of the controul of national councils, made an indelible impreffion on the minds of the Stuarts, who meditated and afpired after nothing lefs for England ; and they never believed but that they fhould finally accomplifh it, and eftablifh an uncontrouled defpotifm. They were miftaken. The convening the parliament of 1641, as of the national affembly of 1789, brought on difquifitions and convulfions, which involved the death of Kings indeed, while the recovery of long loft liberty will juftify the vigorous public exertions in both cafes. And though many tumults and cruel events may arife in the caufe of a juft revolution, which would be unjuftifiable, and which no friend to order, no judicious and upright civilian would juftify, but reprobate, in an ordinary and righteous courfe of government : yet the caufe itfelf, and *every thing effentially fui fervient to it*, is juftifiable on the higheft principles of public right. The caufe is good, though it should sometimes be improperly carried on, and even though it should be unsuccessful and defeated. I think this collation of the houses of Stuart and Bourbon in point to justify resistance to the Stuarts.

Posterity must judge, or rather we may now judge ourselves, whether the negociation between the parliament and Charles I. in 1647, and pacification, was then safe for liberty ? Whether such being the delusory heart of Charles, that like his son, he would have duped the nation, and necessitated the resuming a future struggle for the recovery of their rights ? and in a word, whether it would not have undoubtedly taken effect, if it had not been for the patriotic and ever faithful army ; and so have defeated the end, the justifiable end, for which the parliament had taken up arms ? No man now doubts it.

Such was the change in the minds of the patriots themselves in parliament, who herein coincided with the cavaliers and royalists, all the while in parliament, that even Cromwell and Ireton despaired and gave up the cause as gone, and would in 1648 have acceded to terms of peace. Happy was it that at this critical time, Ireton discovered in the saddle the King's letter, which informed their certain destiny, and that of their most courageous and active compatriots. This with the sense of the ever faithful army turned the tables, and produced the resolute, the violent and daring, the justifiable resolution of the army to purge the house, and by the residuary parliament to institute a high court of justice, and bring the King to a trial. Liberty and the cause were overthrown and gone, unless some efficacious and extraordinary measures were adopted by enterprizing and courageous patriots. Effectual measures then ought in that case to be taken, constitutional and regular if possible, otherwise if this was impossible as it was, then irregular but at all events effectual ones became justifiable and so ultimately regular. Such measures were adopted. And the reasons of them will juftify and vindicate the purgation of parliament by violence, the inftitution of the high court of juftice by three hundred members left, though deferted by the Lords ; and the Judges in the trial and juft condemnation of the King. "There is but one ftep between pardoning a tyrant, and pardoning tyranny."† Charles was a tyrant in heart, Louis XVI. was not.

In contemplating this fubject and its appendages comprehenfively, and in this variety of views, in the lights of the hiftory of nations, and on the great principles of public right, it appears that, in great revolutions and national exertions for the refcue and recovery of unqueftionable and acknowledged but loft rights, criminal tribunals muft be inftituted in a different mode from that of their ordinary appointment : and that there being no alternative between their juftification and the furrendry of liberty, they become legal, juft and right : that Charles I for renouncing and ruling without parliament for twelve years, for levying taxes without the confent of the people, and for other violations of the public laws of the realm, and for levying a war againft a legal and regular parliament, forfeited not only his crown but his life : that if a King of England was now to do what he did, the nation would not doubt but that he merited death, and would certainly originate a revolutionary tribunal and inflict it : and that if neither lords and commons conjunctly, nor either feparately would dare to do it, there muft be fome other manner practical and legal , in which cafe it would reft with the people to do it ; and that almoft any manner of inftituting it, with the general voice of the community, would render it legal and authoritative. It is idle, in this age of light, to combat and elude the legality of fuch a tribunal by arguments, whofe force will conclude in nothing fhort of an abfolute and certain everfion, proftration and furrendry of liberty. In a review of the whole, this is the fummary refult.

† *Polit. ftat. Europ.* 1792, *p.* 961.

D d

1. That the judiciary tribunals in different policies, and in the same policy in different ages, have been very differently inftituted, while yet any or all of them muft be deemed legal and authoritative.

2. That in great revolutions, and national refcues of partial and entire liberty, thefe tribunals, may be and have been as differently inftituted, and yet become vefted and cloathed with juft, legal and plenary authority : and that the high court of 1649 was fuch a legal tribunal. And

3d. That their fentence was righteous and juft. All which will inure to the juftification of the Judges.

They atchieved a great and important work, and it was well done. Four years after this legal expulfion of tyranny, a national convention furnifhed the nation with Oliver's excellent polity, which fubfifted till his death in 1658. But fuch was the fatal and miftaken verfatility of the nation, that they availed not themfelves of this noble foundation, fo happily laid, on principles which Englifhmen will ever revere and in every exigence recur to, and ultimately eftablifh. And with the downfal and overthrow of this beautiful polity, they brought down upon thofe illuftrious heroes, who had enterprized the glorious though unfinifhed work, and overwhelmed them with a load of infamy and reproach which a century and half has not been fufficient to remove. Thus the volcano, deluge and eruptions of Vefuvius buried in ruins the beautiful Herculaneum : which after having been loft for feventeen ages, is now emerging into light and admiration. So likewife the firft chriftian martyrs were covered with infamy and ethnical reproach, until the fourth century gave their merits opportunity to relieve and fhine with glory in the public eftimation ever fince. The republican martyrs and heroes of the twenty years period from 1640 to 1660, are now in referred or in France, Poland, and America, they are beheld with fpreading eftimation, and will in future be contemplated with juftice and veneration by all nations, who in the vindications of their liberties, will find themfelves neceffitated to have recourfe to the fame great, eternal principles of public right, which actuated thefe great patriots. Among thefe will be confidered the enlightened upright and intrepid Judges of Charles I , who will hereafter go down to pofterity with increafing renown, among the Jepthas, the Baracks, the Gideons, and the Wafhingtons, and others raifed up by providence for great and momentous occafions : whofe memories, with thofe of all the other fuccefsful and unfuccefsful, but intrepid and patriotic defenders of real liberty, will be felected in hiftory, and contemplated with equal, impartial and merited juftice : and whofe names, and atchievments, and SUFFERINGS will be tranfmitted with honor, renown and glory, through all the ages of liberty and of man.

CHAP. VI.

Memoirs of THEOPHILUS WHALE.

THERE was a very fingular man, who lived and died at Narraganfet, whofe hiftory arrefted my attention, when I firft fettled at Newport, 1755 ; and upon whom I have fpent much pains in making inquiries, becaufe he is univerfally confidered there as one of the regicides, and I always and uniformly difbelieved it. I was told much about him by Jeremiah Niles, Efq. the honorable Simon Peas, of Newport, the reverend Mr. Jofeph Torry, minifter of South Kingfton, and the honorable Francis Willet, on whofe farm Whale lived, and who knew him well. When detained from time to time, efpecially about 1758 and 1760, at Narraganfet ferry, I ufed often to talk with a Mr. Smith

of that vicinity, and other aged perfons, who knew
Whale, and believed him to have been one of the
the Judges. They all faid he came the.e from Virginia, at the beginning of the Petaquamfcot fettlement,
which was foon after Philips' War, 1657, and the
Great Swamp Fight. But as my beft information came
from Colonel Willet, I will give fome account of this
gentleman.

Colonel FRANCIS WILLET, of North Kingfton,
Rhode-Ifland, died and was buried in the family burying place on his own eftate, one mile north of Narraganfet ferry, February 6, 1776, aged 83. He was defcended from Thomas Willet, the firft mayor of New-
York, who died at Barrington, Rhode-Ifland, 1674,
aged 64. He came a young merchant to Plymouth,
1629, was converfant in the fur and Indian trade of the
whole coaft from Kennebec to Hudfons River, became
very opulent, and fettled on a plantation at Swanzey,
now Barrington, where remains his grave fix miles below Providence. Being an intelligent and refpectable
perfon he went as a counfellor on board Col. Nicols'
fleet, at the reduction of Manhados 1664; and was by
him appointed mayor of the new conquered city. He
owned noufes in New-York and Albany. The Dutch
refuming the government. He afterwards returned to
his fettlement and died at Barrington.

On the ftones at his grave there is this infcription.

(*Head Stone.*)	(*Foot Stone.*)
" 1674.	
Here lyeth the Body	*Who was the*
of the worthy	FIRST MAYOR
THOMAS WILLET, Efq.	*of New-York ;*
Who d·ed Aug. the 4th,	*And twice did*
in the 64th year of his age,	*fuftain that place.*"
Anno."	

He had three fons, Hezekiah, James and Andrew,
by his wife Mary the daughter of John Brown, Efq.

Hezekiah was killed by the Indians 1675. James lived on the paternal estate. Andrew was first a merchant in Boston till 1686: he then removed and settled on Boston Neck at Narraganset ferry and died there 1712, Æ 56, leaving two sons Francis and Thomas, and a daughter. Thomas died a batchelor and left the whole family estate to the possession of Col. Francis Willet, who married and died without issue. This is the gentleman with whom I was intimately acquainted. He was educated a merchant, but did not pursue commerce. He had a good genius and was a man of much reading and information. And settling himself on his paternal estate, being very opulent he lived the life of a private gentleman; he was hospitable and generous, of excellent moral, and a very estimable and highly respected character. The fine tract of Boston Neck was principally owned by the Sewalls and other gentlemen in Boston. This with his father's former residence in Boston, and transacting business for these Boston landholders and for Harvard College brought him into an acquaintance with the first characters at Boston, who often visited him thro' life, and gave him great public information. Once a year these gentlemen visited their estates and at his father's house; and after his father's death 1712, the management and superintendance of these estates and of the college estate, together with the extensive Willet family acquaintance fell unto Col. Francis Willet, whose aunts had married into minister's families, Wilson in Massachusetts, and Hooker in Connecticut. The Willet farm was a tract extending from Narraganset ferry northward perhaps one mile and an half in length, on the Bay, and about one mile or more east and west from the Bay, across to the oblong pond called Petequamscot, and was the original seat of the great Sachem, Miantinomy. At the north end of this pond and on the Willet farm, was settled Theophilus Whaley, or Theophilus Whale, who came there from Virginia, about 1679, or 1680. He affected to live in

poverty and obfcurity and retirement: and built himfelf a little under-ground hut in a high bank, or fide
hill, at the north end or head of the pond, and fubfifted
by fifhing and writing for the Petequamfcot fettlers.—
He was foon found to be a man of fenfe and abilities;
and it was a matter of wonder, that he refufed to live
otherwife than in a mean and obfcure manner. From
his name he was early fufpected to be the regicide; and
being queftioned upon it, his anfwers were fo obfcure
and ambiguous, that they confirmed his acquaintance
in that belief; which I found fixt and univerfal at Narraganfet in 1755, and which remains ftill fo there and
at Rhode Ifland to this day; and among the reft, indubitable in the mind of the fenfible and intelligent Colonel Willet. This made me curious to inquire the
hiftory of this fingular good old man, as the Colonel
ufed to call him, and of whom he talked with great pleafure, and feemed as if he could never fay enough of
him. He told me many anecdotes. And when I
ufed to fay that Whalley died at Hadley, he always
denied it, faying that one indeed of the Judges died at
Hadley, but the other went off to the weftward, fecreted himfelf awhile at Virginia, but being in danger there,
he fecretly fled and buried himfelf in Narraganfet woods,
and lived a reclufe life to the end, and that this Theophilus Whale was the man, notwithftanding the change
of the chriftian name, which the Colonel fuppofed he
did defignedly. In confirmation of this opinion, he
told me many anecdotes. When he was a boy, he faid,
feveral Bofton gentlemen ufed once a year to make an
excurfion and vifit at his father's houfe. As foon as
they came they always enquired eagerly after the welfare of the good old man: and his father ufed to fend
him, when a boy, to call him to come and fpend the
evening at his houfe. As foon as Mr. Whale came in
the gentlemen embraced him with great ardour and affection, and expreffed great joy at feeing him, and treated him with great friendfhip and refpect. They fpent

the evening together with the most endearing familiarity, so that the Colonel said, he never saw any gentlemen treat one another with such apparently heart-felt cordiality and respect. He used to wonder at it, and could not account for it. They kept shut up in a room by themselves, and there seemed to be an air of secrecy about the matter. Their interviews were in the evening only, and continued late in the night. Just before they broke up, he used to observe that one of gentlemen would take Mr. Whale by the hand, and they walked out into the lot, and returning, another took him out, and so all the others singly and by themselves. He did not know for what reason this was done. But when the gentlemen were gone, Whale always had plenty of money. And the Colonel told me that he did not doubt but that they all gave him money in this private and secret manner. He frequently mentioned the names of the gentlemen, and they were some of the first characters in Boston about the beginning of this century. The Secretary was one, and Judge Sewall another. Whale never let Colonel Willet know his true history; but comparing this singular treatment with Whale's manner of life, he was convinced, he said, that he was a secreted regicide.

Colonel Willet told me that, in Queen Ann's war, he remembered a ship of war came up the Bay and anchored before his father's door. The name of the captain was Whale, and he was a kinsman of Mr. Whale, who lived but one mile off, and made him a visit, when they recognized one another with the affection of kindred. After an agreeable interview, the captain invited Mr Whale to dine with him on board ship; he accepted the invitation, and promised to come. But upon considering further of it, he did not adventure on board, rendering as a reason, that this was truely his cousin, yet he did not know but possibly there might be some snare laid for him to take him. Colonel Willet was personally acquainted with this fact, and indeed it was known to all the inhabitants around, who tell of it to this day. This confirmed them all that this was Whalley the regicide.

Many other anecdotes he has told me, and that he wrote Whale's will ; that he lived to a great age, and that he died 104 years old , that a little before his death he removed to his daughter's, about ten miles off, where he died and was buried.

Governor Hutchinfon's hiftory was firft printed 1764, and Colonel Willet foon read it. Dining with him foon after, he faid to me at table, "Tell Governor Hutchinfon, I know more about Whalley than he does —I perfonally knew him, and was intimately acquainted with him—he lived and died at Narraganfet, and not at Hadley." As I had a correfpondence with the Governor, who had fent me his book ; I wrote and informed him what his friend Willet faid. The next year the Governor was on a vifit to Newport, and brought with him a volume of Goffe's original journal and an original letter, and fhewed me and convinced me what I did not doubt before, that Whalley lived and died at Hadley. This he alfo fhewed to Colonel Willet, who became convinced that Theophilus Whale was not Edward Whalley ; but never to his death gave up the belief that Whale was one of Charles's Judges,, altho' why he fhould upon changing his name affume that of fo obnoxious a perfou as Whalley, was to him a paradox.

I have often converfed with him upon it. And we went into the fuppofition that Whale was really Goffe, whom general tradition fpoke of as leaving Hadley and going off weftward toward Virginia, and fo from thence might abdicate into Rhode-Ifland. But the name was an infuperable difficulty. I converfed with feveral of the defcendants of Whale at different times for a dozen years after, but could get no fatisfactory lights. Hutchinfon left with me for half a year an original letter of Goffe to his wife, that I might compare the hand wri-

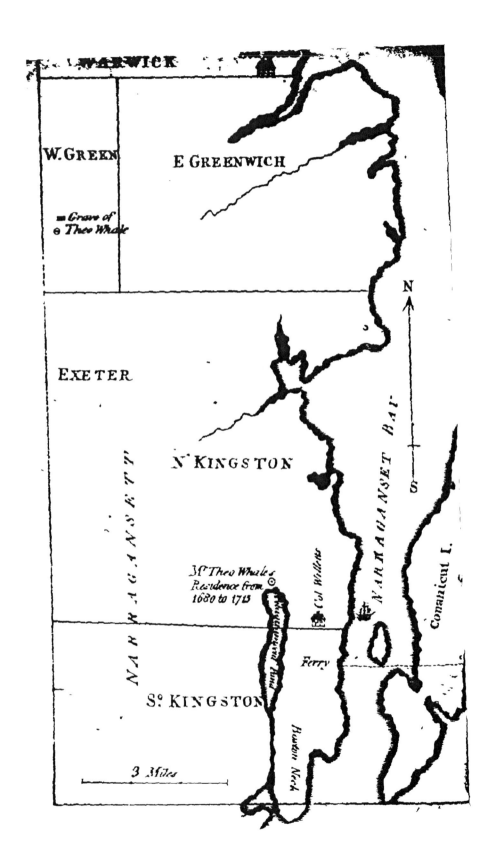

ting with some of Mr. Whale's among the people of Narraganset, where Colonel Willet told me it might eafily be found, and engaged to procure me one of his deeds. He did not do this till Goffe's letter was fent for and I returned it. Since that I have made fundry fruitlefs attempts to fee fome of his writing with his name to it: and fo long ago as 1766, one of the family brought me a piece which he faid was his grandfather's writing, but there was nothing which proved it, and I doubted it. I did not give up the inquiry till 1785. The defcendants of all the families fpringing from Theophilus Whale univerfally believe their anceftor was one of the regicides; but concur in it that he never revealed it to his family or any one elfe. Colonel Willet ufed to tell me of a Mrs. Spencer, about 90 years old, a daughter of Mr. Whale. She furvived to 1793. I always intended to have feen her, but never did. I got her fonin-law, Othniel Gorton, Efq. to inquire of her in her life time, who fent me word, fhe did not doubt her father was one of the Judges, but that he never revealed himfelf to his family.

At length turning out of my way on a journey, I vifited, in 1783, Samuel Hopkins, Efq. aged 81, of Weft Greenwich, a grandfon of Whale, and living on his grandfather's farm. He was a man of good fenfe and accurate information, had been in civil improvement, a member of affembly and judge of the court. He freely and readily communicated all he knew.—— From his mouth I wrote down the following information:

Mr. Theophilus Whale, and Elizabeth his wife, came from Virginia and fettled in Kingfton in Narraganfet. He married his wife in Virginia; her name was Elizabeth Mills. Their children were,

Joane Whale—ob. aged 60 or 70.

Anna Whale—ob. fingle, no iffue.

Theodofia Whale, married Robert Spencer, ob. before 1741.

Elizabeth Whale, married Charles Hazelton. ob.

Martha Whale, married Joseph Hopkins, father of Judge Hopkins, and then married Robert Spencer. ob. 1773, aged 93—so born 1680, and born in Narraganset, as the Judge told me.

Lydia Whale, married John Sweet. ob.

Samuel Whale, married 1st Hopkins, 2d Harrington.

Judge Hopkins, son of Martha Whale, was born in Kingston, January 1705, and is now aged 81, (1785) and remembers his grandfather Whale, who died aged 103, the year he could not ascertain, but it was when the Judge was a young man grown, of age 16 or 18.—He said his grandfather talked Hebrew, Greek and Latin, as he well remembers often to have heard him; that he had a Greek bible, which he constantly used, and which has been in Judge Hopkins's keeping almost ever since, but is now lost, or he knows not what is become of it. He had a great desire to teach his grandson, Samuel Hopkins, Latin and Greek when a boy, and used to try to persuade him to learn it, and did begin to instruct him in it; and that he wrote much in the Petaquamscot purchase, and also that he was a large tall man, six feet high when 100 years old, and then walked upright; not fat, but thin and lathy;—an officer, a captain in the Indian wars in Virginia, and had been an officer in the parliamentary army in England.

Judge Hopkins remembers his grandmother Whale, a smart tight little woman, a mighty doctress, as he said. She died aged perhaps 70 or 60, and perhaps seven or ten years before Mr. Whale, and was buried in Kingston not far from the church. After his wife's death, Mr. Theophilus Whale removed up to West Greenwich to his daughter Spencer and died there, and was buried in Judge Hopkins's lot, where he shewed me his grave, but cannot remember the year of his death, though he well remembers his attending his fu-

neral and faw him depofited in his grave; he was buried
with great refpect, and the Judge told me with military
honors.   His grave lies in Weft Greenwich, about fix
miles nearly due fouthweft from Eaft Greenwich court-
houfe and Narraganfet Bay, one mile weft from Eaft
Greenwich line, and a mile north of Exeter line.   It
has no ftone or monument.

The Judge told me his chief refidence was at the head
of Petaquamfcot Pond, at the north-weft corner of Col.
Willet's farm, and that there he brought up his children.
For his writing for the north Patafquamfcot purchafe,
the proprietors gave him a tract of land, the farm on
which the Judge now lives, of 120 acres, lying in Weft
Greenwich, though then a part of Eaft Greenwich.——
He fhewed me the original deed, dated 1709, under the
hands and feals of perhaps fifteen or twenty proprietors:
Indorfed with an affignment dated February 20, 1711,
to his fon Samuel Whale, by Theophilus Whale, in
his own hand writing, in which he figned his name
Theophilus Whale, in good free writing, but his wife
figned by her mark.   It was indorfed with another affignment under it, on the fame deed, by exchange
from Samuel Whale to Jofhua Hopkins, the Judge's
father; but Samuel Whale figned by his mark.   As this
was the firft certain writing of Theophilus Whale which
I had ever feen, I viewed it with clofe attention, to fee
if I could recognize the writing of Goffe's letters fhewn
me by Governor Hutchinfon near twenty years before,
but I could not recollect a fimilitude.   This was a fharp
running hand; Goffe's, according to my memory, was
more of a blunt round hand.

The Judge told me that old Mr. Whale never would
tell his true hiftory.   The moft he talked about as to
himfelf was, that he was of good defcent and education
in England, and I think of univerfity education, that
in Virginia he was much in the Indian wars, and an
officer; that he there married a young wife when he

was old, but no tradition that he was ever married before in England or America; that he had some difficulty
in Virginia about the diffenting way of worfhip, but
was permitted to come away, as Mr. Hopkins expreffed it, who alfo faid he was a Firft Day Baptift. For
the firft years of his living at Narraganfet he followed
fifhing in Petaquamfcot Pond—at length *weaving*, and
in this he fpent moft of his life. After about thirty
years his children fettled off and left him alone. His
wife ufed alfo to make long vifits to her daughters, efpecially Spencer, and leave the old man to fhift for himfelf. He at length was to have a dozen acres of land
off the Northorp's farm, not far from the head of Petaquamfcot, who were to build a houfe for him and his
wife, and he was to keep fchool for the Northorp family. But his wife dying perhaps about 1715, he gave
up the project of the houfe and fchool, and went to live
with his daughter Spencer at Greenwich, where he
died. His laft years were fpent in folitude and without
labour; yet his body and mind were found to the laft.
The Judge could not recover the year of his death,
though his age, he faid, was 103 when he died. This
is the fubftance of the Judge's information. He faid
that Joane and one or two of the firft children were born
in Virginia.

Judge Hopkins further told me that Samuel Whale,
the only fon of Theophilus, fettled and lived and died at
South Kingfton, on a farm which his father Hopkins
exchanged for Samuel's farm in Greenwich, upon
which his father removed and fettled on the Whale farm
in Greenwich, and Samuel fettled in Kingfton towards
Point Judith. He faid that Samuel married two wives,
firft Hopkins, and then Harrington. By the firft or
Hopkins venter, he had children, fons, for he faid nothing of daughters †

† *Mrs No', Hazelton, living 1793, fays Samuel
Whale had five fons and two daughters.*

Thomas Whale, } By Hopkins venter.
Samuel Whale,

Theophilus Whale,
James or Jeremy Whale, } By Harrington venter.
John Whale,

And that from thefe all the Whales in Narraganfet and Connecticut defcended : and there is a number of families of this name, feveral of whom I have feen and converfed with, but their family information is only general and not accurate ; although they all believe their anceftor was one of Charles's judges to this day, for none of them have accurately inveftigated the matter.

Mr. Spencer married two fifters, firft Theodofia Whale, and after her death he married her fifter, widow Martha Hopkins, mother of the Judge, and mother of the wife of Othniel Gorton, Efq. with whom fhe died.

There was indeed another Whale from Theophilus, but not from Samuel. Joane, the eldeft daughter of old Theophilus never was married : yet had two children, who went by the name of Whale, Lawrence Whale and Mary Whale. Lawrence lived many years in Narraganfett, and afterwards went away towards Hudfon's river. Judge Hopkins did not know his birth, but if then living in 1785, he judged he would be aged 95, or certainly 12 or 15 years older than Judge Hopkins was, and fo his birth about 1690. Doctor Torry, who was born October 19, 1707, was well acquainted with Lawrence, and judged him 15 years older than himfelf, which would bring his birth 1692, which fhews Joane of the age of parturition, 1692, aged 15 or 20, implying her nativity as far back as 1670, or 1671, for Elizabeth, her fifter, younger than Joane, was born in Virginia about 1672, fhewing that Theophilus Whale was married in Virginia fo long ago as 1670, or before. Though Judge Hopkins knew it not, yet Mr. Northrop, of North Kingfton, afterwards told me that Lawrence died before the war 1775, near Ticonderoga, and I

E e

think was never married, fo that no White proceeded from him ; but all the New-England Whales defended from Samuel, of South Kingfton, the only fon of Theophilus. Judge Stephen Potter, of Coventry, was perfonally acquainted with Samuel Whale, and told me that he died about 1782, aged 77, fo born 1705. Yet I believe he was of age 1712, when he made the affignment of his farm, and fo was born 1691, the laft of Theophilus's children. As we can get no records or family writings, we are obliged to ufe thefe deductions and inferrences from traditional ages.

Upon my requeft, Ray Green, Efq. fon of Governor Green, of Warwick, fent me this information in a letter, dated September 30, 1785—" The grand-daughter Nelly, by Elizabeth Hazelton, a communicative old maiden, informs me that Mr. Theophilus Whale, her grand-father, was derived of a very genteel family in England, and very opulent ; but through fome mis-ftep he was fuppofed to be difaffected to royalty ; which occafioned his quitting England and retiring to America ; in a province of which, Virginia, he married Elizabeth Milis, and removed to Narraganfet ; having firft had two children in Virginia, *Joane* and *Elizabeth*. The other children were born in Narraganfet, except Martha, the place of whofe nativity is uncertain. Elizabeth, who married a Hazelton, lived to the age of 79, and died in 1752. The old gentleman having loft his wife and fettled his children, refided the remainder of his days with his daughter Hopkins, afterwards Spencer, in Weft Greenwich, where he finifhed his days at 110 years."

October 29, 1782, I fell in with the aged Mr. Hamilton, aged 86, at North Kingfton, fo born 1696, who told me he was at the funeral of old Theophilus Whale, who died when he was a young man, though married, and then aged about 23, fo about 1719 to 1722, that he was about 100 years old, and had five daughters, whom he well knew: and that Mrs. Spencer (once Hopkins) died at East Greenwich, August 1781, aged 96, or would have been 98 in September 1782, that she always enjoyed good health, and died a Quaker. Her son says she died 1773, aged 93.

Col. Willet and the reverend Mr. Torrey used to tell me many other anecdotes of Theophilus and his wife. The wife was a notable woman, a woman of high spirits, and often chastised her husband for his inattention to domestic concerns, and spending so much of his time in religion and contemplation, neglecting to repair and cover his house, which was worn out and become leaky and let in rain in heavy storms, which used to set her a storming at him. He used to endeavor to sooth her with placid mildness, and to calm her by observing in a storm, while the rain was beating in upon them, that then was not a time to repair it, and that they should learn to be contented, as it was better than sinners deserved, with other religious reflexions; and when the storm was over, and she urged him, he would calmly and humourously reply, it is now fair weather, and when it did not rain they did not want a better house. He was often asked, why he always lay on a deal board, and refused a feather bed; he replied, that a feather-bed was too good for him, for he was a man of blood, and ought to mortify himself. He led a pious, but recluse and austere life. He had not many books. This from Colonel Willet. He sometimes said that when he was young he was brought up delicately, and that till he was eighteen years old, he knew not what it was to want a servant to attend him with a silver ewer and knapkin whenever he wanted to wash his hands. The true character of Whale remains unknown. It is most probable that, like Axtel and others, he had a command among the guards that attended the King's trial and execution, and was very active in compassing the King's death. That afterwards, like Lord,

Say and others, he relented and confcientioufly condemned himfelf, thinking he had committed a heinous
crime, and that blood guiltinefs was upon him, which
made him go mourning all the reft of his days with for-
row, contrition and penetential humility. Others concerned in that tranfaction were afterwards deeply affected in the fame manner all their days; while thofe
who are fatisfied the caufe was good, and the fentence
on the King was highly juft and righteous, will as humbly truft and confide in it that thefe immediate actors
have long ago found; at the tribunal of Eternal Juftice,
that their heartfelt and fincere repentance was founded
in miftake and mifconception of atrocious wickednefs
and high criminality, in what was one of the moft meritorious acts of their lives.

And now that I am collecting the flying rumours and
anecdotes concerning Whale, I will in this connexion
bring together fcattered rumours concerning fome others
—In different parts of the country we come acrofs flying traditions and furmifes ventilated abroad, of three
other perfons believed by fome to have been alfo Charles's
judges who fled to America. One was George Fleetwood, who was tried, condemned and pardoned, and
certainly came over to Bofton and lived there in an
open manner, and died in Bofton.† He, and Whalley
and Goffe and Dixwell, were unqueftionably of the real
judges, and thofe four were the only real and true judges that ever have been known to have come to America.
It is however believed by fome, that Adrian Scroope,
who certainly lived at Hartford in Connecticut, 1666,
and foon after returned to England, was the real judge
Scroope. In evidence of which, this is adduced.—Su-
peradded to a certain inftrument or deed, dated March
21, 1663—4, recorded in Hartford records, is an at-
teftation dated March 8, 1666—7, and recorded March
11, 1666—7, figned by the names of Robert Peirce and
Adrian Scroope, as witneffes, with their own hand

† *Noble V.* 2. 334.

writing in the very book of records, though this is fingular and unufual. I infpected and examined the manufcript records and autographical fignatures in 1792.
The hand writing of the name of Scroope, upon comparifon, fo nearly refembles that in the copper-plate
fac fimile of King Charles's death warrant figned and
fealed by all the judges, that one would not much doubt
but that it was the fame. It might have been the régi-
cide's fon, or fome other perfon of the fame name ; but
certainly it was not the true and real judge Adrian
Scroope, becaufe he was condemned and executed
1661, as appears from all the hiftories, ‡ and particularly from the trial of the regicides, in which there is a
particular account of his execution with Colonel Jones.

Befides Fleetwood and Scroope, Solicitor Cook is a
third perfon fuppofed to have been one of the Judges,
and to have abfconded from England to America, and
to have died on Staten-Ifland. Mr. Cook was not one
of the judges, but the Solicitor at the King's trial and
adjudication, and was among thofe who were condemned and executed, as appears by all the hiftories, and by
the trial of the regicides. The fuppofition of another
regicide dying in America, led me to profecute an inquiry upon what I had been told by a perfon of veracity
and good intelligence, as received many years ago from
the mouth of Mrs. Watkins, a widow lady of Harlem,
near New-York, that fhe gloried in being a defcendant
from an anceftor, who had fuffered in the caufe of liberty, who was one of the regicides, and who fled and died at Staten-Ifland, or fomewhere in America. Accordingly I wrote a letter to her, and received the following anfwer ; which I infert, that in cafe any fhould
meet the fame ftory, they might be enabled to correct
and rectify it. I have fince feen this very refpectable
lady, who is ftill living at Harlem, and in converfation
with her, received even more ample information upon
the fubject.

‡ *Smollet.*

E e 2

"Harlem Heights, 4th January, 1793.

" Reverend Sir,

" The letter you did me the honor of writing me by Mr. Broome, of 20th December laft, I have received, and would have anfwered fooner, but being fearful of fome errors creeping into my account of the late *Solicitor* Cooke, I endeavored to obtain as accurate an account from fome of his defcendants, who are here, as time would permit. Madam Woofter has mifunderftood me in what fhe has related as having received from me relative to Solicitor Cooke, who was my greatgrand-father, and was tried and condemned, hanged, burt and quartered in England, on Charles the fecond's coming to the throne, for the part he had taken in having his predeceffor brought to that punifhment he fo richly merited. His daughter who was married to my grand-father Stillwell, which was an affumed name, came to Bofton with him (that is my grand-father) which place they removed from and lived in New-York, from whence they went to Staten-Ifland, where they died.— They had feveral children, amongft whom was my father, previous to my grand-mother's arrival in this country, and during fome part of the life of her father fhe was one of the maids of honor to the then Queen, and was obliged to leave England for the active part her father had taken.

As to what has been related by Madam Woofter relative to Fifhers and Shelter Iflands, I had a grand-father named Ray who was a clergyman) who lived on Block-Ifland, but was driven from there by the pirates, who at that time infefted thefe places, and the natives of the country, and went into fome of the then provinces of New-England, where he died.

I am, reverend Sir, with refpect and efteem,

Your friend and very humble fervant,

LYDIA WATKINS."

. But to return, I have collected and thrown together
thefe difconnected anecdotes and traditions concerning
Theophilus Whale, in this confufed manner, though
fomething as they at various times came to my knowledge, having been above thirty years in picking them
up here and there, as I accidentally came acrofs them.
From all which we may make the following deductions.

1. That Theophilus Whale, dying about 1719 or
1722, aged 103, was born in England about 1616 or
1619, of a good family, and well educated in grammar
learning, and other ftudies of a young gentleman. That
when aged about 18, or 1637, he came over to Virginia, a fpirited young gentleman, and went an officer
into the Indian wars ; but returned to England and
became an officer in the parliament wars, and through
the Protectorate. And after the Reftoration, 1660, he
might abdicate to Virginia, having by fome action or
other rendered himfelf obnoxious to the royalifts. Noble, in his memoirs of the houfe of Cromwell,† gives
the hiftory of Major-General Whalley, the Judge, and
enumerates others of the fame family concerned in the
public affairs, " during the government of Charles I.
the commonwealth and the Protectors." One he mentions was " Lieutenant Whalley, who ferved in Hacker's regiment." Hacker, though not a judge, yet commanding at the execution of the King, was himfelf executed in 1660. And Goffe's journal mentions Robert
Wale. Suppofing Theophilus then an officer in Hacker's regiment, and active at the King's execution, he
might be in danger, and fo fled to efcape from vengeance, and confidered himfelf a man of blood.

2. Though it cannot be afcertained when he came
to Virginia a fecond time, yet he muft have been there,
and married about 1670. For he had certainly two
and probably four children at Virginia. Joane was the
oldeft, and old enough to have a child by 1692, as fhe
was the mother of Lawrence by Hill, and Elizabeth

† Noble V. 2. P. 188.

dying 1752, aged 79, must have been born in Virginia about 1673. I remember Judge Hopkins seemed a little at a loss concerning the order of the children from Joane to his mother. It is enough, however that Joane and Elizabeth were born in Virginia before the year 1680, when Martha was born in Narraganset.

3. It is thus at length ascertained that Theophilus Whale could not have been William Goffe, or one of the Hadley Judges, as Colonel Willet formerly conceived. For though Whale's appearance at Narraganset might agree well enough with Goffe's evanescence from Hadley, both being about 1680, yet it is certain that Whale was in Virginia, and had a wife and children there in 1673, while Goffe was at Hadley, and from thence wrote a letter to his wife in England, 1674, and another 1679, and never was out of Hadley from 1664 to 1679, when he wrote his last letter to his wife then still living. I never was able to determine this to certainty till 1785 from Judge Hopkins; having for twenty years before entertained some apprehension that this Whale and Goffe might possibly be the same.

4. Any other abdicating Judge would not have taken the name of Whale; and therefore whatever Theophilus was, he was not one of the King's Judges, as Colonel Willet and all Narraganset uniformly believed — There is a mystery in Theophilus's character which can never be cleared up, further than to ascertain that he was not one of the Judges. He was doubtless a disappointed and mortified man; but what his true history and disappointments were must remain in oblivion.

5 That he was however of respectable character and connexions, and that there were those here during his life who knew his history, seems justly and conclusively to be inferred from the singularly respectful treatment he received from the Boston gentlemen who used to visit him at Colonel Willet's father's, and which convinced Colonel Willet, who was knowing to it, nor can this treatment be accounted for on any other supposition.

Thus I have collected and brought together all the various and scattered information to be found concerning this singular person :- whose history is not even hitherto known by his family and the inhabitants of Rhode-Island, nor by any one else, in the light in which I have now set it : while however I trust I have exhibited such documents and proofs as will enable every one to make a decided judgment, that Mr. Theophilus Whale, whoever he was, was not one of King Charles's Judges.

FINIS.

ADVERTISEMENT.

As the size of this book is altered from that mentioned in the proposals, although the quantity of type condensed in a page, and the contents of the whole are the same ; it is but just that the subscribers should be left at their liberty to take the books, or not, as they please.

CPSIA information can be obtained at www.ICGtesting.com
Printed in the USA
LVOW100733220412

278585LV00005B/65/P

9 781170 775